FIRST-YEAR GERMAN
Third Edition

ROBERT E. HELBLING
University of Utah

WOLF GEWEHR
Universität Münster

DIETER JEDAN
University of California, Los Angeles

WOLFF A. VON SCHMIDT
University of Utah

FIRST-YEAR GERMAN
Third Edition

HOLT, RINEHART AND WINSTON
New York Chicago San Francisco
Philadelphia Montreal Toronto London
Sydney Tokyo Mexico City
Rio de Janeiro Madrid

Photograph Credits are on page 464.

Publisher: Rita Perez
Project Editor: Arthur Morgan
Production Manager: Lula Schwartz
Design Supervisor: Renée Davis
Text Design: Ben Kann

Library of Congress Cataloging in Publication Data
Main entry under title:

First-year German.

   Includes index.
   1. German language—Grammar—1950–   . I. Helbling,
Robert E.
PF3112.IV 1983   438.2′421   82-21210
ISBN 0-03-062506-8

CBS COLLEGE PUBLISHING
Holt, Rinehart and Winston
The Dryden Press
Saunders College Publishing

CONTENTS

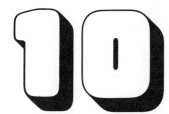

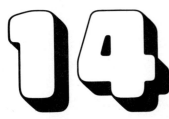

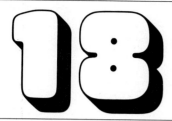

INTRODUCTION

In preparing the *third* edition of *First-year German* we have adhered to the pedagogic goals of the first two editions but have introduced a few new features, and slightly changed others, to make it a still more accessible and useful text. Its aim is to give the students a firm control of the four language skills—listening comprehension, speaking, reading, and writing—while introducing them to various cultural aspects of the German-speaking countries. Throughout, we have endeavored to use a natural, contemporary German within the confines of the given grammatical structures.

In comparison with the second edition, the following significant changes have been made:

—Mini-dialogues are provided at the beginning of each chapter.

—In the first six chapters, brief pronunciation exercises have been inserted.

—The Model Sentences are now directly placed before the discussion of the grammatical structures which they illustrate.

—The Vocabulary Development has been moved forward to follow directly the Practice section.

—New Communicative Exercises making extensive use of the vocabulary contained in the Practice, Conversation, and Vocabulary Development have been devised and replace the former Guided Conversation while incorporating some of its features.

—The Useful Phrases no longer have a separate listing, and they now appear under the Conversation so that they are better integrated visually with the conversational texts.

—The questions following the Conversations have been clearly separated into a "content" and a "personal" category.

—A few Conversations have been up-dated and simplified.

—Some Readings have been altered, not thematically but substantively, and others have been edited to remove complexities or up-date facts.

—Where deemed necessary, the Grammar Explanations have been streamlined and clarified.

—The Chapter Vocabulary is now clearly divided into three groups: "Nouns," "Verbs," and "Other Words."

—Most of the photographs and cultural realia are new. As to the supplements accompanying *First-year German,* the following changes should be noted:

—In place of the *Instructor's Edition* we have written a concise *Instructor's Manual* that should prove more useful, generally, in the teaching process and in the classroom presentation of certain specific points.

—The two former readers, *Current Issues* and *Arts and Letters,* have been shortened and merged under the title: *Aspekte: Kultur, Literatur, Politik, Alltag,* containing twelve "cultural" and four "literary" selections.

—The *Laboratory and Exercise Manual* and the *Tape Program,* though not changed in format, have been carefully coordinated with the changes made in the basic text.

Chapter Organization

Each of the 18 chapters consists of the following sections:

Mini-dialogues

These consist of a few conversational exchanges, making use of everyday phraseology which illustrates some grammatical points of the lesson, thus introducing the student in a natural way to the new structures and to useful vocabulary. These Mini-dialogues can be easily memorized.

Pronunciation (in the first six chapters)

This section consists primarily of exercises that illustrate the differences in pronunciation of the vowels and a number of consonants in certain positions within a word and will serve as a reinforcement of the pronunciation drills contained in the laboratory program.

Grammar Explanations preceded by Model Sentences

Each point of grammar discussed is preceded by Model Sentences translated into English that contain previous and new vocabulary in about equal measure. No more than three grammar topics are presented in each chapter. They are explained in English and in many places supported by diagrams and paradigms. At strategic intervals, the explanations are followed by brief Check Your Comprehension exercises that allow students to test their understanding of the material step by step.

Conversation

Preceding each conversation, there is a short series of everyday expressions (idioms with unusual grammatical structures, exclamations, interjections, etc.) with their approximate English equivalents. The Conversations themselves revolve around situations that students can identify with. They contain examples of the grammatical material in the chapter, and their topics relate to elements and motifs found in the subsequent Reading. The Conversations are followed by two sets of Questions, one set designed to check the students' understanding of the text as well as their mastery of the new vocabulary, the other addressed to their personal experience in relation to the topic under discussion.

Practice

This section is made up of a series of various types of exercises, including a German-English translation, to help the students assimilate the new grammar along with the new vocabulary. These exercises can be done either orally or in writing.

Vocabulary Development

In this section etymological relationships between words, the use of certain idioms, the recognition of gender in certain noun endings, etc., are discussed. Suggestions for class interaction are given that anticipate the Communicative Exercises.

Communicative Exercises

These are designed to stimulate dialogues among students and between students and teacher that use the new vocabulary and the new grammatical structures, in a context that approximates "real life" situations. In some lessons, specific suggestions for conversations between two or more students are given.

Reading

The Readings illustrate interesting aspects of modern life in the German-speaking countries and make ample use of the grammatical principles studied up to that point. It has been our goal to give realistic glimpses of the cultures of West and East Germany, and Austria as well as Switzerland. Historical and other references are explained in the Cultural Notes that follow the Readings. The Questions test the students' understanding of the text and may be answered orally or in writing.

A modified version of part of the Reading is used as the second listening comprehension passage in the tape program.

Review

A final series of diversified exercises reinforce the application of all the grammar principles and the vocabulary presented in the chapter and in preceding lessons. An English-German translation passage is included.

Guided Composition

The topics of the Guided Compositions are largely based on the subject matter of the Readings. Suggestions are made to help students and instructors with the topics. Occasionally visuals are used as catalysts. Guided Compositions are included only from Chapter 7 on, at a point when the students have a modicum of vocabulary to work with.

Chapter Vocabulary

Each Chapter Vocabulary is divided into three word groups: "Nouns," "Verbs," and "Other Words." The components of the everyday phrases occurring in the Conversation are listed in the Chapter Vocabulary when deemed necessary. But the words and expressions glossed in the margins of the Conversations and Readings have been entered only in the End Vocabulary.

Appendix and End Vocabulary

The *Appendix* is made up of the following elements:
A *Supplementary Guide to Pronunciation* to be used as a quick reference section and as the basis of drills of individual sounds. It can be used throughout the year and/or in conjunction with the Introductory Chapter.
Translations of all Conversations appearing in the text. All translations are in idiomatic English.
A *List of Important Strong and Irregular Weak Verbs.*
A *List of Common Units of Measurement* providing the equivalents between the American system and the metric system.
Four *maps* which provide students with the basic geography of Europe, Germany, Switzerland and Austria.
A complete *German-English End Vocabulary,* combining all vocabulary items and idiomatic expressions used throughout the text.
A thorough *Index* to all grammar points covered in the text is also included.

Supplementary Materials

Laboratory and Exercise Manual and Tape Program

The following supplementary materials complete the *First-year German* package.
The Laboratory and Exercise Manual and the accompanying *Tape Program* follow the chapter structure of the main text. There are two parts for each chapter. Part I, representing approximately twenty minutes of lab work, can most profitably be done after the Practice exercises and the Communicative Exercises in the corresponding chapter of the main text. It features pronunciation drills, reinforcement exercises for each point covered in the text and a listening comprehension passage based on the Conversation in the text. Part II, which lasts approximately fifteen minutes, is to be done at the very end of the chapter and consists of one exercise reviewing all the grammatical structures covered, a listening comprehension passage based on the Reading in the text, and a short dictation, also taken from the Reading. The Manual gives

all directions heard on tape, all examples and for approximately half the exercises (asterisked), the sentences and cues. The latter allows students to prepare for the tape session and/or for the instructor to assign the exercises as additional written work. Other exercises are entirely on tape. The listening comprehension passages as well as the Dictations are included in the Instructor's Manual.

Instructor's Manual

The Manual contains chapter by chapter suggestions for classroom presentation of the material in the text, as well as a general lesson plan, sample examinations, and the listening comprehension exercises and dictations from the tape program.

Reader

The new *First-year German* package includes one reader, *Aspekte: Kultur, Literatur, Politik, Alltag.* Twelve selections focus on aspects and problems of contemporary life in the German-speaking countries and four selections are brief stories, in their original form, written by well-known writers.

The reader is primarily designed to develop the students' reading comprehension skills. However, questions checking comprehension and encouraging the students' personal reactions have been added, which may be used for oral practice at the instructor's discretion. The grammar and vocabulary are sufficiently controlled so as not to pose vexing problems for the beginning student.

We suggest that the reader be used starting with Chapter 7 of the main text. Although a number of topics are coordinated with those of the text's Conversations and Readings, the reader may be used with any other introductory German program.

Acknowledgments

We gratefully acknowledge the many experts teaching at various institutions throughout the country whom the publisher called on to give us valuable advice at different stages in our work. A special word of thanks is due to the following reviewers for their most helpful comments:

Gerhard F. Strasser, *Pennsylvania State University*   Paul F. Dvorak, *Virginia Commonwealth University*   Ruth H. Firestone, *University of Mis-*

souri Hans Gilde, *University of Nebraska*   Marianne Heinicke Gupta, *Purdue University*   Evelyn M. Jacobson, *University of Nebraska* Harvey L. Kendall, *California State University, Long Beach*   Meredith McClain, *Texas Tech University*   Anthony K. Munson, *Hamline University*   Claus Reschke, *University of Houston*   Ursula Ritzenhoff, *University of Tennessee*   Claudia Scharfenstein, *Universität Münster* Juliette Victor-Rood   Ronald W. Walker, *Colorado State University* Herbert F. Wiese, *Coe College*

INTRODUCTORY CHAPTER

The Introductory Chapter will teach you to say a few common things right away. Study the words and expressions carefully and imitate the pronunciation of your instructor closely. (A guide to the rules of pronunciation is in the Appendix and pronunciation exercises are given in chapters 1 to 6.)

I. Cardinal numbers

0	null	19	neunzehn
1	eins (ein–)	20	zwanzig
2	zwei	21	einundzwanzig
3	drei	30	dreißig
4	vier	40	vierzig
5	fünf	50	fünfzig
6	sechs	60	sechzig
7	sieben	70	siebzig
8	acht	80	achtzig
9	neun	90	neunzig
10	zehn	100	(ein)hundert
11	elf	101	(ein)hunderteins
12	zwölf	200	zweihundert
13	dreizehn	1000	(ein)tausend
14	vierzehn	1100	(ein)tausendeinhundert
15	fünfzehn	1101	(ein)tausendeinhunderteins
16	sechzehn	2000	zweitausend
17	siebzehn	1 000 000	eine Million
18	achtzehn	2 000 000	zwei Millionen

Compound numbers are always written as one word. Notice that the unit number precedes the ten number.

66	sechsundsechzig	4210	viertausendzweihundertzehn
124	hundertvierundzwanzig	1925	neunzehnhundertfünfundzwanzig

CHECK YOUR COMPREHENSION

1. Count from one to ten.
2. Give all even numbers from one to twenty.
3. Give all odd numbers from eleven to thirty-one.
4. Count by tens to one hundred.
5. Give the number 345.
6. Give the number 1066.
7. Give your age.
8. Give the year.
9. Give the year of your birth.

Some everyday phrases

Some useful phrases which you will hear from the very beginning are listed below. Memorize them as quickly as possible.

Guten Tag!	*Hello!*
Guten Morgen!	*Good morning.*
Guten Abend!	*Good evening.*
Auf Wiedersehen!	*Good-bye.*
Wie geht es Ihnen?	*How are you?*
Gut!	*Fine.*

Schlecht!	*Bad.*
Und Ihnen?	*And yourself?*
Danke!	*Thank you.*
Bitte!	{ *Please.* *You're welcome.*
Wieviel Uhr ist es? } Wie spät ist es?	*What time is it?*
Es ist acht Uhr.	*It is eight o'clock.*
Es ist halb neun.	*It is eight-thirty.*
Es ist Viertel vor zwei.	*It is a quarter to two.*
Es ist Viertel nach zwölf.	*It is a quarter past twelve.*

CHECK YOUR COMPREHENSION

Engage in a conversation with a classmate.

1. Say good day (morning, evening), and get an answer.
2. Ask each other how you are, and answer.
3. Ask what time it is, and get an approximate answer.
4. Thank the classmate, and get an answer.
5. Say good-bye to each other.

II. Days of the week

The days of the week are:

der Montag	*Monday*
der Dienstag	*Tuesday*
der Mittwoch	*Wednesday*
der Donnerstag	*Thursday*
der Freitag	*Friday*
der Samstag or Sonnabend	*Saturday*
der Sonntag	*Sunday*
Was ist heute?	*What is today?*
Heute ist Sonntag.	*Today is Sunday.*
Was war gestern?	*What was yesterday?*
Gestern war Mittwoch.	*Yesterday was Wednesday.*

Was ist morgen?   *What's tomorrow?*

Morgen ist Freitag.   *Tomorrow is Friday.*

CHECK YOUR COMPREHENSION

1. Recite the days of the week.
2. Ask a classmate what today is, and get an answer.
3. Ask a classmate what yesterday was, and get an answer.
4. Ask a classmate what tomorrow will be, and get an answer.

III. Seasons, months, weather

The seasons of the year are:

der Frühling	*spring*	der Herbst	*fall*
der Sommer	*summer*	der Winter	*winter*

Es ist Frühling.   *It is spring.*

Es ist Herbst.   *It's fall.*

Es ist warm.

Es ist kalt.

The months of the year are:

der Januar	January	der Juli	July
der Februar	February	der August	August
der März	March	der September	September
der April	April	der Oktober	October
der Mai	May	der November	November
der Juni	June	der Dezember	December

Es ist Januar.	*It is January.*
Es ist Juli.	*It's July.*

Some common expressions of weather are:

Wie ist das Wetter?	*What's the weather like?*
Es ist schön.	*It's nice (beautiful).*
Es ist warm.	*It's warm.*
Es ist heiß.	*It's hot.*
Es ist kalt.	*It's cold.*

Es regnet.	{ *It rains.* *It's raining.*
Es schneit.	{ *It snows.* *It's snowing.*
Es ist warm, und es regnet.	*It's warm and it's raining.*
Es regnet oder es schneit.	*It rains or it snows.*

CHECK YOUR COMPREHENSION

1. Practice the seasons and months with a classmate.
2. Ask a classmate what the weather is like, and get an answer.
3. Tell a classmate it is a certain season or month, ask what the weather is like, and get an appropriate answer.

EXAMPLES: Es ist Winter. Wie ist das Wetter?
    Es ist kalt, und es schneit.

    Es ist April. Wie ist das Wetter?
    Es ist warm oder kalt. Es regnet.

Mini-dialogues

Practice the following mini-dialogues with your neighbor(s).

Student(in) A Guten Tag!
         B Wie geht es Ihnen?
         A Danke, gut! Und Ihnen?
         B Danke, gut!

         A Wie spät ist es?
         B Es ist neun Uhr.
         A Danke!
         B Bitte!

Bitte – please
– Thank you

A Hello!
B How are you?
A Thank you, fine. And you?
B Fine, thanks.

A What time is it?
B It is nine o'clock.
A Thank you.
B You're welcome.

Pronunciation

Repeat each word after your instructor and pay close attention to the contrast in sounds. Then listen to your instructor again pronounce each word.

Long ä	vs. Short ä	Long a	vs. Long ä	Short a	vs. Short ä
Gespräch	Schwäche	Name	nämlich	Mann	Männer
Mädchen	Männer	Sprache	spräche	lang	Länge
nämlich	Klänge				
Fähre	ändern				
Gerät	hätte				

Long ö	vs. Short ö	Long o	vs. Long ö	Short o	vs. Short ö
König	können	schon	schön	kommen	können
Höhle	Hölle	hohe	Höhe	offen	öffnen
Öl	öffnen				
schön	nördlich				
rötlich	rösten				

Long ü	vs. Short ü		Long i	vs. Long u	vs. Long ü
fühlen	füllen		vier	fuhren	führen
grüßen	küssen		Tier	Kultur	Tür
für	füttern				
Mühle	Müller		Short i	vs. Short u	vs. Short ü
glühen	Glück		Mitte	Mutter	Mütter
			Kissen	Kuß	küssen

Grammar explanations

I. Personal pronouns: nominative case

Study the following sentences carefully. Note the German words in bold-face in each set of sentences. Their function and structure are explained following each set of examples.

Ich suche das Buch.
I am looking for the book.

Es ist hier.
It's here.

Wir studieren Deutsch.
We are studying German.

The subject of a sentence is in the *nominative case;* it usually answers the question *"Who?"* or *"What?"*

Ulrike studiert eine Sprache.	*Ulrike studies a language.*
Das Buch ist hier.	*The book is here.*

The subject can be a noun, as in the preceding sentences, or a pronoun:

Sie studiert eine Sprache.	*She (Ulrike) studies a language.*
Es ist hier.	*It (the book) is here.*

In German as in English, these pronouns can be in the first person (*I, we*), the second person (*you*), or the third person (*he, she, it, they*).

Person	Singular		Plural		
1st	ich	*I*	wir	*we*	*Personal pronouns: nominative case*
2nd (familiar)	du	*you*	ihr	*you*	
3rd	er	*he*			
	sie	*she*	sie	*they*	
	es	*it*			
2nd (formal)	Sie	*you*	Sie	*you*	

Note these differences between the two languages.

1. The 1st person singular, **ich,** is not capitalized in German, except at the beginning of a sentence.

2. The 2nd person singular and plural have two forms in German, the familiar and the formal. Use the familiar form to address relatives, close friends, and children: in speaking to one person, use **du;** in speaking to more than one, use **ihr.** Use the formal **Sie** to address all other people, especially people you meet for the first time. **Sie** is identical in the singular and plural.

3. In both the 2nd person singular and plural, the formal **Sie** is always capitalized.

Familiar

Peter, du bist so jung.	*Peter, you are so young.*
Peter und Doris, ihr seid klug.	*Peter and Doris, you are bright.*

Formal

Was studieren Sie, Fräulein Müller?	*What are you studying, Miss Müller?*
Herr und Frau Keller, sind Sie aus Amerika?	*Mr. and Mrs. Keller, are you from America?*

CHECK YOUR COMPREHENSION

Complete the sentence with the personal pronoun indicated.

1. _____ suchen das Buch. (*we*)
2. _____ bist klug. (*you, fam. sing.*)
3. _____ heißt Peter. (*he*)
4. _____ heißt Doris. (*she*)
5. _____ studiere hier Deutsch. (*I*)
6. Studiert _____ Englisch, Peter und Doris? (*you, fam. pl.*)
7. _____ ist interessant. (*it*)
8. Sind _____ Herr und Frau Müller? (*you, formal pl.*)
9. Ja, und _____ sind Herr Meyer? (*you, formal sing.*)

II. Present tense of regular verbs and *SEIN*

Ulrike sucht das Buch.
Ulrike is looking for the book.

Was studieren Sie, Fräulein Müller?
What do you study, Miss Müller?
What are you studying, Miss Müller?

Sie findet das Buch.
She finds the book.

Wie heißt das Mädchen?
What is the girl's name?

Wie heißt du?
What's your name?

Sind Sie aus Deutschland?
Are you from Germany?

Ich bin aus Bonn.
I'm from Bonn.

Das ist interessant.
That's interesting.

A. Formation

The infinitive is the form of the verb given in vocabulary lists and dictionaries. In English the infinitive consists of *to* + a form of the verb: *to be, to study.* In German it normally ends in **-en,** as in **kommen** (*to come*). In some cases, for phonetic reasons it ends in **-n,** as in **sein** (*to be*).

hoffen	*to hope*
kommen	*to come*
suchen	*to look for*
studieren	*to study*

The present tense of most German verbs is formed by dropping the infinitive ending **-en** and adding personal endings to the verb stem.

	Singular	Plural	
1st	**-e**	**-en**	*Present tense:*
2nd (fam.)	**-st**	**-t**	*personal*
3rd	-t	**-en**	*endings*
2nd (formal)	**-en**	**-en**	

The present tense of a regular German verb is as follows:

	Singular	Plural	
1st	ich hoff**e**	wir hoff**en**	**hoffen** (*to hope*)
2nd (fam.)	du hoff**st**	ihr hoff**t**	
3rd	er sie } hoff**t** es	sie hoff**en**	
2nd (formal)	Sie hoff**en**	Sie hoff**en**	

If the verb stem ends in a hissing sound, such as **s, ss, or ß,**[1] (as in **heißen**), add only **-t** and not **-st** to the stem of the **du** form: **du heißt** (*you are called*). Thus the **du, er,** and **ihr** forms are identical: **du heißt, er (sie, es) heißt, ihr heißt.**

If the stem of the verb ends in **-t** or **-d,** as in **arbeiten** (*to work*) or **finden** (*to find*), insert **-e-** between the stem and the endings **-st** and **-t.** This makes it easier to hear and pronounce the endings.

du	arbeitest		du	findest
er sie } arbeitet es			er sie } findet es	
ihr	arbeitet		ihr	findet

---

[1]The **-ss-** changes to **-ß-** (1) if the preceding vowel is long, (2) at the end of a word, and (3) before a **-t-.**

Also insert **-e-** before these endings when the stem ends in **-n** or **-m,** preceded by a consonant other than **l** or **r,** as in **öffnen** (*to open*).

du   öffnest

er
sie } öffnet
es

ihr   öffnet

The verb **sein,** like its equivalent *to be* in English, is the most frequently used verb in German.

	Singular		Plural		sein (to be)
1st	ich **bin**	I am	wir **sind**	we are	
2nd (fam.)	du **bist**	you are	ihr **seid**	you are	
3rd	er sie } **ist** es	he she } is it	sie **sind**	they are	
2nd (formal)	Sie **sind**	you are	Sie **sind**	you are	

B. Usage

1. There are no special verbal structures in German that correspond to the forms of the English progressive (*I am hoping*) and emphatic (*I do hope*). The German present tense may therefore have the following meanings in English:

ich hoffe	*I hope*
	I am hoping
	I do hope

2. The present tense can also express an action projected into the near future. This implied future is often used with a time phrase such as **heute abend** (*this evening*) or **gleich** (*right away*).

Ich komme **gleich**.	*I'm coming right away.*
Er arbeitet **heute abend**.	*He's working tonight.*

CHECK YOUR COMPREHENSION

Supply the appropriate present-tense form of the verb in parentheses.

1. Ulrike _____ eine Sprache. (*studieren*)
2. Herr Meyer _____ das Buch. (*suchen*)
3. Ihr _____ aus Berlin. (*sein*)
4. Ich _____, das Buch ist da. (*hoffen*)
5. Fritz _____ heute abend. (*arbeiten*)
6. Wir _____ gleich. (*kommen*)
7. Wie _____ das Fräulein? (*heißen*)
8. _____ du aus England? (*sein*)
9. Ulrike _____ die Tür. (*öffnen*)
10. Fräulein Meyer, _____ Sie aus Deutschland? (*sein*)

III. Article, gender, and number of nouns

Der Tag ist lang.
The day is long.

Die Tür ist da drüben.
The door is over there.

Hier ist **ein** Buch von Kafka.
Here's a book by Kafka.

Das Buch heißt „Amerika".
The book is called Amerika.

Das Mädchen studiert eine Sprache.
The girl is studying a language.

Die Bücher sind interessant.
The books are interesting.

German nouns are always capitalized, no matter where they appear in the sentence.

Das Buch ist hier.
Hier ist das Buch.

A. Article and gender of nouns

In German as in English, a noun may be preceded by either a definite or an indefinite article. The definite article refers to a specific entity: **der Mann** (*the man*). The indefinite article does not refer to any one particular person or thing: **ein Mann** (*a man*).

The article in German indicates the grammatical gender of a noun. Here "gender" is a linguistic rather than a biological term. All German nouns have a gender, even those which do not denote persons.

A German noun is either masculine, feminine, or neuter.

masculine	**der** Mann		*man*	**der** Tag		*day*	*Definite article*
feminine	**die** Frau	*the*	*woman*	**die** Tür	*the*	*door*	
neuter	**das** Kind		*child*	**das** Buch		*book*	

masculine	**ein** Mann		*man*	**ein** Tag		*day*	*Indefinite article*
feminine	**eine** Frau	*a*	*woman*	**eine** Tür	*a*	*door*	
neuter	**ein** Kind		*child*	**ein** Buch		*book*	

Sometimes biological and grammatical gender are the same, as in **der Mann, die Frau;** but most often there is no way of telling what grammatical gender a noun is: **der Tag, das Buch, das Kind, die Tür.** It is therefore necessary to memorize the definite article with each noun.

Nouns are normally preceded by either a definite or an indefinite article. However, when the noun indicates a *nationality* or *occupation*, the article is omitted.

Judy ist Amerikanerin.   *Judy is an American.*

Er ist Student.   *He's a student.*

CHECK YOUR COMPREHENSION

Supply the definite or indefinite article as indicated.

1. _____ Mädchen heißt Ulrike.   (*def.*)
2. Hier ist _____ Tür.   (*indef.*)

3. _____ Tag ist lang.   (*def.*)
4. Hier ist _____ Buch.   (*indef.*)
5. _____ Mann ist aus Amerika.   (*def.*)
6. _____ Frau ist da.   (*indef.*)
7. _____ Kind ist klug.   (*def.*)
8. Ich studiere _____ Sprache.   (*indef.*)

B. Number of nouns

In German, the article also indicates the number of a noun—that is, whether it is singular or plural. While in English the plural of nouns is normally formed by adding -s, in German the plurals vary. Since there is no standard rule for forming the plural of a German noun, it is best to learn the plural along with the singular. In the vocabulary sections of this book, plural forms are indicated as follows:

der **Tag,** -e	*day*
die **Tür,** -en	*door*
das **Buch,** ¨er	*book*
das **Mädchen,** -	*girl*
die **Studentin,** -nen	*female student*

The plural form of the definite article is the same for all three genders: **die.** So the plural forms of the preceding nouns are: **die Tage, die Türen, die Bücher, die Mädchen, die Studentinnen.**

However, the indefinite article is dropped in the plural.

Sie studiert eine Sprache.	*She is studying a language.*
Sie studiert Sprachen.	*She is studying languages.*

Notice that nouns ending in **-chen** and **-lein** (diminutive) are always neuter and take no additional endings in the plural.

die Tür ⟶ das Türchen, die Türchen
das Buch ⟶ das Büchlein, die Büchlein

In addition, the feminine singular of nouns denoting persons, including nouns of nationality, is in most cases formed by adding **-in** to the masculine form; for the feminine plural, add **-innen.**

CHECK YOUR COMPREHENSION

Change these sentences to the plural. If you do not know the plural of a noun, look for it in the Chapter Vocabulary.

EXAMPLE: Das Buch ist interessant.
      Die Bücher sind interessant.

1. Der Mann arbeitet heute abend.
2. Das Mädchen ist aus Berlin.
3. Wir studieren eine Sprache.
4. Das Kind ist hier.
5. Der Tag ist lang.

6. Sie suchen ein Buch.
7. Das Fräulein kommt gleich.
8. Die Frau ist klug.
9. Der Student ist aus England.
10. Die Studentin ist jung.

C. Use of pronouns

Be careful to replace a noun by the appropriate pronoun according to grammatical gender and number.

Noun		*Pronoun*
der Tag	⟶	er
die Tür	⟶	sie
das Buch	⟶	es
die Bücher	⟶	sie

However, under certain circumstances **sie** is used in reference to **das Mädchen** or **das Fräulein,** especially when a first or family name is mentioned.

Das Mädchen heißt Ulrike. **Sie** ist hier.
Fräulein Meyer studiert Sprachen. **Sie** ist aus Deutschland.

   But:

Das Kind kommt heute abend. **Es** ist aus Berlin.

CHECK YOUR COMPREHENSION

Substitute the appropriate personal pronoun for the noun.

1. Die Tage sind lang. _____ sind lang.
2. Das Kind ist aus England. _____ ist aus England.
3. Das Buch ist interessant. _____ ist interessant.
4. Fräulein Meyer studiert in Amerika. _____ studiert in Amerika.
5. Herr Meyer und Fräulein Keller arbeiten in Deutschland. _____ arbeiten in Deutschland.
6. Das Kind heißt Fritz. _____ heißt Fritz.
7. Die Amerikanerin sucht das Institut. _____ sucht das Institut.
8. Das Mädchen kommt heute. _____ kommt heute.

Conversation

Memorize the following everyday phrases.

Wie heißen Sie bitte?   *What is your name, please?*

Ich heiße Ulrike Müller.   *My name is Ulrike Müller.*

Es ist gleich da drüben.   *It's right over there.*

Viel Glück!   *Good luck.*

Read the following conversation several times, both silently and aloud. Commit to memory the new words, phrases, and structures.

EINE AUSKUNFT

Judy is an American who has a scholarship to study at a German university. She stops at the information desk of the library and talks with Mr. Keller, a librarian.

Judy   Guten Tag! Ich suche das „Institut für deutsche Sprache und Literatur".

Herr Keller   Adenauer[1]-Straße eins. Es ist gleich da drüben. Sind Sie aus Amerika?

Judy   Ja, ich bin aus Buffalo, New York. Ich heiße Judy Miller.

Herr Keller   Und Sie studieren jetzt hier in Deutschland?

Judy   Ja, ich studiere Deutsch und Soziologie.

[1]Konrad Adenauer (1876–1967) was the first chancellor of the Federal Republic of Germany. He presided over Germany's reconstruction after World War II.

Herr Keller   Das ist interessant.
Judy   Ich suche ein Buch von Kafka.[2]
Herr Keller   Wie heißt das Buch?
Judy   Es heißt „Amerika". Ich hoffe, es ist da.
Herr Keller   Ich bin nicht sicher. Der Katalog ist gleich da drüben.
Judy   Danke für die Auskunft. Auf Wiedersehen!
Herr Keller   Bitte! Auf Wiedersehen, Fräulein Miller! Viel Glück!

QUESTIONS ON THE CONVERSATION

Answer in complete sentences.

1. Wie heißt die Studentin?
2. Wie heißt der Mann?
3. Was (*what*) sucht die Studentin?
4. Ist sie aus Deutschland?
5. Was studiert sie?

6. Wo (*where*) studiert sie?
7. Wie heißt das Buch von Kafka?
8. Was hofft Judy Miller?
9. Wo ist der Katalog?

PERSONAL QUESTIONS

1. Wie heißen Sie?
2. Sind Sie aus Deutschland oder Amerika?
3. Sind Sie Student (Studentin)?

4. Studieren Sie Deutsch oder Soziologie?
5. Wo studieren Sie?

Practice

A. Supply an appropriate personal pronoun.

EXAMPLES: _____ seid aus England.
Ihr seid aus England.

_____ ist hier.   (*Herr Meyer*)
Er ist hier.

1. _____ arbeitet in Bonn.   (*Fräulein Meyer*)

2. _____ öffnest die Tür.

[2]Franz Kafka (1883–1924) was one of the most influential writers of the present age. A Czech who wrote chiefly in German, he was the author of three major novels and many short stories.

3. Sucht _____ ein Buch? (*Herr Keller*)

4. _____ ist da drüben. (*das Buch*)

5. _____ studieren Deutsch. (*1st person pl.*)

6. _____ heißt Peter.

7. Bist _____ aus Deutschland?

8. _____ sind hier. (*die Kinder*)

9. _____ komme gleich.

10. _____ bin aus Hamburg.

B. Complete the definite or indefinite articles.

EXAMPLES: D_____ Studentin ist aus Deutschland.
Die Studentin ist aus Deutschland.

1. D_____ Institut ist da drüben.

2. Ich suche e_____ Buch von Kafka.

3. Er öffnet d_____ Tür.

4. D_____ Mädchen kommen gleich.

5. E_____ Studentin heißt Keller.

6. Wo sind d_____ Bücher?

7. E_____ Herr sucht das Institut.

8. D_____ Auskunft ist da drüben.

9. D_____ Tage sind lang.

10. Wie heißen d_____ Kinder?

C. In the following sentences change everything possible to the plural—nouns, verbs, and pronouns.

EXAMPLE: Der Mann kommt aus Bonn.
Die Männer kommen aus Bonn.

1. Die Studentin ist aus Deutschland.

2. Sie sucht ein Buch von Kafka.

3. Wo ist der Katalog?

4. Die Straße ist lang.

5. Wie heißt das Kind?

6. Ich studiere eine Sprache.

7. Arbeitest du heute abend?

8. Das Mädchen hofft, du kommst heute abend.

D. Fill in the blank with the appropriate present-tense form of the verb indicated in parentheses.

EXAMPLE: Der Mann _____ das Institut. (*suchen*)
Der Mann sucht das Institut.

1. Wir _____ sicher. (*sein*)

2. Das Fräulein _____ morgen. (*arbeiten*)

3. _____ du Fritz? (*heißen*)

4. Wer (*who*) _____ die Tür? (*öffnen*)

5. Die Kinder _____ gleich. (*kommen*)

6. Was _____ du? (*suchen*)

7. Ihr _____ aus England. (*sein*)

8. Die Studentinnen _____ Sprachen. (*studieren*)

9. Die Mädchen _____ das Buch. (*öffnen*)

10. Wo _____ die Straße? (*sein*)

E. Answer the following questions with complete sentences. Use the cue and replace nouns with pronouns whenever possible.

EXAMPLE: Wo ist Fräulein Meyer? *(in Hamburg)*
          Sie ist in Hamburg.

1. Wie heißt die Studentin aus Amerika? *(Fräulein Miller)*
2. Was ist interessant? *(das Buch)*
3. Wo studieren die Studenten? *(in Köln)*
4. Wer sucht das Institut? *(die Studentin aus Amerika)*
5. Wo ist die Adenauer-Straße? *(in Hamburg)*
6. Was studieren Sie? *(Deutsch)*
7. Ist der Student aus Deutschland? *(aus England)*
8. Was ist Herr Meyer? *(Student)*

F. Give the English equivalent of the following sentences, paying special attention to the various uses of the German present tense.

1. Du studierst Deutsch in Deutschland.
2. Die Frauen arbeiten heute abend.
3. Wer öffnet die Tür?
4. Was suchen Sie?
5. Ich komme gleich.
6. Er hofft, die Bücher sind da.

Vocabulary development

A. The masculine singular of nouns indicating nationality is usually formed by adding **-er** to the name of the country. The masculine plural form of the noun is the same.

	Singular	*Plural*
die Schweiz *Switzerland*	**der Schweizer** *the Swiss*	**die Schweizer** *the Swiss*
Österreich *Austria*	**der Österreicher** *the Austrian*	**die Österreicher** *the Austrians*
England *England*	**der Engländer** *the Englishman*	**die Engländer** *the English, the Englishmen*

But note these exceptions:

Deutschland	der Deutsche	die Deutschen
Germany	*the German*	*the Germans*
Rußland	der Russe	die Russen
Russia	*the Russian*	*the Russians*
Frankreich	der Franzose	die Franzosen
France	*the Frenchman*	*the French, the Frenchmen*

If the name of a country ends in a vowel, it adds **-ner: Amerika, der Amerikaner, die Amerikaner.**

B. The feminine singular of nouns denoting persons, including nouns of nationality, is in most cases formed by adding **-in** to the masculine form; for the feminine plural, add **-innen.**

Masc. sing.	*Fem. sing.*	*Fem. pl.*
der Student	die Studentin	die Studentinnen
der Amerikaner	die Amerikanerin	die Amerikanerinnen
der Engländer	die Engländerin	die Engländerinnen
der Franzose	die Französin	die Französinnen
der Russe	die Russin	die Russinnen

But:
Masc. sing.	*Fem. sing.*	*Masc. & fem. pl.*
der Deutsche	die Deutsche	die Deutschen

Form the feminine singular and plural of **der Schweizer, der Österreicher.** Practice these nouns by engaging in a short dialogue with your neighbor(s). For instance:

Sylvia, bist du **Engländerin?**

Nein, ich bin **Deutsche.**

Communicative exercises

A. *Student A asks:* Wie heißt das Mädchen? sie, er? das Kind? die Straße?
Student B answers: Sie heißt . . .
Student C says: Nein, sie heißt . . .

B. *Student A asks:* Was studierst du?
Student B answers: Ich studiere . . .

C. *Student A asks:* Sind Sie (bist du) aus New York?
Student B answers: Nein, ich (wir) . . .

Studenten diskutieren vor der Universität Münster.

D. *Student A asks:* Wo ist das Buch?
Student B answers: Es ist hier.
Student C says: Nein, es ist da drüben.

Then change roles and ask the question in the plural. Do the same with your books closed, with as many words as you can remember from the lesson.

Reading

Read the following passage and note all new words, phrases, and structures. When you have finished reading the passage and fully understand what it says, answer the questions that follow it.

INSTITUT FÜR GERMANISTIK

Herr Keller informiert Judy Miller über das Institut für Germanistik, Adenauer-Straße 1. Judy sucht die Straße. Sie hat Glück.° Sie findet *is lucky*
die Adenauer-Straße gleich. Hier ist das Institut für Germanistik.

Fräulein Miller öffnet die Tür. Ein Student und eine Studentin kommen gleich. Sie verteilen Programme.° Judy hat jetzt ein Programm. *leaflets*
Es heißt da:° *it says there*

informieren
diskutieren
veränder°   *vost stress enlout*

change

Judy studiert das Programm. Es informiert Judy über das Studenten-
parlament.° Sie findet es wirklich interessant. Der Student heißt
Bernd. Er informiert Judy jetzt über das Institut. Sie diskutieren über
Politik in Deutschland und Amerika. Verändern: ja oder nein? Was
und wie? Der Student und die Amerikanerin diskutieren fast eine
Stunde.

student senate

Judy und Bernd suchen jetzt das Buch „Amerika" von Kafka. Die
Bibliothek ist gleich da drüben. Da ist der Katalog. Sie finden das
Buch unter° „K". Es ist in Zimmer neun unter „Literatur". Bernd sagt°:
„Auf Wiedersehen." Er hat jetzt eine Vorlesung.°

under / says
lecture

Judy öffnet die Tür von Zimmer neun. Sie hat Glück. Das Buch ist
da. Die Amerikanerin öffnet das Buch und arbeitet fast eine Stunde.
Sie findet „Amerika" wirklich interessant.

QUESTIONS

Answer in complete sentences.

1. Was sucht Judy Miller?
2. Wie heißt die Straße?
3. Wer öffnet die Tür?
4. Wer verteilt Programme?
5. Wie findet sie das Programm?
6. Wie lange (*how long*) diskutieren
   sie über Politik?

7. Was sucht Judy jetzt?
8. Wo ist die Bibliothek?
9. Wo findet Judy das Buch?
10. Wie lange arbeitet sie?
11. Wie findet sie „Amerika"?

Review

A. Form questions about the following statements, using the cue in parentheses.

EXAMPLES: Das Fräulein studiert in Berlin. (*wo?*)
Wo studiert das Fräulein?

Ich suche ein Buch. (*was?*)
Was suchst du?

1. Die Studenten verteilen die Bücher. (*was?*)
2. Ich finde das Institut interessant. (*wie?*)
3. Die Adenauer-Straße ist gleich da drüben. (*wo?*)
4. Die Studentinnen studieren Soziologie. (*was?*)
5. Das Mädchen sucht das Buch von Kafka. (*was?*)
6. Die Studenten suchen die Bücher von Kafka. (*was?*)
7. Literatur ist interessant. (*wie?*)

B. Answer the following questions as well as you can.

1. Studieren Sie eine Sprache?
2. Finden Sie die Klasse wirklich interessant?
3. Finden Sie das Buch interessant?
4. Sind Sie sicher?
5. Arbeiten Sie heute abend?

C. Answer the following sentences, using the cue provided.

EXAMPLES: Wo sind die Kataloge? (*da drüben*)
Die Kataloge sind da drüben.

1. Was studiert die Studentin? (*Englisch*)
2. Wer kommt gleich? (*die Mädchen*)
3. Wie lange studierst du? (*zwei Stunden*)
4. Wer öffnet die Tür? (*die Herren*)
5. Wie heißt sie? (*Luise*)
6. Wer diskutiert über Politik? (*der Franzose und die Schweizerin*)
7. Wo ist das Institut? (*in Köln*)
8. Wer findet die Klasse wirklich interessant? (*die Engländer*)

D. Change the following sentences to the plural.

EXAMPLE: Wo ist die Tür?
Wo sind die Türen?

1. Ich studiere das Buch.
2. Der Student kommt morgen.
3. Findest du das Institut?
4. Der Mann informiert die Frau.

5. Wo ist das Kind?
6. Sie sucht die Deutsche.
7. Der Herr findet die Straße.

8. Die Amerikanerin sucht eine Auskunft.

E. Supply the appropriate pronoun.

1. Kommt Fräulein Meyer heute abend? Ja, _____ kommt heute abend.
2. Was findet der Student? _____ findet Bücher.
3. Ist Frau Keller aus Bonn? Nein, _____ ist aus Hamburg.
4. Sucht die Engländerin die Bibliothek? Ja, _____ sucht die Bibliothek.
5. Ist die Auskunft interessant? Ja, _____ ist interessant.
6. Heißt das Mädchen Ulrike? Ja, _____ heißt Ulrike.
7. Ist der Tag lang? Ja, _____ ist lang.
8. Ist das Kind aus Deutschland? Nein, _____ ist aus Amerika.
9. Diskutieren die Amerikaner über Politik? Nein, _____ diskutieren über Soziologie.
10. Sind die Französinnen klug? Ja, _____ sind klug.

F. Express in German.

1. She is working this evening.
2. We'll come right away.
3. You (*fam. pl.*) are discussing literature.
4. He does study sociology.
5. They are looking for books by Kafka.
6. The room is right over there.
7. What's your name, please?
8. My name is Müller.
9. Good-bye.
10. Good luck.
11. Thank you for the information.
12. You're welcome.
13. He informs the class.
14. The Russians are studying languages.

Chapter vocabulary

Nouns _____

(das)[1]	**Amerika**	*America*
der	**Amerikaner, -**	*American (male)*
die	**Amerikanerin, -nen**	*American (female)*

die	**Auskunft, ⸚e**	*(piece of) information; information desk*
die	**Bibliothek, -en**	*library*
das	**Buch, ⸚er**	*book*
das	**Büchlein, -**	*the little book*

[1]With some exceptions such as **die Schweiz,** the names of countries do not require an article. In vocabulary lists the article appears in parentheses so as to indicate the gender of a pronoun replacing the noun.

'er' - almost always masculine → change to die
'erinn' - " " " for feminine → add nen for plural

(das)	Deutsch	German (language, subject)
(das)	Deutschland	Germany
(das)	England	England
(das)	Englisch	English (language, subject)
(das)	Frankreich	France
die	Frau, -en	woman, wife, Mrs.
das	Fräulein, -	young lady, Miss
die	Germanistik	Germanics
das	Glück	luck
	— haben	to be lucky
der	Herr, -en	man, gentleman, Mr.
das	Institut, -e	institute
der	Katalog, -e	(card) catalogue
das	Kind, -er	child
die	Klasse, -n	class
die	Literatur, -en	literature
das	Mädchen, -	girl
der	Mann, -̈er	man
(das)	Österreich	Austria
die	Politik	politics
(das)	Rußland	Russia
die	Schweiz	Switzerland
die	Soziologie	sociology
die	Sprache, -n	language
die	Straße, -n	street
der	Student, -en	student (male)
die	Studentin, -nen	student (female)
die	Stunde, -n	hour
der	Tag, -e	day
die	Tür, -en	door
das	Türchen, -	the small door
die	Uhr, -en	o'clock, watch, clock
das	Zimmer, -	room

Verbs

arbeiten	to work
diskutieren (über)	to discuss
finden	to find
haben	to have
heißen	to be called
hoffen	to hope
informieren (über)	to inform (about)
kommen	to come

öffnen	to open
sein	to be
studieren	to study
suchen	to look for
verteilen	to distribute

Other words

aus	from
bitte	please, you're welcome
da	there
da drüben	over there
danke	thank you
deutsch	German (adj.)
fast	almost
für	for
gleich	right (directly), right away
gut	good, well
heute abend	this evening
hier	here
in	in, into
interessant	interesting
ja	yes
jetzt	now
jung	young
klug	intelligent, bright
lang; lange (in respect to time)	long; for a long time
morgen	tomorrow
nein	no
nicht	not
sicher	sure
spät	late
über	about (concerning)
viel	much
von	by, of
was	what
wer	who
wie	how
wirklich	really
wo	where

See the nouns of nationality on pp. 22–23.

Mini-dialogues

Student(in) A   Fritz, hast du einen Plattenspieler?
          B   Nein, leider nicht.
          A   Spielst du Klavier?
          B   Nein, auch nicht. Aber ich spiele gern Tennis.

          A   Herr Meier, trinken Sie Kaffee?
          B   Ja, sehr gern.
          A   Mit oder ohne Zucker und Sahne?
          B   Mit Sahne, aber ohne Zucker, bitte.
          A   Ohne Zucker?
          B   Ja, Zucker ist nicht gut für die Gesundheit.

          A   Guten Tag, Günter, wie geht's?
          B   Danke, nicht sehr gut.
          A   Warum, bist du krank?
          B   Nein, nein, aber ich arbeite zuviel.

          A   Arbeitest du heute abend?
          B   Nein, ich spiele Karten mit Hansjörg und Dora. Kommst
              du auch?
          A   Nein, leider habe ich keine Zeit.

A   Fritz, do you have a record player?
B   No, unfortunately not.
A   Do you play the piano?
B   Neither. But I like to play tennis.

A   Mr. Meier, do you drink coffee?
B   Yes, very much (so).
A   With or without cream and sugar?
B   With cream but without sugar, please.
A   Without sugar?
B   Yes, sugar isn't good for one's health.

A   Hello, Günter, how are you?
B   (Thanks), not too well.
A   Why, are you sick?
B   No, no, but I'm working (studying) too much.

A   Are you studying tonight?
B   No, I'm playing cards with Hansjörg and Dora.
    Are you coming, too?
A   No, unfortunately I have no time.

Pronunciation

au	vs. ei/ai	vs. eu/äu		ei	vs. ie
Frau	mein	heulen		Wein	Wien
Aufschrift	nein	Deutschland		arbeiten	bieten
Raum	Mai	Freund		heiraten	hier
glauben	arbeiten	Fräulein		Bein	Bier
auch	gleich	Häuser		sein	sieben

back ch	vs. front ch		k	vs. ch
nach	nicht		Acker	acht
noch	schlecht		Flak	flach
Koch	Köche		Lack	lachen
schwach	Schwäche		Fleck	Fläche
auch	Architekt		flicken	Pflicht

Grammar explanations

I. The accusative case of the definite and indefinite articles, and *kein*

Ich suche **den** Katalog.
I'm looking for the catalog.

Monika findet **einen** Freund.
Monika finds a friend.

Er spielt **eine** Platte.
He is playing a record.

Wir kaufen **ein** Buch.
We are buying a book.

Ich habe **keine** Zeit.
I have no time.

Er hat **keine** Freundinnen.
He has no girlfriends.

   The direct object receives the action expressed by the verb and is in the *accusative case:*

Subject		*Direct object*
Nominative		*Accusative*

Wir	suchen	den Katalog.
Franz	spielt	die Platte.
Erika	kauft	das Buch.

The feminine, neuter, and plural forms are the same as the nominative. Only the masculine changes from **der** to **den** and **ein** to **einen:**

Accusative:	Masc.	Fem.	Neut.	Plural
definite	**den**	die	das	die
indefinite	**einen**	eine	ein	—

Remember, the indefinite article has no plural forms:

| **Kaufst du ein Buch?** | *Are you buying a book?* |
| **Kaufst du Bücher?** | *Are you buying books?* |

Kein, meaning *no, not a,* or *not any,* is used to negate nouns and has the same endings as **ein,** but also has a plural: **keine** for all genders.

| **Judy findet keinen Freund.** | *Judy doesn't find a friend.* |
| **Judy findet keine Freunde.** | *Judy doesn't find any friends.* |

The accusative of **wer** (*who*) is **wen** (*whom*).

| **Wen kennt ihr?** | *Who(m) do you know?* |

CHECK YOUR COMPREHENSION

A. Supply the appropriate article or **kein,** as indicated in parentheses.

1. Wir suchen _____ Straße. (*def.*)
2. Sie kauft _____ Buch. (*def.*)
3. Wer hat _____ Telefon? (*indef.*)
4. Die Studenten öffnen _____ Bücher. (*def.*)
5. Der Herr hat _____ Zeit. (*kein*)
6. Die Studentinnen suchen _____ Bibliothek. (*def.*)
7. Die Mädchen finden _____ Freunde. (*kein*)
8. Der Student sucht _____ Freundin. (*indef.*)

9. Ihr habt _____ Probleme. (*kein*)
10. Das Fräulein trinkt _____ Kaffee. (*kein*)
11. Ich studiere _____ Sprachen. (*indef.*)
12. Die Studenten finden _____ Katalog. (*def.*)
13. Findest du _____ Institut? (*def.*)
14. Kennt ihr _____ Herren? (*def.*)

B. Use **wer** or **wen** in the following sentences.

1. _____ sind Sie?
2. _____ sucht der Student?
3. _____ sucht den Amerikaner?
4. _____ kennt er?

II. Present tense of *HABEN*

Hast du eine Gitarre?
Do you have a guitar?

Ihr **habt** ein Telefon.
You have a phone.

Sie **hat** ein Kind.
She has a child.

Like **sein** (*to be*), **haben** (*to have*) is a much used verb.

	Singular		Plural		**haben** (*to have*)
1st	ich	**habe**	wir	**haben**	
2nd (fam.)	du	**hast**	ihr	**habt**	
3rd	er sie es	**hat**	sie	**haben**	
2nd (formal)	Sie	**haben**	Sie	**haben**	

CHECK YOUR COMPREHENSION

Supply the appropriate form of **haben.**

1. Wir _____ einen Freund.
2. Die Studenten _____ keine Freundinnen.
3. Ich _____ keine Bücher.
4. Du _____ kein Telefon.
5. Der Mann _____ keine Zeit.
6. Sie _____ ein Buch. (*you, formal*)
7. Ihr _____ kein Klavier.

III. Word order

Ich kenne den Amerikaner nicht.
I don't know the American.

Kennst du die Französin?
Do you know the French woman?

Leider **kenne ich** die Französin nicht.
Unfortunately, I don't know the French woman.

Wen **kennen Sie?**
Whom do you know?

Ist die Platte neu?
Is the record new?

Nein, neu **ist sie** nicht, aber gut.
No, it is not new, but it is good.

There are three basic patterns of word order in German, two of which are[1]:

A. Subject-Verb or "S-V" word order

The sentence begins with the subject and the *verb follows:*

S   V

Wir suchen ein Zimmer.   *We are looking for a room.*

B. Verb-Subject or "V-S" word order

The subject follows the verb. As you have already seen, this happens in *questions:*

  V   *S*

Studierst du Deutsch?   *Are you studying German?*
Wo arbeitet   **Herr Moser?**   *Where does Mr. Moser work?*

The first question requires a "yes" or "no" answer; the second involves an interrogative. Other frequently used interrogatives are:

Wer (*who*), **wen** (*whom*), **wann** (*when*), **wo** (*where*), **wie** (*how*), **warum** (*why*).

Note: **Wer** is automatically the subject in a question, **wen** the object. Therefore:

---

[1]The third basic word order (verb last) will be discussed in chapter 9.

S   V

| **Wer** kennt Herrn Moser? | *Who knows Mr. Moser?* |

    V   S

| **Wen** kennt Herr Moser? | *Whom does Mr. Moser know?* |

The V-S word order must also be used in a *statement* beginning with an element *that is not the subject.* This may be a single word or a phrase (at times called the "front field"):

"front field" **V**   **S**

Natürlich arbeitet sie viel.	*Of course, she works a lot.*
Heute abend kommt er nicht.	*He isn't coming tonight.*
Neu ist sie nicht, aber gut.	*It is not new, but it is good. (In answer to a question such as:* Ist die Platte neu? *Is the record new?)*

However, **und** (*and*), **aber** (*but, however*), and **oder** (*or*) do *not* require the V-S order when placed at the beginning of a clause:

| Ich studiere Deutsch, und | *I'm studying German and she studies English.* |

S V

sie studiert Englisch.

    S V

| Aber er kommt heute abend nicht. | *But he isn't coming tonight.* |

Note: In a negative sentence **nicht** usually comes before the word or phrase that is negated:

| Er ist **nicht** krank. | *He isn't sick.* |
| Sie arbeitet **nicht** zuviel. | *She doesn't work too much.* |

If the idea expressed in the whole sentence is negated, **nicht** usually comes at the end:

| Ich studiere heute abend **nicht.** | *I'm not studying tonight.* |

CHECK YOUR COMPREHENSION

A. Put the word in italics at the beginning and use the appropriate word order.

EXAMPLE: Er spielt *leider* nicht gern Tennis.
Leider spielt er nicht gern Tennis.

1. Wir arbeiten *morgen* nicht.
2. Die Freundinnen kommen *gleich*.
3. Das Buch ist nicht *neu*.
4. Sie arbeitet *natürlich* zuviel.
5. Sie spielt *aber* auch Klavier.

B. Form questions that elicit the following responses.

EXAMPLES: Die Freunde kommen heute abend.
Wer kommt heute abend?
Or: **Wann kommen die Freunde?**

Ja, ich komme heute abend.
Kommst du (Kommen Sie) heute abend?

1. Der Student studiert in Berlin.
2. Die Studentin heißt Jutta.
3. Claudia kommt morgen nicht.
4. Wir studieren Sprachen.
5. Ja, ich arbeite sehr viel.
6. Nein, ich habe keinen Plattenspieler.
7. Die Frau sucht das Kind.
8. Ja, ich trinke Kaffee ohne Zucker.
9. Die Bibliothek ist da drüben.
10. Ich kenne die Amerikanerin sehr gut.

Conversation

Verzeihung!	*Excuse me.* / *Pardon me.*
Hast du einen Moment Zeit?	*Do you have a minute?*
zum Beispiel	*for example*
Ich habe die Platte wirklich gern.	*I really like the record.*
Tschüß!	*So long.*
Bis gleich!	*See you later.*

AM° TELEFON

on the

Klaus Hier Schönberg.
Monika   Klaus, hier ist Monika. Verzeihung! Hast du einen Moment Zeit?

Klaus	Sicher.[1] Warum?
Monika	Wir haben jetzt einen Plattenspieler. Er ist ganz neu.
Klaus	Wirklich? Toll°!
Monika	Den Klang finde ich ganz fantastisch. Hast du vielleicht eine Platte von Peter Alexander?
Klaus	Von Alexander habe ich leider keine Platte, aber ich habe ein paar Jazz-Platten, zum Beispiel von Louis Armstrong.
Monika	Toll! Kennst du die Platte „Aber bitte mit Sahne"[2] von Udo Jürgens?
Klaus	Nein, ist sie neu?
Monika	Neu ist sie nicht, aber ich habe die Platte wirklich gern.
Klaus	Prima°! Ich komme gleich. Tschüß, Monika!
Monika	Tschüß, Klaus! Bis gleich!

Great!

Wonderful!

[1]In German, adjectives can also serve as adverbs; **sicher** can mean both *certain* and (as here) *certainly*.

[2]The title means *With whipped cream, please.* Germans have a marked liking for whipped cream in coffee and on desserts.

QUESTIONS ON THE CONVERSATION

1. Wer ist am Telefon?
2. Hat Klaus einen Moment Zeit?
3. Was hat Monika jetzt?
4. Wie findet Monika den Klang?
5. Hat Klaus eine Platte von Alexander?
6. Wie findet Monika die Platte von Udo Jürgens?

PERSONAL QUESTIONS

1. Haben Sie einen Plattenspieler?
2. Ist der Plattenspieler alt oder neu?
3. Wie finden Sie den Klang?
4. Haben Sie Jazz-Platten?
5. Haben Sie Platten von Mozart oder Richard Wagner?
6. Welche (*which*) Platten finden Sie ganz fantastisch?
7. Haben Sie die Platten von Louis Armstrong gern?

Practice

A. Restate the following sentences using the word in parentheses to replace the word in italics. Use the appropriate form of the article.

EXAMPLE: Er hat *ein Buch.*   *(Freund)*
     Er hat einen Freund.

1. Das Mädchen sucht *das Institut.*   *(Plattenspieler)*
2. Ich habe *kein Buch.*   *(Freund)*
3. Das Fräulein öffnet *die Tür.*   *(Katalog)*
4. Monika findet *den Klang* fantastisch.   *(Platte)*
5. Der Mann findet *die Straße* nicht.   *(Bücher)*
6. Ich kenne *keine Studenten.*   *(Studentinnen)*
7. Else hat *einen Freund.*   *(Freundinnen)*
8. Hast du *kein Kind?*   *(Kinder)*

B. Form questions that elicit the following answers.

EXAMPLES: Ja, Ulrike hat einen Freund.
     Hat Ulrike einen Freund?

       Er studiert in England.
     Wo studiert er?

1. Ja, Monika hat einen Plattenspieler.
2. Ja, Klaus studiert Deutsch.
3. Herr Meyer arbeitet in Berlin.
4. Ja, die Freunde kommen heute abend.
5. Nein, ich kenne die Straße nicht.
6. Ja, die Studenten haben die Platten gern.
7. Die Freundin heißt Barbara.
8. Frau Keller öffnet die Tür.
9. Wir kommen morgen.
10. Ich suche die Kinder.

C. Put the word in parentheses at the beginning of the sentence. Change the word order, if necessary.

EXAMPLE: Er kommt.   *(jetzt)*
     Jetzt kommt er.

1. Ich habe kein Buch von Kafka.   *(leider)*
2. Die Engländerinnen kommen.   *(heute abend)*
3. Die Studenten haben einen Moment Zeit.   *(jetzt)*
4. Du rauchst zuviel.   *(manchmal)*
5. Die Studentin studiert Sprachen.   *(natürlich)*
6. Sie arbeitet nicht.   *(morgen)*

D. Construct sentences with the given cues. Start the sentence with the word in italics, use the appropriate word order, and make the necessary changes.

EXAMPLE: suchen / der Mann / *das Fräulein*
     Das Fräulein sucht den Mann.

1. kennen / ich / *leider* / das Buch / nicht

2. studieren / die Studentin / *wo?*
3. sein / *das Institut* / neu /nicht.
4. kommen / *der Amerikaner* / gleich
5. *finden* / das Kind / die Straße?

E. Give the English equivalent of the following sentences, paying special attention to word order in German.

1. Wo arbeitest du?
2. Kennen Sie die Platte?
3. Heute abend kommen die Freunde.
4. Leider haben wir keine Zeit.
5. Natürlich rauche ich zuviel.
6. Aber ich trinke keinen Alkohol.
7. Ich studiere, und er spielt Klavier.
8. Wen suchen Sie?
9. Wer arbeitet zuviel?
10. Findet der Student den Katalog?

Vocabulary development

A. Spielen may be used with games or instruments.

ein Instrument **spielen**	*to play an instrument*
sie **spielt** Klavier	*she plays the piano*
er **spielt** Violine	*he plays the violin*
wir **spielen** Karten	*we play cards*
ihr **spielt** Tennis	*you play tennis*

Ask your neighbors whether they play the guitar or another instrument, and if they play tennis. Ask if they play well (**gut**).

B. The adjective of **die Gesundheit** is **gesund** (*healthy*); the opposite is **ungesund** (*unhealthy*) or **krank** (*sick, ill*). A thing or activity is **gesund** or **ungesund**; a person is **gesund** or **krank.**

Ask your neighbor if cigarettes, cigars, alcohol, etc., are healthy or unhealthy, and whether he or she is in good or bad health.

Communicative exercises

A. Ask one or several of your classmates anything from the following suggestions and have them answer your question.

(Name) _____, gern Tennis spielen
          Kaffee mit oder ohne Zucker trinken
          viel arbeiten
          heute abend studieren

Kinder haben
das Buch gut finden
Zeit haben
Zigaretten rauchen
ein Instrument spielen
viele Studenten (-innen) kennen

B. Address some of the above questions to your instructor.

Herr   ————————,   ————————————————

Frau   ————————,   ————————————————

Fräulein ————————,   ————————————————

C. Make some plausible statement about yourself or others by combining the expressions given below. Start with the expressions given at the left.

Heute abend	studieren
Manchmal	Freunde kommen
Vielleicht	Karten spielen
Leider	keine Zeit haben
	zuviel trinken
	Zigaretten rauchen
	ein paar Platten spielen
	krank sein

D. Carry on a brief conversation with your classmate(s) about records they may have. Suggestions:

Hast du Platten von . . .?

Wie findest du die Platten von . . .?

Kennst du Platten von . . .?

Verzeihung, wie heißt die Platte?

E. Do the same with respect to books and change the grammatical person. **Habt ihr Bücher von . . .?** etc.

Reading

DAS PROBLEM

„Fritz, Verzeihung, hast du eine Zigarette?" „Leider nicht." Ach, ja!°   *Oh yes!*
Fritz raucht nicht. Er trinkt auch nicht. Hat er eigentlich° eine Schwäche?   *actually*
Ja, vielleicht. Er studiert nicht viel, aber er spielt immer Gitarre.

Sicher habe ich ein Problem. Nein, nein, ich trinke nicht. Wirklich, ich trinke fast keinen Alkohol, nur manchmal ein Bier. Und ich spiele auch nicht immer Gitarre. Aber ich rauche zuviel, besonders wenn° *when, if* ich studiere. Und ich studiere viel!

Ich rauche keine Zigarren, auch keine Pfeife.° Ich rauche meistens° *pipe / mostly* Zigaretten ohne Filter. Sie kommen aus Deutschland oder Amerika. In Amerika haben die Zigaretten eine Warnung: Zigaretten sind gefährlich für die Gesundheit. Aber ich rauche trotzdem.° Andere° *all the same / other* Dinge sind auch gefährlich. Zuviel Zucker, zuviel Kaffee, zum Beispiel.

Aha, Fritz hat wirklich eine Schwäche. Er trinkt immer Kaffee mit sehr viel Zucker. Das ist sein° Problem! *his*

Ist hier ein Automat? Jetzt kaufe ich eine Packung° Roth-Händle.[1] *pack* Eine Schwäche ist so gut wie eine andere.° *as good as another*

[1]A popular brand of rather strong, unfiltered cigarettes.

der Rauche — smoke
die Glaube — a belief!

das Spieler — player

QUESTIONS

1. Glauben Sie, Fritz hat eine Schwäche?
2. Was ist die Schwäche?
3. Was trinkt der Sprecher (*speaker*)?
4. Spielt er immer Gitarre?
5. Hat er kein Problem?
6. Was haben die Zigaretten in Amerika?
7. Sind andere Dinge gefährlich? Zum Beispiel?

Review

A. Fill in the blanks with an article as indicated.

1. D__er__ Amerikaner raucht k__ein__ Zigaretten.
2. Wie finden d__ie__ Mädchen d__en__ Klang?
3. Sind d__ie__ Kinder gesund oder krank?
4. Hast du e__in__ Telefon?
5. D__ie__ Zigarren haben k__eine__ Warnung.
6. D__ie__ Studentin hat e__inen__ Freund.
7. Wo arbeiten d__ie__ Männer?
8. Ich hoffe, er findet e__ine__ Freundin.
9. D__ie__ Tür ist da drüben.
10. Natürlich habe ich e__inen__ Plattenspieler.

B. Replace the words in each sentence as indicated, making any necessary changes.

EXAMPLE: Habt ihr eine Platte?   (*kaufen / du*)
         Kaufst du eine Platte?

1. Wie heißt die Studentin aus Amerika? (*Studenten / Deutschland*)
2. Findet ihr die Bücher? (*du / Zimmer*)
3. Er raucht nicht. (*ihr / trinken*)
4. Kennst du eine Studentin aus England? (*haben / Freunde*)
5. Die Männer finden das Bier wirklich gut. (*Frau / Kaffee*)

C. Form the sentences with the words supplied. Add any other necessary grammatical elements and start the sentence with the word in italics.

EXAMPLE: suchen / Institut / Frau / *jetzt*
         Jetzt sucht die Frau das Institut.

1. trinken / Alkohol / *der Student* / zuviel
2. kommen / die Freundin / nicht / *leider*
3. kaufen / Plattenspieler / ich / *vielleicht*
4. *spielen* / immer / Sie / Gitarre?
5. *kennen* / Studentinnen / ihr / aus / Amerika?
6. haben / ein paar / er / Freunde / *natürlich*
7. studieren / zuviel / immer / *wer?*
8. arbeiten / in Berlin / das Fräulein / *aber*

D. Answer the following questions in complete sentences. Wherever possible, use pronouns for the subject in the answer.

1. Wer kennt das Buch von Kafka?
2. Rauchen die Frauen Zigarren?
3. Hat Klaus einen Plattenspieler?
4. Findet das Fräulein den Klang gut?
5. Arbeitet Klaus, oder ist er Student?

E. Express in German, *paying special attention to word order.*

1. Unfortunately, they are ill.
2. Who always drinks too much beer?
3. Do you (*du*) know students from England?
4. No, the record is really not new.
5. Where do you (*ihr*) work?
6. Do the students play tennis?
7. Pardon me, do you (*Sie*) have a moment?
8. Are you (*du*) coming tonight? Great! So long!

Chapter vocabulary

Nouns

der	Alkohol	*alcohol*
der	Automat, -en	*automat*
das	Beispiel, -e	*example*
das	Bier, -e	*beer*
das	Ding, -e	*thing*
der	Filter, -	*filter*
der	Freund, -e	*friend (male)*
die	Freundin, -nen	*friend (female)*
die	Gesundheit	*health*
die	Gitarre, -n	*guitar*
das	Instrument, -e	*instrument*
der	Kaffee	*coffee*
die	Karte, -n	*card*
der	Klang, ⸚e	*sound*
das	Klavier, -e	*piano*
der	Moment, -e	*moment*
die	Platte, -n	*record*
der	Plattenspieler, -	*record player*
das	Problem, -e	*problem*
die	Sahne	*cream*

die	Schwäche, -n	weakness, vice
das	Telefon, -e	telephone
(das)	Tennis	tennis
(die)	Verzeihung	pardon
die	Violine, -n	violin
die	Warnung, -en	warning
die	Zeit, -en	time
die	Zigarette, -n	cigarette
die	Zigarre, -n	cigar
der	Zucker	sugar

Verbs

glauben	to believe, think
haben	to have
kaufen	to buy
kennen	to know (someone or something), be acquainted with
rauchen	to smoke
spielen	to play
trinken	to drink

Other words

aber	but
alle	all
alt	old
auch	also

besonders	especially
bis	until
ein paar	a few
fantastisch	fantastic
ganz	quite, completely
gefährlich	dangerous
gern (+ verb)	to like to . . .
gesund	healthy
immer	always
kein	no; not a; not any
krank	sick, ill
leider	unfortunately
manchmal	sometimes, once in a while
mit	with
morgen	tomorrow
natürlich	naturally, of course
neu	new
nur	only
oder	or
ohne	without
sehr	very
tschüß	bye-bye
und	and
ungesund	unhealthy
vielleicht	perhaps, maybe
wann	when
warum	why
zuviel	too much

Mini-dialogues

Student(in) A   Guten Tag! Fährt der Bus alle fünfzehn Minuten?
            B   Nein, alle zwanzig Minuten.
            A   Wie spät ist es jetzt?
            B   Es ist halb vier.
            A   Vielen Dank!
            B   Bitte!

            A   Verzeihung! Wo ist der Kurfürstendamm?
            B   Fahren Sie drei Straßen weiter und dann nach rechts.
            A   Und das ist der Kurfürstendamm?
            B   Ja, das ist der Kurfürstendamm.
            A   Vielen Dank.
            B   Bitte!

A   Hello! Does the bus run every fifteen minutes?
B   No, every twenty minutes.
A   What time is it now?
B   It's three-thirty.
A   Thank you.
B   You're welcome.

A   Pardon me. Where is the Kurfürstendamm?
B   Drive three blocks and then turn right.
A   And that's the Kurfürstendamm?
B   Yes, that's the Kurfürstendamm.
A   Thank you.
B   You're welcome.

Pronunciation

English l vs. German l		*English r vs. German r*		*Final r*
land	Land	right	richtig	wir
literature	Literatur	rule	Regel	der
ball	Ball	correct	korrekt	pur
tunnel	Tunnel	arrogant	arrogant	Rohr
also	also	pair	Paar	Bar

Initial sp, st vs. mid., final sp, st		*z, tz, and -tion*	
sprechen	Wespe	Zucker	Nation
Beispiel	Aspekt	Medizin	Sensation
Studium	Fenster	kurz	Reaktion
Stand	fast	Blitz	
bestellen	gestern	jetzt	

Grammar explanations

I. Present tense: stem-vowel changes

Nimmst du den Bus?
Are you taking the bus?

Nein, ich **nehme** ein Taxi.
No, I'm taking a cab.

Ich **fahre** nach Frankfurt, und Hilde **fährt** nach Hannover.
I'm driving to Frankfurt, and Hilde is driving to Hannover.

Liest du das Programm?
Are you reading the program?

Nein, ich **lese** ein Buch.
No, I'm reading a book.

In the 2nd- and 3rd person singular of the present tense, the stem vowel **e, a,** or **au** of many common verbs undergoes a change known as "vowel variation."

e changes to **i** or **ie**
a changes to **ä** (Umlaut)[1]
au changes to **äu** (Umlaut)

[1]For a discussion of the Umlaut, see the Guide to Pronunciation section in the Appendix.

	sprechen (to speak)	sehen (to see)	fahren (to drive)	laufen (to run)	*Present tense: stem-vowel changes of strong verbs*
singular					
1st	ich spreche	ich sehe	ich fahre	ich laufe	
2nd (fam.)	du sprichst	du siehst	du fährst	du läufst	
3rd	er spricht	er sieht	er fährt	er läuft	
plural					
1st	wir sprechen	wir sehen	wir fahren	wir laufen	
2nd (fam.)	ihr sprecht	ihr seht	ihr fahrt	ihr lauft	
3rd	sie sprechen	sie sehen	sie fahren	sie laufen	
singular/plural					
2nd (formal)	Sie sprechen	Sie sehen	Sie fahren	Sie laufen	

Infinitive	2nd person singular	3rd person singular		*Other common verbs with vowel variation include:*
a>ä				
halten (*to stop*)	du hältst	er hält		
lassen (*to let*)	du läßt[1]	er läßt		
verlassen (*to leave*)	du verläßt[1]	er verläßt		
e>i or **ie**				
essen (*to eat*)	du ißt[1]	er ißt		
nehmen (*to take*)	du nimmst	er nimmt		
lesen (*to read*)	du liest[1]	er liest		
sprechen (*to speak*)	du sprichst	er spricht		
vergessen (*to forget*)	du vergißt[1]	er vergißt		

The verb **nehmen,** in addition to changing **e>i,** also undergoes a consonant change:

ich nehme	wir nehmen
du nimmst	ihr nehmt
er nimmt	sie nehmen

The vocabulary sections of this text and most dictionaries indicate the vowel variation of a verb by listing the 3rd person singular after the infinitive: **halten, hält.**

[1]Note that verbs with a stem ending in a hissing sound have the same form in the 2nd and 3rd person singular. The **ihr**-form is different, since it has no vowel variation: **ihr laßt, ihr eßt,** etc.

CHECK YOUR COMPREHENSION

Complete the sentence with the correct form of the verb in parentheses.

1. Fräulein Lang _____ sehr gut Englisch. (*sprechen*)
2. _____ du ein Buch von Thomas Mann? (*lesen*)
3. Der Student _____ zuviel. (*essen*)
5. Ihr _____ immer den Kaffee. (*vergessen*)
6. _____ Sie Deutsch? (*sprechen*)
7. Peter _____ heute nach Salzburg. (*fahren*)
8. Was _____ du? (*nehmen*)
9. Er _____ das Taxi nicht. (*sehen*)
10. Das Mädchen _____ nicht schnell. (*laufen*)
11. _____ ihr das Institut? (*verlassen*)
12. Wo _____ der Bus? (*halten*)

II. Present tense: verbs with separable prefixes

Steigen Sie bitte **ein!**
Step in, please.

Franz, **mach** die Tür **zu!**
Franz, close the door.

Der Taxifahrer **hält an.**
The cab driver stops.

Wo **fährst** du heute abend **hin?**
Where are you going tonight?

Fräulein Heller **geht** die Treppe **hinauf.**
Miss Heller is going upstairs.

Many German verbs consist of the verb itself and a particle known as a prefix. This particle is placed directly in front of the infinitive to form a unit: **einsteigen,** *to get in (a vehicle).*

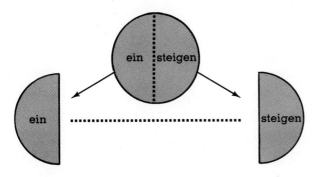

In the present tense, separable prefixes are detached from the verb and placed at the end of the clause.

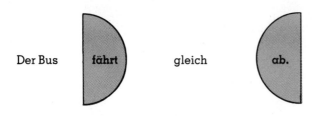

Der Bus   **fährt**   gleich   **ab.**

The bus is leaving right away.

Robert   **steigt**   in ein Taxi   **ein.**

Robert is getting into a taxi.

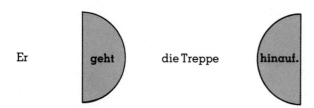

Er   **geht**   die Treppe   **hinauf.**

He's going upstairs.

In pronunciation the separable prefix receives the stress accent: **eínsteigen; er steigt eín.**

A separable prefix adds an important nuance to the meaning of a verb. Sometimes the meaning may be changed altogether. In the beginning of your studies, you cannot easily anticipate a separable prefix when you see a verb. So to understand the verb correctly, be sure to glance at the end of the clause or sentence.

Er kommt aus Amerika.	*He comes from the United States.*
Er kommt in Deutschland an.	*He arrives in Germany.*
Wir fahren nach Frankfurt.	*We're going to Frankfurt.*
Wir fahren ab.	*We're leaving.*

Here are some common separable prefixes:

ab	**ab·fahren** *to depart, drive off, leave*
an	{ **an·halten** *to stop*
	an·kommen *to arrive*
aus	**aus·steigen** *to get out (of a vehicle), get off*
ein	**ein·steigen** *to get in*
weiter	{ **weiter·fahren** *to drive on*
	weiter·gehen *to go on, continue*
zu	**zu·machen** *to close*
zurück	**zurück·laufen** *to run back*

auf·machen — to open

In dictionaries and vocabularies, a separable prefix is indicated by a dot (·), as in **ein·steigen.** However, the dot is not part of the spelling; it is merely an aid to the student.

CHECK YOUR COMPREHENSION

Answer the following sentences in the affirmative, then translate your answers into English.

EXAMPLE: Fährt der Bus ab?
Ja, der Bus fährt ab.
Yes, the bus is leaving.

1. Kommt das Taxi an?
2. Fahren die Herren weiter?
3. Steigt Hilde in das Auto ein?
4. Machst du die Tür zu?
5. Läuft der Student in die Bibliothek zurück?
6. Steigt ihr hier aus?
7. Geht Franz immer weiter?
8. Hält der Bus hier an?
9. Fährt der Bus ab?
10. Steigst du ein?

A special group of separable prefixes is constructed with **hin** (or **hinein, hinauf, hinunter,** etc.), suggesting a movement **away from** the position of the speaker, and with **her** (or **herein, herauf, herunter, heran,** etc.), suggesting a movement *toward* the speaker.

Away from the speaker

hin·fahren *to drive (there)*
hinein·lassen *to let in (there)*
hinauf·gehen *to go up (there)*
hinunter·gehen *to go down (there)*

Toward the speaker

her·fahren *to drive (here)*
herein·lassen *to let in (here)*
herauf·kommen *to come up (here)*
herunter·kommen *to come down (here)*

Away from   *Toward*

Er geht hinauf.   **Sie kommt herunter.**
He's going up (there).   *She's coming down (here.)*

Notice that **gehen** expresses *movement toward* and **kommen** *movement away from;* the separable prefix expresses the direction more specifically.

Hin and **her** should not be confused with **hier** (*here*) and **dort** or **da** (*there*), which indicate fixed position only and not movement:

Position

Fritz ist hier.   *Fritz is here.*

Monika arbeitet dort.   *Monika works there.*

Movement

Er kommt gleich her.   *He's coming (here) right away.*

Wir fahren gleich hin.   *We'll drive there right away.*

With verbs of movement, *where?* is expressed by either **wohin,** *where to?* or **woher,** *from where?* **Wo** (*where*) is used when no movement is implied.

	Wohin fahren Sie?	*Where are you going?*
	Woher kommt er?	*Where is he coming from?*
But:	**Wo** sind wir?	*Where are we?*
	Wo arbeitest du?	*Where do you work?*

Wohin and **woher** can be "split":

Wo fahren Sie **hin?**
Wo kommt er **her?**

In this case, **hin** and **her** act as separable prefixes of their respective verbs:

hin·fahren
her·kommen

A. Form the questions to which the following statements are the answer, then translate the answer into English.

EXAMPLE: Ja, ich gehe die Treppe hinauf. *(du)*
> **Gehst du die Treppe hinauf?**
> *Are you going upstairs?*

1. Ja, wir gehen die Treppe hinunter. *(Sie)*
2. Ja, Herr Kunz fährt hin.
3. Ja, ich lasse die Studenten herein. *(du)*
4. Ja, das Fräulein geht schnell hinauf.
5. Ja, Karl kommt jetzt herunter.
6. Ja, wir lassen die Amerikanerin hinein. *(ihr)*
7. Ja, die Männer fahren auch hin.
8. Ja, sie kommt die Treppe herauf.

B. Form the questions to which the following statements are the answer. Use **wo, wohin,** or **woher.**

EXAMPLE: Sie geht in das Institut.
> **Wohin geht sie?** *or:* **Wo geht sie hin?**

1. Die Studenten fahren nach Salzburg.
2. Da arbeitet er.
3. Sie kommt aus England.
4. Sie studieren in Berlin.
5. Fritz geht in die Bibliothek.
6. Die Frauen fahren nach Hamburg.

III. The imperative

Komm schnell, Peter!
Come quickly, Peter.

Geht weiter, Peter und Monika!
Continue, Peter and Monika.

Herr Kunz, **nehmen Sie** bitte Platz!
Mr. Kunz, please have (take) a seat.

The imperative form of the verb is used to give a command or make a suggestion. German distinguishes between three forms of direct address in the imperative: the **Sie, du,** and **ihr** forms. Usually they are followed by an exclamation mark.

The formal or **Sie** form of the imperative is identical with the present-tense form, except that pronoun and verb are inverted.

Kommen Sie, bitte!	*Please come.*
Gehen Sie, bitte!	*Please go.*
Lesen Sie, bitte!	*Read, please.*

The imperative of the plural familiar or **ihr**-form is identical with the present-tense form, except that the pronoun is dropped.

Kommt, bitte!	*Please come.*
Geht, bitte!	*Please go.*
Lest, bitte!	*Read, please.*

The imperative of the 2nd person singular (familiar or **du**-form) consists of the stem of the 2nd person singular of the present tense; the ending **-st** is dropped. However, if the stem ends in **-s** or **-ß,** only the **-t** is dropped and the insert **-e-** in verbs like **antworten** and **öffnen** is retained.

Present tense	*Imperative*
du kommst	komm!
du gehst	geh!
du sprichst	sprich!
du nimmst	nimm!
du liest	lies!
du fährst	fahr!
du läßt	laß!
du läufst	lauf!
du antwortest	antworte!
du öffnest	öffne!

Note that verbs with the vowel variation **a>ä** or **au>äu** do not carry the umlaut into the imperative of the 2nd person singular.

In all three forms of the imperative, the separable prefixes always move to the end of the phrase.

du form:	Steig bitte **ein!**	*Get in, please.*
ihr form:	Lauft bitte **weiter!**	*Run on, please.*
Sie form:	Gehen Sie bitte **zurück!**	*Go back, please.*

The verb **sein** (*to be*) has the following irregular imperative forms:

du form:	**Sei** so gut!	
ihr form:	**Seid** so gut!	*Be so kind (good).*
Sie form:	**Seien** Sie so gut!	

The infinitive may be used as an impersonal imperative form to give instructions to the public. A bus driver, for instance, might call out the following:

Bitte, einsteigen!	*Please step in.*
Weitergehen, bitte!	*Please move on.*
Bitte, aussteigen!	*(Everybody) out, please.*

CHECK YOUR COMPREHENSION

Use the appropriate imperative form of the verb in parentheses. Watch the position of the separable prefix.

EXAMPLE: Klaus, _____ gleich! (*herunterkommen*)
Klaus, komm gleich herunter!

1. Peter und Lotte, _____ die Bücher nicht! (*vergessen*)
2. Herr Mayer, bitte _____! (*einsteigen*)
3. Richard, _____ nicht so schnell! (*sprechen*)
4. Fräulein Schmidt, bitte _____! (*heraufkommen*)
5. Fritz, _____ schnell in die Klasse! (*zurücklaufen*)
6. Ulrike, _____ die Tür! (*öffnen*)
7. Franz _____ hier nicht! (*anhalten*)
8. Karl, _____ bitte Platz! (*nehmen*)
9. Anna, _____ die Treppe! (*hinuntergehen*)
10. Herr Wegner, _____ die Mädchen! (*hereinlassen*)

Conversation

Er bittet um Auskunft.	*He asks for information.*
alle (fünfzehn) Minuten	*every (fifteen) minutes*
Ich bin nicht in Eile.	*I'm not in a hurry.*
Vielen Dank!	$\left\{\begin{array}{l}\textit{Thank you very much.}\\ \textit{Thanks a lot.}\end{array}\right.$
das nächste Mal	*next time*
Moment mal!	*Just a moment.*

BUS ODER TAXI?

Flugplatz Berlin-Tegel. Robert kommt gerade in West-Berlin an. Er nimmt das Gepäck und verläßt die Halle°. Draußen° stehen Taxis. Er bittet einen Taxifahrer um Auskunft.   terminal / outside

Robert   Guten Tag! Verzeihung! Fährt ein Bus von hier zum°   to the
Kurfürstendamm?[1]

[1]The main shopping street in West Berlin, called "Kudamm" by the Berliners.

Taxifahrer Nicht direkt° von hier. Aber sehen Sie die Bus-   *directly*
Haltestelle da drüben? Nehmen Sie den Bus Nummer acht!

    Dort fährt gerade ein Bus Nummer acht ab.

Robert Wie oft fährt der Bus zum Kurfürstendamm?
Taxifahrer Moment mal, ich glaube, alle fünfzehn Minuten.
Robert Wirklich?
Taxifahrer Aber nehmen Sie doch ein Taxi! Da, steigen Sie ein!
Robert Danke, ich bin nicht in Eile und habe auch nicht genug
Geld für ein Taxi. Vielen Dank für die Auskunft.
Taxifahrer Bitte.

    *Nach fünfzehn Minuten kommt ein Bus Nummer acht an und
Robert steigt ein.*

Robert Fahren Sie zum Kurfürstendamm?
Busfahrer Nein, nein. Steigen Sie schnell wieder aus und nehmen
Sie Bus Nummer fünfzehn.

    An die Passagiere°:   *to the passengers*

    Einsteigen, bitte. Gehen Sie weiter! Weitergehen, bitte!

    Der Busfahrer macht die Tür zu.

Robert (*zu sich*)° Das nächste Mal nehme ich ein Taxi.   *to himself*

QUESTIONS ON THE CONVERSATION

1. Wo kommt Robert an?
2. Wen bittet er um Auskunft?
3. Fährt Bus Nummer acht oder fünfzehn zum Kurfürstendamm?
4. Nimmt er den Bus oder das Taxi? Warum?

5. Wie oft fährt der Bus zum Kurfürstendamm?
6. Steigt Robert in den Bus ein?
7. Was sagt der Busfahrer zu Robert?

PERSONAL QUESTIONS

1. Bist du in Eile?
2. Nimmst du heute einen Bus? Wohin?
3. Hast du genug Geld für ein Taxi?
4. Kennst du West-Berlin?
5. Bittest du oft Taxifahrer oder Busfahrer um Auskunft?

Practice

A. Substitute the appropriate form of each verb in parentheses for the verb in the sentence.

1. Friederike nimmt das Auto. (sehen / verlasssen / anhalten / fahren)
2. Du fährst sehr schnell, Angelika. (laufen / sprechen / lesen / essen)
3. Herr Steiner, fahren Sie bitte ab! (einsteigen / heraufkommen / weitergehen / anhalten)

B. Use the appropriate form of the verb in parentheses. Watch the position of the separable prefix.

EXAMPLE: Albert, _____ nicht so schnell!   *(laufen)*
          Albert, lauf nicht so schnell!

1. Else, _____ Deutsch, nicht Englisch!   *(sprechen)*
2. Wo _____ die Busse?   *(anhalten)*
3. _____ ihr den Bus oder das Taxi?   *(nehmen)*
4. Bitte, Herr Schmidt, _____!   *(aussteigen)*
5. Erich, _____ das Buch nicht!   *(vergessen)*
6. _____ du oft Bücher von Thomas Mann?   *(lesen)*
7. Er _____ manchmal.   *(hinuntergehen)*
8. Wer _____ die Treppe?   *(heraufkommen)*
9. Der Freund _____ heute abend in Berlin.   *(ankommen)*
10. Viktor und Thomas, bitte _____ die Tür.   *(zumachen)*
11. _____ ihr die Bus-Haltestelle da drüben?   *(sehen)*
12. Der Student _____ viel zuviel.   *(essen)*
13. _____ du den Bus oder ein Taxi?   *(nehmen)*
14. Hans, _____ den Mann!   *(hereinlassen)*
15. Die Frau _____ gleich den Flugplatz.   *(verlassen)*

C. In the following sentences use the appropriate separable prefix with the verb given in parentheses, and place it in the appropriate position. The direction is indicated by the arrow, and the position of the speaker by ●.

EXAMPLE: Die Studentin _____ die Treppe.   (_____ kommen ↗ ●)
Die Studentin kommt die Treppe herauf.

1. Wo _____ ihr morgen?   (_____ fahren ● ——→)
2. Wo _____ du?   (_____ kommen ——→ ●)
3. Hier _____ wir die Treppe.   (_____ gehen ● ↘)
4. _____ du den Freund nicht?   (_____ lassen ——→ ●)
5. Herr Frisch _____ in das Haus.   (_____ gehen ● ——→)

D. Construct sentences with the following cues. Watch the punctuation to determine whether the sentence is a statement, question, or command.

EXAMPLE: weiterfahren / bitte / Herr Bunzle!
Fahren Sie bitte weiter, Herr Bunzle!

1. fahren / Fräulein Heller / nach Frankfurt?
2. anhalten / der Bus / hier?
3. zumachen / Paul / die Tür!
4. abfahren / wir / heute abend.
5. heraufkommen / wer / die Treppe?
6. fahren / Herr Müller / immer / sehr schnell.
7. zurücklaufen / die Studentin / in das Institut.
8. aussteigen / ich / hier.
9. essen / Hans / zuviel / Zucker.
10. vergessen / Dieter / das Gepäck / nicht!

E. Use the appropriate imperative form of the verbs in parentheses. Watch the position of the separable prefix.

EXAMPLE: Arnold, _____ so gut und _____ das Zimmer! (*sein, verlassen*)
Arnold, sei so gut und verlaß das Zimmer!

1. Fräulein Ottinger, _____ bitte die Warnung! (*lesen*)
2. Joachim, _____ doch nicht so schnell! (*essen*)
3. Monika and Jürgen, _____ so gut und _____ das Geld! (*sein, suchen*)
4. Herr Brandt, bitte _____! (*hinfahren*)
5. Willy, _____ bitte die Treppe _____ und _____ die Tür! (*hinaufgehen, öffnen*)

F. Give the English equivalent of the following sentences.

1. Oskar, halt hier nicht an; fahr weiter!
2. Lauf schnell zurück in das Institut!
3. Er ist krank, ißt nicht genug und vergißt sehr viel.
4. Vielleicht kommt Gretchen heute abend an.
5. Robert ist nicht in Eile und nimmt den Bus.
6. Der Bus fährt alle zwanzig Minuten ab.
7. Moment mal! Warum steigt ihr hier aus?
8. Wer kommt die Treppe herauf?
9. Er läßt die Frauen nicht hinein.
10. Das nächste Mal vergessen Sie das Gepäck nicht!
11. Wo kommst du her?
12. Wo fahrt ihr hin?

Vocabulary development

A. German is versatile in combining separable prefixes with verbs. For instance:

weiter·lesen	*to go on reading*
weiter·machen	*to go on doing*
weiter·sprechen	*to go on talking*

Give some commands with these compounds, such as: **Sprich weiter!**

Here are some compounds with **mit** (*with*):

mit·fahren	*to travel along with*
mit·lesen	*to read along with*
mit·nehmen	*to take along with*

Form a few questions or commands with these verbs, such as: **Nimmst du die Zeitung nicht mit? Rudolf, lies mit!**

B. The opposite of **rechts** (*right*) is **links** (*left*), which also occurs frequently with **nach;** for instance:

Fahren Sie nach links!	*Drive to the left.*

Construct a few short sentences with the two expressions, using the verbs **fahren** and **gehen.**

C. German uses many "flavoring particles," such as **doch** and **mal,** which must be understood within a given context; there is no one translation for all instances.

Nehmen Sie Platz!	*Have a seat.*
Nehmen Sie doch Platz!	*Do sit down.*
Nehmen Sie ein Taxi!	*Take a taxi.*
Nehmen Sie doch ein Taxi!	*Well then, take a taxi!*

The particle **mal** can be combined with numerals: **einmal, zweimal, dreimal,** etc. (*once, twice, three times,* etc.) It may also be used as a noun: **das nächste Mal** (*next time*). As a flavoring particle it takes on the sense of *just* or *even:*

Moment mal!	*Just a moment.*
Sie sieht den Mann nicht mal an.	*She doesn't even look at the man.*

In multiplications **mal** means *times:*

$2 \times 2 =$ **zwei mal zwei**	*two times two*

Communicative exercises

A. Ask your classmate a question with the following elements and have him/her answer:

wann / abfahren	Ich fahre . . .
hier / aussteigen	
der Bus / hier / anhalten	
wer / die Treppe / heraufkommen	
wohin / fahren	
mitkommen	

B. Give commands with the following elements to a classmate with whom you are on **du**- terms:

verlassen	das Zimmer	_____
sprechen	nicht so schnell, bitte	_____
essen	nicht so viel	_____
fahren	nach rechts	_____
hinaufgehen	die Treppe	_____
zumachen	die Tür, bitte	_____
anhalten	hier, bitte	_____
vergessen	die Zeitungen nicht	_____
nehmen	das Gepäck	_____
bestellen	doch eine Tasse Kaffee	_____

C. Give the same commands in the **ihr** and **Sie** forms.

D. Use the following expressions in commands given to your neighbors in the **du** and **ihr** forms and then have them give the opposite command.

die Tür öffnen	_____	_____
Platz nehmen	_____	_____
hier einsteigen	_____	_____
nach links fahren	_____	_____
die Treppe herunterkommen	_____	_____
schnell abfahren	_____	_____

Reading

ZIMMER NUMMER DREIZEHN

Robert verläßt das Hotel „Conti". Es ist fünf Uhr. Er sieht einen Kiosk°, kauft eine Zeitung und geht in ein Café. Aber er geht nicht hinein. Er findet einen Platz auf dem Bürgersteig° und bestellt eine Tasse Kaffee. Dann kommt eine Studentin heran und fragt: „Ist hier noch ein Platz frei?"[1] „Oh ja, natürlich, nehmen Sie bitte Platz!" sagt er. Sie bestellt eine Tasse Tee und ein Stück Kuchen. Dann öffnet sie ein Buch, liest und spricht nicht. „Na schön",° denkt Robert, „dann lese ich die Zeitung und trinke den Kaffee."

Plötzlich hört er eine Sirene.° Ein Feuerwehrwagen° kommt heran. Alle Autos fahren nach rechts und halten an. Robert sieht Rauch aufsteigen.° „Ist das möglich?" denkt er. „Ist das nicht das Hotel Conti?"

Er läuft schnell zurück, aber die Polizei läßt ihn nicht hinein. „Halt! Nicht hineingehen!" hört er. Er protestiert. Vergeblich.° Endlich ist

newsstand

on the sidewalk

well, then

siren / fire engine

smoke rising

in vain

das Feuer unter Kontrolle. Robert geht schnell die Treppe hinauf und öffnet die Tür von Zimmer Nummer dreizehn. Die Daunendecke[2], das Gepäck, alles ist ganz naß.° Er macht die Tür wieder zu und geht lang- *wet* sam die Treppe hinunter. „Heute habe ich wirklich kein Glück", denkt er. „Das nächste Mal nehme ich nicht wieder Zimmer Nummer dreizehn!"

CULTURAL NOTES

1. „**Ist hier noch ein Platz frei?**"   In Germany it is customary to sit down at a partially occupied table in a crowded restaurant or café.

2. **Daunendecke**   Eiderdown. This is much used bedding in Germany.

QUESTIONS

1. Was macht Robert um (*at*) fünf Uhr?
2. Was kauft er?
3. Wohin geht er?
4. Was bestellt er?
5. Wer kommt an?
6. Was fragt sie?
7. Kennt Robert die Studentin?
8. Was macht dann die Studentin?
9. Was denkt Robert?
10. Was hört er plötzlich?
11. Was machen alle Autos?
12. Wohin läuft Robert schnell?
13. Wer läßt Robert nicht in das Hotel?
14. Was ist in Zimmer dreizehn ganz naß?
15. Was denkt Robert?

Review

A. Construct sentences with the cues given below; watch the punctuation to see whether the sentence is a statement, question, or command. Start the sentence with the word in italics, where so indicated. Watch the word order.

EXAMPLE: ankommen / der Freund / morgen früh / *sicher*
    Sicher kommt der Freund morgen früh an.

1. sein / Zucker / gefährlich / für die Gesundheit?
2. essen / du / sehr viel / Kuchen?
3. nehmen / Adolf / das Buch / und / lesen / das Beispiel!
4. arbeiten / der Freund / sehr viel / aber / weiterkommen / er / nicht.
5. spielen / Monika / die Platte / von Louis Armstrong!
6. ankommen / Fräulein Ohlendorf / heute / nicht / *leider*.

7. zurücklaufen / Ernst / doch / und / kaufen / eine Zeitung!
8. nehmen / Herr Schwarzkopf / doch / bitte / Platz!
9. hinfahren / er / morgen / *vielleicht*.
10. sprechen / er / viel / zu langsam / *immer*.

B. Fill in each blank with a form of the appropriate verb listed at the right.

1. Adalbert, du _____ viel zu schnell; das _____ nicht gut für   a. verlassen
   die Gesundheit.   b. sein
2. Der Student _____ immer das Deutschbuch.   c. essen
3. Die Polizei _____ die Studentin nicht in das Hotel.   d. lassen
4. Sie (*sing.*) _____ das Institut.   e. vergessen

C. Express in German.

1. Please have a seat.
2. We're getting out here.
3. Mrs. Ottinger, when are you going downstairs?
4. We aren't in a hurry.
5. Ulrike eats too much cake.
6. The police let Robert in.
7. He asks the taxi driver for information.
8. The children are coming up again.
9. Now the men are leaving the hotel.
10. The bus stops every twelve minutes.
11. Erika, please drive slowly.
12. Where is Hilde running to?

Chapter vocabulary

Nouns _____

das	Auto, -s	car, automobile
der	Bus, -se	bus
der	Busfahrer, -	bus driver
das	Café, -s	coffeehouse, restaurant
der	Dank	gratitude
die	Eile	hurry
das	Feuer, -	fire
der	Flugplatz, ⸚e	airport
das	Geld, -er	money
das	Gepäck	luggage
die	Haltestelle, -n	(bus, streetcar or train) stop
das	Haus, ⸚er	house
das	Hotel, -s	hotel
die	Kontrolle, -n	control

der	Kuchen, -	cake
das	Mal, -e	occasion, time, times
das	nächste —	next time
die	Minute, -n	minute
der	Moment	moment
	— mal!	Just a minute!
die	Nummer, -n	number
der	Platz, ⸚e	place, seat
	— nehmen	to take (have) a seat
die	Polizei (*sing.*)	police
das	Stück, -e	piece
die	Tasse, -n	cup
das	Taxi, -s	taxi, cab
der	Taxifahrer, -	taxi driver
der	Tee	tea
die	Treppe, -n	stairs
die	Zeitung, -en	newspaper

Verbs

ab•fahren (fährt)	to leave, depart, drive off
an•halten (hält)	to stop
an•kommen	to arrive (at a place)
antworten	to answer
aus•steigen	to get out (of a vehicle), get off
bestellen	to order
bitten (um)	to ask (for)
denken	to think
ein•steigen	to get in or into (a vehicle)
essen (ißt)	to eat
fahren (fährt)	to drive, go (by vehicle)
fragen	to ask (a question)
gehen	to go
halten (hält)	to stop
hören	to hear
lassen (läßt)	to let, let go
laufen (läuft)	to run, go (on foot)
lesen (liest)	to read
machen	to do
nehmen (nimmt)	to take
protestieren	to protest
sagen	to say
sehen (sieht)	to see
sprechen (spricht)	to speak
stehen	to stand
vergessen (vergißt)	to forget
verlassen (verläßt)	to leave (behind)
weiter• (+ *verb*)	to continue to (doing)
zu•machen	to close
zurück•laufen (läuft)	to run back

Other words

alles	all, everything
dann	then
das	that
dort	there
einmal	once
endlich	finally
frei	free, vacant
genug	enough
gerade	just now, just then
halt (!)	stop (!)
langsam	slow(ly)
links	left, on the left
nach —	to the left
mal	times (multiplication)
mit	with
möglich	possible
nach	toward; after
noch	yet; still
oft	often
plötzlich	suddenly
rechts	right, on the right
nach —	to the right
schnell	quickly, fast
von	of
wieder	again
woher	where, from what place
wohin	where, to what place
zu	to; too

See also the **hin** and **her** verbs on p. 53.

Mini-dialogues

Student(in) A   Sind Sie heute abend zu Hause?
           B   Ja, ich arbeite heute abend nicht und fahre um halb fünf nach Hause.
           A   Wie spät ist es jetzt?
           B   Es ist Viertel vor vier.
           A   Fahren Sie mit der Straßenbahn, oder sind Sie mit dem Auto in der Stadt?
           B   Ich fahre mit der Straßenbahn.
           A   Warum fahren Sie nicht mit mir?
           B   Danke, sehr gern. Bis halb fünf.

           A   Guten Morgen! Bitte sehr?
           B   Ich suche ein Zimmer.
           A   Sind Sie Student?
           B   Ja.
           A   Warum nehmen Sie nicht ein Zimmer direkt bei der Universität?
           B   Ja, sehr schön! Wieviel kostet es monatlich?
           A   Mit Kochgelegenheit und Heizung zweihundertfünfzig Mark.
           B   Das ist nicht teuer. Wie ist die Adresse, bitte?

A   Will you be home tonight?
B   Yes, I'm not working tonight and will be going home at four-thirty.
A   What time is it now?
B   It's a quarter to four.
A   Are you taking the streetcar or do you have your car with you?
B   I'm taking the streetcar.
A   Why don't you come along with me?
B   Thank you, gladly. Till four-thirty.

A   Good morning. May I help you?
B   I'm looking for a room.
A   Are you a student?
B   Yes.
A   Why don't you take a room right by the University?
B   Yes, very nice. How much is it per month?
A   With cooking privileges and heat included, two hundred fifty marks.
B   That's not expensive. What's the address, please?

Pronunciation

Final -ig	ng	f-sound	vs. v-sound
hungrig	bringen	**V**ater	**V**anille
langweilig	gingen	**v**ergessen	**V**ase
wenig	hängen	wie**v**iel	**V**illa
Ewigkeit	Wohnung	**V**olk	Uni**v**ersität
Heiligtum	Heizung	**v**öllig	Offensi**v**e

Grammar explanations

I. Dative case

Das Kind bringt **den Männern** einen Schlüssel.
The child brings the men a key.

Der Taxifahrer zeigt **den Frauen** den Bahnhof.
The taxi driver shows the women the railroad station.

Das Mädchen gibt **dem Busfahrer** das Geld.
The girl gives the bus driver the money.

Wem bringst du die Zeitung?
To whom do you take the newspaper?

Another important part of a sentence is the *indirect object*, which tells *to whom* or *for whom* something is done. For instance, in the act expressed by the verb **geben** (*to give*), three elements are involved:

the one who gives	= subject
the one to whom something is given	= indirect object
the thing that is given	= direct object

The case of the indirect object is called the *dative*.

Thomas gibt   dem Mann   das Buch.
Thomas gives the man the book.

In German, if the two objects are nouns, the dative precedes the accusative. But for emphasis the indirect object can be placed at the beginning: **Dem Mann gibt Thomas das Buch.**

In English the indirect object is recognized by the prepositions *to* or *for*, expressed or understood. In German the indirect object occurs without a preposition, and is indicated by the dative forms of the definite and indefinite articles and the negative **kein.**

Er bringt **der** Frau eine Zeitung.	*He brings the woman a newspaper.*
Er öffnet **einem** Freund die Tür.	*He opens the door for a friend.*
Thomas gibt **keinem** Kind die Schlüssel.	*Thomas doesn't give the keys to any child.*
Wir bezahlen **den** Männern das Bier.	*We'll buy the men the beer.*

In the dative plural, all nouns add **-n** (or **-en** for phonetic reasons), unless their nominative plural forms already end in **-n.**

	Nominative plural	Dative plural
masc.	die Männer	den Männer**n**
fem.	die Städte	den Städte**n**
neut.	die Kinder	den Kinder**n**
But:	die Studentinnen	den Studentin**nen**
	die Frauen	den Frau**en**

Singular	Def. article	Indef. article	**kein**		Articles, **kein,**
masc.	de**m** Mann	ein**em** Mann	kein**em** Mann		*and nouns:*
fem.	de**r** Frau	ein**er** Frau	kein**er** Frau		*dative case*
neut.	de**m** Kind	ein**em** Kind	kein**em** Kind		

Plural					
masc.		Männer**n**	—Männer**n**		Männer**n**
fem.	**den**	Frau**en**	—Frau**en**	**keinen**	Frau**en**
neut.		Kinder**n**	—Kinder**n**		Kinder**n**

Foreign words like **das Auto, das Café,** and **das Hotel,** which end in **-s** in the nominative plural, do *not* add **-n** in the dative plural:

nom. sing.	das Auto
nom. pl.	die Autos
dat. pl.	den Autos

Singular	Nominative	Accusative	Dative	
masc.	der	den	dem	*Articles and*
	ein	einen	einem	**kein:**
	kein	keinen	keinem	*nominative,*
fem.	die	die	der	*accusative,*
	eine	eine	einer	*and dative*
	keine	keine	keiner	*cases*
neut.	das	das	dem	
	ein	ein	einem	
	kein	kein	keinem	
Plural				
all genders	die	die	den	
	—	—	—	
	keine	keine	keinen	

The interrogative **wer** (*who*) also has a dative form: **wem** (*to whom*).

Wem gibt er das Geld?

To whom does he give the money?
Whom does he give the money to?

CHECK YOUR COMPREHENSION

A. Fill in the appropriate accusative or dative of the noun indicated in parentheses. Determine first whether the noun is a direct or indirect object, singular or plural.

1. Karl öffnet _____. (*die Tür*)
2. Geben Sie _____ da drüben das Buch. (*das Fräulein*)
3. Die Frau zeigt _____ das Gepäck. (*der Taxifahrer*)
4. Heute essen wir _____. (*ein Kuchen*)
5. Sie bringt _____ ein Bier. (*der Mann*)
6. Wir zeigen _____ die Platte. (*eine Freundin*)
7. Warum öffnest du _____ die Tür nicht? (*die Kinder*)
8. Hans sieht _____. (*die Freundin*)
9. Er bringt _____ die Karten. (*die Studentinnen*)

B. Use **wer, wen,** or **wem** in the following sentences.

1. _____ ist da?
2. _____ bringst du das Buch?
3. _____ kennst du gut?
4. _____ gibst du eine Zeitung?
5. _____ öffnet sie die Tür?
6. *Wer* bringt den Tee?

Wen bringt er den Tee?

Salzburg

II. Prepositions with the dative

Wir kommen gerade **aus dem Hotel.**
We're just coming from the hotel.

Die Herren gehen **zur Haltestelle.**
The gentlemen are going to the bus stop.

Die Freundinnen fahren **mit dem Auto nach Hause.**
The girlfriends are going home by car.

Heute abend bin ich **zu Hause.**
I'll be home tonight.

A preposition is usually followed by a noun or a pronoun. In German, a preposition governs a specific case, most often the dative or accusative.

The following is a list of prepositions that are always followed by an object in the *dative case*. Memorize them, for they occur frequently. The English translations given here are general and flexible; sometimes they must be adjusted to the context of the sentence.

aus	out of, from	Er kommt gerade **aus dem Hotel.**
		He is coming from the hotel.
		Jürgen kommt **aus der Stadt Köln.**
		Jürgen comes from the city of Cologne.
außer	except, besides	Helga kennt die Studenten, **außer dem Amerikaner.**
		Helga knows the students, except the American.
bei	near, at (the place of)	Sie steht **bei der Tür.**
		She is standing near the door.
		Heinz wohnt **bei Frau Becker.**
		Heinz lives at Mrs. Becker's (place).
mit	with, by (means of)	Sie spricht **mit den Kindern.**
		She's talking with the children.
		Wir fahren **mit dem Auto.**
		We're traveling by car.
nach	after, to (referring to cities and countries)	**Nach dem Abendessen** liest er die Zeitung.
		After dinner he reads the newspaper.
		Sie **fahren nach Berlin.**
		They are going to Berlin.
seit	since, for (in reference to time)	**Seit dem Feuer** ißt er hier.[1]
		(Ever) since the fire he has been eating here.
		Sie ist **seit Tagen** krank.[1]
		She has been ill for days.
von	from, by, of, about	Kommt ihr **von der Haltestelle?**
		Are you coming from the bus stop?
		Wir sprechen gerade **von dem Feuer.**
		We're just now talking about the fire.
zu	to (referring to persons and public places), at	Die Frau geht **zu den Kindern.**
		The woman goes to the children.
		Er geht **zu der Haltestelle.**
		He is going to the (bus) stop.

[1]Note that **seit** is used here with the present tense in German.

The prepositions **bei, von,** and **zu** are usually contracted with the definite article in the singular:

*With **dem** (masc. and neut.)*   *With **der** (fem.)*

bei dem = **beim**   zu der = **zur**
von dem = **vom**
zu dem = **zum**

Die Kinder stehen **beim** Fenster.
Die Freundin kommt **vom** Bahnhof.
Heidi fährt **zum** Hotel.
Frau Strauß geht **zur** Haltestelle.

✳ Two phrases using prepositions governing the dative have special meanings: **zu Hause** indicates a fixed position, *at home;* **nach Hause** indicates movement *toward home.*

Das Gepäck lasse ich **zu Hause.** *at home*   *I'll leave the luggage at home.*

Wir gehen jetzt **nach Hause.**   *We're going home now.*
↘ *w/ motion*

The interrogative **wem** may occur with a dative preposition.

Mit wem fahren Sie nach Köln?   *With whom are you driving to Cologne?*

CHECK YOUR COMPREHENSION

A. Complete the sentence with the cue in parentheses.

1. Herr Müller kommt _____. *(out of the house)*
2. Heute fahren wir _____. *(to Germany)*
3. Die Mädchen gehen _____. *(to the bus stop)*
4. Robert wohnt _____. *(at Mrs. Lang's)*
5. Die Studenten sprechen _____. *(about the fire)*
6. Werner, spiel jetzt nicht _____! *(with the children)*
7. Er kennt Frau Klein _____. *(since July)* *seit Juli*
8. Der Bus fährt _____. *(from Cologne to Dortmund)*
9. Wir gehen gleich *nach hause*. *(home)*

Wir sind zu hause

B. Complete the sentences by using either **zu Hause** or **nach Hause.**

1. Ich bin heute abend ___*zu*___.
2. Das Kind geht gerade ___*nach*___.

3. Der Student ißt heute vielleicht _____. *zu*
4. Heute abend fahre ich ___*nach*___.

just, just now

heute - today
abend - evening

III. Special noun declensions

Ich zeige **dem Studenten** die Stadt.
I am showing the student the city.

Gib **dem Herrn** die Adresse!
Give the address to the gentleman.

Although most nouns do not add any endings in the nominative, accusative, and dative singular, certain masculine nouns add **-en** to *all* cases *except* the *nominative singular*. These nouns maintain the **-en** ending throughout the plural. In this group are **der Student, der Mensch, der Präsident** (*president*), **der Tourist** (*tourist*), and **der Junge**[1] (*boy*).

	Singular	Plural	
nom.	der Student	die Studenten	*Special masculine declension*
acc.	den Studenten	die Studenten	
dat.	dem Studenten	den Studenten	

The common noun **der Herr** deviates slightly from this special declension; it adds **-n** in the accusative and dative singular, and **-en** in all plural forms.

	Singular	Plural	
nom.	der Herr	die Herren	*Declension:* **der Herr**
acc.	den Herrn	die Herren	
dat.	dem Herrn	den Herren	

CHECK YOUR COMPREHENSION

Use the appropriate case of the noun in parentheses.

1. Wir bringen _____ die Gitarre.   (*der Student*)
2. Kennst du _____? (*der Mensch*)
3. Wo sind _____? (*die Herren*)
4. Sag _____, ich gehe nach Hause.   (*der Junge*)
5. Fräulein Schell sucht _____.   (*der Student*)

die Menschen — the people

[1]A frequently used plural of **der Junge** is the colloquialism **die Jungens** (*boys*); **die Jungen** not only means *boys* but also *the young*.

after the verb 'to be' the noun is in the NOMINATIVE

6. Er spricht mit _____. (*die Touristen*)
7. Wir sehen _____ nicht. (*der Präsident*)

Conversation

Bitte sehr?	{ *What can I do for you?* *May I help you?*
Moment bitte!	*One moment, please.*
Das ist nicht gerade billig.	*That is not particularly cheap.*
zu Hause sein	*to be at home*
nach Hause gehen	*to go home*
Wie steht es mit . . .?	*What can you tell me . . .?*

DAS STUDENTENZIMMER

Heinz ist in Köln zu Hause, aber er studiert in Marburg. Er sucht ein Zimmer. Er liest die Zeitung und geht dann zum Ver-mittlungsbüro°. Dort spricht er mit Fräulein Schell.   rental agency

Frl.[1] *Schell*   Guten Morgen! Bitte sehr?

Heinz   Ich bin Student hier in Marburg und suche ein Zimmer.

Frl. Schell   Wieviel können° Sie monatlich bezahlen?   can

Heinz   Ungefähr zweihundert Mark monatlich.

Frl. Schell   Moment bitte! Warum nehmen Sie nicht ein Zimmer
direkt bei der Universität? Es kostet zweihundertvierzig Mark
mit Heizung.°   heat

Heinz   Das ist nicht gerade billig! Ist das mit Kochgelegenheit?°   cooking facilities

Frl. Schell   Ja, ich bin sicher.

Heinz   Hat das Zimmer auch eine Dusche oder ein Bad?

Frl. Schell   Nein, aber es hat ein Waschbecken.

Heinz   Und wie steht es mit der Toilette?

Frl. Schell   Sie ist direkt beim Zimmer.

Heinz   Nicht schlecht! Wie ist die Adresse, bitte?

Frl. Schell   Frau Becker, Lindenstraße fünf. Beim Hindenburg-
Platz.[2]

Heinz   Danke! Was kostet das?

Frl. Schell   Acht Mark. (Sie bringt dem Studenten ein Formular.°)   form (sheet)
Unterschreiben° Sie das Formular bitte und geben Sie es Frau   sign
Becker!

Heinz unterschreibt und bezahlt.

Heinz   Vielen Dank! Auf Wiedersehen!

Heinz geht nach Hause.

[1]**Frl.** is the abbreviation for **Fräulein.**

[2]Named for Paul von Hindenburg (1847–1934), a famous general who was president
of the German Republic from 1925 until his death.

QUESTIONS ON THE CONVERSATION

1. Wo ist Heinz zu Hause?
2. Was liest Heinz?
3. Was sucht er?
4. Wohin geht Heinz, und mit wem spricht er dort?
5. Wieviel möchte (*would like*) Heinz monatlich bezahlen?
6. Hat das Zimmer bei der Universität Heizung?
7. Was ist direkt beim Zimmer?
8. Wieviel bezahlt Heinz beim Vermittlungsbüro?

PERSONAL QUESTIONS

1. Wo sind Sie zu Hause?
2. Haben Sie ein Zimmer mit Heizung?
3. Ist es billig oder teuer?
4. Wieviel bezahlen Sie monatlich?
5. Hat das Zimmer eine Dusche oder ein Bad oder ein Waschbecken?
6. Ist es direkt bei der Universität?

Practice

A. Substitute the items in parentheses for the noun in italics and make the necessary changes. Note that only nouns in which singular and plural forms are the same have been marked "*sing.*" and "*pl.*".

1. Bringt ihr *der Frau* das Gepäck?
   (*Fräulein / Freundin / Mädchen, pl. / Studenten / Junge*)

2. Zeigst du *dem Fräulein* das Haus?
   (*Busfahrer, pl. / Kinder / Freund / Herren / Mädchen, sing. / Polizei*)

3. Wir öffnen *einem Studenten* immer die Tür.
   (*Mädchen, sing. / Studentin / Freund / Frauen / Kinder / Freundinnen*)

B. Form sentences with the following elements. Be careful to use the right case ending. First form the question and then the answer.

EXAMPLE: er / geben / der Herr / das Geld.
        Gibt er dem Herrn das Geld?
        Ja, er gibt dem Herrn das Geld.

1. das Mädchen / bestellen / die Freunde (or die Freundin) / ein Buch.
2. der Busfahrer / zeigen / die Studentin (or der Student) / die Haltestelle.

3. das Kind / bringen / der Mann (or der Herr) / die Zeitung.
4. der Herr / öffnen / die Frauen (or das Fräulein) / die Tür.
5. der Student / geben / die Studentinnen (or die Männer) / das Geld.

C. Substitute the noun in parentheses for the noun in italics, and make the necessary changes.

1. Außer der *Zeitung* bringt er Paul ein Buch.   (Geld)
2. Ich gehe sicher zur *Polizei*.   (Haltestelle)
3. Der Freund fährt mit dem *Bus*.   (Auto)
4. Er kommt aus der *Bibliothek*.   (Zimmer)
5. Sie wohnt nicht bei der *Universität*.   (Flugplatz)

D. Supply the appropriate phrase, either **zu Hause** or **nach Hause**.

1. Heute abend sind wir _____.
2. Kommt ihr bald _____?
3. Fahren wir jetzt _____?
4. Das Mädchen ist _____.
5. Herr und Frau Müller sind heute nicht _____.

E. Answer the following questions.

1. Bei wem wohnen Sie?
2. Wohnen Sie direkt bei einer Bus-Haltestelle?
3. Fahren Sie oft mit dem Bus? Wohin?
4. Gehen Sie heute abend nach Hause?
5. Kommen Sie morgen zur Universität?
6. Mit wem kommen Sie zur Universität?
7. Gehen Sie oft zur Bibliothek? Was finden Sie da?
8. Geben Sie manchmal Freunden Geld?

F. Now ask your neighbor the same questions in the **du**-form and get an answer.

G. Give the English equivalent of the following sentences.

1. Geht ihr jetzt mit dem Studenten nach Hause?
2. Bezahlen Sie bitte das Buch da drüben!
3. Beim Bahnhof finden Sie ein Zimmer mit Bad.
4. Er bestellt den Touristen kein Bier.
5. Wir suchen den Herren ein Hotel.

Vocabulary development

A. The adverb derived from **der Monat** (*month*) is **monatlich** (*monthly*). Similar constructions (with the umlaut, however):

die Stunde (*hour*)	stündlich
der Tag (*day*)	täglich
die Woche (*week*)	wöchentlich
das Jahr (*year*)	jährlich

Ask your neighbor how much he or she pays for a room per day, per week, per month, per year.

B. The expression **es gibt,** meaning *there is, there are*, is always followed by the accusative case.

Es gibt hier keinen Katalog.	*There is no catalogue here.*
In Salzburg **gibt es** viele Gasthäuser.	*In Salzburg there are many inns.*

But by itself the question **Was gibt es?** (often abbreviated to **Was gibt's?**) means *What's the matter? What's up?* What then would be the meaning of: **Was gibt's heute zum Abendessen?**

The shades of meaning of this expression have to be carefully observed through the context.

C. The word for *meal* in German is **das Essen.** Here are the names of the three main meals:

das Frühstück, -e	*breakfast*
das Mittagessen, -	*lunch, dinner*
das Abendessen,-	*dinner, supper*

Der Mittag means *noon*, therefore **das Mittagessen** is the midday meal, whether one calls it *lunch* or *dinner*. Similarly, **der Abend** means *evening*, so **das Abendessen** is the *evening meal*, whether one calls it *dinner* or *supper*.

The prepositions **bei** and **zu** are often used with these words, meaning *at* and *for*, respectively.

Beim Frühstück liest er die Zeitung.	*At breakfast he reads the paper.*
Zum Frühstück essen die Deutschen Brötchen und trinken Kaffee.	*For breakfast the Germans have rolls and coffee.*

Ask some classmates when they eat their meals.

Communicative exercises

A. Imagine you are in a travel agency in a foreign city. Ask an employee:

Wie komme ich von . . .	zu	das Hotel
der Bahnhof		die Universität
die Stadtmitte		die Bushaltestelle
das Hotel		der Flugplatz
die Haltestelle		die Kirche
das Institut		?

B. Ask your classmate the question: **Wem gibst du . . .** and the words on the left and have him/her answer with: **Ich gebe es (ihn, sie) . . .** and the words on the right.

Wem gibst du . . .	Ich gebe . . .
das Buch	die Studentin
das Geld	der Busfahrer
die Zeitung	der Student
der Kuchen	das Kind
das Gepäck	der Junge

C. Now, ask the same questions in the **ihr**-form and have your classmates answer with **wir** and have them put the nouns on the right in the plural.

D. Ask your neighbor the following questions and have him/her answer with the suggestions on the right.

Seit wann	rauchst	du?	Ich . . . seit	ein Jahr
	trinkst	du?		ein Monat
	spielst	du Klavier?		eine Woche
	arbeitest	du?		eine Stunde
	studierst	du?		

E. Ask some classmates if they read books or papers or talk a lot at breakfast. Ask them what they have for breakfast, lunch, or dinner. In addition to other words that you already know, these words will help in the answers.

das Brot, -e	*bread*	**die Kartoffel, -n**	*potato*
das Brötchen, -	*roll*	**die Milch**	*milk*
das Ei, -er	*egg*	**das Obst**	*fruit*
der Fisch, -e	*fish*	**der Salat, -e**	*salad*
das Fleisch	*meat*	**die Suppe, -n**	*soup*
das Gemüse, -	*vegetable*		

F. Pretend with your neighbor that one of you is a student looking for a room and the other is a representative of a rental agency. Consider location, price, and quality of the rooms under consideration.

Reading

GASTHAUS „WEIßES RÖßL"

Susan und Lynn wohnen in Amerika und reisen seit Juni in Europa. Sie kommen mit dem Zug aus München in Salzburg (Österreich) an. Da finden sie viele Touristen, denn° in Salzburg gibt es das Geburtshaus° von Mozart, Schloß° Mirabell, die Festung° Hohensalzburg und Kirchen aus der Barockzeit°.

for
the house of birth / castle / fortress
from the baroque period

Zuerst suchen sie ein Hotel. Es gibt viele Hotels in Salzburg, aber sie sind nicht gerade billig. Der Herr bei der Zimmervermittlung sagt den Amerikanerinnen, das Gasthaus „Weißes Rößl" ist nicht zu groß oder zu teuer. Es liegt nicht weit von der Stadtmitte beim Mozart-Platz. Susan und Lynn fahren mit dem Bus vom Bahnhof zum Gasthaus.

Nach ein paar Minuten kommen sie beim Gasthaus an. Sie sehen ein Schild bei der Tür—„Zimmer frei". Lynn liest die Worte „Zimmer frei" laut°, und Susan sagt sofort: „Nein, nein, das bedeutet nicht, es kostet nichts; das bedeutet, ein Zimmer ist noch frei". Das Haus ist hübsch, es hat auch einen Garten.

aloud

Frau Strauß, die Besitzerin°, begrüßt° die Studentinnen. Susan und Lynn unterschreiben die Formulare°. Dann fragen sie nach dem Schlüssel und gehen die Treppe hinauf. Sie haben Zimmer Nummer neun.

owner / greets
forms

Das Zimmer ist nicht groß, aber sehr hübsch. Beim Fenster stehen ein Tisch mit zwei Stühlen und ein Sessel. Rechts von der Tür steht ein Doppelbett. Es ist sehr groß und alt. Links von der Tür ist das Waschbecken. Susan denkt, außer dem Bad und der Toilette ist alles hier. Sie stellen das Gepäck in die Ecke und öffnen die Koffer.

Hotel "Weißes Rößl"
am Wolfgangsee

Dann verlassen sie das Zimmer und machen die Tür zu. Rechts von Zimmer Nummer neun finden sie das Badezimmer mit Dusche. Beim Badezimmer ist ein Telefon. Die Toilette ist auch da, mit einem Schild—WC.[1] Das Gasthaus hat nur ein Badezimmer und eine Toilette pro Etage°, aber das ist genug.   *per floor*

Sie gehen die Treppe hinunter und geben Frau Strauß den Zimmerschlüssel. Dann verlassen sie das Gasthaus und gehen zum Abendessen.

QUESTIONS

1. Seit wann reisen Susan und Lynn in Europa?
2. Wohin fahren sie?
3. Wo liegt Salzburg?
4. Was suchen die zwei Studentinnen zuerst?
5. Was sagt der Herr von der Zimmervermittlung?
6. Wo liegt das Gasthaus?
7. Nehmen die Mädchen ein Taxi oder einen Bus zum Gasthaus?
8. Was bedeutet das Schild „Zimmer frei"?

[1]Derived from the English *watercloset*; pronounced *veh-tseh*.

Salzburg

9. Wer begrüßt die zwei Studentinnen?
10. Wie ist das Zimmer?
11. Was finden sie da?
12. Wie ist das Bett?
13. Was stellen sie in die Ecke?
14. Wohin gehen sie jetzt?
15. Wem geben die Studentinnen den Schlüssel?

Review

A. Express in German.

1. Karl drives from Hamburg to Berlin.
2. The girls give the key to Mr. Klein.
3. We have no rooms today.
4. Are you (**du**) going home tonight?

5. Please, give (**du**) the address to the boy.
6. Order Mr. Schmidt a beer, please.
7. First we'll talk with the tourists.
8. Are you (**Sie**) coming from the railroad station?
9. The girls live at Mr. and Mrs. Braun's.
10. There is everything here except hotels and an airport.
11. Show (**Sie**) the (girl) students the garden.
12. When are you (**ihr**) home?

B. Use the following sentence elements in a question and an answer. Watch the word order and the case endings and use the right pronoun for the subject in the answer.

EXAMPLE: das Mädchen / geben / der Brief / der Herr
        Gibt das Mädchen dem Herrn den Brief?
        Ja, es gibt dem Herrn den Brief.

1. der Freund / geben / das Geld / der Busfahrer.
2. du / sehen / die Busfahrerin (*pl.*).
3. die Mädchen / sprechen / von / die Amerikanerin (*pl.*).
4. Barbara / zeigen / das Auto / der Freund.
5. ich / geben / die Zeitung / das Fräulein.
6. du / kennen / der Herr.
7. Herr Meyer / lesen / ein Buch.
8. ihr / fahren / zu / der Flugplatz.

Am Wolfgangsee (Österreich)

C. Complete the following sentences with the appropriate form of the suggested definite or indefinite article or **kein**. Make any contractions that are possible.

1. D_____ Fräulein gibt d _____ Mann e_____ Schlüssel.
2. E_____ Busfahrer fährt d _____ Bus zu d _____ Flugplatz.
3. D _____ Frau öffnet e _____ Koffer.
4. Franz kauft d _____ Freundin k _____ Gitarre.
5. Er gibt e _____ Taxifahrer e _____ paar Zigaretten.
6. Außer d _____ Bad findet d _____ Mädchen alles.
7. D _____ Mädchen da drüben kennen d _____ Bücher nicht.
8. Bei d _____ Bett steht k _____ Tisch.
9. D _____ Herren kommen d _____ Treppe herunter.
10. E_____ Student zeigt d _____ Fräulein d _____ Stadt.
11. Links von d _____ Fenster steht e _____ Doppelbett.
12. Leider liegen d _____ Gasthäuser weit von d _____ Bahnhof.

Chapter vocabulary

Nouns

das	Abendessen, -	supper, dinner
die	Adresse, -n	address
das	Bad, ⸚er	bath
das	Badezimmer, -	bathroom
der	Bahnhof, ⸚e	railroad station
das	Bett, -en	bed
der	Brief, -e	letter
das	Doppelbett, -en	double bed
die	Dusche, -n	shower
die	Ecke, -n	corner
(das)	Europa	Europe
das	Fenster, -	window
das	Formular, -e	form, document
der	Garten, ⸚	garden
das	Gasthaus, ⸚er	inn, restaurant
das	Jahr, -e	year
der	Junge, -n	boy
die	Kirche, -n	church
der	Koffer, -	suitcase
die	Mark	mark: the unit of German currency
der	Mensch, -en	human being
der	Monat, -e	month
der	Präsident, -en	president
das	Schild, -er	sign

der	Schlüssel, -	key
der	Sessel, -	armchair, chair
die	Stadt, ⸚e	city
die	Stadtmitte	city center
der	Stuhl, ⸚e	chair
der	Tisch, -e	table
die	Toilette, -n	lavatory, toilet
der	Tourist, -en	tourist
die	Universität, -en	university
das	Waschbecken, -	wash basin, sink
die	Woche, -n	week
das	Wort, ⸚er	word
die	Zimmervermitt-lung, -en	rental agency
der	Zug, ⸚e	train

Verbs

bedeuten	to have the meaning, mean
bezahlen	to pay
bringen	to bring
fragen nach	ask for
geben (gibt)	to give
es gibt	there is, there are
kosten	to cost
liegen	to lie, be situated

reisen	*to travel*	monatlich	*monthly, per month*
stellen	*to put, set*	nichts	*nothing*
unterschreiben	*to sign*	sofort	*at once*
wohnen	*to reside, live*	stündlich	*hourly*
zeigen	*to show*	täglich	*daily*
		teuer	*expensive*

Other words _____

		ungefähr	*approximately*
		viele	*many*
bald	*soon*	weit	*far*
billig	*cheap*	wieviel	*how much*
direkt	*directly, right*	wieviele	*how many*
groß	*big, large*	wöchentlich	*weekly*
hübsch	*attractive, pretty*	zu	*too (in excess of)*
jährlich	*yearly*	zuerst	*first of all, at first*

See also the words for meals and food on pp. 82–83.

See also the prepositions on pp. 74–76.

Mini-dialogues

Student(in) A Wo seid ihr gestern abend gewesen?
         B Warum?
         A Ich habe euch angerufen, aber keine Antwort erhalten.
         B Wir haben eine Party bei Freunden besucht.
         A Und was macht ihr heute abend?
         B Heute abend bleiben wir zu Hause und gehen früh zu Bett.

         A Wer hat dir geschrieben?
         B Ein Freund von mir.
         A Kenne ich ihn?
         B Ich glaube kaum.
         A Wo hast du ihn getroffen?
         B Oh, kürzlich bei Gürtlers.

           (*Am Telefon*)
         A Wie ist das Wetter bei euch?
         B Furchtbar, seit zwei Wochen regnet es.
         A Bei uns scheint endlich einmal die Sonne. Aber sehr wahrscheinlich nicht lange.
         B Kommt ihr bald wieder zu uns?
         A So bald wie möglich, aber nicht bei dem Regen.

A Where were you last night?
B Why?
A I called you but received no answer.
B We went to a party at some friends'.
A And tonight?
B Tonight we'll stay home and go to bed early.

A Who wrote you?
B A friend of mine.
A Do I know him?
B I doubt it.
A Where did you meet him?
B Recently at the Gürtlers'.

(*On the phone*)
A How is the weather there?
B Dreadful, the past two weeks it's been raining.
A Here, we finally had some sunshine. But probably not for very long.
B Are you coming to us again soon?
A As soon as possible. But not in this rain.

Pronunciation

pf	*ps*	*kn*
Pfeffer	**Psychologie**	**Knie**
Pfosten	**Pseudonym**	**Knopf**
Pflicht	**Psalm**	**Knabe**
Apfel	**Schnaps**	**knurren**
Topf		**geknackt**

j	*y*
jetzt	**Physik** (cf. "ü" in chapter 1)
jung	**System**
Jugend	**Psychiatrie**

Grammar explanations

I. Present perfect tense

Ich habe ein Auto **gekauft.**
I have bought a car.

Ich habe Kaffee **getrunken.**
I drank coffee.

Der Zug hat angehalten.
The train stopped.

Du hast alles wieder **vergessen.**
You forgot everything again.

Warum ist er nicht **gekommen?**
Why didn't he come?

Kürzlich ist bei uns viel **passiert.**
A lot has happened here recently.

Seit Montag **arbeitet** er wieder.
He's been working again since Monday.

German and English have several tenses to express past time; these tenses are used differently in the two languages and must be studied with care. This chapter introduces the present perfect tense.

A. Formation

The present perfect tense consists of two parts: (1) the present tense of an auxiliary verb, and (2) the past participle of the principal verb. For this reason, it is often called a compound tense. For most verbs, the auxiliary is **haben.**

	Singular	Plural	
1st	ich habe gekauft	wir haben gekauft	*Present*
2nd (fam.)	du hast gekauft	ihr habt gekauft	*perfect:* **kaufen**
		sie haben gekauft	*(to buy)*
3rd	er, sie, es } hat gekauft		
2nd (formal)	Sie haben gekauft	Sie haben gekauft	

Ich habe ein Auto gekauft.   { *I have bought a car.*
                                    { *I bought a car.*

Notice that the past participle is placed at the end of a clause.

German verbs can be classified as *weak, irregular weak,* or *strong.* These three types form the past participle differently.

1. *Weak verbs* form the past participle by placing the unchanged verb stem within the frame **ge—t.**

Infinitive		*Past participle*	
kaufen	*to buy*	**gekauft**	*bought*
haben	*to have*	**gehabt**	*had*
sagen	*to say*	**gesagt**	*said*

If the stem of a weak verb ends in **-d** or **-t,** as in **arbeiten** (*to work*), or in **-m** or **-n** when preceded by a consonant other than **l** and **r,** as in **öffnen** (*to open*), **-e-** is inserted between the stem and the **-t** of the participle to make the word easier to pronounce: gearbeit**et**, geöffn**et**. Verbs ending in **-ieren** do not add **ge-** to the past participle, but always take the suffix **-t.**

Infinitive		*Past participle*	
studieren	*to study*	**studiert**	*studied*
passieren	*to happen*	**passiert**	*happened*

2. *Irregular weak verbs* form the past participle by placing a changed form of the stem within the frame **ge—t.** These verbs are few in number, and include:

Infinitive		Past participle	
brennen	*to burn*	**gebrannt**	*burned*
bringen	*to bring*	**gebracht**	*brought*
denken	*to think*	**gedacht**	*thought*
kennen	*to know*	**gekannt**	*known*

The past participles of all irregular weak verbs are indicated both in the chapter and in the end vocabulary sections.

CHECK YOUR COMPREHENSION

A. Form the past participle of the following weak verbs:

1. zeigen   *gezeigt*
2. hören   *gehört*
3. protestieren
4. fragen   *gefragt*
5. suchen   *gesucht*
6. rauchen   *geraucht*
7. diskutieren
8. kosten   *gekostet { d,t*
9. wohnen
10. spielen   *arbeiten — gearbeitet*

B. Answer the following questions affirmatively in the present perfect tense.

EXAMPLE: Haben Sie ein Auto gekauft?
       Ja, ich habe ein Auto gekauft.

1. Hast du eine Zigarette geraucht?
2. Hat er viel protestiert?
3. Habt ihr viele Freunde gehabt?
4. Haben Sie den Schlüssel gebracht?
5. Haben sie bei einem Flugplatz gewohnt?
6. Hast du manchmal über Politik diskutiert?

7. Hat er den Mann gekannt?
8. Hat sie oft Karten gespielt?

---

3. *Strong verbs* form the past participle by placing a changed form of the stem, or occasionally the unchanged stem, within the frame **ge—en: trinken** (*to drink*), **getrunken** (*drunk*); **geben** (*to give*), **gegeben** (*given*).

It is important to memorize the past participle of each strong verb when you learn the infinitive. Here are some strong verbs that you have already encountered.

Infinitive		*Past participle*	
bitten (um)	*to ask (for)*	**gebeten**	*asked*
essen	*to eat*	**gegessen**	*eaten*
finden	*to find*	**gefunden**	*found*
geben	*to give*	**gegeben**	*given*
halten	*to stop*	**gehalten**	*stopped*
heißen	*to be called*	**geheißen**	*been called*
lassen	*to let*	**gelassen**	*let*
lesen	*to read*	**gelesen**	*read*
liegen	*to lie, be situated*	**gelegen**	*lain*
nehmen	*to take*	**genommen**	*taken*
sehen	*to see*	**gesehen**	*seen*
sprechen	*to speak*	**gesprochen**	*spoken*
stehen	*to stand*	**gestanden**	*stood*
trinken	*to drink*	**getrunken**	*drunk*

The past participles of all strong verbs are indicated both in the chapter and in the end vocabulary section.

CHECK YOUR COMPREHENSION

Change the following sentences to the present perfect tense. Pay special attention to the position of the past participle.

EXAMPLE: Wir trinken Milch.
  Wir haben Milch getrunken.

1. Wir nehmen ein Taxi.
2. Er sieht das Feuer.
3. Ich bitte um Auskunft.
4. Findest du ein Zimmer?
5. Warum spricht sie mit dem Busfahrer?
6. Eßt ihr viel Fleisch?
7. Wir geben dem Herrn das Geld.
8. Sie lesen viele Bücher.
9. Warum hält der Zug?
10. Wo steht das Bett?

B. Past participles of verbs with prefixes

German has two types of compound verbs: (1) the verbs with a separable prefix discussed in Chapter 3: **abfahren, einsteigen,** etc.; and (2) the verbs with an inseparable prefix, such as **be-, emp-, ent-, er-, ge-, ver-,** and **zer-: bestellen, vergessen,** etc. Inseparable prefixes always remain attached to the verb.

separable prefix	zu·machen	Er **macht** das Fenster **zu.**
inseparable prefix	bestellen	Sie **bestellt** eine Tasse Tee.

Verbs with separable prefixes are stressed on the *prefix*: **éinsteigen.** But verbs with inseparable prefixes are stressed on the *stem*: **bestéllen, vergéssen.**

Both separable and inseparable prefix verbs are found among the weak, irregular weak, and strong verbs. The formation of their past participle differs from the normal pattern.

1. *Verbs with separable prefixes* insert the **ge-** of the past participle between the separable prefix and the stem.

	Infinitive	Past participle
weak	zu·machen *to close*	zu**ge**macht
irreg. weak	herein·bringen *to bring in*	herein**ge**bracht
strong	an·halten *to stop*	an**ge**halten
	weiter·lesen *to go on reading*	weiter**ge**lesen
	weiter·sprechen *to go on speaking*	weiter**ge**sprochen

Der Zug hat angehalten.   *The train has stopped.*

2. *Verbs with inseparable prefixes* do not add **ge-** to the past participle.

	Infinitive	Past participle
weak	bezahlen *to pay*	bezahlt
irreg. weak	erkennen *to recognize*	erkannt
strong	bekommen *to get, receive*	bekommen
	vergessen *to forget*	vergessen
	verlassen *to leave*	verlassen

Du hast alles vergessen.   *You have forgotten everything.*

CHECK YOUR COMPREHENSION

A. Form the past participle of the following verbs.

* past part = infinitive

1. erkennen
2. zumachen
3. hereinbringen
4. bekommen ***
5. anhalten

6. verlassen ***
7. bedeuten
8. weiterlesen
9. bezahlen
10. vergessen ***

B. Change the following sentences to the present perfect tense. Pay special attention to the position of the past participle.

EXAMPLE: Wir bestellen eine Tasse Kaffee.
Wir haben eine Tasse Kaffee bestellt.

1. Er vergißt die Adresse.
2. Die Studentin liest weiter.
3. Der Busfahrer erkennt die Männer.
4. Was bedeutet das Schild?
5. Wann verlassen sie das Hotel?

6. Hier hält der Zug an.
7. Anna macht das Fenster zu.
8. Was bringt sie herein?
9. Fräulein Lerner bezahlt dem Herrn das Buch.

C. Verbs taking **sein** as an auxiliary

Though most verbs use the auxiliary **haben** to form the present perfect tense, some verbs use the auxiliary **sein.** To use **sein** as the auxiliary, a verb must meet two criteria: (1) it must not take a direct object (that is, it must be intransitive), and (2) it must indicate a change in the position or condition of the subject.

	Singular	Plural
1st	ich bin gekommen	wir sind gekommen
2nd (fam.)	du bist gekommen	ihr seid gekommen
	er ⎫	sie sind gekommen
3rd	sie ⎬ ist gekommen	
	es ⎭	
2nd (formal)	Sie sind gekommen	Sie sind gekommen

Warum ist er gekommen?
⎧ *Why did he come?*
⎨ *Why has he come?*

Verbs taking **sein** include the following:

Infinitive		*Past participle*
ab·fahren	*to depart*	ist abgefahren
an·kommen	*to arrive*	ist angekommen
aus·steigen	*to get out*	ist ausgestiegen
ein·steigen	*to get in*	ist eingestiegen
fahren	*to drive*	ist gefahren
gehen	*to go*	ist gegangen
herunter·kommen	*to come down*	ist heruntergekommen
hinunter·gehen	*to go down*	ist hinuntergegangen
kommen	*to come*	ist gekommen
laufen	*to run*	ist gelaufen
passieren	*to happen*	ist passiert
reisen	*to travel*	ist gereist
weiter·fahren	*to drive on*	ist weitergefahren
weiter·gehen	*to move on*	ist weitergegangen
zurück·laufen	*to run back*	ist zurückgelaufen

The verbs **sein** (*to be*) and **bleiben** (*to stay*), though inherently expressing a *lack* of change or movement, are also conjugated with **sein.**

Ich bin dort gewesen.	*I have been there.*
Er ist dort geblieben.	*He's stayed here.*

To avoid asking yourself constantly whether to use **sein** or **haben**, memorize the auxiliary along with the past participle. In the vocabulary sections of this book, verbs taking **sein** have their past participles indicated thus: **fahren, ist gefahren.** Verbs taking **haben** do not have the auxiliary indicated: **trinken, getrunken.**

CHECK YOUR COMPREHENSION

A. Answer the following questions affirmatively in the present perfect tense.

EXAMPLE: Bist du kürzlich angekommen?
        Ja, ich bin kürzlich angekommen.

1. Sind Sie sofort weitergegangen?
2. Bist du ungefähr vier Wochen geblieben?
3. Ist Herr Müller mit dem Zug gefahren?
4. Seid ihr endlich hinuntergegangen?
5. Sind wir auch dort gewesen?
6. Ist Jürgen schnell zurückgelaufen?
7. Bist du zuerst ausgestiegen?
8. Sind die Busse gerade abgefahren?

B. Change the following sentences to the present perfect tense. Pay special attention to the choice of the auxiliary verb.

EXAMPLE: Wir fahren ab.
Wir sind abgefahren.
Wieviel bezahlt das Mädchen?
Wieviel hat das Mädchen bezahlt?

1. Wo essen Sie?
2. Ich fahre sofort nach links.
3. Leider hält der Zug an.
4. Die Menschen kommen von der Stadtmitte.
5. Plötzlich erkennt sie den Amerikaner.
6. Hans geht direkt zum Bahnhof.
7. Frau Keller findet kein Gasthaus.
8. Immer bittet er um Geld.

D. Use of the present perfect tense

In German the present perfect is most often used as a conversational past in the spoken language and in informal writing, such as a letter to a friend. It denotes an action that was completed at a point in the past, and is rendered by the English past tense.

Ich habe das Auto gesehen.	*I saw the car.*
Ich bin schnell nach rechts gefahren.	*I quickly turned to the right.*

The present perfect may also emphasize a stretch, rather than a point, of time in the past. This occurs when an action or situation starting in the past lasts or has an effect right up to the more recent past or the present. In this case the present perfect carries the same connotation in German as in English.

Kürzlich ist bei uns viel passiert.   *A lot has happened here recently.*

When such a stretch of time is expressed, the present perfect is often used with **schon** (*already*) in the affirmative and **noch nicht** (*not yet*) in the negative.

Haben Sie schon gegessen?   *Have you already eaten?*

Ja, ich habe schon gegessen.   *Yes, I have already eaten.*

Nein, ich habe noch nicht gegessen.   *No, I have not yet eaten.*

Compare the two uses of the present perfect:

Past time   *Present time*

Point of time:
   Ich habe das Auto gesehen.
   I saw the car.

Stretch of time:
   Kürzlich ist bei uns viel passiert.
   A lot has happened here recently.

In many instances the time span expressed stretches through the present into the future. In that case, German uses the present tense, often with the preposition **seit,** whereas English uses the present perfect tense.

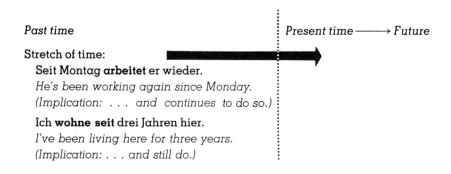

Past time   *Present time ——→ Future*

Stretch of time:
   Seit Montag arbeitet er wieder.
   He's been working again since Monday.
   (Implication: . . . and continues to do so.)
   Ich wohne seit drei Jahren hier.
   I've been living here for three years.
   (Implication: . . . and still do.)

CHECK YOUR COMPREHENSION

Express in German.

1. We found a hotel.
2. You (*du*) forgot the newspaper.
3. I have already read the book.
4. What happened here?
5. The children recognized the man.
6. The students have lived here for four years.
7. Paul has been reading for ten minutes.
8. Where did the children get off?

II. Personal pronouns: accusative and dative cases

Hast du ihn vergessen?
Did you forget him?

Ich kenne dich.
I know you.

Gib mir eine Antwort!
Give me an answer.

Kennst du mich?
Do you know me?

The personal pronouns, introduced in the nominative case in Chapter 1, also have accusative and dative case forms.

Singular

Acc.	**Er kennt mich nicht.**	*He doesn't know me.*
Dat.	**Sie hat oft mit mir gesprochen.**	*She often talked with me.*
Acc.	**Er hat dich nicht gesehen.**	*He didn't see you.*
Dat.	**Sie schreibt dir oft.**	*She writes (to) you often.*
Acc.	**Er findet ihn (sie) nicht.**	*He doesn't find him (her).*
Dat.	**Sie hat** $\left\{ \begin{array}{l} \textbf{ihm} \\ \textbf{ihr} \end{array} \right\}$ **den Brief gegeben.**	*She gave* $\left\{ \begin{array}{l} him \\ her \end{array} \right\}$ *the letter.*

Plural

Acc.	**Er sieht uns nicht.**	*He doesn't see us.*
Dat.	**Sie schreibt uns oft.**	*She writes (to) us often.*
Acc.	**Er hat euch nicht gesehen.**	*He didn't see you.*
Dat.	**Sie spricht oft mit euch.**	*She talks with you often.*
Acc.	**Er kennt sie nicht.**	*He doesn't know them.*
Dat.	**Sie trinken oft mit ihnen.**	*They often drink with them.*
Acc.	**Er kennt Sie nicht.**	*He doesn't know you.*
Dat.	**Sie schreibt Ihnen oft.**	*She writes (to) you often.*

Singular	Nominative	Accusative	Dative	*Personal*
1st	ich	**mich**	**mir**	*pronouns:*
2nd (fam.)	du	**dich**	**dir**	*nominative,*
	er	**ihn**	**ihm**	*accusative,*
3rd	sie	sie	**ihr**	*and dative*
	es	es	**ihm**	*cases*

Plural				
1st	wir	**uns**	**uns**	
2nd (fam.)	ihr	**euch**	**euch**	
3rd	sie	sie	**ihnen**	

Singular/plural				
2nd (formal)	Sie	Sie	**Ihnen**	

Notice that in the 1st and 2nd person plural, the pronouns are the same in the *dative* and *accusative:* **uns, euch.** The same forms occur in the *nominative* and *accusative* in the 3rd person sing. fem. and neut. and 3rd person plural.

To determine the position of dative and accusative nouns and pronouns, the simplest rule is as follows: the dative precedes the accusative unless the accusative is a pronoun.

	Dat.	*Acc.*
Jürgen bezahlt	dem Mann	das Buch
Jürgen bezahlt	ihm	das Buch

But:

	Acc.	*Dat.*
Jürgen bezahlt	es	dem Mann.
Jürgen bezahlt	es	ihm.

CHECK YOUR COMPREHENSION

A. Substitute the appropriate personal pronouns for all nouns. Watch the word order.

1. Karl gibt dem Herrn eine Zigarre.
2. Herr und Frau Schmidt bringen den Studenten den Tisch.
3. Der Taxifahrer zeigt den Studentinnen die Haltestelle.
4. Gib dem Herrn die Adresse!
5. Bei Frau Schell wohnen drei Mädchen.
6. Wir haben den Frauen die Koffer gebracht.

B. Use the appropriate form of the pronoun for the nouns or pronouns given in parentheses.

1. Ich kenne _____ nicht. (*das Gasthaus*)
2. Die Studentin sieht _____ nicht mal an. (*der Herr*)
3. Albert, zeig _____ _____! (*das Zimmer, die Frau*)
4. Kürzlich haben die Freunde _____ geschrieben. (*wir*)
5. Hans, spiel doch mit _____! (*die Kinder*)
6. Ich habe _____ _____ gegeben. (*der Schlüssel, der Student*)
7. Haben Sie _____ gelesen? (*die Zeitung*)

III. Position of *nicht*

Ich kenne ihn nicht.
I don't know him.

Das Auto ist nicht neu.
The car isn't new.

Fräulein Schell ist nicht zu Hause.
Miss Schell isn't at home.

Der Zug fährt noch nicht ab.
The train isn't leaving yet.

Sind die Männer nicht angekommen?
Haven't the men arrived?

Frau Steinhoff hat die Schlüssel nicht.
Mrs. Steinhoff doesn't have the keys.

The position of **nicht** (*not*) varies considerably in German. It should be gradually learned through careful observation. Here are a few useful guidelines.

1. Nicht is usually placed at the end of a sentence.

Er kommt heute nicht.	*He's not coming today.*
Er verläßt sie nicht.	*He isn't leaving her.*

But it precedes
(a) parts of verbs—that is, separable prefixes, and the past participle in the present perfect tense.

Wir steigen nicht ein.	*We aren't getting in.*
Er ist gestern nicht angekommen.	*He didn't arrive yesterday.*

(b) predicate adjectives and predicate nouns.

Das Haus ist nicht neu.   *The house is not new.*

Er spielt nicht Tennis.   *He doesn't play tennis.*

   (c) prepositional phrases.

Wir gehen nicht nach Hause.   *We aren't going home.*

2. Nicht can also be placed before any element in the sentence that one wants to emphasize.

Die Party ist nicht heute, sie ist   *The party isn't today, it's tomorrow.*
morgen.

CHECK YOUR COMPREHENSION

Place **nicht** in the correct position within each sentence.

1. Er hört mich.
2. Die Betten sind alt.
3. Die Studentinnen sind zu Hause.
4. Ich finde die Adresse.
5. Sie spricht sehr schnell.
6. Wir zeigen ihm die Kirche.
7. Wir arbeiten heute.
8. Hier steigen wir aus.
9. Haben Sie die Adresse vergessen?
10. Ist er abgefahren?

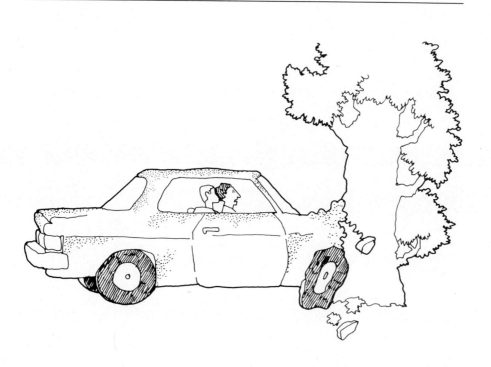

Conversation

Ich glaube, ja.	*I think so.*
Wie ist das passiert?	*How did it happen?*
Ich habe keine Ahnung.	*I have no idea.*

VOR GERICHT°

in court

Staatsanwalt°   Herr Steinhoff, jetzt sagen Sie uns bitte: Wie ist der Unfall passiert? — *district attorney*

Steinhoff   Ja, ich habe eine Party bei Freunden besucht.° — *went to*

Staatsanwalt   Was haben Sie denn[1] getrunken?

Steinhoff   Wir haben Wein, Bier und Orangensaft getrunken.

Staatsanwalt   Aha! Und Sie haben natürlich Orangensaft getrunken.

Steinhoff   Ich glaube, ja.

Staatsanwalt   Wie bitte?° Ich verstehe Sie nicht. Die Polizei hat Sie angehalten und eine Blutprobe° gemacht. — *How is that?* / *blood test*

Steinhoff   Das ist richtig.

Staatsanwalt   Haben Sie wirklich nur Orangensaft getrunken?

Steinhoff   Jemand hat mir vielleicht etwas Wodka° hineingemischt, aber ich habe nichts gemerkt. — *vodka*

Staatsanwalt   Herr Steinhoff, haben Sie es schon vergessen? Sie haben Staatseigentum° beschädigt!° — *public property/damaged*

Steinhoff   Ach, Sie meinen den Baum?

Staatsanwalt   Ja, wie ist das eigentlich passiert?

Steinhoff   Ein Porsche[2] hat mich überholt und ich bin sofort nach rechts gefahren.

Staatsanwalt   Und da hat ein Baum gestanden?

Steinhoff   Ja, leider.

Staatsanwalt   Und Sie haben ihn nicht gesehen?

Steinhoff   Nein, leider nicht.

Staatsanwalt   Warum nicht, Herr Steinhoff?

Steinhoff   Ich habe keine Ahnung.

Staatsanwalt   Dann gebe ich Ihnen die Antwort: Sie haben leider etwas zuviel Orangensaft im Blut° gehabt! — *in your blood*

---

[1] **Denn** is a "flavoring particle" that cannot be translated directly. It is frequently used to give a question more emphasis.

[2] The brand names of cars are always masculine.

QUESTIONS ON THE CONVERSATION

1. Wen hat Herr Steinhoff besucht?
2. Was hat er getrunken?
3. Was haben die Freunde von Herrn Steinhoff getrunken?
4. Wer hat Herrn Steinhoff angehalten?
5. Was hat jemand mit dem Orangensaft von Herrn Steinhoff gemacht?
6. Was hat Herr Steinhoff beschädigt?
7. Warum ist er sofort nach rechts gefahren?
8. Wo hat der Baum gestanden?
9. Hat Herr Steinhoff den Baum eigentlich gesehen?
10. Was hat er zuviel im Blut gehabt?

PERSONAL QUESTIONS

1. Haben Sie auch schon einen Unfall gehabt?
2. Trinken Sie viel Orangensaft?
3. Mischen Sie manchmal etwas Wodka hinein?

Practice

A. Change the sentences to the present perfect.

1. Wie passiert der Unfall?
2. Ich besuche eine Party bei Freunden.
3. Was trinken Sie denn dort?
4. Wir trinken da Wein, Bier und Orangensaft.
5. Die Polizei hält Sie an.
6. Sie macht eine Blutprobe.
7. Ich merke nichts.
8. Da kommt plötzlich ein Volkswagen von links und überholt mich.
9. Trinken Sie wirklich keinen Wein?
10. Mischt jemand etwas Wodka hinein?
11. Ich sehe den Baum nicht.
12. Sprechen Sie mit der Polizei?

B. Change the sentences to the present.

1. Wann sind sie angekommen?
2. Wir sind gleich hinunter-gegangen.
3. Habt ihr das Fenster zugemacht?
4. Sie haben das Zimmer verlassen.
5. Hast du ihn erkannt?
6. Du bist sehr schnell gefahren.
7. Wo seid ihr gewesen?
8. Sie sind sehr weit gereist.
9. Wo bist du ausgestiegen?
10. Wir haben den Wein bezahlt.

C. Answer the following questions in the affirmative or negative, substituting appropriate pronouns for nouns (or other pronouns) wherever possible.

EXAMPLE: Sind die Freunde gestern bei Ihnen gewesen?
Ja, sie sind gestern bei uns gewesen.
Wohnt Sylvia bei Frau Meyer?
Nein, sie wohnt nicht bei ihr.

1. Hast du dem Herrn das Buch bezahlt?
2. Habt ihr Fräulein Müller das Zimmer gezeigt?
3. Sind die Freunde schon bei Ihnen angekommen?
4. Haben Sie die Adresse vergessen?
5. Kauft Fritz die Gitarre?
6. Sehen Sie die Kirche da drüben?
7. Hat Robert der Frau den Schlüssel gegeben?
8. Habt ihr den Salat schon gegessen?
9. Bist du gestern bei Karl gewesen?
10. Hat die Polizei den Autofahrer angehalten?

D. Complete the following text by supplying the appropriate personal pronoun in either the accusative or the dative case.

Herr Steinhoff, jetzt sagen Sie es _____ (*wir*) endlich! Sie sind bei Freunden gewesen. Was haben Sie bei _____ (*sie, pl.*) gemacht? Die Freunde haben Sie doch gut gekannt. Ist der Wodka vielleicht von _____ (*sie*) gewesen? Ist das möglich? Sie kennen _____ (*sie*) besser als wir. Glauben Sie mir doch! _____ (*Sie*) passiert wahrscheinlich nicht viel! Verstehen Sie _____ (*ich*)? Die Polizei hat _____ (*Sie*) angehalten und bei _____ (*Sie*) eine Blutprobe gemacht. Was ist das Resultat? Hier, lesen Sie _____ (*es*)! Sie sagen: „Ein Porsche hat _____ (*ich*) von rechts überholt." Ich sage _____ (*Sie*): Das ist nicht möglich!

E. Give the English equivalent.

1. Bei uns ist kürzlich sehr viel passiert.
2. Hast du das nicht gemerkt?
3. Ich arbeite seit zwei Jahren hier in Berlin.
4. Wie ist der Unfall eigentlich passiert?
5. Wahrscheinlich haben sie es ihr noch nicht geschrieben.

Vocabulary development

A. When used by itself, the adverb **gern** means *gladly*. For instance, in a short reply to a request: **Hans, gib mir doch bitte den Schlüssel!—Ja, gern.** But most often **gern** is used with a verb, and should be translated as *to like to (do something)*.

Ich lese gern.	*I like to read.*
Er studiert nicht gern.	*He doesn't like to study.*
Herr Steinhoff trinkt gern Orangensaft.	*Mr. Steinhoff likes to drink orange juice.*

B. An important verb is **tun**, past participle: **getan** (*to do*), often used as a synonym of **machen:**

Was tust (machst) du?	*What are you doing?*

Tun occurs with **es** and the dative of the person involved in the frequently used expression:

Es tut **mir** leid.	*I am*	
dir	*You are*	} *sorry.*
ihm etc.	*He is* etc.	

Note that, structurally, this expression cannot be directly rendered into English (lit. "*it does suffering to me*").

The full conjugation of **tun:**

ich tue	wir tun
du tust	ihr tut
er tut	sie tun

C. The verb **gehen** occurs with **es** in one of the most frequently used expressions in German:

Wie geht es?

> *How's it going?*
> *How are you?*

Often the expression is shortened to **Wie geht's?**

If a pronoun or noun is used with this expression, it is in the *dative case.*

Wie geht es dir?
Wie geht es Ihnen?

How are you?

Danke, es geht mir gut.

Thanks, I'm fine.

Wie geht es den Kindern?

How are the children?

Leider geht es ihnen nicht so gut.

Unfortunately they don't feel so good.

Notice that **es** is the grammatical subject; therefore the verb is 3rd person singular: **geht.**

In this context the opposite of **gut** is **schlecht.**

Wie geht es Frau Müller?

How is Mrs. Müller?

Es geht ihr leider schlecht.

She's not well, unfortunately.

Quite often one enounters **besser** with **es geht:**

Es geht ihm wieder besser.

He's better again.

Ask your neighbors how they or friends of theirs are.

Communicative exercises

A. Ask the questions below and have your classmate(s) answer in the negative, starting the sentence with „**Es tut mir leid, ich (wir) . . .**" Use pronouns wherever possible.

Kennst du Fräulein Gieseke?   Es tut . . .
Kennen Sie Herrn Schultze?
Haben Sie das Buch gelesen?
Hast du die Amerikanerinnen getroffen?
Hat er Sie schon angerufen?

Sind die Freunde bei euch gewesen?   Es tut . . .
Haben Sie den Baum gesehen?
Hat er dir schon eine Antwort gegeben?

B. Ask a classmate what he or she likes to do. You may use the suggestions given on the right or make up your own answers.

Was tust du gern?   Sprachen lernen
     tun Sie   Bücher (Zeitungen) lesen
              Gitarre spielen
              Politik diskutieren
              mit Freunden reisen
              Briefe schreiben
              Orangensaft trinken
              mit dem Zug fahren

C. Have your classmate(s) answer the following questions:

Seit wann   wohnst du   hier?   Ich wohne seit . . . hier.
           wohnen Sie   etc.
           studierst du Deutsch?
           regnet es bei euch?
           kennst du Irmgard?
           arbeitest du bei der Polizei?
           ist sie krank?

D. Tell your classmates what you did at a recent party at your friend's house. Suggestions:

lange über Politik diskutieren
Karten spielen
Wein, Bier, Coca Cola trinken
viel essen
von einem Unfall sprechen
Platten von . . . spielen.
tanzen (= *to dance, weak verb*)

Reading

EIN BRIEF

Bonn, den 19. März

Liebe Elke, lieber Hans,

Schon lange habe ich Euch[1] keinen Brief geschrieben. Leider habe ich nie genug Zeit, und ich schreibe nicht gern.

Bei uns ist viel passiert. Anfang Februar ist Peter zwei Wochen krank gewesen. Er ist beim Skilaufen° hingefallen.° Resultat: Gehirnerschütterung.° Fünf Wochen hat er nicht gearbeitet. Aber seit Montag arbeitet er wieder. Außerdem hat Gisela Masern° bekommen. Deshalb habe ich natürlich viel Arbeit gehabt. Aber jetzt geht es auch ihr wieder besser.

while skiing / fell
brain concussion
measles

Das Wetter bei uns ist furchtbar. Seit zwei Wochen regnet es. Wir sind oft zu Hause geblieben und haben Karten gespielt. Peter hat nicht gut gespielt. Er hat immer verloren. Er sagt, es ist die Gehirnerschütterung. Hoffentlich ist das Wetter bald wieder schön.

Aber die Nachrichten von uns sind nicht nur schlecht. Kürzlich sind wir bei Müllers gewesen. Dort haben wir die Kapps getroffen. Sie sind wirklich nett! Bei° viel Wein und Bier haben wir lange geredet. Herr Kapp ist gerade aus Amerika zurückgekommen. Er ist in New York und Washington gewesen und hat auch Boston kurz besucht. Er hat sehr interessant erzählt. Leider hat er sonst° nicht viel gesehen, aber er glaubt, er kennt Amerika. Wir sind bis sehr spät bei Müllers geblieben. Peter und ich sind dann noch mit dem Auto nach Hause gefahren; das ist bei° dem Wetter gefährlich gewesen. Wir haben aber keinen Unfall gehabt.

while drinking

otherwise

because of

Noch eine° Nachricht: wir haben gerade Möbel für das Schlafzimmer und Wohnzimmer gekauft. Sehr schön, aber natürlich ist alles furchtbar teuer gewesen. Leider ist heutzutage nichts billig.

another

Hoffentlich seid Ihr alle gesund geblieben. Ich habe lange nichts von Euch gehört. Schreibt mir bald mal wieder.

Seid herzlich gegrüßt

Jutta

P.S. Grüße auch von Peter.

---

[1]All 2nd person pronouns in a letter are capitalized.

QUESTIONS

1. Wer hat den Brief geschrieben?
2. Wo hat Jutta den Brief geschrieben?
3. Was ist Peter beim Skilaufen passiert?
4. Was ist das Resultat gewesen?
5. Was macht Peter seit Montag?
6. Was hat Gisela bekommen?
7. Wie ist das Wetter in Bonn gewesen?
8. Was haben Peter und Jutta zu Hause gemacht?
9. Wer hat immer verloren?
10. Wo sind Peter und Jutta kürzlich gewesen?
11. Wen haben Peter und Jutta bei Müllers getroffen?
12. Wo ist Herr Kapp gerade gewesen?
13. Was hat Herr Kapp in Amerika gesehen?
14. Was haben sie bei Müllers getrunken?
15. Was haben Peter und Jutta gerade gekauft?
16. Sind die Möbel teuer oder billig gewesen?

Review

A. Express in German (use the present perfect tense).

1. Have you been in Salzburg recently?
2. How did the accident happen?
3. A car passed me on the left.
4. Have you forgotten the letter?
5. I drank a cup of coffee and ate a piece of cake.
6. He found it (the hotel) right away.
7. The bathroom was on the left of room number nine.
8. I paid two hundred marks a month.
9. Was the furniture attractive?
10. The fire was not very dangerous.

B. Answer the following questions with complete sentences. Use pronouns wherever possible.

1. Sind die Schmidts bei Frau Becker gewesen?
2. Hat Elke dem Amerikaner den Brief geschrieben?
3. Hast du Peter das Buch gebracht?
4. Seid ihr bei den Studentinnen gewesen?
5. Gibst du den Kindern die Platten?

6. Wohin sind Sie gestern gefahren?
7. Was hat Frau Wegner Ihnen gezeigt?
8. Wer hat euch oft besucht?
9. Wem hat sie die Briefe geschrieben?

C. First add **nicht** to each sentence. Then change all nouns in the sentence to pronouns.

EXAMPLE: Thomas hat das Haus erkannt.
          Thomas hat das Haus nicht erkannt.
          Er hat es nicht erkannt.

1. Ich kenne das Resultat.
2. Frau Ottinger redet gern.
3. Gestern hat sie das Hotel verlassen.
4. Klaus hat den Touristen verstanden.
5. Wir bringen die Möbel herein.
6. Lotte hat die Kinder begrüßt.
7. Ich habe dem Taxifahrer die Koffer gegeben.
8. Die Antworten sind richtig.

D. Change the following sentences into the present or present perfect, whichever is applicable.

1. Ich habe nichts gemerkt.
2. Der Student kommt zu Hause an.
3. Die Frau hat dem Taxifahrer den Koffer gegeben.
4. Peter hat immer alles vergessen.
5. Der Mann bringt das Kind nach Hause.
6. Wo ist die Zeitung?

Chapter vocabulary

Nouns

die	Ahnung, -en	*idea, notion*
der	Anfang, ⸚e	*beginning*
die	Antwort, -en	*answer*
die	Arbeit, -en	*work*
der	Autofahrer, -	*(car) driver*
der	Baum, ⸚e	*tree*
der	Gruß, ⸚e	*greeting*
die	Möbel (pl.)	*furniture*
die	Nachricht, -en	*news*
der	Orangensaft, ⸚e	*orange juice*
die	Party, -ies	*party*
das	Resultat, -e	*result*
das	Schlafzimmer, -	*bedroom*
die	Sonne	*sun*
der	Unfall, ⸚e	*accident*
der	Wein, -e	*wine*
das	Wetter	*weather*
die	Woche, -n	*week*
das	Wohnzimmer, -	*living room*

Verbs

an·rufen (angerufen)	*to call (by phone)*
begrüßen	*to greet*
bekommen (bekommen)	*to get, receive*
besuchen	*to visit*
bleiben (ist geblieben)	*to stay*
brennen (gebrannt)	*to burn*
erhalten (erhielt, erhalten)	*to receive*
erkennen (erkannt)	*to recognize*
erzählen	*to tell (stories)*
grüßen	*to greet*
herein·bringen (hereingebracht)	*to bring in*
hinein·mischen	*to mix in*
lernen	*to learn*
meinen	*to mean*
merken	*to notice*
passieren (ist passiert)	*to happen*
reden	*to talk*

regnen	*to rain*
scheinen (geschienen)	*to shine*
schreiben (geschrieben)	*to write*
tanzen	*to dance*
treffen (trifft, getroffen)	*to meet*
tun (getan)	*to do*
überholen	*to pass*
vergessen (vergißt, vergessen)	*to forget*
verlieren (verloren)	*to lose*
verstehen (verstanden)	*to understand*

Other words

außerdem	*besides, in addition*
besser	*better*
deshalb	*therefore*
eigentlich	*actually*
einmal	*ever; once*
etwas	*a little, something*
früh	*early*
furchtbar	*awful, dreadful*
gern	*gladly*
etwas gern haben	*to like*
herzlich	*cordial(ly)*
heutzutage	*these days, nowadays*
hoffentlich	*it is to be hoped; I hope so*
jemand	*someone*
kaum	*hardly*
kürzlich	*recently*
lange	*for a long time*
leid: es tut (mir) —.	*(I) am sorry*
lieb	*dear*
nett	*pleasant*
nie	*never*
nur	*only*
richtig	*right, correct*
schon	*already*
spät	*late*
tatsächlich	*indeed*
wahrscheinlich	*probably*

Mini-dialogues

Student(in) A Wo hast du denn das Strafmandat bekommen?
          B In der Lindenstraße. Ich wollte gerade zum Café
             Rosenkranz.
          A Wie ist es denn passiert?
          B Ich suchte einen Parkplatz und konnte keinen finden. Da
             habe ich den Wagen schließlich bei der Bäckerei
             geparkt.
          A Und da hast du natürlich ein Strafmandat bekommen.
          B Ja, leider!

          A Kannst du auch mit uns kommen?
          B Wo wollt ihr denn hin?
          A In die Stadt. Wir müssen zur Bäckerei.
          B Ich weiß nicht. Wann wollt ihr denn wieder zu Hause
             sein?
          A Um fünf.
          B Ja, dann komme ich mit.
          A Gut. Bis gleich!

A Where did you get the ticket?
B On Lindenstraße. I just wanted to go to the Café
   Rosenkranz.
A How did it happen?
B I was looking for a parking space and couldn't
   find one. Finally, I parked the car by the
   bakery.
A And there you got a ticket, of course.
B Yes, unfortunately.

A Can you come along with us?
B Where do you want to go?
A Downtown. We have to go to the bakery.
B I don't know. When do you want to be back
   again?
A At five (o'clock).
B Yes, then I'll come along, too.
A OK. See you soon.

Pronunciation

Repeat each sentence after your instructor and pay close attention to the
contrast in sounds. Then listen to your instructor read each sentence again.

1. **Wann kam Tante Anna?**   *(When did Aunt Anna come?)*
2. **Nach dem Kaffee gehen Peter und Werner an den See.**   *(After coffee [time]
   Peter and Werner go to the lake.)*

3. **Liebe Lili, willst du wissen, wie ich dich liebe?** *(Dear Lili, do you want to know how much I love you?)*

4. **Bitte, gib dem Klavierspieler noch ein Bier!** *(Please give the piano player another beer.)*

5. **Mein Sohn, dort oben ist das Telefon.** *(My son, the telephone is up there.)*

6. **„Morgenstund[1] hat Gold im Mund."** *("The early bird catches the worm.")*

7. **„Nach dem Essen sollst du ruhn[1] oder tausend Schritte tun."** *(After dinner you should either rest or go for a short walk.)*

8. **Unser Koch kocht auch gut nach einem Kochbuch.** *(Our cook also cooks well by following a cookbook.)*

9. **Zehn Zigeuner ziehen zehn Zentner Zuckerrüben.** *(Ten gypsies are pulling a thousand pounds of sugar beets.)*

[1]In these sayings, the **e** in -stund**e** and in ruh**e**n has been dropped.

Grammar explanations

I. Past tense

Das Mädchen **bezahlte** den Taxifahrer.
The girl paid the taxi driver.

Klaus **ging** die Treppe **hinunter.**
Klaus went downstairs.

Ich **kannte** ihn nicht.
I didn't know him.

Wir **hatten** kein Geld bei uns.
We had no money on us.

Du **fuhrst** zu schnell.
You drove too fast.
You were driving too fast.

Da **kam** ein Polizist.
A policeman came (on the scene).

Wir **gingen** nach Hause.
We went home.

Karl **war** krank.
Karl was sick.

Die Studentin **brachte** ihm ein Buch.
The student brought him a book.

As discussed in Chapter 5, the present perfect tense is generally preferred in conversation. The past tense, on the other hand, is used primarily in writing as the so-called "narrative past," when the narrator enumerates step by step the events that form part of a sequence, as in a story. Yet the past tense may be used in the spoken language, too, when the speaker turns narrator.

Ich **suchte** einen Parkplatz und konnte keinen finden.	*I looked for a parking space and couldn't find one.*
Schließlich **parkte** ich den Wagen bei der Bäckerei.	*Finally I parked the car by the bakery.*

A. Formation

Like the present, the past is a "simple" tense, because it does not need an auxiliary. In this tense the difference in conjugation between the weak and strong verbs is particularly apparent.

1. *Weak verbs* form the past tense by inserting **-t-** between the *unchanged stem* and a personal ending. In English the equivalent of the weak-verb endings is *-ed*, as in to *play, played.*

Singular	Plural	*Past tense:*
		sagen *(to say)*
ich sagte	wir sagten	
du sagtest	ihr sagtet	
er ⎫	sie sagten	
sie ⎬ sagte		
es ⎭		
Sie sagten	Sie sagten	

Privatgrundstück
Parken verboten !
Widerrechtlich geparkte Fahrzeuge
werden kostenpflichtig
abgeschleppt

Since the **-t-** of the past tense must be clearly audible, verbs with a stem ending in **-d** or **-t** insert **-e-** between the stem and the ending.

Ich arbeitete heute.   *I worked today.*

The same is true for verbs with a stem ending in **-m** or **-n** preceded by a consonant other than **l** or **r**.

Du öffnetest die Tür.   *You opened the door.*

Remember that these verbs also insert **-e-** in the present tense and in the past participle: **du öffnest, geöffnet.**
The verb **haben** shows an irregularity in its simple past forms.

Singular	Plural		*Past tense:* **haben**
ich hatte	wir hatten		
du hattest	ihr hattet		
er ⎫	sie hatten		
sie ⎬ hatte			
es ⎭			
Sie hatten	Sie hatten		

---

2. *Irregular weak verbs* take the same past-forming element **-t-** and the same personal endings as weak verbs, but feature a *stem-vowel change* similar to the strong verbs.

Infinitive	*Past*	*Past participle*
brennen *to burn*	**brannte**	gebrannt
bringen *to bring*	**brachte**	gebracht
denken *to think*	**dachte**	gedacht
kennen *to know*	**kannte**	gekannt

Note that irregular weak verbs have the same stem vowel in the past and the past participle.

CHECK YOUR COMPREHENSION

Supply the appropriate past-tense form of the verb in parentheses.

1. Die Autofahrer _____ einen Parkplatz. (*suchen*)

2. Der Student _____ zu Hause. (*arbeiten*)

3. Du _____ wirklich
   Probleme. (*haben*)
4. Wir _____ ihm kein
   Geld. (*bringen*)

5. Ich _____ dich. (*meinen*)
6. Er _____ uns immer. (*grüßen*)
7. Er _____ ihn nicht. (*kennen*)

---

3. *Strong verbs*, instead of using **-t-,** change their *stem vowel* and add *different personal endings* to the changed stem.

Singular	Plural		Past tense:
			fahren
ich **fu**hr	wir **fu**hren		
du **fu**hrst	ihr **fu**hrt		
er			
sie } **fu**hr	sie **fu**hren		
es			
Sie **fu**hren	Sie **fu**hren		

Other strong verbs:

Infinitive	Past	Past participle
halten	**hielt**	gehalten
nehmen	**nahm**	genommen
bleiben	**blieb**	ist geblieben
kommen	**kam**	ist gekommen
tun	**tat**	getan

Note that the stem change in the past tense is not necessarily the same as that in the past participle.

The verb **sein** has a special form for the past tense: **war** plus the usual endings for strong verbs.

Singular	Plural		Past tense:
			sein
ich **war**	wir **waren**		
du **warst**	ihr **wart**		
er			
sie } **war**	sie **waren**		
es			
Sie **waren**	Sie **waren**		

It is important to memorize the past of each strong verb along with the infinitive and past participle: **sein, war, ist gewesen; fahren, fuhr, ist gefahren,** etc. The strong verbs without prefixes that you have already

encountered include those listed on page 95, plus **bleiben, fahren, gehen, kommen, laufen, schreiben, treffen,** and **tun.**

listed on page 95

CHECK YOUR COMPREHENSION

Change the following sentences to the past tense.

1. Peter ist furchtbar krank.
2. Er schreibt mir einen Brief.
3. Wir bitten um Wein.
4. Anja findet keinen Bus.
5. Spricht Maria mit euch?

6. Frau Scholz nimmt ein Taxi.
7. Wir fahren nach Köln.
8. Sie bleibt zu Hause.
9. Er trifft uns bei Jens.

B. Past forms of verbs with prefixes

1. Verbs with separable prefixes have their prefixes detached from the verb and placed at the end of the clause. This applies no matter whether the verb is weak, irregular weak, or strong.

	Infinitive	Past	Past participle
weak	zu·machen *to close*	**machte zu**	zugemacht
irreg. weak	herein·bringen *to bring in*	**brachte herein**	hereingebracht
strong	an·halten *to stop*	**hielt an**	angehalten

Die Polizei **hielt** uns **an.**   *The police stopped us.*

2. Verbs with inseparable prefixes, such as **be-, emp-, ent-, er-, ge-, ver-,** and **zer-,** are governed by the respective rules for weak, irregular weak, and strong verbs in the past tense.

Infinitive		Past	Past Participle
weak	bezahlen *to pay*	**bezahlte**	bezahlt
irreg. weak	erkennen *to recognize*	**erkannte**	erkannt
strong	bekommen *to get, receive*	**bekam**	bekommen

Er **bekam** keine Antwort.   *He got no answer.*

CHECK YOUR COMPREHENSION

Supply the appropriate past-tense form of the verb in parentheses.

1. Herr Klein _____ die Zeitungen. (*vergessen*)
2. Erika _____ das Auto. (*anhalten*)
3. Der Polizist _____ die Treppe. (*hinaufgehen*)
4. Wir _____ bei der Haltestelle. (*aussteigen*)
5. Wen _____ Karl? (*hereinbringen*)
6. Die Herren _____ die Kinder. (*erkennen*)
7. Leider _____ ich den Brief. (*verlieren*)
8. Er _____ nach Köln. (*weiterfahren*)
9. Anna _____ keinen Brief. (*bekommen*)
10. Natürlich _____ Jürgen gleich. (*zurücklaufen*)

C. The three principal parts of verbs

The *inifitive, past,* and *past participle* are called the "three principal parts" of the verb. From this point on, you should memorize the three principal parts of strong and irregular weak verbs, and then add the necessary personal endings. As a matter of convention, the past-tense form is indicated by the 3rd-person singular. In verbs with vowel variation in the present tense, the 3rd-person singular will also be listed. If the present perfect is formed with **sein, ist** will precede the past participle.

denken	dachte	gedacht
lesen (liest)	las	gelesen
kommen	kam	ist gekommen

The forms of weak verbs, however, need not be memorized individually, since they can easily be derived from the infinitive stem.

In the Appendix you will find a list of the most important strong and irregular verbs with their principal parts. Look there for verbs whose forms you do not know; if a verb does not occur there, it is weak.

II. Modals and *wissen* (to know)

Peter will nicht hier bleiben.
Peter doesn't want to stay here.

Können Sie Deutsch (sprechen)?
Do you know German?

Ich möchte nach Hause (gehen).
I would like to go home.

Durften Sie mit dem Auto kommen?
Were you allowed to come by car?

Viktor mußte zu Hause arbeiten.
Viktor had to work at home.

Renate weiß es noch nicht.
Renate doesn't know it yet.

Wußtet ihr es?
Did you know it?

A. Modal auxiliaries

In German as well as in English, certain verbs function as *modal auxiliaries*, describing how an action is viewed. In the sentences *I must go home now* and *You may leave now*, for instance, the verbs *must* and

may show how the speaker feels (his mode or manner of feeling) about going or leaving.

German has six modal auxiliaries: **dürfen, können, mögen, müssen, sollen,** and **wollen,** expressing permission, ability, desire or preference, necessity, obligation, and intention. Remember their basic meanings, rather than any direct word-for-word translation.

Modal	Sample sentence	Approximate translation	Basic meaning
dürfen	Du **darfst** heute hier bleiben. *You may (are allowed to) stay here today.* **Du darfst** das nicht tun. *You mustn't (!) do that.*	to be allowed to	permission
können	Er **kann** nicht kommen. *He cannot come.* **Sie kann** Deutsch. *She knows (how to speak) German.*	to be able to, can	ability
mögen	Ich **mag** hier nicht bleiben. *I don't like to stay here.* **Sie möchte** hier bleiben. *She would like to stay here.*	to like to / would like to	desire, preference
müssen	Ich **muß** nach Hause (gehen). *I must (have to) go home.*	to have to, must	necessity, compulsion
sollen	Er **soll** nach Köln fahren. *He is supposed to go to Cologne.* **Sollen** wir nach München gehen? *Shall we go to Munich?*	to be supposed to, ought to, shall	imposed obligation (in questions: suggestion)
wollen	Ich **will** hier bleiben. *I want (intend) to stay here.* Ich **will** morgen nach Frankfurt fahren. *I want to drive to Frankfurt tomorrow.*	to want to	intention, strong desire

Modals most often occur with the infinitive of another verb placed at the end of the phrase. Sometimes the infinitive is understood, as in **Ich kann Deutsch** or **Ich muß nach Hause.**

Möchten, a special form of **mögen,** is used frequently. It has the meaning *would like to,* and expresses a statement or request more politely.

Ich möchte kommen.   *I would like to come.*

In the *present tense,* the modals undergo vowel changes in the singular (except **sollen**), but do not change in the plural.

Infinitive to the end of the sentence

dürfen	können	mögen	müssen	sollen	wollen	*Present tense:* *modals*
ich darf	kann	mag/möchte	muß	soll	will	
du darfst	kannst	magst/möchtest	mußt	sollst	willst	
er *sie* } darf *es*	kann	mag/möchte	muß	soll	will	
wir dürfen	können	mögen/möchten	müssen	sollen	wollen	
ihr dürft	könnt	mögt/möchtet	müßt	sollt	wollt	
sie dürfen	können	mögen/möchten	müssen	sollen	wollen	
Sie dürfen	können	mögen/möchten	müssen	sollen	wollen	

[handwritten: singular changes. Plurals based on infinitive]

Notice that **möchten,** adds **-e** in the 1st and 3rd person singular, but not the other modals.

In the *past tense*, the modals add **-t-** and weak verb endings and lose the umlaut.

dürfen	können	mögen	müssen	sollen	wollen	*Past tense:* *modals*
ich durfte	konnte	mochte	mußte	sollte	wollte	
du durftest	konntest	mochtest	mußtest	solltest	wolltest	
er *sie* } durfte *es*	konnte	mochte	mußte	sollte	wollte	
wir durften	konnten	mochten	mußten	sollten	wollten	
ihr durftet	konntet	mochtet	mußtet	solltet	wolltet	
sie durften	konnten	mochten	mußten	sollten	wollten	
Sie durften	konnten	mochten	mußten	sollten	wollten	

[handwritten: lose umlaut add regular endings]

Notice that the **-g-** of **mögen** changes to **-ch-.**

With a modal followed by an infinitive, the simple past is preferred over the present perfect.

Ich **wollte** wirklich pünktlich sein.   *I really wanted to be on time.*

Ich **konnte** keinen Parkplatz finden.   *I couldn't find a parking space.*

B. *wissen* (to know)

The verb **wissen,** meaning *to know* in the sense of knowing facts, is highly irregular in the present tense and must therefore be memorized separately.

Singular	Plural		Present tense:
			wissen

ich weiß   wir wissen

du weißt   ihr wißt

er

sie } weiß   sie wissen

es

Sie wissen   Sie wissen

(handwritten: to know of / have knowledge)

(handwritten: conjugates like auxiliary)

Er weiß nichts.   *He knows nothing.*

The principal parts of this verb are **wissen (weiß), wußte, gewußt.**

Wissen behaves like the irregular weak verbs in the past and present perfect tenses.

Ich wußte es nicht.   *I didn't know it.*

Das hast du leider nicht **gewußt.**   *Unfortunately you didn't know that.*

CHECK YOUR COMPREHENSION

A. Supply the correct present-tense form of the modal in parentheses, then translate into English.

1. Der Herr _____ keine Zigaretten rauchen. (*dürfen*)
2. Der Amerikaner _____ die Zeitung nicht lesen. (*können*)
3. Ich _____ keinen Kuchen. (*mögen*)
4. _____ du mit uns kommen? (*möchten*)
5. Die Studenten _____ heute abend arbeiten. (*müssen*)
6. Wir _____ mit ihr nach Bonn fahren. (*sollen*)
7. Wer _____ den Brief schreiben? (*wollen*)

B. Supply the correct past-tense form of the modal in parentheses, then translate into English.

1. Anita _____ nicht viel essen. (*dürfen*)
2. Wir _____ hier nicht studieren. (*können*)
3. Ich _____ nach Hause (gehen). (*müssen*)
4. Das Mädchen _____ schnell zurückfahren. (*sollen*)
5. Sie (*pl.*) _____ uns verlassen. (*wollen*)

C. Supply the indicated tense of **wissen.**

1. Ich _____ nichts, und ihr _____ alles. (*present*)
2. _____ Sie es auch? (*past*)

3. Das _____ ich lange nicht _____. (*present perfect*)
4. _____ du die Antwort nicht? (*present*)
5. Das _____ wir schon _____. (*present perfect*)

Conversation

Ich wollte wirklich pünktlich sein.   *I really wanted to be on time.*

Das ist nichts Neues.   *That's nothing new.*

Na, und dann?   { *Well?*
                          { *Go on!*

DAS STRAFMANDAT

Georg und Sibille hatten eine Verabredung für neun Uhr morgens in einer Kaffee-Bar.[1] Georg kommt fünfzehn Minuten zu spät.

Sibille   Da bist du ja[2] endlich! Wo bist du so lange gewesen?

Georg   Tag,[3] Sibille! Es tut mir leid. Ich wollte wirklich pünktlich sein. *I'm sorry*

Sibille   Was ist denn wieder passiert?

Georg   Ich suchte einen Parkplatz und konnte keinen finden.

Sibille   Das ist nichts Neues.

Georg   Schließlich parkte ich den Wagen auf dem° Bürgersteig vor der° Bäckerei. *on the / in front of the*

Sibille   Na, und dann?

George   Ich wollte gerade aussteigen, da kam ein Polizist. „Sie dürfen hier nicht parken. Fahren Sie weiter," sagte er.

Sibille   Aber du weißt doch, da kannst du nicht parken.

Georg   „Nur für ein paar Minuten," bat ich. Aber der Kerl blieb unerbittlich° und wollte mir gleich ein Strafmandat geben. *pitiless*

Sibille   Warum wolltest du denn zur Bäckerei gehen?

---

[1] A stand-up bar where one can drink a quick cup of coffee (now very popular in Europe).

[2] **ja** is another "flavoring particle" that cannot be directly translated. It is frequently used to give more emphasis to an affirmative statement, just as **denn** gives more emphasis to a question.

[3] Short for **Guten Tag.**

Georg   Ich sollte doch Brötchen mitbringen!
Sibille   Und wo sind die Brötchen?
Georg   Die Brötchen? Ach, jetzt habe ich sie ganz vergessen!

QUESTIONS ON THE CONVERSATION

1. Wann und wo hatten Georg und Sibille eine Verabredung?
2. Warum konnte Georg nicht pünktlich sein?
3. Wo parkte Georg den Wagen?
4. Wer kam da plötzlich?
5. Was sagte der Polizist zu Georg?
6. Wie lange wollte Georg da parken?
7. Was wollte der Polizist Georg geben?
8. Warum wollte Georg zur Bäckerei gehen?
9. Was hat Georg leider vergessen?

PERSONAL QUESTIONS

1. Können Sie oft keinen Parkplatz finden?
2. Haben Sie schon oft ein Strafmandat bekommen?
3. Wieviel kostet ein Strafmandat bei Ihnen?
4. Kaufen Sie manchmal Brötchen, oder essen Sie nur Brot?

Practice

A. Change the sentence from the present to the past tense.

1. Wo bist du denn?
2. Ich will wirklich pünktlich sein.
3. Ich soll noch ein paar Brötchen mitbringen.
4. Du kannst keinen Parkplatz finden?
5. Georg findet keinen Parkplatz.
6. Ich parke den Wagen auf dem Bürgersteig.
7. Ein Polizist kommt.
8. Der Polizist will mir ein Strafmandat geben.
9. Ich will zur Bäckerei gehen.
10. Georg vergißt leider die Brötchen.

B. Supply the appropriate present-tense form of the modal in parentheses.

1. Ich _____ keinen Kaffee trinken. *(dürfen)*
2. _____ du zu Hause bleiben? *(möchten)*
3. Was _____ er studieren? *(wollen)*
4. Georg _____ keine Antwort finden. *(können)*
5. Wir _____ morgen nach Bonn fahren. *(sollen)*
6. Ihr _____ jetzt zur Arbeit gehen. *(müssen)*

C. Change the sentence from the present perfect to the past tense.

1. Ich habe viel Zeit gehabt.
2. Wir sind pünktlich gewesen.
3. Hat er die Zeitung gleich gefunden?
4. Hat der Baum rechts gestanden?
5. Herr Steinhoff ist schnell aus dem Haus gegangen.
6. Sibille hat nichts gesagt.
7. Die Studentinnen haben heute gearbeitet.
8. Der Polizist hat mich angehalten.
9. Ich habe es wirklich nicht gewußt.
10. Ist er gleich zurückgelaufen?

D. Change the sentences in exercise C from the present perfect to the present.

E. Supply the appropriate past-tense forms of the verbs in parentheses.

Freitag abend _____ (*fahren*) Herr Steinhoff nach Mannheim. Er _____ (*besuchen*) eine Party bei Frau Schumacher. Frau Schumacher _____ (*begrüßen*) ihn herzlich. Bei ihr _____ (*treffen*) er die Kapps. Frau Kapp _____ (*sein*) wirklich nett. Herr Steinhoff _____ (*glauben*), sie zu kennen. Herr Kapp _____ (*erzählen*) sehr interessant von einer Reise (*trip*) nach Amerika. Sie _____ (*bleiben*) bis sehr spät bei Frau Schumacher und _____ (*diskutieren*) über Politik. Natürlich _____ (*wollen*) Herr Steinhoff nur Orangensaft trinken, aber jemand _____ (*hineinmischen*) etwas Wodka. Herr Steinhoff _____ (*merken*) es nicht. Endlich _____ (*müssen*) er die Party verlassen. Er _____ (*zurückfahren*) sehr schnell nach Hause. Plötzlich _____ (*überholen*) ihn ein Porsche. Herr Steinhoff _____ (*fahren*) sofort nach rechts. Leider _____ (*sehen*) er den Baum nicht. Das Resultat _____ (*sein*) ein Unfall. Moral: Für die Gesundheit ist Orangensaft manchmal gefährlich!

F. Change the sentence from the present to the past tense.

1. Können Sie Deutsch?
2. Dürft ihr das?
3. Mögen Sie Wodka mit Orangensaft?
4. Wir müssen nach Hause.
5. Ich will das Buch nicht.

G. Answer the following questions.

1. Kamen Sie heute pünktlich an?
2. Können Sie immer einen Parkplatz finden?
3. Haben Sie einmal einen Wagen auf dem Bürgersteig geparkt?
4. Bekamen Sie dann ein Strafmandat?
5. Müssen Sie manchmal viel studieren?
6. Haben Sie wirklich fast alles vergessen?
7. Wollten Sie heute abend Brötchen essen?
8. Wollen Sie morgen zu Hause bleiben?
9. Möchte eine Freundin zu Ihnen kommen?
10. Dürfen Sie zu Hause rauchen und Alkohol trinken?
11. Möchten Sie gern Orangensaft oder Kaffee?
12. Müssen Sie sofort nach Hause?

H. Now ask your neighbor the same questions in the **du**-form and get an answer.

I. Give the English equivalent of the following sentences.

1. Wolfgang kann nicht English.
2. Ich möchte gern eine Tasse Kaffee.

3. Herr Klein weiß nicht immer alles.
4. Durftest du mit dem Auto nach Hause fahren?
5. Der Unfall passierte bei der Thomas-Kirche.
6. Wo warst du kürzlich mit Frau Kapp?

Vocabulary development

A. Man is a frequently used and versatile word. It can be rendered in English by *people, one,* or the indefinite *they,* depending on context.

Man sagt, die Schweiz ist schön.
$\begin{cases} \textit{People say Switzerland is beautiful.} \\ \textit{They say Switzerland is beautiful.} \end{cases}$

Beim Studieren muß man aufmerksam sein.
When studying, one must be attentive.

In the Reading section of this chapter, underline **man** wherever it is used, and translate the sentence in which it occurs.

B. At times a verb may be used as a *neuter noun,* as for instance **(das) Skilaufen** (*skiing*):

Skilaufen ist hier sehr populär.
Skiing is very popular here.

The verbal noun may be used with a preposition, as in the sentence under A above: **Beim Studieren muß man aufmerksam sein.** Form a few sentences with **lesen, schreiben, (Karten) spielen,** and **rad·fahren,** using them as nouns.

C. In building a vocabulary it is useful to observe word families. In this and earlier lessons, for instance, you have seen the following words involving **fahren** and **Rad: das Fahren, das Radfahren, die Fahrt, der Radfahrer, die Radfahrerin, der Busfahrer, der Taxifahrer.** Take **Auto** and combine it with **fahren** in similar fashion, then use each word in a sentence.

D. Wissen, kennen, and **können** can all mean *to know.* **Wissen** means *to know* in the sense of *knowing a fact.*

Ich weiß das.
I know that.

Wir wissen, Claudia kommt morgen.
We know Claudia is coming tomorrow.

Kennen means *to know* in the sense of *knowing about* or *being acquainted with* a person or thing.

Ich kenne Herrn Meyer seit Jahren.	*I have known Mr. Meyer for years.*
Er kennt München sehr gut.	*He knows Munich very well.*

The modal **können** may also mean *to know,* but in the sense of *having know-how,* of *having mastered something* that one has studied or has a talent for.

Herr Müller kann gut Englisch.	*Mr. Müller knows English well.*
Fritz kann gut Gitarre spielen.	*Fritz knows how to play the guitar well.*

In the following sentences, use the appropriate present-tense form of either **wissen, kennen,** or **können.**

1. I know he's at home.
2. Do you (*du*) know the gentleman?
3. He can play the piano very well.
4. They know the answer.
5. Do you (*Sie*) know Berlin?
6. He knows German well.

Communicative exercises

A. Practice with your neighbors the verbs **kennen, wissen,** and **können** by completing and answering the following statements.

1. Ich kenne . . .
   Wen kennst du?
   Wen kennt er?
2. Ich weiß . . .
   Was weißt du?
   Was weiß er?
3. Ich kann . . .
   Was kannst du?
   Was kann sie?

B. Practice with your neighbor all modal auxiliaries by completing as many statements as possible.

1. Ich will (wollte) . . .
2. Er kann (konnte) . . .
3. Sie muß (mußte) . . .
4. Wir dürfen (durften) . . .
5. Möchtest du . . . ?
6. Wir sollen (sollten) nicht . . .

C. Begin a conversation with someone in your class. Pretend you just arrived in a café to meet a friend. After a short greeting explain why you are late and how you forgot to bring along a book you had promised to buy for the friend. Ask your friend whether he or she would like a cup of coffee and rolls.

Reading

DAS RADFAHREN

Heutzutage fährt man in Deutschland, wie überall in Europa und Amerika, wieder Rad. Natürlich fährt man immer noch mit dem Auto und dem Zug. Aber seit einigen° Jahren ist das Fahrrad wieder populär. Vor° dem Krieg fuhr man mit dem Rad oder der Straßenbahn. Autos und Benzin waren zu teuer. Auch jetzt ist das Benzin wieder teuer. Aber seit dem Krieg verdienen die Deutschen viel Geld und können Autos kaufen. Leider haben die Autos die Luft verschmutzt. Wer weiß das nicht? Das Radfahren verschmutzt die Luft nicht und ist auch gesund. Man kann auch beim Radfahren viel Spaß haben!

several
before

Viele Menschen fahren deshalb wieder mit dem Rad zur Arbeit oder machen kurze Ferienreisen° mit dem Rad. Es gibt sogar Fahrradwege.° Das gab es vor dem Krieg nicht. Es war nicht nötig. Das Radfahren war nicht so gefährlich; es gab nicht so viele Autos.

vacation trips
bicycle paths

Aber nicht nur die Luft ist schmutzig. Seit einigen Jahren sind auch die Seen und Flüsse von den Abwässern° schmutzig. Deshalb sind zweihundert Radfahrer und Radfahrerinnen aus der Schweiz, der Bundesrepublik,[1] Frankreich und Holland kürzlich in Schaffhausen

sewage

zusammengekommen. Sie wollten gegen° die Verschmutzung des Rheins° protestieren. Schaffhausen liegt beim Rheinfall° in der Schweiz. Der Rheinfall ist in Europa so bekannt wie zum Beispiel der Niagarafall in Amerika.

against
of the Rhine / Rhine Falls

Die zweihundert Radfahrer kündigten° die Fahrt in vielen Zeitungen an. Sie fuhren mit dem Rad weit nach Deutschland hinein, bis zur Lorelei,[2] und zurück in die Schweiz. Überall haben sie angehalten, mit vielen Menschen gesprochen und Programme verteilt.° Die Journalisten haben viele Berichte über die zweihundert Radfahrer geschrieben, aber auch über die Verschmutzung des Rheins. Einige Berichte waren satirisch.° „Der Rhein ist nicht mehr voll Gold, er ist voll Schmutz", las man zum Beispiel in Berichten mit Bezug auf° die Oper von Richard Wagner.[3] Tatsächlich fließen° die Abwässer von Industrie und Städten in den Rhein, und jetzt muß man den Rhein wieder säubern.

announced

distributed leaflets

satirical
with regard to
to flow

Das Radfahren kann das natürlich nicht erreichen. Aber die zweihundert Radfahrer haben wenigstens das Publikum auf das Problem aufmerksam gemacht. Deshalb war die Fahrt kein Reinfall!°

failure, flop

Aber was denken Sie, was haben die Fahrer beim Fahren getrunken? Rheinwasser, speziell° vom Wasserwerk° in Zürich (Schweiz) gesäubert!

especially / water works

CULTURAL NOTES

1. The official German term for West Germany is **(die) Bundesrepublik Deutschland.** Frequently just the term **Bundesrepublik** is used. The term for East Germany is **(die) Deutsche Demokratische Republik (DDR).**

Der Rheinfall bei Schaffhausen

Angeschwemmter Müll am Rheinufer bei Bonn

2. A rock on the right bank of the Rhine, noted for the danger it caused to navigation. From this originated the legend of the siren who lured boatmen to destruction. The poet Heinrich Heine (1797–1865) celebrated this rock in his famous poem "Die Lorelei."

3. Richard Wagner (1813–1883) was one of the greatest composers of the nineteenth century. **Das Rheingold** is the first part of his impressive opera tetralogy, **Der Ring des Nibelungen.**

QUESTIONS

1. Was fährt man heutzutage wieder?
2. Was fährt man meistens (*mostly*) in Europa und Amerika?
3. Sind Autos und Benzin billig?
4. Was verschmutzen die Autos?
5. Warum gab es vor dem Krieg keine Fahrradwege?
6. Wo liegt der Rheinfall?
7. Wie bekannt ist der Rheinfall in Europa?
8. Wo kündigten die Radfahrer die Fahrt an?
9. Wer hat Berichte über die Radfahrer geschrieben?
10. Was haben die Radfahrer beim Fahren getrunken?

Review

A. Form sentences by combining each item on the left with an item on the right. Make sure your sentences make sense.

EXAMPLE: Wir müssen   mit vielen Menschen sprechen.
Wir müssen mit vielen Menschen sprechen.

1. Wir müssen	gegen die Verschmutzung protestieren
2. Viele Menschen möchten	nichts tun
3. Ich will	die Städte säubern
4. Die Studenten können	mit dem Rad zur Arbeit fahren
5. Die Industrie muß	das Publikum aufmerksam machen
6. Man soll	die Luft und das Wasser nicht
7. Man kann	verschmutzen
	Spaß beim Radfahren haben
	die Seen und die Flüsse säubern
	mit vielen Menschen sprechen
	die Probleme manchmal vergessen

B. Now eliminate the modal auxiliaries and restate your sentences in the past tense.

EXAMPLE: Wir müssen mit vielen Menschen sprechen.
Wir sprachen mit vielen Menschen.

C. Now restate in the present perfect tense the sentences thus obtained.

EXAMPLE: Wir sprachen mit vielen Menschen.
Wir haben mit vielen Menschen gesprochen.

D. Change the following sentences into the present, past, and present perfect. Omit the tense given.

1. Karl trifft die Freundin beim Bahnhof.
2. Die Möbel waren leider teuer.
3. Die Kinder haben den Brief nicht bekommen.
4. Hoffentlich merkt Karl nichts.
5. Peter fuhr morgens mit der Straßenbahn.
6. Der Student schreibt einen Bericht über die Verschmutzung.
7. Der Unfall passierte in Köln.
8. Der Journalist hat mir die Adresse gegeben.
9. Das Hotel liegt weit von der Stadtmitte.
10. Wieviel kostet das Fahrrad?
11. Jürgen hat eine Verabredung mit Sylvia.

Chapter vocabulary

Nouns

die	Bäckerei, -en	bakery
das	Benzin	gasoline
der	Bericht, -e	news report, account
das	Brötchen, -	roll (bread)
die	Bundesrepublik Deutschland	West Germany (Federal Republic of Germany)
der	Bürgersteig, -e	sidewalk
das	Fahren	driving
der	Fahrer, -	driver
das	Fahrrad, ̈er	bicycle
die	Fahrt, -en	trip
der	Fluß, ̈sse	river
(das)	Holland	Holland
die	Industrie, -n	industry
der	Journalist, -en	journalist
der	Kerl, -e	guy, fellow
der	Krieg, -e	war
die	Luft	air
die	Oper, -n	opera
der	Parkplatz, ̈e	parking space, place
der	Polizist, -en	policeman
das	Publikum	public, people
das	Rad, ̈er	bicycle, wheel
das	Radfahren	cycling
die	Reise, -n	trip, journey
der	Schmutz	pollution, dirt
der	See, -n	lake
der	Spaß	fun
das	Strafmandat, -e	ticket
die	Straßenbahn, -en	streetcar
die	Verabredung, -en	date
die	Verschmutzung	pollution
der	Wagen, -	car
das	Wasser	water

Verbs

erreichen	to achieve
mit·bringen, brachte, mitgebracht	to bring along
parken	to park
säubern	to cleanse, clean up
verdienen	to earn
verschmutzen	to pollute; soil
wissen (weiß), wußte, gewußt	to know (a fact)
zusammen·kommen, kam, (ist) zusammen- gekommen	to gather (come together)

See also the modal auxiliaries on p. 124.

Other words

aufmerksam	alert
— machen	to alert (someone)
bekannt	well known
immer noch	still, yet
man	one, you, we, they, people
mehr	more
meistens	mostly
morgens	in the morning(s)
nicht mehr	not any more
nötig	necessary
populär	popular
pünktlich	on time, punctual
schließlich	finally
schmutzig	dirty
so	so
so . . . wie	as . . . as
sogar	even
überall	everywhere
voll	full (of)
wenigstens	at least

Mini-dialogues

Student(in) A Wohin fährst du während der Ferien?
B Ich weiß noch nicht. Und du?
A Vielleicht nach Spanien.
B Gehst du mit deinem Freund?
A Nein, ohne ihn. Er will nach Jugoslawien.

A Fahrt ihr mit dem Auto nach Italien?
B Nein, die Fahrt ist zu lang.
A Aber jetzt kann man doch mit dem Auto durch den St. Gotthard[1] fahren.
B Das schon. Aber ich werde beim Autofahren immer sehr müde.
A Dann nehmt ihr den TEE?[2]
B Ja, sehr wahrscheinlich.

A Where are you going on your vacation?
B I don't know yet. And you?
A Maybe to Spain.
B Are you going with your friend?
A No, without him. He wants to go to Yugoslavia.

A Are you traveling to Italy by car?
B No, the trip is too long.
A But now you can travel directly by car through the St. Gotthard.
B Yes, indeed. But I always get very tired driving.
A Will you take the TEE then?
B Yes, most likely.

[1]The St. Gotthard Pass in Switzerland connects the north with the south of Europe. In 1980, an automobile tunnel, the longest in the world, was opened to traffic.

[2]**TEE** = Trans European Express, a network of transcontinental luxury express trains.

Das Hospiz auf der Gotthardpasshöhe, Zentralschweiz

Grammar explanations

I. Prepositions with the accusative

Der alte Mann ging durch das Tor.
The old man went through the gate.

Wir haben nicht genug Geld für den Urlaub.
We don't have enough money for vacation.

Ich habe nichts gegen dich.
I have nothing against you.

Der Junge ist ohne einen Koffer angekommen.
The boy arrived without a suitcase.

Fahrt um die Ecke!
Drive around the corner.

The *accusative case* must be used after certain prepositions.

durch *through*		**Wir gingen durch das Haus.** *We went through the house.*
für *for*		**Ich habe eine Nachricht für dich.** *I have news for you.*

gegen *against*	Elfriede hat nichts **gegen ihn.**
	Elfriede has nothing against him.
ohne *without*	Robert ist **ohne einen Koffer** angekommen.
	Robert arrived without a suitcase.
um *around, at (with time of day)*	Sie machen eine Reise **um die Welt.**
	They are taking a trip around the world.
	Der Bus fährt **um neun Uhr** zurück.
	The bus returns at nine o'clock.

Some of these prepositions are contracted.

durch + das = **durchs**	Er geht für sie **durchs** Feuer.
	He will go through fire for her.
für + das = **fürs**	Walter macht alles nur **fürs** Geld.
	Walter does everything merely for money.
um + das = **ums**	Albert lief schnell **ums** Haus.
	Albert ran quickly around the house.

CHECK YOUR COMPREHENSION

Use the appropriate form of the noun or pronoun indicated on the right. Pay attention to the case and use contractions where possible.

1. Ich habe eine Platte für _ihn_ gekauft.   (*er*)
2. Gehst du durch _die Stadt_ ?   (*die Stadt*)
3. Hermann ist ohne _die Kinder_ nach Berlin gereist.   (*die Kinder*)
4. Was hat sie eigentlich gegen _dich_ ?   (*du*)
5. Herr Weber hat lange bei _der Univ._ gewohnt.   (*die Universität*)
6. Erwin fuhr immer zu schnell durch _die Stadt_.   (*die Stadtmitte*)
7. Das Café war gleich um _die Ecke_.   (*die Ecke*)
8. Er hat das Zimmer ohne _einen_ verlassen.   (*ein Gruß*)
9. Frau Mann kommt gerade von _dem Flug._   (*der Flugplatz*)
10. Seit _der Fahrt_ ist sie krank.   (*die Fahrt nach Salzburg*)

II. Genitive case and prepositions

Wilfrieds Freund heißt Jakob.
Wilfried's friend is called Jacob.

Hier ist die Adresse **der Studentin.**
Here's the student's address.

Ferien befreien uns von der Routine **des Alltags.**
Vacations liberate us from the routine of everyday life.

Statt des Autos nimmt er den Bus.
Instead of the car he takes the bus.

Wegen eines Unfalls ist er zu spät angekommen.
Because of an accident he arrived late.

Trotz des Regens sind sie schon abgefahren.
In spite of the rain they have already left.

A. Nouns and the definite article

The fourth case in German, the *genitive case*, usually denotes the possessive relationship of one noun to another, and corresponds to many English expressions with *of*.

With proper names—names of particular people and places—the German genitive is expressed by adding **-s** to the name, without an apostrophe.

Werners Fahrrad ist neu.	*Werner's bicycle is new.*
Der Süden **Frankreichs** ist sehr schön.	*The South of France is very beautiful.*

If no proper name is involved, an article is used.

Das Fahrrad **des Studenten** ist neu.	*The bicycle of the student is new.*

Singular		Plural			*Definite article: genitive case*
masc.	**des**	*all genders*	**der**		
fem.	**der**				
neut.	**des**				

---

1. Masculine and neuter nouns of *more than one syllable* usually add **-s** in the genitive singular.

Das Zimmer **des Mädchens** ist sehr groß.	*The girl's room is very big.*
Ich habe die Adresse **des Hotels** nicht.	*I don't have the address of the hotel.*

2. Masculine and neuter nouns that have only *one syllable*, or that end in **-s** or another hissing sound, usually add **-es** in the genitive singular.

Der Koffer **des Mannes** ist da drüben.

The man's suitcase is over there.

Der Garten **des Gasthauses** ist schön.

The garden of the inn is lovely.

3. Feminine nouns in the singular, and all nouns in the plural, take no special endings in the genitive.

Hier ist die Adresse **der Frau.**

Here's the woman's address.

Die Luft **der Städte** ist verschmutzt.

The air of the cities is polluted.

Wo hast du die Fahrräder **der Kinder** gefunden?

Where did you find the children's bicycles?

4. Some masculine nouns, mostly denoting human beings, which form their plurals by adding **-n** or **-en,** do not add **-s** or **-es** in the genitive singular. Instead, they take **-en** in all forms but the nominative singular. Such nouns include **der Student, der Polizist, der Präsident, der Tourist, der Journalist,** and **der Mensch.**

	Singular	Plural	Declension: **der Student**
nom.	der Student	die Studenten	
acc.	den Studenten	die Studenten	
dat.	dem Studenten	den Studenten	
gen.	**des** Student**en**	**der** Student**en**	

Die Polizei hat den Wagen **des Studenten** gesucht.

The police looked for the student's car.

CHECK YOUR COMPREHENSION

A. Restate in the genitive.

1. der Schlüssel *des Schlüssels*
2. der Baum *des Baumes*
3. die Antwort *der Antwort*
4. der Spaß *des Spaßes*
5. das Benzin *des Benzins*
6. der Polizist *des Polizisten*
7. die Straßenbahn *der* ____
8. der Mensch *des Menschen*
9. das Jahr *des Jahres*
10. die Unfälle *der Unfälle*

B. Use the appropriate form of the noun indicated at the right.

1. Wo ist *Viktors* Adresse? (*Viktor*)
2. Ich las die Berichte *des Journalisten* (*der Journalist*)
3. Die Möbel _____ haben viel Geld gekostet. (*die Familie Kapp*)

der Familie Kapp

4. Sind die Seen *Amerikas* verschmutzt? (*Amerika*)
5. Die Kirchen *der Stadt* sind alt. (*die Stadt*)
6. Die Gärten *die Häuser* beim Hotel sind hübsch. (*die Häuser*)

B. The indefinite article and *kein*

The indefinite article and **kein** also have special genitive forms.

Singular	Indefinite article	kein[1]		*Indefinite article and* **kein**: *genitive case*
masc.	**eines**	**keines**		
fem.	**einer**	**keiner**		
neut.	**eines**	**keines**		
Plural				
all genders	—	**keiner**		

Er gab mir die Adresse eines Hotels.   *He gave me the address of a hotel.*

With the inclusion of the genitive, the list of forms of the definite and indefinite articles and **kein** is complete.

	Singular								*Declension: definite and indefinite articles,* **kein**
	Masculine			**Feminine**					
nom.	der	ein	kein	die	eine	keine			
acc.	den	einen	keinen	die	eine	keine			
dat.	dem	einem	keinem	der	einer	keiner			
gen.	des	eines	keines	der	einer	keiner			
	Neuter						**Plural**		
							All genders		
nom.	das	ein	kein				die	—	keine
acc.	das	ein	kein				die	—	keine
dat.	dem	einem	keinem				den	—	—
gen.	des	eines	keines				der	—	—

---

[1]**Kein** is used in the genitive only in rare cases. But the paradigm is given here for the sake of completeness.

CHECK YOUR COMPREHENSION

A. Restate in the genitive.

1. die Industrie
2. ein Fluß
3. ein Fahrrad
4. das Gasthaus

5. die Häuser
6. ein Brief
7. eine Oper
8. ein Waschbecken

B. Use the genitive form of the noun in parentheses.

1. Zeigen Sie uns das Zimmer _____. (*eine Studentin*)
2. Er fand die Adresse _____. (*ein Gasthaus*)
3. Sie hat eine Gehirnerschütterung; das ist das Resultat _____. (*ein Unfall*)
4. Wir suchen den Brief _____. (*ein Freund*)

C. Prepositions

A number of prepositions always require the genitive in the word that follows.

außerhalb   *outside of*

Außerhalb der Stadt gab es noch viel Land.
Outside of the city there was still much land.

innerhalb   *inside of, within*

Innerhalb der Städte gibt es keinen Platz mehr für Gärten.
Within the cities there is no more room for gardens.

(an)statt   *instead of*

Oskar, nimm doch die Straßenbahn **statt des Autos!**
Oskar, why don't you take the streetcar instead of the car!

trotz   *in spite of*

Trotz des Wetters fuhr Peter mit dem Auto nach Hause.
In spite of the weather Peter drove home by car.

während   *during*

Während der Ferien fahre ich nach München.
During vacation I'll drive to Munich.

wegen   *because of, due to*

Wegen eines Unfalls konnte er nicht arbeiten.
Because of an accident he couldn't work.

CHECK YOUR COMPREHENSION

Use the appropriate form of the noun in parentheses. Analyze the case carefully.

1. Außerhalb _____ gab es nicht viele Taxis. *(die Stadt)*
2. Ich habe nicht genug Geld für _____ . *(der Urlaub)*
3. Siegfried bleibt während _____ zu Hause. *(die Ferien)*
4. Trotz _____ ist der Journalist pünktlich angekommen. *(der Regen)*
5. Frau Keller kommt gerade aus _____ . *(das Haus)*
6. Das Wasser _____ ist verschmutzt. *(die Seen)*
7. Wegen _____ hat er die Brötchen vergessen. *(die Polizistin)*
8. Fahrt nicht durch _____ ! *(die Stadtmitte)*
9. Schließlich kaufte sie ein Fahrrad statt _____ . *(ein Auto)*
10. Innerhalb _____ gibt es keine Parkplätze. *(die Universität)*

III. The uses of werden — to become

Beim Autofahren wird man müde.
Driving is tiring.

Ferien innerhalb der Bundesrepublic sind auch teuer geworden.
Vacations within the Federal Republic have also become expensive.

Eine Stadt kann nicht zu einem Garten werden.
A city cannot become a garden.

Was werden Sie mitnehmen?
What will you take along?

A. werden used with adjectives or nouns

The verb **werden** (*to become*) has many uses in German. For instance, it may occur with an adjective as an independent verb.

Beim Studieren wird man müde.   *While studying one gets tired.*

Ferien sind teuer geworden.   *Vacations have become expensive.*

It may also be used with a noun, often with the preposition **zu.**

Eine Stadt kann nicht **zu einem Garten werden.**	*A city cannot become (turn into) a garden.*
Klaus **wird Polizist.**	*Klaus is going to be a policeman.*

B. *werden* used as an auxiliary for the future tense

Followed by the infinitive of another verb, the present tense form of **werden** is used as an auxiliary to form the **future tense.** In German, the future tense suggests a rather vague future.

Er **wird** sehr spät **ankommen.**	*He will arrive very late.*
Wirst du mir nicht **schreiben?**	*Won't you write to me?*

Notice that the separable prefix in **an·kommen** stays with the verb, since it is in the infinitive.

But the immediate future, especially in connection with an expression of time, is expressed by the present tense (see Chapter 1).

Er kommt heute abend.	*He's coming tonight.*

The principal parts of **werden** are:

werden (wird)   wurde   (ist) geworden

Watch out for the irregularities in the *present* tense:

ich	**werde**	*wir*	**werden**
du	**wirst**	*ihr*	**werdet**
er, sie, es	**wird**	*sie*	**werden**
Sie	**werden**	*Sie*	**werden**

CHECK YOUR COMPREHENSION

A. Give the English equivalent.

1. Fritz wurde plötzlich krank.
2. Wann werdet ihr Urlaub haben?
3. Das Reisen innerhalb der Schweiz ist teuer geworden.
4. Der Parkplatz wird zum Garten.
5. Was wirst du ihm schreiben?
6. Wir gehen morgen zur Universität.
7. Was wollen Sie werden?

B. Put the following sentences into the future tense.

1. Die Polizei gibt dem Fahrer ein Strafmandat.

2. Anstatt des Autos nahm ich das Fahrrad.
3. Endlich ist Thomas zurückgekommen.
4. Er parkte den Wagen auf dem Bürgersteig.
5. Wir haben keine Zeitungen gekauft.

Conversation

Hör mal!	*Listen!*
Das hat doch noch Zeit.	*There's still (ample) time for that.*
Von wegen!	*No! Certainly not! (coll.)*
(Das) stimmt.	*(That's) right.*
Nicht wahr?	*Isn't that so?*
Was hältst du von Südfrankreich?	*How do you feel about southern France?*

DIE FERIENREISE

Jutta und Kurt sind seit fünfzehn Jahren verheiratet und haben zwei Kinder, Walter, 12, und Claudia, 10. Sie machen Pläne für den Urlaub der Familie.[1] Sie möchten zusammen mit den Kindern eine Ferienreise machen.

Jutta Kurt, hör mal, wir müssen jetzt Pläne für die Ferien machen.

Kurt *(liest die Zeitung)* Das hat doch noch Zeit!

Jutta Von wegen! In zwei Monaten wirst du schon Urlaub haben.

Kurt *(läßt die Zeitung fallen)* Das stimmt. Aber wohin sollen wir fahren? Wir haben leider kaum noch Geld für den Urlaub.

Jutta Aber wir können doch nicht zu Hause bleiben. Die Kinder möchten zum Beispiel den Süden Frankreichs sehen.

Kurt Was? Den Süden Frankreichs? Das wird zu teuer. Warum fahren wir nicht zur Nordsee°, vielleicht nach Westerland?[2]

North Sea

---

[1]German workers receive a special allowance for their vacation, the **Urlaubsgeld.** In most cases it is the same for unmarried and married persons, with or without children.

[2]Westerland is a resort on the Isle of Sylt, a long, narrow island near the Danish border. It is popular with Germans as a summer resort, although it has a somewhat windy and rainy climate.

Jutta   Aber du weißt doch, das Reisen innerhalb Deutschlands ist auch nicht billig. Außerdem wird es da oben° wieder regnen.   *up there*

Kurt   Dann nehmen wir Regenschirme statt der Badehosen mit.

Jutta   Sei doch nicht so zynisch! Wir müssen doch schließlich auch etwas für die Kinder tun.

Kurt   Natürlich. Aber während der Ferien möchte ich etwas Ruhe haben. Südfrankreich ist so weit, und beim Autofahren wird man so müde.

Jutta   Ich kann doch schließlich auch fahren, nicht wahr? Also°, was hältst du von Südfrankreich?   *so*

QUESTIONS ON THE CONVERSATION

1. Seit wann sind Jutta und Kurt verheiratet?
2. Wofür (*for what*) machen die zwei Pläne?
3. Wohin möchten die Kinder reisen?
4. Warum will Kurt nicht in den Süden Frankreichs fahren?
5. Wohin will er fahren?
6. Wie ist das Wetter in Westerland?
7. Was möchte Kurt während der Ferien haben?

Nizza, im Süden Frankreichs

PERSONAL QUESTIONS

1. Was machen Sie während der Ferien?
2. Haben Sie genug Geld für die Ferien?
3. Werden Sie beim Autofahren auch manchmal müde?
4. Nehmen Sie einen Regenschirm oder Badehosen in die Ferien mit? Sind Sie dann Optimist oder Pessimist?

Practice

A. Fill in the appropriate form of the noun or pronoun in parentheses; use contractions where possible.

1. Der Zug fährt schnell durch _____. (*das Land*)
2. Die Nachricht ist für _____. (*wir*)
3. Während _____ sagte er nichts. (*die Fahrt*)
4. Was hast du eigentlich gegen _____? (*ich*)
5. Wegen _____ bin ich mit _____ gefahren. (*der Regen/die Straßenbahn*)
6. Ist das Reisen innerhalb _____ teuer? (*Deutschland*)
7. Habt ihr genug Geld für _____. (*ein Wagen*)
8. Wegen _____ muß Erich zu Hause bleiben. (*ein Unfall*)
9. Die Familie ist ohne _____ abgefahren. (*er*)
10. Statt _____ bekam er ein Motorrad. (*das Fahrrad*)
11. Innerhalb _____ darf man nicht radfahren. (*der Stadtpark*)
12. Robert stieg aus _____ und ging durch _____. (*das Taxi/der Garten*)
13. Trotz _____ ist die Industrie nötig. (*die Verschmutzung*)

B. Construct sentences in the present tense with the following cues. Watch the punctuation to determine whether they are statements, questions, or commands. Use contractions where possible.

EXAMPLE: gehen / ich / gleich / zu / die Polizei.
    Ich gehe gleich zur Polizei.

1. können / kommen / wegen / ein Unfall / Fritz / nicht.
2. laufen / schnell / das Kind / durch / der Garten.
3. treffen / der Freund (*subj.*)/ ich / bei / der Bahnhof?
4. merken / sie (*sing.*)/ nichts / trotz / die Warnung.
5. fragen (*sing.*) / der Busfahrer / nach / die Straße!

C. Answer each question, using the words in parentheses.

EXAMPLE: Woher sind Sie gekommen? *(von / der Bahnhof)*
   Ich bin vom Bahnhof gekommen.

1. Woher kommt Kurt gerade? *(aus / das Haus)*
2. Wann kann man Ruhe finden? *(während / die Ferien)*
3. Was möchtest du jetzt tun? *(durch / der Garten / gehen)*
4. Wo wohnen Sie? *(außerhalb / die Stadt)*
5. Gehst du durch die Stadt? *(ja, trotz / die Autos)*
6. Wohin ist Erich gegangen? *(zu / die Polizei)*
7. Haben die Leute protestiert? *(ja, gegen / der Krieg)*
8. Haben sie nichts getan? *(nein, trotz / die Warnung)*

D. Fill in the blanks, where necessary, with the appropriate ending of the noun, the suggested article or **kein,** or the indicated pronoun.

1. Frau Zeller _____ Haus liegt sehr schön.
2. Bitte, geben Sie _____ (ich) e_____ Glas Bier!
3. Kennen Sie d _____ Adresse d _____ Student _____?
4. Thomas, sprich doch mit _____ (sie, sing.)!
5. Max, kauf schnell e_____ Zeitung für _____ (ich)!
6. Jakob _____ Fahrrad ist schmutzig.
7. Hast du k _____ Brötchen (plural) für _____ (wir)?
8. D_____ Kinder möchten d _____ Süden Deutschland _____ sehen.

E. Put the following sentences into the future tense.

1. Dann nehmen wir Regenschirme mit.
2. In drei Monaten habt ihr Urlaub.
3. Während der Ferien bleibe ich zu Hause.
4. Die Polizei gibt dem Fahrer ein Strafmandat.
5. Elfriede schreibt dem Freund keine Briefe mehr.
6. Trotz der Krankheit geht er zur Universität.

F. Give the English equivalent.

1. Beim Lesen wird man müde.
2. Das Kind ist groß geworden.
3. Die Gärten sollen nicht zu einem Parkplatz werden.
4. Wann wirst du endlich Urlaub nehmen?
5. Es stimmt. Er kommt schon morgen an.
6. Die Fahrt ist lang. Werdet ihr nicht müde werden?
7. Die Studentin wurde plötzlich krank.
8. Das Kind wird zum Mann.

Vocabulary development

A. Nicht wahr?

This phrase, literally meaning *not true?*, is often added to a statement. It usually expresses a desire to have one's opinion confirmed.

Ich kann doch auch fahren, nicht wahr?	*I can also drive, can't I?*
Die Kinder wollten nicht nach Norddeutschland fahren, nicht wahr?	*The children didn't want to go to northern Germany, did they?*

Note that **nicht wahr?** can be added to a positive or a negative statement. It is much easier to handle than its many equivalents in English (*is it?*, *isn't it?*, *didn't you?*, etc.).

B. Wie ist das Wetter?

In the introductory chapter you learned some expressions referring to the weather such as **es regnet, es schneit,** etc.

Here are a few more:

donnern	Es donnert.	*It's thundering.*
blitzen	Es blitzt.	*There's lightning.*
frieren	Es friert.	*It's freezing.*
scheinen	Die Sonne scheint.	*The sun is shining.*
	Es ist **bewölkt.**	*It's cloudy.*
	Es ist **windig.**	*It's windy.*

Note that with the exception of **scheinen,** these verbs are used with the impersonal **es** (*it*), as in English.

Also learn the nouns: **der Regen, der Schnee, der Frost, die Wolke, -n.**

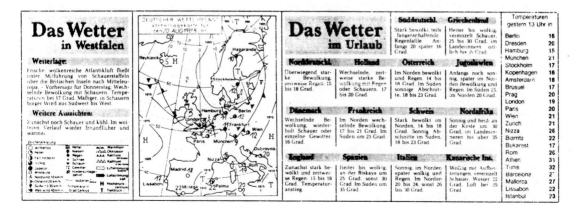

C. Compound nouns

English offers the possibility of gathering up words into compound nouns like *Midsummernight's Dream*, but it does this much less than German, where compound nouns abound.

frei (*free*) + **Zeit** (*time*)	=	**Freizeit** (*free time, leisure*)
Freizeit + **Beschäftigung** (*activity, occupation*)	=	**Freizeitbeschäftigung** (*leisure-time activity*)

Notice that the last noun in the compound determines the gender: **die** Stadt + **der** Park = **der** Stadtpark.

Some words may also be combined with the aid of a *hyphen:* **Freizeit-Gärtner, Nicht-Gärtner, Hindenburg-Platz.** At times an **-s-** is used to connect the two nouns: **Urlaubsgeld.**

No easy rules can be formulated for combining words; learn through observation. Note, however, that all kinds of words may be involved in combinations: noun + noun, adjective + noun, preposition + noun, adverb + noun.

Go through the Conversation and Reading and single out and dissect a few more compound nouns.

A mindteaser: figure out the meaning of this name, which really exists: **Vierwaldstättersee-Dampfschiffahrtsgesellschaft.** Hints: the **Vierwaldstättersee** is a lake in Switzerland. **Dampf** = *steam.* **Gesellschaft** = *company.*

Communicative exercises

A. Ask your classmates **Wie ist das Wetter heute? Wie war das Wetter gestern? Wie war das Wetter in . . . ?** and have them answer with one or two sentences.

B. Answer the following questions about the photo on page 155.

1. Wo liegt das Land?
2. Wie ist der Himmel?
3. Wie ist das Wetter?
4. Was sehen Sie noch auf dem Bild?
5. Was machen die Leute?
6. Schwimmen Sie auch gern?
7. Möchten Sie einmal in dieses Land in die Ferien?

C. You go to a travel agency (**das Reisebüro**) and ask for information about a certain country or region you would like to visit. Construct a short dialogue with a fellow student. Suggestions:

Greetings (Guten Tag, etc.)
Request (Ich möchte gern Auskunft über . . .
   Ich möchte eine Ferienreise nach . . . machen)

Questions by travel agent (Wann möchten Sie fahren?
   Wie lange werden Sie bleiben?
   Möchten Sie allein oder mit einer Gruppe reisen?
   Reisen Sie mit der Familie, mit Freunden, etc.?)

Questions and comments by client (Wieviel kostet der Flug (*flight*), die Fahrt?
   Und die Hotelzimmer für eine, zwei, . . . Person(en)?)
Thanks (Danke vielmals, etc.)

D. Team up with a fellow student and make plans for a mutual vacation or weekend trip. Ask each other where you would like to go. Ask other questions such as: When will we go? What means of transportation will we use? Will it be expensive? Will we go even if it rains? Do you like to cycle a lot? Or do you prefer to read books, relax, do nothing, and forget the world? Do you eat and drink much during a trip? Etc.

Reading

DIE FREIZEIT

Die Beschäftigung während der Freizeit ist für den modernen Menschen durch die Verkürzung° der Arbeitszeit sehr wichtig geworden. Ferien und Freizeitbeschäftigung befreien den Menschen von der Routine des Alltags.

shortening

Eines der beliebten° Hobbies[1] in Deutschland ist der Gartenbau.°[2]   *favorite / gardening*
Heute gibt es in Deutschland über dreizehn Millionen Freizeit-Gärtner.
Außerhalb der Stadt kaufen oder mieten sie ein Stück Land und pflan-
zen Gemüse, Obst und Blumen. Das Gemüse und das Obst aus dem
Privatgarten sind gut für die Gesundheit, sagt man, denn° sie haben   *since*
keine Chemikalien.°   *chemicals*

    Aber es wird schwierig, einen Platz zu finden und billig zu mieten.
Innerhalb der Städte gibt es fast keinen Platz mehr für Gärten, und
außerhalb ist der Boden zu teuer geworden. Was soll man da tun?
Stadtparks in Gärten für Privatleute° umwandeln?° Das tut man   *private individuals / transform*
tatsächlich in Städten wie Dortmund, Hamburg und Bremen.[3] Aber
es gibt nicht genug Parks innerhalb der Städte. Und schließlich kann
nicht eine ganze Stadt zum Gemüsegarten werden!

    Vielleicht muß der Staat intervenieren, den Boden um die Stadt
aufkaufen° und dann billig an° die Freizeit-Gärtner vermieten.°   *buy up / to / rent out*
Alle Einwohner müssen dann mehr Steuern bezahlen. Natürlich sind
die Nicht-Gärtner gegen diese Lösung.° „Etwas mehr Chemikalien   *this solution*
können wir noch verdauen,° aber kaum mehr Steuern", sagen sie.   *digest*
„Trotz der Steuern müssen wir Platz für Gärten machen", antworten
die Gärtner. „Gärtner verbessern die Qualität des Lebens. Was ist
besser: Steuern bezahlen oder Chemikalien essen?" Wer hat recht?

    Aber nicht nur der Gartenbau ist populär als Freizeitbeschäftigung.
Viele Deutsche haben zum Beispiel im Photographieren ein Hobby
gefunden.[4] Oder man macht Reparaturen und Renovierungen innerhalb und außerhalb des Hauses selbst.[5] Und trotz der Popularität des
Fernsehens lesen die Deutschen noch gern Bücher, Zeitschriften°   *magazines*
oder Zeitungen° während der Freizeit.   *newspapers*

Nach° Statistiken der Regierung wird man in Zukunft° noch viel mehr Geld für die Freizeit ausgeben als jetzt. So wird die Freizeit einer Person zur Beschäftigung einer anderen!°

according to / in the future

of another person

CULTURAL NOTES

1. The English "hobby" is now commonly used in German-speaking countries, although **das Steckenpferd** (*hobbyhorse, fad*) can still be heard.

2. The so-called „**Schrebergärten**", small garden plots within the city limits, have been rather popular with city dwellers in German-speaking countries ever since the second half of the nineteenth century. They are named after a certain Dr. Daniel G. M. Schreber, who in the 1860s created the first playgrounds for children. These "children-gardens" later on became "garden-house colonies" for adults.

3. In Bremen, an important port city in northern Germany, for instance, there are 23,000 small gardeners who within the city cultivate roughly 3,000 acres of "green areas" open to the public.

4. Germans spend over three billion DM (= **Deutsche Mark**) annually on photographic equipment and films.

5. Due to the enormous increase in labor costs, the "Do-it-yourself" trend has become a recreational movement in the Federal Republic. There are many "Do-it-yourself Centers," where instruction is given to novices and many new homes have a special „**Hobby-Raum**" (*hobby room*), where home repairs and improvements are carried out as a hobby as much as a necessity.

QUESTIONS

1. Was ist heutzutage für die Deutschen sehr wichtig geworden?
2. Wovon (*from what*), sagt man, befreien die Ferien und die Freizeitbeschäftigung den Menschen?
3. Was machen die Freizeit-Gärtner außerhalb der Stadt?
4. Was wird schwierig für die Freizeit-Gärtner?
5. Was tut man in Städten wie Dortmund, Hamburg und Bremen?
6. Was muß der Staat vielleicht tun?
7. Was sagen die Nicht-Gärtner?
8. Was antworten ihnen die Gärtner?
9. Wer hat recht, die Gärtner oder die Nicht-Gärtner?
10. Was machen die Deutschen noch trotz des Fernsehens?
11. Was wird man wahrscheinlich in Zukunft für die Freizeit tun?

Review

A. Construct sentences with the following cues. Use the tense indicated in parentheses. Use contractions where possible. Watch the punctuation.

1. werden / die Ferien / für / die Europäer / wichtig. (*present perfect*)
2. sein / das Gemüse / aus / der Privatgarten / für / die Gesundheit / gut. (*future*)
3. Geben / doch / die Kinder / Fahrräder / statt / ein Auto! (*imperative*)
4. machen / wann / du / endlich / Urlaub? (*future*)
5. werden / das Wasser / plötzlich / schmutzig. (*past*)
6. werden / der Boden / in Deutschland / teuer. (*present perfect*)

B. Fill in the blanks with the ending or pronoun indicated. Then answer the questions. Use contractions where possible.

Jutta machte e_____ Reise zu d _____ Freund _____ (*pl.*) in Österreich. Während d _____ Fahrt las sie e_____ Buch. Der Zug fuhr schnell durch d _____ Städte. Nur in München hielt _____ (*it*) an. Sie stieg schnell aus d_____ Zug und kaufte e_____ Zeitung. ,,Ich muß schnell wieder einsteigen, oder d_____ Zug fährt ohne _____ (*me*) ab", dachte sie. Außerhalb d_____ Stadt regnete es. Nach e_____ Stunde konnte sie durch d _____ Fenster trotz d_____ Regen _____ die Alpen (*the Alps*) sehen. In Innsbruck schien d ____ Sonne. Jutta stieg aus d _____ Zug und suchte d _____ Freunde. Sie waren schon da. Sie fuhren zusammen mit e_____ Taxi zu_____ Hotel. ,,Für d ____ Skilaufen ist d _____ Wetter nicht gut", sagten sie während d _____ Fahrt, ,,hoffentlich schneit _____ (*it*) morgen."

1. Zu wem fuhr Jutta?
2. Wann las sie ein Buch?
3. Hielt der Zug in vielen Städten an?
4. Was kaufte Jutta in München?
5. Fuhr der Zug ohne Jutta ab?
6. Wo regnete es?
7. Wann konnte sie die Alpen sehen?
8. Wie war das Wetter in Innsbruck?
9. Wohin fuhren sie mit dem Taxi?
10. Was sagten sie während der Fahrt?

C. Answer either set of questions, as directed.

(1) Für den Gärtner:
    1. Pflanzen Sie Gemüse, Obst, Bäume oder Blumen?
    2. Glauben Sie, der Gartenbau (*horticulture*) befreit den Menschen von der Routine des Alltags?

(2) Für den Nicht-Gärtner:
    1. Möchten Sie einen Garten haben?
    2. Wenn ja, was möchten Sie pflanzen? Wenn nein, warum nicht? Was haben Sie gegen den Gartenbau? (*Possibilities:* zuviel Arbeit, keine Zeit, müde werden.)
    3. Was tun Sie während der Freizeit statt des Gartenbaus? Ist das gesund? Verbessert das die Qualität des Lebens?
    4. Geben Sie viel Geld für die Freizeit aus? Warum?

D. Express in German.

1. I always get tired while driving the car.
2. Despite the taxes we must make room for gardens.
3. I had nothing against you (*du*).
4. Gerd stayed home on account of the rain.
5. Unfortunately I can do nothing for the students.
6. Hans, run quickly around the corner and buy me a newspaper.
7. She will stay with us for two months.
8. They went as far as the bus stop.
9. There are not enough parks within the cities.
10. Where will you (*Sie*) go during vacation?

Guided composition

Write a short letter to a friend to tell her/him what you did during a brief vacation. Tell where you went, by what means of transportation, with whom, where you stayed, what you did. Perhaps point out what you liked especially (**besonders**) and state whether you will go back there. At the end, you may express the hope that he/she will go with you next time.

Chapter vocabulary

Nouns

der	Alltag	*everyday life*
die	Badehose, -n	*bathing trunks*
die	Beschäftigung, -en	*activity, occupation*
die	Blume, -n	*flower*
der	Boden, ¨n	*ground, soil, land*
der	Einwohner, -	*resident, inhabitant*
die	Familie, -n	*family*
die	Ferien (pl.)	*vacation*
das	Fernsehen	*television*
die	Freizeit	*leisure (time)*
der	Gärtner, -	*gardener*
das	Glas, ¨er	*glass*
die	Inflation	*inflation*
das	Land, ¨er	*land, country*
das	Leben	*life*
die	Leute (pl.)	*people*
das	Motorrad, ¨er	*motorcycle*
der	Park, -s	*park*
die	Person, -en	*person*
der	Plan, ¨e	*plan*
der	Platz, ¨e	*space, room, place*
die	Popularität	*popularity*
die	Qualität, -en	*quality*
der	Regen	*rain*
der	Regenschirm, -e	*umbrella*
die	Regierung, -en	*government*
die	Renovierung, -en	*renovation*
die	Reparatur, -en	*repair*
die	Routine, -n	*routine*
die	Ruhe	*rest, peace*
der	Staat, -en	*state, country, nation*
der	Stadtpark, -s	*municipal park*
die	Statistik, -en	*statistic*
die	Steuer, -n	*tax*
der	Urlaub	*leave, vacation*
die	Welt, -en	*world*

Verbs

antworten (+ *dat.*)	*to answer*
aus·geben (gibt), gab, ausgegeben	*to spend (money)*
befreien	*to free, liberate*
halten von (hält), hielt, gehalten	*to think about, feel about*
intervenieren	*to intervene*
mieten	*to rent*
mit·nehmen (nimmt), nahm, mitgenommen	*to carry with, along*
pflanzen	*to plant*
photographieren	*to photograph, take pictures*
scheinen, schien, geschienen	*to shine*
stimmen (*impers.*)	*to be right, correct*
verbessern	*to improve*
werden (wird), wurde, (ist) geworden	*to become, get*

Other words

als	*than*
kaum	*hardly*
müde	*tired*
recht haben	*to be right*
schwierig	*difficult*
selbst	*self*
so	*thus*
verheiratet	*married*
von wegen!	*No! Certainly not! (coll.)*
wenn	*if*
wichtig	*important*
wie	*like*
zusammen	*together*
zynisch	*cynical*

See also the prepositions on pp. 140–141, 145–146, and the weather expressions on p. 153.

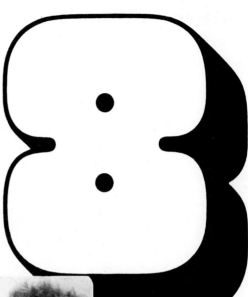

Mini-dialogues

Student(in) A Verzeihung, wie komme ich von hier zum Postamt?

B Das ist sehr einfach. Da vorne fahren Sie rechts um die Ecke in die Domstraße.

A Und da ist das Postamt?

B Ja, aber ganz am Ende der Straße.

A Vielen Dank.

B Bitte.

A Du bist aber sehr schlank geworden.

B Oh, danke. Sehr nett von dir, das zu sagen.

A Wie hast du das denn gemacht?

B Statt am Abend vor dem Fernsehapparat zu sitzen, laufe ich dreimal die Woche vier oder fünf Kilometer.

A Das tue ich auch. Aber es hilft mir nichts.

B Dann darfst du vielleicht nicht soviel essen.

A Pardon me, how do I get from here to the post office?

B That's very simple. Up ahead you turn right, around the corner onto Cathedral Street.

A And that's where the post office is?

B Yes, but at the very end of the street.

A Many thanks.

B You're welcome.

A You've become very slender.

B Oh, thanks. Very nice of you to say that.

A How did you manage to do that?

B Instead of sitting in front of the television set in the evening, I run four or five kilometers three times a week.

A I do that too. But it doesn't do anything for me (. . . doesn't help me any).

B Perhaps you shouldn't eat so much.

Grammar explanations

I. Prepositions with the dative or accusative

Sie halten auf der Straße an.
They are stopping on the street.

Kinder, geht nicht auf die Straße!
Children, don't go into the street!

Die Leute warten in der Bahnhofshalle.
The people are waiting in the entrance hall of the railway station.

Max, lauf schnell in die Bahnhofshalle!
Max, run quickly into (the entrance hall of) the railway station.

Das Auto steht vor dem Haus.
The car is (standing) in front of the house.

Der Vater stellt das Fahrrad vor das Haus.
The father puts the bicycle in front of the house.

Die Eltern warten auf den Zug.
The parents are waiting for the train.

Das Mädchen hört nicht auf die Eltern.
The girl doesn't listen to her parents.

Apart from the prepositions taking the dative or accusative discussed earlier, German also has some prepositions that may take *either* the dative or the accusative. The determining factor is not the preposition itself, but the meaning of the preceding verb.

The *dative* is used after these prepositions when the verb denotes the *location* in which an action takes place. The prepositional phrase then answers the question *where?* or *in what place?*

Peter wartet in der Bahnhofshalle.
Peter is waiting in the entrance hall of the railway station.

Peter geht in der Bahnhofshalle auf und ab.
Peter is pacing up and down in the entrance hall of the railway station (but not going anywhere).

The *accusative* is used after these prepositions when the verb denotes *a motion toward a place.* In this case the prepositional phrase answers the question *where to?*

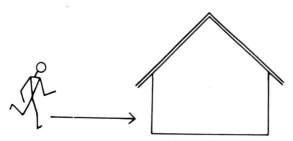

Peter geht in die Bahnhofshalle.
Peter is going into the entrance hall of the railway station.

In German the questions answered by these statements are:

	Wo wartet Peter?	Er wartet in der Bahnhofshalle.
	Wo geht er auf und ab?	Er geht in der Bahnhofshalle auf und ab.
But:	**Wohin geht er?**	Er geht in die Bahnhofshalle.

      dative

      accusative

The prepositions in this category—at times called the "two-way prepositions"—are:

an *at, on, to*

Die Mutter steht **am (an dem) Fenster.**
The mother is standing at the window.

Das Kind geht **ans (an das) Fenster.**
The child goes to the window.

auf *on, upon*

Der Kuchen ist **auf dem Tisch.**
The cake is on the table.

Stell den Kuchen **auf den Tisch!**
Put the cake on the table!

hinter *behind*

Der Park ist **hinter der Kirche.**
The park is behind the church.

Ich fuhr schnell **hinter die Kirche.**
I drove quickly behind the church.

in *in, into*

Der Vater arbeitet **im (in dem) Garten.**
The father is working in the garden.

Der Sohn läuft **in den Garten.**
The son runs into the garden.

All these prepositions relate to 3-D space or arrangements.

neben *beside, next to*

Der Regenschirm steht **neben dem Stuhl.**
The umbrella is (standing) next to the chair.

Sie stellte den Regenschirm **neben den Stuhl.**
She put the umbrella next to the chair.

über *above, over, about*

Siehst du die Sonne **über dem Berg?**
Do you see the sun above the mountain?

Karl fährt **über den Berg.**
Karl is driving over the mountain.

unter *below, under, among*

Ich parkte den Wagen **unter einem Baum.**
I parked the car under a tree.

Ich lief **unter einen Baum.**
I ran under a tree.

vor *in front of, before*

Herr Müller hielt **vor dem Hotel** an.
Mr. Müller stopped in front of the hotel.

Herr Müller fuhr **vor das Hotel.**
Mr. Müller drove in front of the hotel.

zwischen *between*	**Der Koffer ist zwischen den Stühlen.**
	The suitcase is between the chairs.
	Stell den Koffer zwischen die Stühle.
	Put the suitcase between the chairs.

Again, some of these prepositions may be contracted with the definite article.

Dative	*Accusative*
an + dem = **am**	an + das = **ans**
in + dem = **im**	in + das = **ins**
	auf + das = **aufs**

Some of these prepositions plus the accusative may be used with certain verbs that do not denote physical motion toward a place.

Ich denke oft an dich.	*I often think of you.*
Das Kind hört nicht auf die Mutter.	*The child doesn't listen to his (her) mother.*
Wir sprechen über den Unfall.	*We are talking about the accident.*
Die Leute warten auf den Zug.	*The people are waiting for the train.*

[handwritten: — to wait (for someone — auf + acc)]

If you used **warten auf** + dative, as in the phrase „die Leute warten auf dem Zug," it would express the unlikely situation of people waiting on top of the train. But it is possible to say: *[handwritten: (somewhere — auf + dat.)]*

Die Leute warten im Zug.	*The people are waiting inside the train.*

Note also these common expressions with **an:**

am Morgen	*in the morning*
am Nachmittag	*in the afternoon*
am Abend	*in the evening*
am Montag, etc.	*on Monday, etc.*

CHECK YOUR COMPREHENSION

Fill in the appropriate form of the indicated article. Use contractions wherever possible.

EXAMPLE: Ich denke oft an d_____ Geld.

        Ich denke oft ans Geld.

1. Die Mutter liest die Zeitung in d*em* Garten hinter d*em* Haus.
2. Der Schlüssel liegt auf d*em* Tisch.
3. Heute abend gehen wir in d*ie* Stadt.
4. Fritz sprach über e*ine* Reise.
5. Wir fahren mit d*en* Fahrrädern auf d*as* Land. *aufs*
6. Sehen Sie den Wagen zwischen d*em* Garten und d*em* Haus?
7. Stell den Regenschirm neben d*en* Koffer!
8. Der Vater hat das Auto unter e*inem* Baum geparkt.
9. Siehst du das Schild über d*er* Tür?
10. Wollt ihr in e*in* Café gehen?
11. Der Unfall passierte auf d*er* Straße nach Düsseldorf.
12. Oskar wartete lange auf d*em* Bürgersteig vor e*inem* Hotel.
13. Wir haben lange in d*em* Hotel auf e*ine* Freundin gewartet.
14. Essen die Deutschen an d*em* Abend sehr viel? *am*

II. Infinitive clauses

Ich habe vergessen, dir **zu schreiben.**

I forgot to write you.

Die Tochter ging in die Stadt, **um** Einkäufe **zu machen.**

The daughter went downtown in order to shop.

(An)statt zu Fuß **zu gehen,** fahren wir oft im Auto.

Instead of walking (lit., going on foot), we often ride in the car.

Man kann Sport treiben, **ohne** Mitglied eines Sportklubs **zu sein.**

One can engage in sports without being a member of a sports club.

A. Clauses with *zu*

In German as in English, the infinitive is often used with the preposition **zu** (*to*).

Es wird schwierig, einen Parkplatz zu finden.

It's getting difficult to find a parking space.

When the infinitive phrase has an object and/or an adverb, it is set off by a comma.

Wir versuchen, wenigstens einmal in der Woche Sport zu treiben.

We try to engage in sports at least once a week.

Wir werden versuchen, schnell zu parken.	*We'll try to park quickly.*
But: **Er vergaß zu schreiben.**	*He forgot to write.*

If the verb has a separable prefix, **zu** is placed between the prefix and the infinitive, and the whole is written as one word.

Er hat vergessen, an der Bushaltestelle auszusteigen.	*He forgot to get off at the bus stop.*

Three prepositions discussed earlier—**um, ohne,** and **(an)statt**—may be used as conjunctions with **zu** to introduce an infinitive clause.

um . . . zu *in order to*	**Er ging in die Stadt, um Einkäufe zu machen.**
	He went downtown in order to shop
(an)statt . . . zu *instead of*	**(An)statt zu Fuß zu gehen, nehmen wir oft das Auto.**
	Instead of walking, we often take the car.
ohne . . . zu *without*	**Die Studentin sah mich an, ohne mich zu grüßen.**
	The student looked at me without greeting me.

w/o – ING

When introducing an infinitive clause with these conjunctions, commas must be used.

Notice also that in all these infinitive clauses the infinitive is at the end of the clause, immediately preceded by **zu.**

B. Clauses without zu

The modals (see Chapter 6) and a few other verbs, such as **lassen, hören, sehen,** and **bleiben,** do not require **zu** in front of an infinitive that follows.

Ich möchte auf das Matterhorn steigen.	*I would like to climb the Matterhorn.*
Die Frau ließ ihn weiterreden.	*The woman let him go on talking.*
Ich hörte ihn Gitarre spielen.	*I heard him play(ing) the guitar.*
Wir sahen den Sohn das Zimmer verlassen.	*We saw the son leave the room.*
Der Polizist blieb vor dem Hotel stehen.	*The policeman remained standing in front of the hotel.*

CHECK YOUR COMPREHENSION

Supply the appropriate form of the infinitive clause given in parentheses.

1. Die Kinder sind in die Stadt gegangen, _____. (*in order to buy rolls*)
2. Es ist schwierig, _____. (*to rent a house*)
3. Fritz spielte Gitarre, _____. (*instead of studying*)
4. Ich versuchte, _____. (*to close the door*)
5. Franz ist zu mir gekommen, _____. (*without bringing along a record*)
6. Albert ließ sie _____. (*talk about the accident*)
7. Sie sahen Erika _____. (*leave the park*)
8. Wir hörten dich _____. (*arrive in the car*)
9. Sie vergaßen _____. (*to come*)
10. Er blieb lange auf dem Boden _____. (*to lie*)

In the *present perfect*, **lassen, hören,** and **sehen,** when occurring with a dependent infinitive, use the infinitive form as a past participle. This construction is called the *double infinitive*.

	Dependent infinitive	*Past participle*	
Ich habe ihn	kommen	**sehen.**	*I saw him come.*
Wir haben sie	singen	**hören.**	*I heard her sing.*
Sie hat ihn	gehen	**lassen.**	*She let him go.*

With modals, the simple past is usually preferred over the present perfect (double infinitive construction).

Er wollte nicht mit dem Zug nach Hamburg fahren. (Rather than: „Er hat nicht . . . fahren wollen.")	*He did not want to go to Hamburg by train.*

CHECK YOUR COMPREHENSION

Put the following sentences into the present perfect.

1. Laßt ihr euren Sohn studieren?
2. Ich sehe sie gerade losfahren.
3. Wir hören sie die Tür aufmachen.

Conversation

aus Richtung Bielefeld	*from the direction of Bielefeld*
in Richtung Bahnhof	*in the direction of the railroad station*
Kommen wir da am Dom vorbei?	*Will we pass the cathedral?*
Das geht nicht.	$\left\{\begin{array}{l}\textit{That's no good.}\\\textit{That doesn't (won't) work.}\end{array}\right.$
jemand anders	*someone else*
Bitte schön!	*You're welcome.*

AUF DER SUCHE NACH° DER UNIVERSITÄT

looking for

> *Fritz und Rudi, zwei Freunde, kommen in einem Volkswagen aus Richtung Bielefeld in Münster/Westfalen[1] an. Sie fahren in Richtung Bahnhof. Auf einer Straße halten sie an und bitten einen Fußgänger um Auskunft.*

[1]Bielefeld and Münster are both cities in Westphalia, a historic region of northeast Germany now incorporated in the **Land** (State) of **Nordrhein-Westfalen,** one of the eleven States constituting the German Federal Republic.

Fritz   Verzeihung, wie kommen wir von hier zur Universität?

Fußgänger   Zur Universität? Das ist ganz einfach. Sehen Sie den Brunnen da vorne am Ende des Parkplatzes?

Fritz   Oh ja.

Fußgänger   Da fahren Sie gleich nach rechts bis zur Klosterstraße.

Fritz   Sie meinen, gleich da vorne hinter dem Brunnen?

Fußgänger   Hm, ja. Aber passen Sie auf! Auf der Klosterstraße müssen Sie nach links fahren.

Rudi   (*studiert einen Stadtplan*) Kommen wir da am Dom[2] vorbei?

Fußgänger   Nein, der Dom ist geradeaus. Aber das geht nicht. Da ist eine Fußgängerzone.[3]

Fritz   Aber auf der Klosterstraße fahren wir nach links.

Fußgänger   Das müssen Sie. Sie werden sehen, es ist eine Einbahnstraße. Dann kommen Sie an eine Kreuzung.

Fritz   Gut.

Fußgänger   Aber nach der Kreuzung fahren Sie weiter bis zum Ende der Schützenstraße.

Fritz   Und dann?

Fußgänger   Dann fragen Sie vielleicht jemand anders.

Fritz   Vielen Dank.

Fußgänger   Bitte.

Fritz   (*zu Rudolf*) Du, sagte er nun nach rechts oder geradeaus da vorne an der Ecke?

Rudi   Keine Ahnung. Fahr doch mal geradeaus. Wir werden das Universitätsgebäude° schon finden. Man sagt, es ist ein Palast.[4]   *University building*

[2]Münster has a well-known cathedral dating back to the period of late Romanesque and early Gothic architecture.

[3]Many cities in Germany and other European countries now have pedestrian malls, especially in the older sections of towns, where streets are narrow.

[4]The administration building of the University of Münster (**Westfälische Wilhelms-Universität**) is indeed a former episcopal palace.

QUESTIONS ON THE CONVERSATION — *Das Gespräch*

1. Aus welcher (*which*) Richtung kommen die zwei Freunde?
2. Wo halten sie an, und warum?
3. Ist es einfach, die Universität zu finden?
4. Wo steht der Brunnen?
5. Welche Straße erreichen die Freunde an der Ecke?
6. Warum dürfen sie nicht geradeaus zum Dom fahren?
7. Wen sollen die Freunde am Ende der Schützenstraße um Auskunft bitten?
8. Haben die Freunde die Auskunft gut verstanden?

PERSONAL QUESTIONS

1. Wen fragst du um Auskunft auf einer Fahrt durch die Stadt?
2. Gibt es bei dir in der Stadt auch Fußgängerzonen oder Einbahnstraßen? Wenn ja, warum?
3. Gibt es bei dir Dome oder Paläste? Bist du jemals (*ever*) hineingegangen?

Practice

A. Fill in the appropriate form of the indicated article or pronoun. Use contractions wherever possible (for instance: **in** + **dem** = **im**).

1. Der Bus hält hinter d _em_ Bahnhof, aber die Taxis fahren direkt vor d _en_ Bahnhof.
2. Erika nahm d _en_ Regenschirm und verließ d _as_ Zimmer, ohne _ihn_ (er) anzusehen.
3. Der Polizist ging an d _as_ Fenster und sah auf e _inen_ Parkplatz hinunter.
4. Was gibt es denn eigentlich zwischen _dir_ (du) und _ihr_ (sie)? Ihr seht _euch_ (ihr) kaum an.
5. Auf d _er_ Reise in d _ie_ Schweiz wurde er plötzlich krank.
6. Sehen Sie d _as_ Schild über d _er_ Tür? Da gehen Sie durch d _ie_ Tür und d _ie_ Treppe hinauf.
7. Geh nicht in d _em_ Park hinein! Bleib hier neben d _em_ Wagen stehen und warte auf _mich_ (ich)! Ich gehe schnell in d _ie_ Bäckerei.
8. Sie warteten auf d _em_ Bürgersteig vor d _em_ Bahnhof auf e _inen_ Freund. Er kam spät an d _em_ Abend mit e _iner_ Freundin an.
9. Trotz d _es_ Regens ist Herr Weiß schon früh an d _am_ Morgen mit d _em_ Fahrrad zu d _er_ Arbeit gefahren.
10. Er kam spät aus d _em_ Gasthaus und wollte zu d _er_ Haltestelle gehen, aber er blieb an d _er_ Ecke stehen.

B. Answer the following questions with complete sentences using the phrases provided. Be careful to use the right case. Employ pronouns and contractions where possible.

EXAMPLE: Wo ist die Universität? (*an / der Schloßplatz*)
  Sie ist am Schloßplatz.

1. Wohin gehen die Leute? (*zu / der Bahnhof*)
2. Auf wen wartet ihr? (*auf / ein Freund*)
3. Wo werdet ihr auf mich warten? (*vor / das Hotel / unter / der Baum*)
4. Aus welcher (*which*) Richtung kommen die Studenten? (*aus / die Richtung / Münster*)
5. Wo seht ihr einen Brunnen? (*da vorne / an / die Ecke*)
6. Auf wen hörten die Kinder immer? (*auf / die Mutter*)
7. Wohin werden die Studenten reisen? (*mit / der Zug / in / der Süden / Deutschland*)
8. Worüber (*about what*) sprechen die Leute? (*über / die Regierung*)
9. Wo geht er auf und ab? (*in / das Wohnzimmer*)
10. An wen denkt sie? (*an / ein Student / in / die Schweiz*)

C. Complete the sentences with the correct form of the phrases provided. Be careful of word order.

EXAMPLES: Ich möchte immer _____. (*bleiben / hier*)
  Ich möchte immer hier bleiben.

  Es ist einfach, _____. (*fahren / zu / die Universität*)
  Es ist einfach, zur Universität zu fahren.

1. Man muß Geld haben, _____. (*reisen / weit / um*)

2. Ich hörte ihn früh am Morgen _____. (*gehen / auf und ab / in / das Schlafzimmer*)
3. Der Student ließ alles _____. (*liegen / auf / der Boden*)
4. Ich studierte sechs Stunden, _____. (*essen / etwas / ohne*)
5. Er hat vergessen, _____. (*anhalten / vor / das Hotel*)
6. Das Mädchen las weiter, _____. (*antworten / anstatt*)
7. Ich konnte heute nicht _____. (*fahren / auf / das Land*)
8. Wir sahen ihn früh am Morgen _____. (*einsteigen / in / der Bus*)

D. Give the English equivalent.

1. Anstatt mit dem Auto zu fahren, hat er den Zug genommen.
2. Elfriede ist nicht aufmerksam genug, um auf die Kinder aufzupassen.
3. Es ist sehr gefährlich, im Auto schnell über eine Kreuzung zu fahren.
4. Man muß zuerst anhalten, nach rechts und links sehen und dann weiterfahren.
5. Sie warteten auf dem Bürgersteig vor dem Hotel auf einen Freund aus der Schweiz.
6. Die Studenten baten den Fußgänger um eine Auskunft über die Universität.
7. Es ist schwierig für ihn, in der Stadt anstatt auf dem Land zu leben.
8. Der Volkswagen kam um die Ecke und fuhr schnell weiter auf der Einbahnstraße in Richtung Bahnhof.
9. Kinder, geht nicht auf die Straße! Bleibt hier und spielt im Garten!
10. Herr Stolz ließ das Geld für den Kaffee liegen und verließ das Café, ohne auf die Frage zu antworten.
11. Er bleibt immer lange im Bett liegen.
12. Habt ihr ihn ins Haus kommen hören?

Vocabulary development

A. *Die Familie*

The German words for the members of the family are:

der Vater, ⸚	*father*
die Mutter, ⸚	*mother*
die Eltern (pl.)	*parents*
die Tochter, ⸚	*daughter*
der Sohn, ⸚e	*son*
der Bruder, ⸚	*brother*
die Schwester, -n	*sister*

der Großvater, ⸚	*grandfather*
die Großmutter, ⸚	*grandmother*
der Onkel, -	*uncle*
die Tante, -n	*aunt*
der Neffe, -n	*nephew*
die Nichte, -n	*niece*
der Vetter, -n	*cousin (male)*
die Kusine, -n	*cousin (female)*

Describe your family briefly. Tell how many brothers and sisters, etc., you have. State whether your parents or grandparents are still alive (**am Leben**) or deceased (**gestorben**), and whether you have or would like to have children.

B. The gender of nouns and their endings

As we said in the beginning of this course, it is best to memorize the gender and plural of nouns. Nonetheless, in some instances it is possible to determine from certain features of the noun its gender and plural.

For instance, all nouns ending in **-heit, -keit,** and **-ung** are *feminine* and take **-en** in the plural. Often they are derived from an adjective or verb.

krank	*sick*	die Krankheit, -en	*sickness*
möglich	*possible*	die Möglichkeit, -en	*possibility*
bewegen	*to move*	die Bewegung, -en	*movement, exercise*
üben	*to practice*	die Übung. -en	*practice*

Go back to the last three Readings, locate at least three more nouns with these endings, and find their derivation.

Give the nouns derived from **gesund, schwierig,** and **wahr.**

Other feminine nouns ending with a plural in **-en (-n)** are:

die Partei, -en	*(political) party*
die Nation, -en	*nation*
die Mannschaft, -en	*team (especially in sports)*
die Universität, -en	*university*
die Industrie, -n	*industry*

However, these are not derived from adjectives or verbs. Some are in fact of foreign origin.

Communicative exercises

A. Ask a classmate the question below and have him/her answer with the suggestion given on the right. Give as many answers as make sense.

Wo hast du den Wagen geparkt?
hinter	das Hotel
vor	die Kirche
unter	der Dom
auf	die Ecke
an	der Parkplatz
	die Bäckerei
	ein Baum
	der Garten
	das Postamt
	die Bahnhofshalle

B. Do the same with the following question and elements.

Wohin habt ihr den Koffer gestellt?
neben	das Bett
auf	die Tür
hinter	das Zimmer
vor	der Stuhl da
in	der Tisch
	das Fenster

C. Ask your classmates the following two questions and have them answer with the elements given on the right.

Auf wen wartest du?
Auf wen hörst du?
hören Sie?
hört ihr?

die Eltern
die Mutter
der Vater
der Freund
die Freundin
die Schwester
die Brüder
das Mädchen
der Großvater
der Vetter

D. Look at the map on page 177 and ask one of your classmates: **Wie komme ich vom Servatiiplatz zur Voßgasse?** (or any other two points on the map) and have them give you exact directions. You may interrupt them with questions like:

Kommen wir da am Dom, am Postamt, an der Clemenskirche, am Schloßgarten, am Museum etc. vorbei?

Then, thank them for the information.

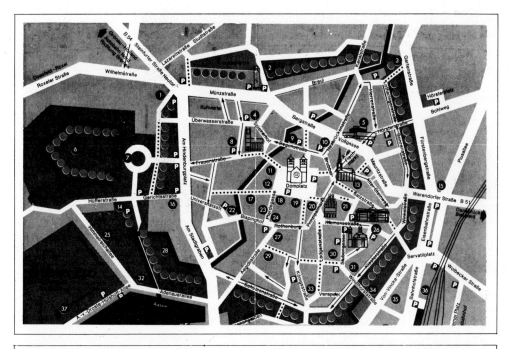

Reading

SPORT UND LEIBESÜBUNGEN

„Im Westen ißt man zu viel. Wir sind zu dick und zu faul geworden. Wir brauchen mehr Körperbewegung, um gesund zu bleiben!" liest und hört man oft in der Presse. Man hört Argumente wie:

„Statt zu Fuß zu gehen, um Einkäufe zu machen, auch nur° um die   *even just*
Ecke, fahren wir mit dem Auto." Oder: „Viele Menschen sitzen den
ganzen° Tag im Büro, gehen nach Hause, essen und trinken gut und   *whole*
sitzen dann noch ein bis zwei Stunden vor dem Fernsehapparat, be-
vor° sie ins Bett gehen. Sie haben zu wenig Körperbewegung."   *before*

   Aber der Mensch von heute treibt auch sehr viel Sport oder versucht, wenigstens einmal oder zweimal die Woche Leibesübungen
zu machen. In Deutschland gibt es zum Beispiel über 43 000 Sportclubs
mit ungefähr 14 Millionen Mitgliedern. Man braucht kein Athlet zu
sein, um Mitglied zu werden. Im Club kann man turnen°, schwimmen,   *do gymnastics*
auch Fußball° und Tennis spielen oder mit Mitgliedern des Clubs   *soccer*
Fußwanderungen machen. Es gibt viele Möglichkeiten.

   In den letzten° Jahren hat man auch außerhalb der Städte „Trimm-   *recent*
dich-Pfade"[1] eingerichtet°, besonders in der Schweiz. Da sieht man *installed*
oft an einem Sonntag oder während der Woche früh am Morgen oder
spät am Nachmittag eine ganze Familie—Vater, Mutter, Söhne und
Töchter—durch einen Wald laufen, über Hindernisse° springen und   *obstacles*
Turnübungen machen. Sie haben viel Spaß, atmen gute Luft ein und
kommen erfrischt nach Hause.

   Auch während der Ferien sucht man Körperbewegung in der Natur.
Aber der Stadtmensch möchte auch den Lärm des Stadtlebens vergessen und auf dem Lande und in den Bergen Ruhe finden. Deshalb
ist das Bergsteigen unter den Europäern sehr populär. Am Matterhorn[2] in der Schweiz, zum Beispiel, hat man bis zu 200 Bergsteiger an
einem Tag gesehen! Aber viele erreichen den Gipfel° nicht. Leider   *peak*
stürzen einige ab.° Andere werden müde und geben auf. Aber zu   *fall off*
Hause sagen sie: „Ich bin auf das Matterhorn gestiegen!" Die Wahrheit ist: Sie sind auf dem Matterhorn herumgestiegen.° Natürlich ha- *climbed around*
ben sie den Gipfel nicht erreicht, aber wenigstens Bewegung, wenn
nicht Ruhe, gefunden.

CULTURAL NOTES

1. These are publicly maintained physical fitness courses, with facilities for gymnastic exercises or simple jogging. „**Trimm dich**" = *trim yourself*. In Switzerland they are called "**Vita Parcours**" (**vita** = Latin for *life*; **parcours** = French for *track*)

2. The Matterhorn is in southern Switzerland; the Swiss-Italian border runs across its peak.

QUESTIONS

1. Was brauchen wir, um gesund zu bleiben?
2. Wo sitzen viele Menschen den ganzen Tag?
3. Wo sitzen sie dann zu Hause, bevor sie ins Bett gehen?
4. Muß man Athlet sein, um Mitglied eines Sportclubs zu werden?
5. Was macht man im Club?
6. Was macht die ganze Familie auf dem Trimm-dich-Pfad?
7. Was atmet man dort ein?
8. Warum ist das Bergsteigen unter den Europäern sehr populär?
9. Warum erreichen viele Bergsteiger den Gipfel nicht?
10. Was sagen sie zu Hause?
11. Was haben sie tatsächlich am Matterhorn gefunden?

Review

A. A sports enthusiast is addressing a group of students. Fill in the blanks as indicated.

1. Die Menschen von heute _____ (*have become too fat*).
2. Statt _____ (*walking*), fahren sie immer _____ (*by car*).
3. Und Sie, liebe Studenten, müssen den ganzen Tag _____ (*sit in the library*) oder _____ (*under trees*) liegen und _____ (*read books*).
4. Und am Abend _____ (*after work*) sitzen Sie zwei oder drei Stunden _____ (*in front of the television set*).
5. Das ist kein Leben! Statt _____ (*sitting at home*), gehen Sie doch _____ (*to the Physical Fitness Track*), springen Sie _____ (*over obstacles*) und laufen Sie _____ (*through forests*)!
6. Sie brauchen nicht _____ (*to be athletes*), _____ gute Luft _____ (*in order to breathe in*), und Sie _____ (*will have much fun*).

B. Fill in the appropriate form of the indicated article or **kein**, and in some cases the ending of the noun, then add the appropriate form of the infinitive clause with the cues given in parentheses. Use contractions where possible.

EXAMPLE: Er versucht, zweimal in d_____ Woche _____. (*machen / eine Leibesübung, pl.*)
Er versucht, zweimal in der Woche Leibesübungen zu machen.

1. Ihr müßt durch d_____ Stadtmitte _____, _____. (*fahren / erreichen / um / die Universität*)
2. Vor k _____ Haus sehe ich _____. (*stehen / ein Wagen*)
3. Statt d_____ Zeitungen sollen wir _____. (*mitnehmen / ein Buch, pl.*)
4. Fahr weiter bis zu (*up to*) d_____ Kreuzung und bleib nicht _____! (*stehen / auf / die Einbahnstraße*)
5. Sie möchten d_____ Lärm d_____ Stadtlebens vergessen und _____. (*finden / Ruhe / auf / das Land*)
6. Wir brauchen mehr Körperbewegung, _____. (*werden / nicht / zu / dick / um*)

C. Fill in the blanks with the appropriate forms of the cues given in parentheses.

EXAMPLE: Geh schnell in _____, da liegt das Buch auf _____. (*das Wohnzimmer / der Tisch*)
   Geh schnell ins Wohnzimmer, da liegt das Buch auf dem Tisch.

1. Frau König lief aus _____ auf _____. (*das Hotel / die Straße*)
2. Wir sahen _____ in _____ über _____ springen. (*ein Mann / der Wald / Hindernis, pl.*)
3. Nach _____ gingen sie in _____ und sprachen über _____. (*das Abendessen / das Wohnzimmer / der Unfall*)
4. Während _____ hat sie immer mit _____ geredet. (*die Fahrt / der Student*)
5. Siehst du _____ nicht? Er liegt gerade vor _____ auf _____ . (*der Schlüssel / du / der Boden*)
6. An _____ haben Sie _____ geschrieben? (*wer / ein Brief*)

D. Express in German.

1. You needn't be an athlete (*in order*) to engage in sports.
2. During vacation the city dweller seeks quiet and exercise in the country.
3. How do we get (*kommen*) to the railroad station from here?
4. Turn left there at the corner.
5. Then drive straight ahead as far as the intersection.
6. Behind the fountain, drive around the corner.
7. Drive on to the end of the street.
8. Be careful of the one-way streets.
9. They have been waiting for some time (*schon lange*) at the bus stop for a friend.
10. Whom are you waiting for?

Guided composition

A pen pal or distant relative of yours in Germany would like to know what you do for physical exercise and/or fun. Write a short letter telling him/her whether you swim, play tennis, run, hike, go mountain climbing; when and how often you do these things, and where—in the city or the country, at the university, in parks, woods, mountains, lakes, rivers. Add whether you do them with friends or by yourself (**allein**).

Talk also about other sports and physical activities you would like to engage in (**Ich möchte gern . . .**).

If you'd rather stay home and play records, drink beer and discuss politics with your friends, watch television or lie under a tree reading a book, don't be afraid to say so.

Chapter vocabulary

Nouns

der	Argument, -e	*argument*
der	Athlet, -en	*athlete*
der	Berg, -e	*mountain*
das	Bergsteigen	*mountain climbing*
der	Bergsteiger, -	*mountain climber*
die	Bewegung, -en	*exercise, movement*
der	Brunnen, -	*fountain*
das	Büro, -s	*office*
der	Dom, -e	*cathedral*
die	Einbahnstraße, -n	*one-way street*
der	Einkauf, ⸚e	*purchase, errand*
die	Eltern (*pl. only*)	*parents*
das	Ende, -n	*end*
der	Fernsehapparat, -e	*television set*
der	Fußgänger, -	*pedestrian*
die	Fußgängerzone, -n	*pedestrian mall*
die	Fußwanderung, -en	*hike*
	Fußwanderungen machen	*to go on hikes*
das	Hindernis, -se	*obstacle*
die	Körperbewegung, -en	*physical activity*

die	Kreuzung, -en	*intersection, crossroads*
der	Lärm	*noise*
die	Leibesübung, -en	*physical exercise*
	Leibesübungen machen	*to do physical exercise*
das	Mitglied, -er	*member (of a club, etc.)*
die	Möglichkeit, -en	*possibility*
das	Museum (*pl.* Museen)	*museum*
die	Mutter, ⸚	*mother*
der	Nachmittag, -e	*afternoon*
die	Natur	*nature*
der	Palast, ⸚e	*palace*
der	Pfad, -e	*track, path*
das	Postamt, ⸚er	*post office*
die	Presse	*press, media*
die	Richtung, -en	*direction*
der	Sohn, ⸚e	*son*
der	Sport	*sport(s)*
der	Sportclub, -s	*sportsclub*
die	Suche	*search, quest*
die	Tochter, ⸚	*daughter*

die	Turnübung, -en	*gymnastic exercise*
der	Vater, -	*father*
die	Wahrheit, -en	*truth*
der	Wald, -er	*forest*
der	Westen	*Western world; west*

Verbs

auf·geben (gibt), gab, aufgegeben	*to give up*
auf·passen (auf + acc.)	*to pay attention (to); to be careful (of)*
brauchen	*to need*
ein·atmen	*to breathe (in)*
erreichen	*to reach, attain*
gehen: zu Fuß gehen	*to go on foot, walk*
hören (auf + acc.)	*to listen to*
schwimmen, schwamm, (ist) geschwommen	*to swim*
sitzen, saß, gesessen	*to sit*
springen, sprang, (ist) gesprungen	*to jump*
steigen, stieg, (ist) gestiegen	*to climb*

treiben, trieb, getrieben	*to practice, work at*
Sport treiben	*to engage in sports, go in for sports*
versuchen	*to try*
vorbei·kommen, kam, (ist) vorbeigekommen	*to pass by*
warten (auf + acc.)	*to wait (for)*

Other words

dick	*fat*
einfach	*simple*
einmal	*once*
einmal die Woche	*once a week*
erfrischt	*refreshed*
faul	*lazy*
geradeaus	*straight ahead*
leicht	*easy*
schlank	*slim, slender*
vorbei	*by, past*
vorn(e)	*in front*
da vorne	*up ahead*
wahr	*true*
wenig	*little, not much*

See also prepositions on pp. 164–166 and words for other members of the family on pp. 174–175.

Mini-dialogues

(*Am Telefon*)

Student(in) A Hallo, Claudia, möchtest du heute abend ins Kino gehen?

B Das möchte ich schon, aber ich habe leider keine Zeit.

A Warum denn nicht?

B Weil ich soviel arbeiten muß.

A Aber du sollst doch nicht immer über den Büchern sitzen, sondern wieder einmal ausgehen.

B Da hast du recht. Aber heute geht es einfach nicht. Vielleicht nächste Woche.

A Hast du Irene gestern abend im Theater gesehen?

B Wie bitte?

A Ob du Irene gestern abend im Theater gesehen hast?[1]

B Nein, warum fragst du?

A Weil sie doch meistens am Donnerstag ins Theater geht.

B Schade, daß ich das nicht wußte.

A Was soll ich ihm sagen, wenn er anruft?

B Sag ihm, daß ich ausgegangen bin.

A Und wenn er wieder anruft?

B Daß ich noch nicht zurück bin.[1]

A Das wird er wohl nicht glauben.

B Dann sag ihm einfach, daß ich ihn vielleicht morgen anrufen werde.

(*On the phone*)

A Hello, Claudia, would you like to go to a movie tonight?

B I'd like to go, all right, but unfortunately I have no time.

A Why not?

B Because I have so much studying to do.

A But you shouldn't always pore over your books, but go out for a change.

B You're right. But it's simply impossible today. Maybe next week.

A Did you see Irene at the theater last night?

B I beg your pardon? What did you say?

A I asked if you saw Irene at the theater last night?

B No, why do you ask?

A Because she usually goes to the theater on Thursdays.

B Too bad I didn't know that.

A What should I tell him if he calls?

B Tell him that I've gone out.

A And if he calls again?

B That I'm not back yet.

A He won't believe that.

B Well, then just tell him that maybe I'll call him tomorrow.

[1]In repeating a question, an introduction such as **ich sagte, wir fragten** is most often omitted in German. But the repeated statement or question remains in the dependent word order.

Grammar explanations

I. Coordinating conjunctions

Sonja ist gerade angekommen, aber sie kommt leider etwas spät.
Sonja has just arrived, but unfortunately she's a little late.

Peter geht nicht zu Fuß in die Stadt, sondern fährt mit dem Fahrrad.
Peter isn't walking downtown but is riding his bike.

Willst du zu Hause bleiben, oder sollen wir ins Theater gehen?
Do you want to stay home, or shall we go to the theater?

Instead of merely juxtaposing words or phrases, we often wish to show their mutual relationship. Conjunctions make it possible to do this. In the following example, note the use of the conjunction **denn:**

Ich kann nicht ins Kino gehen. Ich muß heute abend studieren.	
Ich kann nicht ins Kino gehen, denn ich muß heute abend studieren.	*I can't go to the movies because I have to study tonight.*

There are two kinds of conjunctions: *coordinating conjunctions* like **denn** connect clauses of equal value, whereas *subordinating conjunctions* introduce a clause that is dependent on another clause. In German, the word order of a clause is determined by the kind of conjunction that introduces it.

The *coordinating conjunctions* do not affect the word order of the clause. They leave it in its original sequence, whether normal or inverted. The most important of these conjunctions are:

aber[1] *but, nevertheless, yet*
denn[1] *because, for*
oder *or*
sondern *but, on the contrary*
und *and*

Sie kommt gerade an, aber sie kommt leider etwas spät.	*She's just arriving, but unfortunately she's a little late.*
Ich gehe nicht ins Kino, denn jetzt bin ich zu müde.	*I'm not going to the movies because I'm too tired now.*

---

[1]These conjunctions may also be used as "flavoring particles," as explained earlier.

Sollen wir zu Hause bleiben, **oder** willst du ins Theater gehen?	*Shall we stay home, or do you want to go to the theater?*
Peter fährt nicht mit dem Auto zur Universität, **sondern** mit dem Fahrrad.	*Peter doesn't drive to the university but rides his bike.*
Der Vater arbeitet im Garten, **und** die Tochter liest im Wohnzimmer.	*The father is working in the garden, and the daughter is reading in the living room.*

Sondern means *but* in the sense of correcting a false impression. Usually the first part of the sentence contains **nicht.**

Sie studiert nicht Französisch, sondern Deutsch.	*She doesn't study French, but German.*

Notice also that the word order of the clause following the conjunction may be normal or inverted, or a question, depending on the position of other elements in the sentence.

Ich gehe nicht ins Kino, denn **ich bin** jetzt müde.

Ich gehe nicht ins Kino, denn jetzt **bin ich** müde.

Sollen wir zu Hause bleiben, oder **willst du** ins Theater gehen?

CHECK YOUR COMPREHENSION

Combine each pair of sentences into one by using the conjunction indicated.

EXAMPLES: Moritz braucht mehr Körperbewegung. Er ist zu dick geworden. *(for)*
Moritz braucht mehr Körperbewegung, denn er ist zu dick geworden.

Er war nicht im Haus. Er war im Garten. *(but)*
Er war nicht im Haus, sondern im Garten.

1. Er war kein Athlet. Er war Mitglied eines Sportclubs. *(but)*
2. Gehen wir beim Hotel um die Ecke? Gehen wir geradeaus? *(or)*
3. Der Vater wollte den Zug erreichen. Er gab es auf. *(but)*
4. Wir schwammen nicht im Fluß. Wir schwammen im See. *(but)*
5. Die Schwester lief durch den Wald. Ich blieb zu Hause. *(and)*
6. Er fand die Adresse nicht. Die Fußgänger konnten ihm keine Auskunft geben. *(for)*
7. Fahren Sie nicht nach links. Fahren Sie, bis Sie zu einem Brunnen kommen. *(but)*

II. Subordinating conjunctions and dependent or "Verb Last" word order

Ich weiß, daß sie eine Tochter **hat.**
I know that she has a daughter.

Wir besuchen euch, sobald die Ferien **beginnen.**
We'll visit you as soon as the vacation begins.

Du vergißt, daß der Vater den ganzen Tag im Büro **sitzen muß.**
You forget that Father has to sit in an office all day.

Wenn du Lust **hast,** können wir heute abend in ein Restaurant gehen.
If you're in the mood, we can go to a restaurant tonight.

Margret konnte nichts sagen, weil Oskar die ganze Zeit **redete.**
Margret couldn't say anything because Oskar was talking the whole time.

Als das Mädchen **anrief,** war ich leider nicht zu Hause.
When the girl called, I was, unfortunately, not at home.

Unlike the coordinating conjunctions, the *subordinating conjunctions* affect the word order of the clause they introduce. They require the dependent or "Verb Last" word order. This means that the inflected part of the verb phrase stands at the very end of the clause. One must therefore watch carefully whether the verb is in a simple or compound tense, as in the following examples with **daß** (that).

Du weißt doch, daß ich Urlaub habe.	*You know that I am on leave.*
Du vergißt, daß ich keine Ferien hatte.	*You forget that I had no vacation.*
Ich wußte nicht, daß du keine Ferien gehabt hast.	*I didn't know that you had no vacation.*
Ich glaube, daß er bald Ferien haben wird.	*I think that he'll soon have vacation.*

The sentence may involve a verb with a *separable prefix*. In that case, prefix and verb are united even in the simple tenses.

Ihr wißt doch, daß sie bald abfährt.	*You know that she's leaving soon.*
Wir wissen nicht, ob sie schon abgefahren ist.	*We don't know whether she has already left.*

Or the clause may contain a *modal*, which must be placed at the end:

Du wußtest doch, daß ich am Freitag nicht ins Kino gehen konnte.	*You knew that I couldn't go to the movies on Friday.*

With the conjunctions **wenn** (*if*) and **als** (*when*) the subordinate clause often stands at the beginning. In that case, the main clause which follows has inverted word (V-S) order.

Wenn du Lust hast, **können wir** in einem Restaurant essen.	*We can eat in a restaurant, if you like.*

Notice that clauses introduced by a subordinating conjunction are always set off from the main clause by a comma.

There are many subordinating conjunctions. Here are some of those frequently used.

als *when, as* ~ *in Past*

bevor *before*

daß *that*

nachdem *after*

ob *if (in the sense of whether)*

obwohl *although*

seitdem, seit *since (time)*

sobald *as soon as*

weil[1] *because*

wenn *if, when* *ever*

~ present will be preceded by 's and function as sub- conj.

most ? words within a sentence

Als er ankam, lasen wir die Zeitung.	*When he arrived, we were reading the paper.*
Sie machte die Tür zu, **bevor** sie die Treppe hinaufging.	*She closed the door before she went upstairs.*
Er wußte, **daß** Karl oft auf Berge stieg.	*He knew that Karl often climbed mountains.*
Nachdem wir die Nachrichten gehört haben, sitzen wir immer lange vor dem Fernsehapparat.	*After we've listened to the news, we always sit for a long time in front of the television set.*
Ich weiß nicht, **ob** er gern Bücher liest.	*I don't know if (or: whether) he likes to read books.*
Er redete noch lange weiter, **obwohl** wir alle müde waren.	*He kept on talking a long time, although we were all tired.*
Seitdem sie aus den Ferien zurückgekommen ist, habe ich sie nicht mehr gesehen.	*Since she got back from vacation, I never saw her again.*
Sobald du gegessen hast, fahren wir ab.	*As soon as you've eaten, we'll depart.*
Ich konnte es dir nicht sagen, **weil** du die ganze Zeit redetest.	*I couldn't tell you, because you were talking all the time.*
Wir gehen nach Hause, **wenn** er nicht bald kommt.	*We'll go home if he doesn't come soon.*

Als and **wenn** can both be translated by *when*, but they cannot be used interchangeably. **Als** is used to express *a single action in the past.*

Als er uns anrief, waren wir gerade beim Essen.	*When he called us, we were just eating.*

[1]Note that both **denn** and **weil** may be translated as *because.* (For used to indicate a reason is rather obsolescent in English.) In German, **denn** expresses the "reason for," **weil** the "cause of" something. But be careful: **denn** is a coordinating, **weil** a subordinating conjunction!

Wenn is used to express *an action in the present* (or *in the future*).

Wenn er anruft, gehe ich sofort hin.	*When he calls, I'll go there right away.*

Wenn is also used to express *a repeated action in the past*, especially in conjunction with **immer.**

Immer wenn sie anrief, war ich nicht zu Hause.	*Whenever she called, I was not at home.*

Remember, **wann** is a *question* word.

Wann kommt er nach Hause?	*When is he coming home?*

Now we can briefly compare the three basic word orders in German.

	S.	V.	
Subject-Verb[1] (S-V)	**Sie**	**ist**	in die Stadt gegangen.
Verb-Subject (V-S)	V.	S.	
In a statement with something other than the subject in the "front field"	Heute morgen **ist**	**sie**	in die Stadt gegangen.
In a "yes" or "no" question	**Ist**	**sie**	in die Stadt gegangen?
With a question word	Wann **ist**	**sie**	in die Stadt gegangen?
Dependent or ***Verb Last***	S.		V.
	Ich weiß nicht, ob **sie**	in die Stadt gegangen	**ist.**

CHECK YOUR COMPREHENSION

Combine each pair of sentences into one by using the conjunction indicated. Be careful of word order and punctuation.

EXAMPLE: Er bezahlt. Er steigt aus. (*bevor*)
    Er bezahlt, bevor er aussteigt.

1. Wir lasen die Zeitung. Die Mutter rief aus Düsseldorf an. (*als*)
2. Er ist Mitglied eines Sportclubs geworden. Er ist kein Athlet. (*obwohl*)
3. Ich werde dich anrufen. Ich habe das Gepäck geholt. (*sobald*)

[1]By "verb," the conjugated verb is meant only, not the past participle or infinitive.

4. Mach die Tür zu. Du gehst ins Bett.   (*bevor*)
5. Er kennt uns nicht mehr. Er verdient so viel Geld.   (*seitdem*)
6. Die Eltern gehen nicht ins Theater. Sie sind sehr spät aus der Stadt zurückgekommen.   (*weil*)
7. Kommt doch zu uns. Ihr habt gegessen.   (*nachdem*)
8. Wir wissen nicht. Sie werden bald nach Stuttgart abfahren.   (*ob*)
9. Man muß sehr viel Übung im Bergsteigen haben. Man will auf das Matterhorn steigen.   (*wenn*)
10. Sie verließen das Zimmer. Er spielte Klavier.   (*immer wenn*)

Conversation

vor einer Stunde	*an hour ago*
Hast du Lust, ins Kino zu gehen?	*Do you feel like going to the movies?*
Mach mir nichts vor!	*{ Come on!* *{ Don't kid me!*

interessiert sein (an + *dat.***)**	*to be interested in*
Alles schön und gut.	*That's all fine and dandy.*
Ganz recht!	*That's right.*
Einverstanden?	*Agreed?*
die ganze Zeit	*the whole time, all the time*
Viel Vergnügen!	*Have fun!*

SOLLEN WIR INS KINO GEHEN?

Heinz ist ein Film-Fan. Er ruft einen Freund, Karl Zimmermann, an und versucht, ihn zu überreden, mit ihm am Abend ins Kino zu gehen.

Karl   Zimmermann.

Heinz   Hallo Karl! Hier Heinz. Endlich bist du zu Hause. Ich habe dich schon vor einer Stunde angerufen, aber keine Antwort erhalten.

Karl   Ich war doch heute im Seminar bei Professor Dietrich. Zum Schluß ließ er einen Studenten noch lange reden, obwohl wir alle fast am Einschlafen° waren.   *about to go to sleep*

Heinz   Das ist nichts Neues. Als ich vor einem Jahr bei ihm im Seminar saß, geschah das jede° Woche. Aber hör mal, hast du Lust, ins Kino zu gehen?   *every*

Karl   Lust habe ich sicher, aber ich habe schon eine Verabredung.

Heinz   Mach mir nichts vor! Den Fassbinder[1]-Film im „Odeon" mußt du unbedingt sehen, wenn du wirklich an der Filmkunst interessiert bist.

Karl   Alles schön und gut, aber ich kann doch nicht gleichzeitig an zwei Orten sein.

Heniz   Ganz recht! Also, ich hole dich ab, sobald du gegessen hast. Einverstanden?

Karl   Aber Heinz, heute abend gehe ich mit Irene ins Theater zu einer Faust[2]-Vorstellung. Verstehst du?

Heinz   Aber warum hast du denn das nicht gleich gesagt?

Karl   Weil du die ganze Zeit redest.

Heinz   Na, gut. Viel Vergnügen! Dann gehe ich ohne dich ins Kino.

QUESTIONS ON THE CONVERSATION

1. Wen ruft Heinz an?
2. Was versucht er zu tun?

[1]Rainer-Werner Fassbinder, a well-known German film maker (1946–1982).

[2]*Faust*, by Johann Wolfgang von Goethe (1749–1832), is probably the most eminent work of German literature. It is a dramatic poem in two parts, only the first of which is widely known abroad.

Der deutsche Regisseur
Rainer-Werner Fassbinder

3. Warum hat er Karl nicht erreicht, als er anrief?
4. Wann will Heinz den Freund abholen?
5. Warum kann Karl nicht mit Heinz ins Kino gehen?
6. Warum hat Karl das nicht gleich gesagt?

PERSONAL QUESTIONS

1. Haben Sie Lust, heute abend ins Kino zu gehen? *Ja, ich habe Lust, ins Kino zu gehen*
2. Gehen Sie oft ins Kino oder ins Theater? *Ja, Ich gehe oft ins Kino*
3. Mit wem gehen Sie meistens ins Kino oder Theater? *Ich gehe meistens mit der Freundin.*
4. Sind Sie ein Film- oder Theater-Fan? Wenn nein, was für ein (*what kind of a*) Fan sind Sie? *Ja, Ich bin ein Film-Fan,*

Practice

A. Complete each sentence with the item in parentheses. Be careful of word order.

1. Rudi gab das Bergsteigen auf. Er wird leicht müde. (*denn*)

2. Es regnete. Ich konnte keinen Parkplatz beim Hotel finden.   (*und*)
3. Herr Dietrich geht zur Arbeit. Er ist kürzlich sehr krank gewesen.   (*obwohl*)
4. Du vergißt. Ich kann nicht gleichzeitig an zwei Orten sein.   (*daß*)
5. Nichts Neues ist geschehen. Die zweihundert Radfahrer sind in Schaffhausen zusammengekommen.   (*seitdem*)
6. Hör doch auf zu reden. Wir schlafen alle ein.   (*bevor*)
7. Ich weiß nicht. Ferien befreien den Menschen von der Routine.   (*ob*)
8. Passen Sie auf. Die Polizei hält Sie an.   (*oder*)
9. Sie sah uns nicht an. Wir fragten nach dem Schlüssel.   (*als*)
10. Frau Heller hat die Polizei angerufen. Sie hörte den Lärm im Schlafzimmer.   (*sobald*)

B. Combine the two sentences with the conjunction listed on the right, and put the verb in parentheses in the indicated tense. Watch word order and punctuation.

EXAMPLE: Sie (*pl.*) / noch nicht ins Bett   (*gehen, pres. perf.*)   es / erst neun Uhr   (*sein, pres.*)   *denn*
          Sie sind noch nicht ins Bett gegangen, denn es ist erst neun Uhr.

1. Die ganze Familie / immer gern in die Berge   (*reisen, pres. perf.*)   man / da gute Luft   (*einatmen können, pres.*)   *weil*
2. Wir / erst heute   (*hören, pres. perf.*)   Herr Meyer / so lange krank   (*sein, past*)   *daß*
3. Er / Mitglied eines Sportclubs   (*werden, pres. perf.*)   er / kein Athlet   (*sein, pres.*)   *obwohl*
4. Er / das Haus wieder   (*vermieten, future*)   es / frei   (*werden, pres. perf.*)   *sobald*
5. Die Schwester / lange in Hamburg   (*wohnen, past*)   der Bruder / außerhalb der Stadt   (*wohnen, past*)   *und*

C. Form sentences with the given cues and combine them first with **denn** and then with **weil** in the indicated tenses. Watch word order and punctuation.

EXAMPLE: sein / die Schwester / noch / sehr schwach   (*pres.*) / sein / sie / lange / krank.   (*pres. perf.*)
          Die Schwester ist noch sehr schwach, denn sie ist lange krank gewesen.
          Die Schwester ist noch sehr schwach, weil sie lange krank gewesen ist.

1. haben / wir / jetzt / kein / Geld   (*pres.*)
   ausgeben / zuviel / für die Möbel.   (*pres. perf.*)
2. Können / fahren / du / nicht / auf / die Klosterstraße / geradeaus   (*pres.*)
   sein / eine Einbahnstraße   (*pres.*)

3. trinken / ich / viel (*pres. perf.*) sein / sehr / durstig. (*past.*)
4. abholen / ich (*subject*) / er / an / der Bahnhof (*future*)
   haben / er / immer noch / kein Wagen. (*pres.*)

D. Fill in the asterisked blank with **aber** or **sondern**. Also fill in the indicated articles, contracted where possible.

1. Der Bruder wohnt nicht in d_____ Stadt, _____* auf d_____ Land.
2. Der Vater hat in d_____ Garten hinter d_____ Haus viel Gemüse, _____*
   auch viele Bumen gepflanzt.
3. An d_____ Kreuzung da vorne müssen Sie nach links fahren, _____* passen
   Sie auf, denn Sie werden auf e_____ Einbahnstraße kommen.
4. Sie wartet nicht auf d_____ Vater, _____* auf d_____ Freunde.
5. Er hielt bei d_____ Fußgängerstraße an, _____* er stieg nicht aus d_____
   Wagen.
6. Der Parkplatz ist nicht vor d_____ Bahnhof, _____* neben d_____
   Bushaltestelle.

E. Fill in the blanks with **als** or **wenn**. Fill in also the appropriate form of the indicated article, contracted where possible.

1. _____ ihr k_____ Sport treibt, werdet ihr zu dick.
2. _____ er gestern in d_____ Stadt fuhr, hatte er e_____ Unfall.
3. Immer_____ wir in d_____ Restaurant gingen, vergaß er, Geld mitzubringen.
4. _____ sie kürzlich nach Westerland in d_____ Ferien reisten, hatten sie viel
   Spaß.
5. _____ ihr gute Luft einatmen wollt, geht auf d_____ Land!

F. Having used certain subordinating conjunctions in dependent word order, you will readily understand sentences and phrases containing other subordinating conjunctions, such as:

falls *in case, if*
so daß *so that*
solange *as long as*

sooft *as often as, whenever*
während *while*
wie *as*

Now give the English equivalents of the following sentences.

1. Falls du wirklich an dem Problem interessiert bist, kannst du das Buch
   mitnehmen.
2. Wie ich gerade in den Nachrichten im Fernsehen hörte, ist auf der Straße vor
   dem Theater ein Autounfall passiert.
3. Sooft er versuchte, mich zu überreden, hörte ich nicht auf ihn.
4. Während der Student weiterredete, schliefen wir fast alle ein.
5. Elfriede treibt sehr viel Sport, so daß sie nicht oft krank ist.
6. Solange man gesund ist, treibt man oft keinen Sport.

Vocabulary development

Wortfamilien

If you are observant, you will develop a certain flair in detecting relationships between words and in making deductions from the known to the unknown. It can be fun. For instance:

1. holen
(etwas) **holen** = *to fetch, to go and get something.*

Hol mir doch schnell die Zeitung!   *Please go and quickly get me the paper.*

(jemand) **ab·holen** = *to go or come get, to pick up someone*

Wir holen euch am Flughafen ab.   *We'll pick you up at the airport.*

wiederholen (wieder: here an inseparable prefix) = *to repeat (lit.: to retrieve again and again)*

Wiederholen Sie die Übung!   *Repeat the exercise!*

So, what would a **Wiederholungsübung** be?

Wieder (*again*) may occur as an adverb with **holen:**

Hol mir doch wieder das Buch, bitte!   *Please, fetch me that book again.*

or as a separable prefix with many verbs:

Wann kommen sie wieder?   *When are you coming again?*
Wann sehe ich dich wieder?   *When will I see you again?*

from which is derived **Auf Wiedersehen!**

2. schlafen has the frequently used compound **ein·schlafen** and **aus·schlafen.**
But be careful: **ein·schlafen** means *to fall asleep* (*not: to sleep in!*) and takes the auxiliary **sein** in the perfect tense:

Der Junge ist in der Kirche   *The boy fell asleep in church.*
eingeschlafen.

aus·schlafen = *to get a good night's sleep or rest,* takes **haben** in the perfect tense:

Hast du ausgeschlafen?   *Did you get a good night's rest?*

> REISEN – AUFBRECHEN!
> Ferien sind der Umbruch im Jahr...
> Da heißt es, vor dem Zusammenbrechen
> den Trott unterbrechen und aufbrechen...
> Aber bitte dabei auf brechend vollen
> Autobahnen nicht einbrechen...
> Den bahnbrechenden Fortschritt nutzen...
> Schnell die Fahrkarte her – und die
> Zelte abbrechen...(Mit der Bahn kann man
> oft die Fahrt unterbrechen...)
> Also: Nicht mehr den Kopf zerbrechen...
> Alles dicht,(damit keine Einbrecher einbrechen...)
> Los geht die Reise: aufbrechen und für
> lange Zeit nicht mehr abbrechen ... !

3. drücken = *to press, as in the idiom*

Er hat mir die Hand gedrückt.   *He shook hands with me.*

has some frequently used derivatives:

aus·drücken = *to express* > **der Ausdruck, ¨e** = *expression:*

Der Film drückt etwas über das   *The film expresses something about*
Problem der Luftverschmutzung aus.   *the problem of air pollution.*

Kennen Sie den Ausdruck?   *Do you know the expression?*

unterdrücken (inseparable prefix) = *to suppress, oppress* > **die Unterdrückung** = *suppression, oppression:*

Wer unterdrückt wen?   *Who is oppressing whom?*

Man spricht und liest viel von der   *One talks and reads a lot about the*
Unterdrückung der Frauen.   *oppression of women.*

beeindrucken (without umlaut!) = *to impress, make an impression* > **der
Eindruck, ¨e** = *impression:*

Sie hat mich sehr beeindruckt.   *She impressed me very much.*

Er hat einen guten Eindruck auf uns   *He made a good impression on us.*
gemacht.

4. Der Anzug, ¨e = *suit (of clothes)* is derived from **an·ziehen, zog, angezogen** = *to pull or put on (clothes):*

Heute abend ziehe ich einen Anzug   *Tonight I'll put on a suit to go to*
an, um ins Theater zu gehen.   *the theater.*

Communicative exercises

A. Ask your classmates the following question and have them answer with the suggestions given on the right, starting the dependent clause with **weil**.

Warum kommst du (kommt ihr) heute
abend nicht zu uns, um Karten zu
spielen?

wir müssen arbeiten
ich gehe mit einem Freund ins Kino
wir haben leider keine Zeit
ich gehe bei dem Regen nicht gern
    aus
ich bin zu müde, um auszugehen
ich habe keine Lust, Karten zu spielen

B. Ask your classmates the questions below with **ob** and have them answer with:
Nein, leider weiß ich (wissen wir) nicht, ob . . .

| Weißt du, | ob | sie liest gern Bücher | Nein, etc. |

Wissen Sie,
Wißt ihr,

sie liest gern Bücher
sie machen gern
    Wanderungen
er ist Mitglied eines Sportclubs
sie ist schon abgefahren
sie treiben gern Sport
er wird uns abholen
der Bus hält hier an
sie haben das Geld mitgebracht

C. Ask your classmate **Was machst du, wenn du etwas Geld hast?** and have him/
her answer in a complete statement, using the suggestions on the right.

Wenn ich etwas Geld habe,   ins Kino gehen
im Restaurant essen
Kleider kaufen
Urlaub machen
mit der Freundin (dem Freund) ins Theater gehen
den Freunden das Kino bezahlen

D. Give the same answers to the above question, but place **Wenn ich etwas Geld habe** after the other clause.

E. Ask your classmates the following questions, starting with **Glaubst du,** etc. . . . and have them answer with **Nein, ich glaube (wir glauben) kaum, daß . . .**

Glaubst du, daß	er wird kommen	Nein, ich (wir), etc.
Glauben Sie, daß	sie hat Lust, ins Theater zu gehen	
Glaubt ihr, daß	er ist auf das Matterhorn gestiegen	
	sie haben den Brief schon geschrieben	
	sie hat den Film schon gesehen	
	er wird auf uns warten	

F. You are standing with your friend in front of the advertising poster below and are trying to persuade him/her to come and see the film with you. He/she gives evasive answers and finally declines. Suggestions:

A.

B.

Der Film soll wirklich gut sein.
Möchtest du ihn sehen?

Ja, gern.

Dann hole ich dich heute abend um 7 Uhr ab.

Es tut mir leid, aber heute ist es mir nicht möglich.

Warum nicht?

Weil ich . . .

Aber das kannst du auch morgen tun.

Nein, wirklich nicht.

Mach mir doch nichts vor!

—

B. finally admits that he/she is already busy (going out to dinner with a friend, to a play, to a party at another friend's, etc.). A. regrets and says that he/she will go alone or with another friend.

    When you have developed a conversation along these lines, try to memorize and repeat it.

*Schauspieler Gustaf Gründgens als
Mephistopheles*

Reading

THEATER, FILM UND FERNSEHEN

Man hört oft, daß der Film das Theater ersetzt hat und das Fernsehen bald den Film ersetzen wird. Aber das ist natürlich eine Übertreibung.° Man kann das Problem nicht so einfach ausdrücken, sondern man muß viele Faktoren betrachten. Zum Beispiel darf man sagen, daß das Theater eine lange Tradition hat und seit den Anfängen tief° in der Kultur des Volkes verwurzelt° ist. Obwohl es später oft zum Unternehmen° einer Elite wurde, ist das Theater auch heute noch, besonders in Europa, sehr populär. In Deutschland, Österreich und in der Schweiz gibt es viele „Stadttheater" oder „Staatstheater".[1] Das sind Theater, die° von der Stadt oder vom Staat Subventionen° erhalten. Das heißt, man verwendet° einen Teil der Steuern, um das Theater zu unterstützen. So wird das Theater fast zum Eigentum° des Publikums.

Während der Vorstellung hat man auch im Theater selber° das Gefühl, ein Teil des Geschehens° zu sein, denn oft kennt man das

exaggeration

deep / rooted
undertaking

which
subsidies / uses

property
itself
event

Theaterstück oder auch die Schauspieler, und man weiß, ob sie es
gut machen oder nicht. Während der Pause geht man ins Foyer, trinkt
Sekt[2], ißt Kuchen und spricht mit Freunden über die Vorstellung. Man
ist da, nicht nur um zu sehen, sondern auch, um gesehen zu werden.° — *to be seen*
Deshalb geht man sehr oft im besten Anzug ins Theater.

Man will im Gespräch auch zeigen, daß man etwas vom Theaterstück versteht. Manchmal ist zum Beispiel der erste° Teil von Goethes — *first*
„Faust"[3] auf dem Programm. Aber die Interpretation des Stückes läßt
viele Möglichkeiten offen, und meistens glaubt das Publikum, „Faust"
gut zu verstehen. So hörte man kürzlich bei einer Faust-Vorstellung
im Residenztheater[4] in München Gespräche wie: „Du, Fritz, zum Teufel noch mal,° der Mephistopheles[5] schien mir am Anfang doch etwas — *what the devil*
zu kriecherisch".° „Ja, vielleicht, aber der Teufel braucht ja nicht im- — *fawning*
mer so selbstsicher° zu sein. Er hat schließlich auch Probleme mit — *self-assured*
Gott". „Du bist aber zynisch° heute." — *cynical*

Man trinkt noch schnell einen Schluck° und geht dann in den Thea- — *sip*
tersaal zurück.

Im Film ist der Intellekt vielleicht nicht so stark beschäftigt. Viele
Leute sagen, daß der Film das Auge ebenso° beschäftigen soll wie — *as much as*
den Intellekt. Es ist richtig, daß im Film die Kunst des Photographie-
rens°—Licht, Farben, Bewegungen°—sehr wichtig ist. Aber viele — *photography / light, colors, action*
Filme verbinden die Kunst des Photographierens mit einem ernsten° — *serious*
Thema. In Deutschland haben einige Filmproduzenten° diese — *film producers*
Kunstform sehr gefördert,° und der Staat unterstützt sie auch. — *promoted*

Im Fernsehen muß man aber mit dem Thema vorsichtig sein. Viele
Fernsehfilme sind in Deutschland sehr lehrhaft.° Sie drücken etwas — *instructional*
über ein Problem aus, wie zum Beispiel die Emanzipation der Frau
oder die Unterdrückung von Randgruppen.° Aber, wie in Amerika, — *minorities*
sind „Krimis", Shows und Quizzes[6] sehr populär, denn wenn man am
Abend nach Hause kommt, will man die Probleme des Tages vergessen.

CULTURAL NOTES

1. „Staatstheater" are subsidized by each of the ten **Bundesländer** (corresponding roughly to the individual states in the USA); „Stadttheater" receive their subsidies from a city or town. There are close to 100 such establishments in the **Bundesrepublik (BRD)**, including opera and operetta houses as well as ballet theaters. Although the average attendance is approximately 75 per cent of capacity, the public funds these houses receive—well over one billion DM per year—amount to 83% of their budgets. There are also many private repertory theaters and amateur groups in small communities, most of which are also recipients of some public subsidies. Altogether, there are approximately 350 theatrical establishments in the **Bundesrepublik**.

FERNSEHEN

Programmauswahl vom 17. bis 23. Febr.

ARD	ZDF	III.
20.15 Auf los geht's los Wieder gesund, in neuer Kulisse und mit Änderungen im Programm: Joachim ›Blackie‹ Fuchsberger ist wieder da!	**20.15 Der Kurier des Zaren** Spielfilm nach Jules Verne mit internationaler Besetzung und Curd Jürgens in der Hauptrolle des Draufgängers Strogoff	**20.15 Karl III. und Anna von Österreich** Ein Wiedersehen mit dem unvergeßlichen Robert Graf. Partnerin im heiteren Spiel: Gerlinde Locker
20.15 Giganten Start für eine Reihe von Filmen mit dem 1955 tödlich verunglückten James Dean. In ›Giganten‹ spielt er mit Liz Taylor (Foto)	**20.00 Die Ratten** »Ein großer Abend«, urteilte Friedrich Luft über die Aufführung der Freien Volksbühne beim Berliner Theatertreffen 1978	**21.45 Düsseldorf Helau** Jede Stadt hat ihre eigene karnevalistische Tradition. Heute kommt das närrische Treiben aus der Düsseldorfer Stadthalle
20.15 Liebe zu Lydia (13) Letzte Folge der englischen Fernsehserie. Dr. Baird, Lydias Arzt, macht Edward Richardson klar, daß die Kranke jetzt seine ganze Zuneigung braucht. Sie hatte einen gefährlichen Rückfall. Noch ist sich Edward unsicher über seine Gefühle zu Lydia	**21.20 Die Münze** In einer süddeutschen Kleinstadt taucht Falschgeld auf. Schwank mit Gustl Bayrhammer, Mogens von Gadow	**21.15 Der falsche Torero** Eddie Cantor, umjubelter Komiker der US Music Halls und von 1927 – 1948 Star vieler Filme, als unfreiwilliger Matador
21.45 Detektiv Rockford: Anruf genügt In dem Zweiteiler ›Computer hört mit‹ versucht Jim Rockford, den Tod eines Kollegen zu klären	**22.45 Zwei Särge auf Bestellung** Italienisches Gesellschaftsporträt im Gewand eines Krimis mit Gian Maria Volonté und Gabriele Ferzetti	**20.15 Fast ein Ofen für Naturschwärmer** Einmalig ist eine Entstaubungsanlage in Duisburg: Der Hochofen hinterläßt keine Schmutzwolken mehr
20.15 Was wären wir ohne uns Im Jahre 1952 können die Baumanns (Horst Bollmann, Margret Homeyer) endlich einen eigenen Friseursalon aufmachen	**21.20 Heinz Erhardt: Noch ne Oper** Musikalischer Spaß zum 70. Geburtstag von Heinz Erhardt: eine Ritter-Oper mit Rudolf Schock u. a.	**20.15 Mittwochs in Düsseldorf** Meyer's Dampfkapelle heizt musikalisch ein – fröhliche Randbemerkungen machen Narren und Nicht-Narren
21.00 Café in Takt Zum zweiten Male die musikalische Abendunterhaltung live aus dem Studio Hamburg. Peter Horton hat u. a. Sylvia Vrethammar und Siegfried Schwab eingeladen. Weitere Gäste: Kevin Johnson aus Australien, der Franzose Richard Clayderman und Dalida	**19.30 Dalli-Dalli** Mal sehen, ob der Segler-Experte den Radfahr - Fachmann vom letzten Mal im ›Abräumen‹ bei Hans Rosenthal schlägt	**20.15 Atemlos nach Florida** Ein übermütiges, bittersüßes Märchen von der Jagd nach Erfolg. In der Hauptrolle die bezaubernde Claudette Colbert
20.00 Lord Nelsons letzte Liebe Der berühmte Spielfilm mit Laurence Olivier und Vivien Leigh (Foto) als Lord Nelson und Lady Hamilton	**20.00 Mainz bleibt Mainz, wie es singt und lacht** Zum 25. Mal die Karnevalsitzung aus der Narrenhochburg Mainz. Sitzungspräsident: Rolf Braun	**22.00 Ich, Claudius, Kaiser und Gott** Germanicus ist in Syrien gestorben. Der Statthalter Piso (Stratford Jones) muß sich in Rom verantworten

2. German champagne.

3. Usually only the first part of *Faust* is performed on stage. Most directors consider the second part, almost five times as long as the first, too immense for a stage performance.

4. A well-known state theater in Munich, occupying a part of the former residence of the Bavarian kings.

5. Mephistopheles, the devil in Goethe's *Faust*, is a clever schemer who contends with God for Faust's soul and is ultimately defeated.

6. **Krimis** (from **Kriminal**) is an abbreviation for murder mysteries and detective stories. The terms **Shows** and **Quizzes** are now commonly used in Germany.

QUESTIONS

1. Was hört man oft?
2. Warum kann man das Problem nicht so einfach ausdrücken?
3. Was darf man über das Theater sagen?
4. Wer unterstützt ein Stadttheater? ein Staatstheater?
5. Was tut man im Theater in Deutschland während der Pause?
6. Was will man im Gespräch über das Theaterstück zeigen?
7. Was ist im Film sehr wichtig?
8. Was verbinden viele Filme?
9. Was drücken viele Fernsehfilme in Deutschland aus?
10. Warum wollen viele Leute solche (*such*) Filme am Abend nicht sehen?

Review

A. Combine each pair of sentences into one by using the conjunction indicated.

EXAMPLE: Ich gehe heute nicht ins Kino. Ich muß noch sehr viel studieren. (*for*)
   Ich gehe heute nicht ins Kino, denn ich muß noch sehr viel studieren.

1. Wir haben keinen Brief von ihm erhalten. Er weiß die Adresse nicht. (*for*)
2. Es war nicht möglich einzuschlafen. Die Studenten machten so viel Lärm auf der Straße. (*because*)
3. Man weiß nicht. Das Fernsehen wird bald den Film ersetzen. (*whether*)
4. Das Publikum weiß. Die Schauspieler machen es gut. (*if*)
5. Er sprach mit Freunden über die Vorstellung. Er ging während der Pause ins Foyer. (*when*)

6. Wir trinken Sekt. Wir gehen in den Theatersaal zurück.   (*before*)
7. Ich habe ihn nicht gesehen. Wir sind zusammen ins Theater gegangen.   (*since*)
8. Man sagt. Man muß mit dem Thema vorsichtig sein.   (*that*)

B. Form sentences with the given cues in the a./b. sequence. Watch the word order and punctuation.

EXAMPLE: a. sprechen / der / Professor / obwohl / lange über das Problem   (*past*)
 b. verstehen / ich / nichts   (*pres. perf.*)
 Obwohl der Professor lange über das Problem sprach, habe ich nichts verstanden.

1. a. unterstützen / die Regierung / obwohl / es   (*pres.*)
   b. sein / das Theater / teuer.
2. a. können / ausdrücken / man / das Problem / nicht / so einfach   (*pres.*)
   b. müssen / betrachten / man / denn / viele Faktoren.   (*pres.*)
3. a. anrufen / er (*subject*) / sobald / ich   (*pres. perf.*)
   b. abholen / ich (*subject*) / er.   (*future*)
4. a. sagen / ich / nichts   (*past*)
   b. reden / er (*subject*) / weil / die ganze Zeit.   (*past*)
5. a. zurückgehen / das Theater / bis zu / die Anfänge / die Kultur   (*pres.*)
   b. sein / die Filmkunst / aber / neu.   (*pres.*)
6. a. wissen / du   (*pres.*)
   b. verwenden / man / in Deutschland / daß / Steuern / für / das Theater? (*pres.*)

C. Put the second clause at the beginning of the sentence and adjust the word order of the other clause. At the same time fill in the blanks with the appropriate forms and endings, using contractions where possible.

1. Er ging lange in d_____ Zimmer auf und ab, weil er nicht einschlafen konnte.
2. Ich werde nicht in d_____ Theater gehen, wenn ihr nicht mitkommt.
3. Er sah _____ (wir) nur an, während wir versuchten, _____ (er) zu überreden.
4. Sie sind nicht an d_____ Film interessiert, obwohl der Film zu e_____ Kunstform geworden ist.
5. Er hat _____ (ich) nicht geschrieben, seitdem er bei d_____ Freunden wohnt.
6. Wir werden _____ (ihr) anrufen, sobald wir gegessen haben.

D. Express in German.

1. Although I like to go to the theater, I can't go there (*hin·gehen*) very often.
2. It is said that television will soon replace the movies.
3. Are you in the mood to go to a movie, or do you wish to stay home?
4. I don't know whether she has already arrived.
5. Don't try (*ihr*) to persuade us.
6. While they were talking about God and the devil, we fell asleep.
7. Although the play is very good, the performance was bad.
8. I can't go with you this evening because I already have a date.
9. When he called an hour ago, we were sitting in front of the television set.

Guided composition

State whether you are interested in the theater, cinema, or television, or all three.

If you like television, state whether you like **Krimis**, sit-coms (**Situationskomödien**), cultural programs (**Kulturprogramme**), or the news (**die Nachrichten**) and when you usually watch such programs. Do you watch television largely to forget the problems of the day or do you wish to learn something once in a while (**manchmal**)?

If you like plays or films, describe briefly a visit to the theater or the movies. Where was it? Were there many people there? Were you interested in the theme of the play or movie? Are you interested in the photography of the film? Was there an intermission? What did people say and do during intermission? Did you go home directly or did you go to a café or restaurant first? With whom did you go? Are you in a mood to go with that person again?

Chapter vocabulary

Nouns

der	Anzug, ⸚e	(men's) suit
das	Auge, -n	eye
der	Ausdruck, ⸚e	expression
der	Eindruck, ⸚e	impression
die	Elite	elite
der	Faktor, -en	factor
der	Fan, -s	fan
der	Film, -e	film, movie
die	Form, -en	form
das	Foyer, -s	lobby
das	Gefühl, -e	feeling
das	Gespräch, -e	conversation, discussion
der	Gott, ⸚er	god
der	Intellekt	intellect
die	Interpretation, -en	interpretation
das	Kino, -s	movie theater
	ins Kino gehen	to go to the movies
das	Kleid, -er	dress
die	Kultur, -en	culture
die	Kunst, ⸚e	art

die	Lust	desire, joy
	Lust haben	to be in the mood, feel like (doing something)
der	Ort, -e	place, spot
die	Pause, -n	intermission
der	Professor, -en	professor
das	Restaurant, -s	restaurant
der	Saal (pl. Säle)	hall, large room
der	Schauspieler, -	actor
der	Schluß	end
das	Seminar, -e	seminar
der	Teil, -e	part
der	Teufel, -	devil
das	Theater, -	theater
das	Theaterstück, -e	play
das	Thema (pl. Themen)	theme
die	Tradition, -en	tradition
die	Übung, -en	practice
die	Unterdrückung, -en	suppression, oppression
die	Verabredung, -en	date, appointment
das	Vergnügen	pleasure
das	Volk, ⸚er	people
die	Vorstellung, -en	performance

Verbs

ab·holen	to come or go for, come or go get
an·ziehen, zog, angezogen	to get dressed, put on
auf·hören	to stop
aus·drücken	to express
aus·gehen, ging, (ist) gegangen	to go out
aus·schlafen (schläft), schlief, ausgeschlafen	to get a good night's sleep
beeindrucken	to impress
beschäftigen	to occupy
betrachten	to consider
drücken	to press
ein·schlafen (schläft), schlief, (ist) eingeschlafen	to go to sleep
erhalten (erhält), erhielt, erhalten	to receive
ersetzen	to replace
geschehen (geschieht), geschah, (ist) geschehen	to happen
holen	to fetch, get
scheinen (+ *dat.*), schien, geschienen	to seem

überreden	to persuade
unterdrücken	to suppress, oppress
unterstützen	to support
verbinden, verband, verbunden	to join, unite, combine
wiederholen	to repeat

Other words

also	therefore
durstig	thirsty
erst	only, not until
gleichzeitig	at the same time
interessiert (an + *dat.*)	interested (in)
leicht	easy
nachmittags	in the afternoon
offen	open
schade	too bad; it's a pity
solange	as long as
sondern	but, on the contrary
soviel	so much
später	later on
unbedingt	absolutely, definitely
vor (+ *dat.*)	ago
vorsichtig	careful

See also the conjunctions on pp. 186 and 189.

Mini-dialogues

Student(in) A   Seit wann haben Sie denn einen Wagen?
  B   Er gehört mir seit drei Wochen.
  A   Was für ein Wagen ist es eigentlich?
  B   Es ist ein Volkswagen. Er ist nicht groß, aber solch ein
        Wagen genügt mir.
  A   Ja, wenige Autos aus Deutschland sind so gut wie der VW.
  B   Es ist mir auch gelungen, ihn billig zu bekommen.

  A   Ist das Ihr Buch?
  B   Welches?
  A   Dieses hier.
  B   Ja, das ist meins. Kennen Sie es?
  A   Nein. Gefällt es Ihnen? Was für ein Buch ist es denn?
  B   Oh ja, es gefällt mir sehr gut. Es ist über Amerika und
        wirklich interessant.

A Since when do you have a car?	*A* Is that your book?
B I have owned one for three weeks.	*B* Which one?
A What kind of car is it?	*A* This one here.
B It's a Volkswagen. It's not big, but a car like this is good enough for me.	*B* Yes, it's mine. Are you familiar with it?
A Yes, few cars from Germany are as good as the VW.	*A* No. Do you like it? What kind of book is it?
B I was also able to get it at a good price.	*B* Oh yes, I like it very much. It's about the U.S. and really interesting.

Grammar explanations

I. *Der-* and *Ein-*words

Dieses Gespräch war interessant.
This conversation was interesting.

Welchen Film möchtet ihr sehen?
Which film would you like to see?

Ich suche **meinen** Anzug.
I'm looking for my suit.

Wo habt ihr **eure** Fahrräder hingestellt?
Where did you put your bikes?

In **dieser** Stadt gibt es viele Hochhäuser.
In this city there are many high-rise buildings.

Sie wohnen seit **mehreren** Jahren in Österreich.
They have been living in Austria for several years.

Der- and **ein-**words are two groups of noun modifiers. The first group is declined like the definite article **der, die, das;** the second like the indefinite article **ein, eine, ein.**

A. *Der*-words

The most common **der**-words are:

dieser *this, that*
jeder *each, every (used only in the singular)*
mancher *many a; pl. some*
welcher *which*

Dieser Film ist sehr interessant.	*This film is very interesting.*
Heinz ging **jede**[1] Woche ins Kino.	*Heinz went to the movies every week.*
Mancher Student schreibt nicht gern.	*Many a student doesn't like to write.*
Manche Leute gehen jede Woche ins Theater.	*Some people go to the theater every week.*
Welches Theaterstück möchtest du sehen?	*Which play would you like to see?*

[1]Expressions of definite time with no prepositions are in the accusative case: **jede Woche** (*every week*); **nächsten Montag** (*next Monday*); **letzten Monat** (*last month*); etc. This usage occurs throughout the chapter.

To determine the form of a **der**-word, take the stem—for instance **dies**—and add the appropriate case endings of the definite article.

		Singular		Plural	*Declension of*
	Masculine	Feminine	Neuter	All genders	**der**-*words:* **dieser**
nom.	dies**er**	dies**e**	dies**es**	dies**e**	
acc.	dies**en**	dies**e**	dies**es**	dies**e**	
dat.	dies**em**	dies**er**	dies**em**	dies**en**	
gen.	dies**es**	dies**er**	dies**es**	dies**er**	

Deutsche Bundesbahn
Panorama-Wagen

CHECK YOUR COMPREHENSION

Fill in the appropriate form of the **der**-words indicated in parentheses.

1. In _Welche_ Richtung müssen wir fahren? *(welch—)*
2. In _manchen_ Städten gibt es Fußgängerzonen. *(manch—)*
3. Kennen Sie _diesen_ Schauspieler? *(dies—; sing. & pl.)*
4. Was bedeutet _dieses_ Wort? *(dies—)*
5. Wir arbeiten _jeden_ Tag im Büro. *(jed—)*
6. _Mancher_ Fernsehfilm drückt etwas über _dieses_ Problem aus. *(manch—, dies—)*
7. _Welche_ Vorstellung _dieses_ Theaterstückes habt ihr gesehen? *(welch—, dies—)*

[handwritten margin notes: jeden Tag / jede Woche / jede Jahre / Time expressed in acc]

B. *Ein-words*

The **ein**-words include all the possessive adjectives.

Singular

1st Person	**mein**	*my*	Dort ist **mein** Vater.	*There is my father.*
2nd Person	**dein**	*your*	Suchst du **deinen** Anzug?	*Are you looking for your suit?*
3rd Person	**sein**	*his*	Kennst du **seine** Tochter?	*Do you know his daughter?*
	ihr	*her*	Wo ist **ihr** Regenschirm?	*Where is her umbrella?*
	sein	*its*	Dieses Dorf ist nicht groß; **seine** Einwohner arbeiten fast alle in der Stadt.	*This village isn't large; almost all its inhabitants work in the city.*

Plural

1st Person	**unser**	*our*	Wir werden in **unserem** Garten arbeiten.	*We will work in our garden.*
2nd Person	**euer**	*your*	Wann werdet ihr **euren** Urlaub haben?	*When will you have your vacation?*
3rd Person	**ihr**	*their*	Ist das **ihr** Klavier?	*Is that their piano?*
2nd (formal)	**Ihr**	*your*	Wo sind **Ihre** Freunde?	*Where are your friends?*

The other **ein**-words are the negative **kein, solch ein** (*such a*), **was für ein** (*what a, what kind of a*) and **welch ein** (*what a, what kind of a*).

Solch einen Film muß man sehen!	*One ought to see such a film!*
Was für ein Glück!	*What luck!*
Was für ein Buch hat er geschrieben?	*What kind of a book did he write?*
Welch ein Vergnügen!	*What a pleasure!*

Notice that **was für ein** can be used in either exclamations or questions and that in this instance **für** does not function as an accusative preposition.

To determine the form of an **ein**-word, take the stem—for instance, **mein**—and add the appropriate case ending of the indefinite article in the singular and of **kein** in the plural (since the indefinite article does not have a plural form).

		Singular		Plural
	Masculine	Feminine	Neuter	All genders
nom.	mein	mein**e**	mein	mein**e**
acc.	mein**en**	mein**e**	mein	mein**e**
dat.	mein**em**	mein**er**	mein**em**	mein**en**
gen.	mein**es**	mein**er**	mein**es**	mein**er**

Declension of ein *words:* **mein**

Notice that the **ein**-words differ from the **der**-words only in the *nominative masculine singular* and the *nominative and accusative neuter singular* (as is to be expected from the declension of **der** and **ein**).

When **euer** takes a declensional ending, it drops **-e-** in front of **-r.** For instance:

| euere > **eure** | Wo sind **eure** Fahrräder? | *Where are your bikes?* |
| eueren > **euren** | Wo habt ihr **euren** Koffer hingestellt? | *Where did you put your suitcase?* |

The **ein**-words, especially the possessives, may replace a noun and so become *pronouns*. In that case the *nominative masculine singular* adds **-er** and the *nominative and accusative neuter singular* add **-s** or **-es.** The other cases remain the same.

Sein Wagen ist auf der Straße.	*His car is on the street.*
Meiner steht vor dem Hotel.	*Mine is in front of the hotel.*
Hast du mein Buch?	*Do you have my book?*
Nein, ich habe **seins** (or: **seines**).	*No, I have his.*
Ist das sein Auto?	*Is that his car?*
Nein, es ist **unseres.**	*No, it's ours.*

In connection with the **der-** and **ein**-words, you should learn a number of words, most of them called *indefinite numerical adjectives*, that occur in the plural. They take the endings of the **der-** or **ein-**words (which are the same in the plural, as you can tell from the charts above).

alle[1] *all*	**mehrere** *several* ~~many~~ ~~viele~~
andere[2] *other*	**solche** *such* (plural of **solch ein**)
beide *both*	**viele**[3] *many* ~~mehrere~~
einige *some; several* ~~a few~~	**wenige**[3] *(a) few*

Alle Einwohner sind gegen diesen Plan.

All inhabitants are against this plan.

Es gibt **andere** Möglichkeiten.

There are other possibilities.

Ich kenne **beide** Teile von Goethes „Faust".

I know both parts of Goethe's Faust.

Herr Härtling ist schon seit **einigen** Tagen krank.

Mr. Härtling has been sick for several days.

Sie hatten **mehrere** Wochen Urlaub.

They had several weeks of vacation.

Solche Leute sind gefährlich.

Such people are dangerous.

Auf **vielen** Bergen stehen Burgen.

There are castles on many mountains.

In **wenigen** Tagen wird unser Sohn zurückfahren.

In a few days our son will drive back.

CHECK YOUR COMPREHENSION

A. Fill in the appropriate form of the **ein-**word or numerical adjective indicated in parentheses.

1. Wohin fuhr _eure_ Tochter in die Ferien? *(euer)*
2. _Mehrere_ Mitglieder _unseres_ Clubs haben einen Unfall gehabt. *(mehrere, unser)*
3. Die Interpretation _seines_ Theaterstückes läßt _viele_ Möglichkeiten offen. *(sein, viele)*
4. Was für _einen_ Wagen hat _dein_ Bruder gekauft? *(ein, dein)*
5. In _____ Orten sah man _____ Touristen. *(solche, wenige)*

[1]There is also an undeclined singular form: **alles,** which does not refer to specific items, but rather to a general idea. **Was bedeutet das alles?** *What does all that mean?*

[2]**Andere** is also used in the singular and plural as an attributive adjective with an article: **Der andere Wagen ist besser.** *The other car is better.* For attributive adjectives, see Chapter 11.

[3]**Viele** and **wenige** may also occur in the singular, but then they remain undeclined:

Er hat wenig Zeit.   *He has little time.*
Er hat nicht viel Geld.   *He doesn't have much money.*

6. Das ist _____ Tisch, nicht _____. (*ihr, mein*)
7. Seit _____ Tagen sucht die Polizei _____ Sohn. (*einige, ihr*)

B. Fill in the appropriate form of the **der-** or **ein-**word or numerical adjective indicated in English.

1. _____ Anzug ziehst du an? (*which*)
2. Wo habt ihr _____ Regenschirme hingestellt? (*your, fam.*)
3. _____ Woche geht Franz einmal ins Kino. (*every*)
4. _____ Gärtner hat _____ Glück mit _____ Garten. (*Many a, no, his*)
5. _____ Freund ist das? (*What kind of a*)
6. Das ist nicht _____ Auto, es ist _____. (*their, ours*)
7. _____ Eltern leben seit _____ Jahren in _____ Schweiz. (*My, several, the*)
8. Ich spiele nicht gern auf _____ Klavier. (*his*)
9. Wir haben in _____ Garten _____ Blumen gepflanzt. (*our, many*)
10. _____ Töchter werden in _____ Tagen aus _____ Ferien zurückkommen. (*her, a few, the*)

II. Reflexive pronouns and verbs

Im Rheinland **befinden sich** viele Burgen.
In the Rhineland there are many castles.

Ich **erinnere mich** sehr gut an diesen Film.
I remember this film very well.

Fritz, geh und **wasch dir** die Hände!
Fritz, go wash your hands.

Haben Sie **sich** von Ihrer Krankeit **erholt?**
Have you recovered from your illness?

Ich **hole mir** schnell eine Zeitung.
I'm quickly going to pick up (to get myself) a newspaper.

Reflexive pronouns refer the action of the verb back to its subject.

Subject	Verb	Reflexive Pronoun	
Er	fragte	**sich**	= *he asked himself* (not somebody else)

In German, a number of verbs occur only as reflexives.

Er hat **sich** von seiner Krankheit **erholt.**   *He has recovered from his illness.*

Im Rheinland **befinden sich** viele Burgen.	*There are many castles in the Rhineland.*
Sie **kümmern sich** kaum um ihre Eltern.	*They hardly take care of their parents.*

Most verbs can be made reflexive without change of basic meaning.

Ich frage **dich, was das bedeutet.**	*I'm asking you what that means.*
Ich frage **mich, was das bedeutet.**	*I'm asking myself (or: I wonder) what that means.*

Some verbs have a different (though related) meaning in the reflexive form.

Ich **erinnerte mich** gut an das Gespräch.	*I remembered the conversation well.*

But:

Ich **erinnerte ihn** an das Gespräch.	*I reminded him of the conversation.*

Notice that in some of the above sentences the reflexive verb is followed by a preposition such as **von, um, an.**[1]

Usually the reflexive pronoun is in the *accusative*. However, if the verb already has an accusative object, the reflexive is in the *dative* case. That happens especially with reference to *parts of the body* or with *articles of clothing*. In that case one uses the reflexive pronoun in the dative and the definite article of the accusative object, rather than the possessive adjective.

Ich wasche **mir die Hände.**	*I wash my hands.*
Zieh **dir die Schuhe an!**	*Put on your shoes!*

Or one may use this structure to emphasize the significance of an action to its performer:

Ich kaufe **mir ein Auto.**	*I'm buying myself a car.*
Ich hole **mir eine Zeitung.**	*I'm going to get myself a paper.*

Notice the position of the reflexive pronoun.

S-V:	{ Ich kaufe **mir** einen Anzug.
	Ich habe **mir** einen Anzug gekauft.
V-S:	Morgen kaufe ich **mir** einen Anzug.
Verb-Last:	Ich glaube, daß ich **mir** bald einen Anzug kaufen muß.

[1]Some reflexive verbs must always be used with a preposition, such as **sich kümmern um** + *acc.*; these verbs are listed in vocabularies with the preposition not in parentheses. Other verbs may or may not be used with a prepositional object such as **sich erholen (von** + *dat.*); these verbs are listed with the preposition in parentheses.

In the first and second persons, the reflexive pronouns are identical with the dative and accusative object pronouns. In the third person, singular and plural, and formal address, the reflexive has a special form: **sich.**

	Singular Accusative	Dative	Plural Accusative and Dative	Reflexive pronouns
1st	mich	mir	uns	
2nd fam.	dich	dir	euch	
3rd	**sich**	**sich**	**sich**	
2nd formal	**sich**	**sich**	**sich**	

CHECK YOUR COMPREHENSION

A. Supply the appropriate form of the reflexive pronoun.

1. Kurt, wasch _____ die Hände.
2. Herr Graf, haben Sie _sich_ von der Reise erholt?
3. Ihr müßt _euch_ mehr um eure Eltern kümmern.
4. Wo hat Albert _sich_ Zigaretten geholt?
5. Endlich kann ich _mir_ ein Fahrrad kaufen!
6. In welchem Land befinden _sich_ viele Burgen?
7. Wir fragen _uns_, wann die Kinder zurückkommen werden.

B. Translate into German.

1. I remember her very well.
2. We reminded him of our appointment.
3. He washed his hands.

III. Verbs requiring the dative

Antworten Sie **mir** doch!
Answer me, please.

Ich **danke Ihnen** sehr.
I thank you very much.

Es **ist mir** nicht **gelungen,** ihn zu überreden.
I did not succeed in persuading him.

A number of important German verbs cannot have an accusative object and are most often followed by an object in the dative.

antworten *to answer*	Sie antwortete **ihm** nicht. *She didn't answer him.*
danken *to thank*	Ich danke **Ihnen** sehr. *I thank you very much.*
folgen (ist gefolgt) *to follow*	Ich konnte **seinem** Argument nicht folgen. *I couldn't follow his argument.*
gefallen *to please*	Das Theaterstück gefiel **mir** nicht. *I didn't like the play.*
gehören *to belong*	Dieses Fahrrad gehört **der** Tochter meines Freundes. *This bike belongs to my friend's daughter.*
helfen *to help*	Hilf **ihr** doch ein wenig! *Please help her a little.*
zu·hören *to listen*	Wir hören **ihm** gern zu. *We like to listen to him.*

The verb **glauben** takes the *dative with a person*, but the *accusative with a fact* or at times a *thing*.

    Wir glauben **ihr** nicht.   *We don't believe her.*

But:

    Ich glaube **das** nicht.   *I don't believe that.*

    Er glaubt **die Geschichte** nicht.   *He doesn't believe the story.*

Some verbs are primarily used with the impersonal subject **es** (or **das**); the person concerned is in the dative.

gelingen (ist gelungen) *to succeed*	**Es** ist **ihnen** nicht gelungen, ihn zu überreden. *They did not succeed in convincing him.*
genügen *to be enough, be sufficient*	**Das** genügt **uns.** *That is sufficient for us.*

CHECK YOUR COMPREHENSION

Fill in the appropriate form of the indicated words.

1. Ich kann _____ leider mit _____ Arbeit nicht helfen. (*du, diese*)
2. Es ist _____ Bergsteiger nicht gelungen, auf das Matterhorn zu steigen. (*der*)
3. Hat _____ der Film gefallen? (*Sie*)

4. _____ gehört diese Zeitung? (wer)
5. Wir danken _____ für _____ Bericht. (ihr, 2nd fam.; dieser)
6. Ich kann _____ nicht glauben. (er)
7. Ich habe _____ noch nicht geantwortet. (sie, 3rd sing.)
8. Danke sehr, das genügt _____. (ich)

Conversation

im Vergleich mit	in comparison with
Meine Güte!	Good grief! / My goodness!
Wart mal!	Just a second!
ganze (fünf) Mark!	a whole (five) Marks!

DER UMRECHNUNGSKURS°

rate of exchange

Herr und Frau Kohler, Deutschamerikaner, befinden sich auf
einer Ferienreise durch ihre alte Heimat.° Sie sind vor zwei   homeland
Tagen im Flugzeug aus Chicago in Frankfurt angekommen

und haben sich inzwischen von ihrer Reise erholt. Nun kommen sie ins Frühstückszimmer ihres Hotels und setzen sich an einen Tisch. Sie haben gerade ihr Frühstück bestellt und fangen an, sich zu unterhalten.

Frau K.   Du, da hat einer[1] seine Zeitung vergessen.

Herr K.   Das glaube ich nicht. Sie gehört sicher dem Hotel. Siehst du die Zeitungen auf dem Tisch da drüben? Die sind alle für die Gäste da.

Frau K.   Ach ja, ich muß mich wieder an die Bräuche hier gewöhnen.

Herr K.   Moment bitte, ich hole mir schnell die „Frankfurter Allgemeine"[2]! Welche Zeitung möchtest du dir ansehen?

Frau K.   „Die Süddeutsche"[2], bitte. Wir müssen uns unbedingt über den Umrechnungskurs des Dollars informieren.

Herr Kohler geht zu dem Tisch und kommt mit beiden Zeitungen zurück.

Herr K.   Hoffentlich ist der Kurs° nicht noch weiter gefallen. Für Amerikaner hat das Wirschaftswunder[3] leider auch seine Schattenseiten.°   *rate*

     dark side(s)

[1]Often **einer** (the **ein**-word as a noun) is used for **jemand** (*someone*).

[2]A well-known daily in the **Bundesrepublik.**

[3]**Wirtschaftswunder** (*economic miracle*) is the term commonly used to describe the amazing economic recovery of West Germany from the Second World War in the fifties and sixties. In its initial stages the recovery was greatly stimulated by Marshal Plan aid from the United States. At the beginning of the eighties, however, Germany is also feeling the sting of the worldwide recession.

Frau K.   Fantastisch! Hier steht:° Dollar erholt sich an der Frank-   *it says*
furter Börse.°   *money and stock
                                                                       exchange*
Herr K.   Gut, dann gehen wir zur Bank, sobald wir gegessen haben, und wechseln noch einige Reiseschecks.

Eine Stunde später vor der Bank.

Frau K.   Wieviel Mark auf zweihundert Dollar haben wir nun gewonnen im Vergleich mit dem Kurs von gestern?

Herr K.   Wart mal! Ich rechne es schnell aus.° Meine Güte! Ganze   *I'm figuring*
fünf Mark! Das genügt vielleicht gerade für das Taxi ins Hotel
zurück.

QUESTIONS ON THE CONVERSATION

1. Was haben Herr und Frau Kohler getan, seitdem sie in Frankfurt angekommen
   sind?
2. Was machen Herr und Frau Kohler, nachdem sie ins Frühstückszimmer gekommen sind?
3. Wem gehören die Zeitungen im Hotel?
4. Was hofft Herr Kohler?
5. Warum sagt Frau Kohler „fantastisch!"?
6. Was wollen die beiden nach dem Frühstück tun?
7. Ist es ihnen gelungen, etwas Geld zu gewinnen? Wieviel?

PERSONAL QUESTIONS

1. Sind Sie schon einmal in Deutschland, Österreich oder in der Schweiz gewesen?
2. Lesen Sie oft beim Frühstück eine Zeitung?
3. Haben Sie schon einmal Dollars in Mark umgewechselt? Wo haben Sie die Reiseschecks umgewechselt?
4. Wie ist jetzt der Umrechnungskurs des Dollars?

Practice

A. Substitute the appropriate form of the words in parentheses for the word in italics.

1. In *dieser* Stadt gibt es viele Brunnen.
   (euer / mancher / welcher / Ihr / was für ein / solch ein / unser)

2. Ich kenne die Einwohner *mancher* Städte.
   (mehrere / viele / andere / alle / beide / wenige / einige / dieser)

3. Wir erinnern uns an *den* Freund.
   (dein / sein / ihr / mancher / jeder / euer / mein / solch ein)

4. Ich glaube *diesen* Menschen nicht.
   (viele / solche / einige / mehrere / alle / mancher)

5. Sie kümmern sich sehr um *ihre* Kinder.
   (sein / euer / mehrere / dein / viele / unser / alle / beide / einige)

B. Substitute the words in parentheses for the word in italics, make the possessive adjective agree with the new subject, and put the verb in the appropriate form.

1. *Ich* habe meine Steuern noch nicht bezahlt.
   (die Eltern / der Vater / wir / ihr / die Einwohner / du)

2. *Er* tut etwas in seinem Zimmer.
   (die Mutter / die Kinder / wir / ihr / du / beide)

C. Fill in the blank with a possessive pronoun corresponding to the pronoun in parentheses.

EXAMPLE: Ist das Ihr Wagen?—Nein, es ist _____.   (er)
   Ist das Ihr Wagen?—Nein, es ist seiner.

1. Fährst du mit seinem Wagen nach Frankfurt?—Nein, mit _____.   *(ich)*

2. Hast du mein Buch schon gelesen?—Nein, aber _____ habe ich gelesen. (er)
3. Hier stehen unsere Regenschirme. Wo habt ihr _____ hingestellt? (ihr)
4. Ich sehe Ihr Auto da vorne. _____ steht auf dem Parkplatz hinter dem Hotel. (wir)

D. Insert the appropriate form of the verb in parentheses, putting it in the indicated form. Watch the word order.

EXAMPLE: Marie / gut mit unseren Eltern. (*sich unterhalten, pres. perf.*)
      Maria hat sich gut mit unseren Eltern unterhalten.

1. Bitte, Frau Kohler / an diesen Tisch! (*sich setzen, imperative*)
2. Gestern / wir nach dem Umrechnungskurs. (*sich erkundigen, past*)
3. Ich / schnell die Reiseschecks. (*sich holen, future*)
4. Wir / nicht mehr an sie. (*sich erinnern, past*)
5. Wir wissen, daß er / nie um seine Eltern. (*sich kümmern, pres. perf.*)
6. Hans, wie schmutzig du bist! Geh und / das Gesicht und die Hände! (*sich waschen, imperative*)
7. Wart mal, ich / schnell eine Tasse Kaffee. (*sich holen, pres.*)
8. Ich / gut von meiner Krankheit. (*sich erholen, pres. perf.*)
9. Vor vielen Jahren / hier ein Theater. (*sich befinden, past*)
10. Helga / die Haare! (*sich waschen, imperative*)

E. Fill in the appropriate form of the indicated words.

1. Der Film gefällt _____ nicht. (*wir*)
2. Ich danke _____ für _____ Bericht. (*Sie, der*)
3. Dieser Schlüssel gehört nicht _____, sondern _____. (*er; sie, sing.*)
4. Folgst du _____ Wagen in die Einbahnstraße? (*dieser*)
5. _____ hört der Junge zu? (*wer*)
6. Ich glaube _____ einfach nicht. (*du*)
7. Es gelingt _____ Autofahrer nicht, _____ Polizisten zu überreden. (*der, der*)

F. Put each of the sentences in exercise E into the past and the present perfect.

G. Give the English equivalent.

1. Erika und Hans, geht und zieht euch die Schuhe an!
2. Setz dich an den Tisch und fang an zu essen!
3. Warum hast du mich nicht an die Vorstellung erinnert?
4. Ich kann mich nicht an dieses Theaterstück erinnern.
5. Was für ein Fernsehprogramm möchten Sie sich ansehen?
6. Du, da hat einer seine Badehose vergessen.
7. Ich muß mich zuerst an dieses Klavier gewöhnen.
8. Wir können ihm einfach nicht glauben.
9. Während des Essens haben sie sich sehr gut unterhalten.
10. Fährt Ihr Freund in Ihrem Auto?—Nein, in seinem.

Vocabulary development

A. *Sitzen* and *sich setzen; liegen* and *sich legen*

Sich setzen denotes the action of sitting down, while **sitzen (saß, gesessen)** denotes the position of sitting or being seated. The first is a motion toward, the second a position in. Therefore, what cases will they take?

Accusative: Ich setze mich an **den** Tisch.   *I sit down at the table.*

Dative: Ich sitze **am** Tisch.   *I'm sitting at the table.*

Now ask a classmate if he or she is standing or sitting, and get an answer. Then ask someone else if they sat down at a table in the dining room (**das Eßzimmer**) today.

The same distinction has to be made between **legen** and **liegen (lag, gelegen)**, namely between *to lay* in the sense of *to put*, and *to lie* in the sense of *to recline*. Translate:

Sie legt ihren Schlüssel auf **den** Tisch.
Ihr Schlüssel liegt auf **dem** Tisch.

Use the same pair of sentences with other nouns that you know.

B. *Heben, hob, gehoben*

In its basic form this verb means *to lift:*

Sie hob das Kind auf den Stuhl.   *She lifted the child onto the chair.*

But separable prefixes can do much to extend the basic meaning of a verb. Among other things, **auf·heben** can mean *to lift* or *pick up*, or *to preserve, keep.*

Bitte, heb das Geld auf!   *Please pick up the money.*

Ich werde dein Bild für immer aufheben.   *I will keep your picture forever.*

But **sich erheben** means *to rise:*

Die Hochhäuser erheben sich gegen den Horizont.   *The high-rise buildings rise on the horizon.*

Many other verbs lend themselves to the same manipulation with prefixes. In the Reading of this chapter you will encounter **aus dem Fenster**

schauen und **zu den Burgen auf·schauen.** What do you think the following phrase means?

Er hat mich durchschaut.

C. The time of your life: *die Vergangenheit, die Gegenwart, die Zukunft*

You already know **gestern** (*yesterday*) and **morgen** (*tomorrow*). What then do **vorgestern** and **übermorgen** mean? Use each in a sentence.

Communicative exercises

A. Ask a classmate the following questions with **dein** . . . and have him/her answer with: **Mein** . . . ? **Er (es, sie,** *etc.***) ist** . . . etc.

Wo ist dein Wagen?   Mein Wagen? Er ist . . .

Wo ist _____ Fahrrad?

Wo befindet sich _____ Haus?

Wo hast du _____ Regenschirm hingestellt?

Wie geht es _____ Schwester?

Hast du Nachrichten von _____ Freunden?

B. Ask the same questions with **euer** . . . and answer with **unser** . . .

C. Make a statement about yourself with the elements listed below and then ask your neighbor whether he/she is doing the same:
EXAMPLE: Ich erinnere mich sehr gut an Paul.
          Erinnerst du dich auch an ihn?

(*present*)	sich ein Fahrrad kaufen	_____
(*present*)	sich um die Eltern kümmern	_____
(*present perfect*)	sich eine Zeitung holen	_____
(*present*)	sich über das Buch freuen	_____
(*present perfect*)	sich an diese Arbeit gewöhnen	_____
(*present perfect*)	sich von der Reise erholen	_____

D. Do the same exercise in the same tenses, but with **wir** and **euch.**

E. Ask your classmates: **Wem gehört (dieses Buch,** *etc.*) with the nouns listed below, changing the definite article to **dies . . . ,** and have them answer: **Es** (*etc.*) **gehört mir, ihr, dem Freund,** *etc.*

Wem gehört/gehören   der Wagen?   _____
                     der Scheck?   _____
                     die Uhr?   _____
                     der Regenschirm?   _____
                     die Möbel?   _____
                     das Gepäck?   _____
                     das Geld hier?   _____
                     die Blumen?   _____
                     der Anzug?   _____
                     die Gitarre?   _____

F. Pretend that you and several classmates are American tourists who have just met in a hotel in Germany. Ask one another if you came to Germany by plane, and when. Ask one another if you have recovered from the trip, and if you are having a good time. Ask if the dollar has recovered, or if it has fallen again. Ask one another if you are getting used to the money, the customs, the language, the people, etc.

Reading

VERGANGENHEIT UND GEGENWART DEUTSCHLANDS

Seit dem Ende des Zweiten° Weltkrieges ist Frankfurt a. M.[1] das Finanzzentrum° Deutschlands geworden. In dieser Stadt erheben sich jetzt neben einigen Gebäuden aus dem Mittelalter viele Hochhäuser gegen den Horizont. Da ist zum Beispiel das Rathaus, wo einmal die Kaiser Deutschlands ihre Bankette hielten°; aber es ist nun von einem

second
financial center

held their banquets

Am Rhein

Frankfurt am Main

Bankgebäude und anderen Hochhäusern überschattet.° Sogar der
Dom scheint klein im Vergleich mit diesen Riesen.° Und neben vielen
Brunnen aus dem Mittelalter befinden sich große Parkplätze. Hier
erlebt man gleichzeitig die Vergangenheit und die Gegenwart.

Man gewinnt diesen Eindruck besonders, wenn man mit dem Zug
durch das Rheintal ins Ruhrgebiet[2] fährt. Nachdem der Zug die Bahnhofshalle verlassen hat, fängt man an zu lesen oder aus dem Fenster
zu schauen. Bald öffnet sich dem Auge eine Traumlandschaft.° Der
Rhein windet sich gegen Norden durch Hügel und Weinberge, um
Felsen und an vielen Dörfern mit hübschen Häusern und Kirchen vor-
bei.° Auf vielen Felsen und Hügeln stehen Burgen wie Wächter.° Aber
das Leben auf dem Rhein scheint sich kaum um sie zu kümmern. Viele
Frachter,° mit Kohle° und anderen Industrieprodukten voll beladen,°
fahren langsam den Rhein hinauf oder hinab; der Rhein ist für die
Wirtschaft Deutschlands und Europas sehr wichtig. Im Zug studieren
Geschäftsleute Akten, schreiben Berichte oder unterhalten sich über
Wirtschaftsprobleme. Sie haben keine Zeit, sich über die schöne
Landschaft zu freuen. Sie unterhalten sich über Probleme der Gegenwart. Da sagt einer: „Sobald wir noch mehr° Kernkraftwerke° haben, werden wir nicht mehr soviel Kohle brauchen." Eine Kollegin°
antwortet ihm: „Ha, das wird noch lange dauern,° wenn es überhaupt
möglich ist."

Für einen Moment scheinen Vergangenheit, Gegenwart und Zukunft zusammenzufließen—die Burgen auf den Felsen, die Kohle auf
den Frachtern und die Kernkraftwerke im Gespräch der Geschäftsleute.

overshadowed
giants

dreamland

past / guards

freighters / coal / loaded

still more / nuclear power
plants
colleague
take a long time

Und wenn man aus dem Fenster zu den Burgen aufschaut,° hat man   *looks up*
fast das Gefühl, daß diese Wächter der Vergangenheit sich fragen:
was soll das alles bedeuten?

    Nicht weit hinter Köln fängt das Ruhrgebiet an. Anstatt der Burgen,
Kirchen und Dome des Rheinlandes sieht man die Kamine° vieler Fa-   *smokestacks*
briken, aber in Städten wie Düsseldorf stehen wieder viele Hochhäuser
neben mehreren Gebäuden aus dem Mittelalter. Besonders in
Düsseldorf ist es den Einwohnern gelungen, das Alte mit dem Neuen
zu verbinden. Da ist die „Königsallee",[3] wo sich viele moderne Geschäfte und Banken befinden. Ganz in der Nähe der „Kö", wie die
Düsseldorfer die Königsallee nennen, ist die „Altstadt". Da gibt es
viele Gebäude aus dem Mittelalter und anderen Zeiten, die° man re-   *here: which*
stauriert hat. In diesen Gebäuden befinden sich viele Restaurants
und Geschäfte, wo man gut essen und einkaufen kann. Am Ende der
Königsallee liegt ein Park mit vielen Brunnen, und durch die Allee
fließt ein Kanal mit Brücken. Man erinnert sich, daß Napoleon
Düsseldorf „mein kleines Paris" nannte.

    Man kann wohl sagen, daß man während einer Reise von wenigen
Stunden die Dynamik° mancher Jahrhunderte° erlebt hat—von den   *dynamics / centuries*
Burgen des Mittelalters zu den Hochburgen° der Finanz und Industrie   *strongholds*
unserer Zeit.

CULTURAL NOTES

1. **a. M.** is the abbreviation for **am Main;** the river **Main** flows into the Rhine.

2. The Ruhr district is one of the world's most important industrial areas; its
    financial and banking center is Düsseldorf.

3. This literally means the King's Promenade.

Königsallee, Düsseldorf

QUESTIONS

1. Was ist Frankfurt a. M. seit dem Ende des Zweiten Weltkrieges geworden?
2. Was sieht man in dieser Stadt?
3. Durch was für eine Landschaft fließt der Rhein?
4. Wo befinden sich die Burgen?
5. Was sieht man auf dem Fluß? Womit (*with what*) sind sie beladen?
6. Was tun die Geschäftsleute im Zug?
7. Was scheint zusammenzufließen?
8. Was für ein Gefühl hat man, wenn man aus dem Fenster zu den Burgen aufschaut?
9. Was sieht man überall im Ruhrgebiet statt der Burgen des Rheinlandes?
10. Was ist den Einwohnern Düsseldorfs gelungen?
11. Was befindet sich auf der Königsallee? in der Altstadt?

Review

A. Form sentences with the given cues. Put nouns and pronouns into the appropriate form and use the tense indicated in parentheses.

1. stehen / mehrere / Hochhäuser / neben / Gebäude / aus / das Mittelalter.   (*pres.*)
2. hinstellen / du / wo / dein Regenschirm?   (*pres. perf.*)
3. sich erinnern / können / er (*subject*) / an / ich.   (*past*)
4. sich kümmern / seine Eltern (*subject*) / nie / um / er.   (*past*)
5. sich befinden / Restaurants / in / manche Gebäude.   (*pres.*)
6. stellen / ich (*subject*) / jeder Student / eine Frage.   (*future*)
7. sehen / wir / während / eine Reise / von / wenige Stunden / viel.   (*pres. perf.*)
8. sich ziehen / ein Kanal durch / der Wald.   (*pres.*)
9. sich erholen / du / von / deine Krankheit?   (*pres. perf.*)
10. abreisen / sie (pl.) / schon / vor / einige / Tage.   (*pres. perf.*)
11. sich kaufen / ihr / ein Auto / oder / andere Fahrräder?   (*future*)
12. sich fragen / ich (*subject*) / ob / können / folgen / ihr / das Argument.   (*past*)

B. Answer the following questions with complete sentences.

EXAMPLE: Gehört dieser Regenschirm dir?
        Ja, er gehört mir.

1. Erinnern Sie sich an Ihren Großvater?
2. Hast du mir wirklich zugehört?
3. Ist es euch gelungen, ihn zu überreden?
4. Habt ihr ihm bei seiner Arbeit geholfen?

5. Was gefällt Ihnen besser: eine Stadt mit Gärten und Brunnen, oder eine mit Hochhäusern und Geschäften?

C. Express in German.

1. We came back from Switzerland several weeks ago.
2. May I remind you (*Sie*) of your appointment with your students?
3. We did not succeed in persuading them.
4. Please get yourself a newspaper, sit down on this chair, and don't say a word!
5. The Rhine winds toward the north through hills and vineyards.
6. Peter, go and wash your hands!
7. I can't get used to such buildings.
8. We would like to talk (*sich unterhalten*) with you about the economy of our country!
9. We must inquire about the rate of exchange of the dollar.
10. Don't give me any more vegetables; this is enough for me!

Im Speisewagen

Guided composition

Describe certain features of your city where old and new have been combined successfully. Have old buildings been restored? Are there new buildings nearby? Do they give you the feeling that you are experiencing the past and present simultaneously? Has an old section of the town been rebuilt to house shops, restaurants, movie houses, discothèques, etc.? Are there pedestrian malls, gardens, or parks outside or inside the city? State whether you like to go there or not, and what your favorite pastime is when going there: shopping, talking with friends, having a drink and seeing the world go by, etc. If you do not wish to describe your own town or city, look at the two pictures of Frankfurt a. M. and Köln below and describe some striking features in the scenery of these cities.

Frankfurt

Köln

Chapter vocabulary

Nouns

die	Akte -n	file
die	Bank, -en	bank
der	Brauch, ̈e	custom
die	Brücke, -n	bridge
die	Burg, -en	castle
das	Dorf, ̈er	village
die	Fabrik, -en	factory
der	Felsen, -	rock, cliff
das	Flugzeug, -e	airplane
der	Gast, ̈e	guest
das	Gebäude, -	building
das	Gebiet, -e	region
die	Gegenwart	present
das	Geschäft, -e	business, firm
das	Gesicht, -er	face
das	Haar, -e	hair
die	Hand, ̈e	hand
das	Hochhaus, ̈er	high-rise building
der	Hügel, -	hill
die	Landschaft, -en	countryside, landscape
das	Mittelalter	Middle Ages
die	Nähe	proximity
	in der Nähe	in the neighborhood
das	Rathaus, ̈er	city hall
der	Reisescheck, -s	traveler's check
das	Tal, ̈er	valley
die	Vergangenheit	past
der	Vergleich, -e	comparison
	im Vergleich mit	in comparison with
der	Weinberg, -e	vineyard
die	Wirtschaft	economy

Verbs

an·fangen (fängt), fing, angefangen	to start, begin
sich befinden, befand, befunden	to be (located)
danken (+ dat.)	to thank
ein·kaufen	to buy
sich erheben, erhob, erhoben	to rise
sich erholen (von + dat.)	to recover (from)
sich erkundigen (nach + dat.)	to find out; inquire
erinnern (an + acc.)	to remind of
sich erinnern (an + acc.)	to remember
erleben	to experience
fallen (fällt), fiel, (ist) gefallen	to fall

fließen, floß, (ist) geflossen	to flow
folgen (ist gefolgt) (+ dat.)	to follow
sich freuen (über + acc.)	to be happy (about)
gefallen (gefällt), gefiel, gefallen (+ dat.)	to please, be pleasing to, appreciate
gehören (+ dat.)	to belong to
gelingen, gelang, (ist) gelungen (impers. + dat.)	to succeed
genügen (impers. + dat.)	to suffice
gewinnen, gewann, gewonnen	to win, gain
sich gewöhnen (an + acc.)	to get used to, become accustomed to
helfen (hilft), half, geholfen (+ dat.)	to help
sich informieren (über + acc.)	to inform oneself about
sich kümmern (um + acc.)	to take care of, worry about
legen	to lay, put
nennen, nannte, genannt	to name, call
sich öffnen	to open up
sich dem Auge—	can be seen
restaurieren	to restore
schauen	to look
sich setzen	to sit down
um·wechseln	to exchange (money)
sich unterhalten (über + acc.) (unterhält), unterhielt, unterhalten	to converse, talk about; to have a good time
waschen (wäscht), wusch, gewaschen	to wash
wechseln	to change
sich winden, wand, gewunden	to wind
zu·hören (+ dat.)	to listen (to)

(handwritten annotation next to gefallen: to appeal to / to like)

Other words

inzwischen	meanwhile
klein	small, little
nun	now
überhaupt	anyway
übermorgen	the day after tomorrow
vorgestern	the day before yesterday

See also the noun modifiers on pp. 209, 211–213.

Mini-dialogues

Student(in) A Wie ist das Wetter heute morgen?
        B Kalt und auf jeden Fall sehr windig.
        A Was soll ich denn anziehen?
        B Deinen warmen Mantel, natürlich.
        A Ach nein, der gefällt mir nicht mehr.
        B Dann wenigstens einen dicken Pullover und die braune Jacke. Und setz dir auch eine Mütze auf!

        A Du, wo hast du dir diese neuen Jeans gekauft?
        B Im „Kaufhof". Aber neu sind sie nicht.
        A Aber die eleganten Stiefel müssen neu sein.
        B Stimmt!
        A Die müssen sehr teuer gewesen sein.
        B Allerdings.

        A Wie heißt das Mädchen, mit dem ich dich kürzlich gesehen habe?
        B Hm! Welches Mädchen? Meinst du vielleicht Lotte? Hatte sie blondes Haar?
        A Blondes Haar, sagst du? Nein, ich glaube, sie hatte braunes Haar.
        B Dann weiß ich nicht, wen du meinst.

A What's the weather like this morning?
B Cold and by all means very windy.
A What shall I put on?
B Your warm overcoat, of course.
A Oh no, I don't like that one any more.
B Then at least a heavy sweater and a jacket. Also put on a hat (cap).

A Say, where did you get those new jeans?
B At the "Kaufhof." But they're not new.
A But the fancy boots must be new.
B Yes, they are.
A They must have been quite expensive.
B I should say.

A What's the name of the girl I saw you with recently?
B Hm! Which girl? Do you perhaps mean Lotte? Did she have blond hair?
A Blond hair, you say? No, I think she had brown hair.
B Then I don't know who you mean.

Grammar explanations

I. Declension of adjectives preceded by a der-word

Der neue Bahnhof ist sehr groß.
The new railroad station is very large.

Trotz des schlechten Wetters ist unser Onkel in die Ferien gereist.
Despite the bad weather our uncle left on his vacation.

Schade, daß du dieses schöne Gebiet nicht kennst.
Too bad you don't know this beautiful region.

Von welchen großen Fabriken sprichst du?
Which large factories are you talking about?

A *predicate* adjective is not declined.

Dieses Problem ist wichtig.   *This problem is important.*

In most cases the predicate adjective is separated from the noun it modifies by the verbs **sein, werden,** or **bleiben.**[1]

But an *attributive* adjective—one that immediately precedes the noun—is declined.

Wir dürfen dieses wichtige Problem   *We mustn't forget this important*
nicht vergessen.   *problem.*

If the adjective itself is preceded by a **der**-word, it takes the ending **-e** or **-en** according to the following chart:

	MASC.	FEM.	NEUT.	PLUR.
Nom.				
Acc.		−e		
Dat.				
Gen.		−en		

That is to say, the adjective ending is **-e** in the masculine, feminine, and

---

[1]Remember that German differs from English in not having distinguishable forms for the predicate adjective and the adverb.

ADJECTIVE: Meine Freundin ist immer sehr **vorsichtig.**
                                             My girlfriend is always very careful.

ADVERB: Meine Freundin fährt immer sehr
                                             vorsichtig.
                                             My girlfriend always drives very carefully.

neuter nominative singular, and the feminine and neuter accusative singular. It is **-en** in all other instances.

Here then is what is sometimes called the "weak" declension of adjectives:

		SINGULAR						
	MASC.			FEM.			NEUT.		
nom.	der	neu**e**	Bahnhof	diese	schön**e**	Farbe	welches	groß**e**	Dorf
acc.	den	neu**en**	Bahnhof	diese	schön**e**	Farbe	welches	groß**e**	Dorf
dat.	dem	neu**en**	Bahnhof	dieser	schön**en**	Farbe	welchem	groß**en**	Dorf
gen.	des	neu**en**	Bahnhofs	dieser	schön**en**	Farbe	welches	groß**en**	Dorfes

	PLURAL		
nom.	manche	hübsch**en**	Häuser
acc.	manche	hübsch**en**	Häuser
dat.	manchen	hübsch**en**	häusern
gen.	mancher	hübsch**en**	Häuser

Adjectives ending in **-el** or **-er** drop **-e-** in front of a declensional ending: **teuer** > **der teure Wagen** (*the expensive car*); **dunkel** > **das dunkle Bier** (*the dark beer*).

Fill in the blanks with the appropriate adjective endings.

1. Ich will nicht über diese alt _e_ Brücke fahren.
2. Hast du dir den neu _en_ Anzug schon einmal angezogen?
3. Diese schmutzig _en_ Hosen gehören nicht mir. → once already → ever
4. Trotz des schlecht _en_ Wetters ist sie abgefahren.
5. Ich erinnere mich an dieses klein _e_ Dorf.
6. Welches groß _e_ Haus habt ihr gemietet?
7. Von welchem teuer _en_ Restaurant sprichst du?
8. Manche schön _en_ Wagen sind zu teuer.
9. Wer hat dieses alt _e_ Rathaus so gut restauriert?
10. Wir konnten die Fragen dieser jung _en_ Leute nicht verstehen.

II. Declension of adjectives preceded by an *ein*-word

Hast du mein schönes neues Auto schon gesehen?
Have you already seen my beautiful new car?

Hinter dem Hügel befindet sich ein tiefer See.
Behind the hill there is a deep lake.

Wir kennen Ihre hübsche Tochter.
We know your pretty daughter.

Wo habt ihr unsere alten Fahrräder hingestellt?
Where did you put our old bikes?

As you know, **ein**-words have no endings in the masculine nominative singular and the neuter nominative and accusative singular.

Ein Mann ist gekommen.
Ein Kind ist gekommen.
Ich habe **ein** Kind gesehen.

When an attributive adjective is inserted in these instances, it takes the endings of the **der**-word, in order to show the gender of the noun it modifies.

Ein groß**er** Mann ist gekommen.
Ein hübsch**es** Kind ist gekommen.
Ich habe ein hübsch**es** Kind gesehen.

The endings in all other cases are the same as for adjectives preceded by a **der**-word.

	MASC.	FEM.	NEUT.	PLUR.
Nom.	-er	-e	-es	
Acc.				
Dat.		-en		
Gen.				

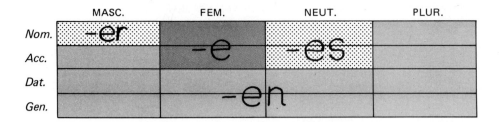

This so called "mixed" declension of adjectives is as follows:

		SINGULAR							
	MASC.			FEM.			NEUTER		
nom.	ein	tiefer	See	seine	hübsche	Tochter	ihr	krankes	Kind
acc.	einen	tiefen	See	seine	hübsche	Tochter	ihr	krankes	Kind
dat.	einem	tiefen	See	seiner	hübschen	Tochter	ihrem	kranken	Kind
gen.	eines	tiefen	Sees	seiner	hübschen	Tochter	ihres	kranken	Kindes

		PLURAL	
nom.	deine	lieben	Eltern
acc.	deine	lieben	Eltern
dat.	deinen	lieben	Eltern
gen.	deiner	lieben	Eltern

CHECK YOUR COMPREHENSION

Fill in the blanks with the appropriate endings of the **der**-words, **ein**-words, and adjectives.

1. Auf dies__em__ groß__em__ Hügel steht ein__e__ schön__e__ Burg.
2. Neben d__em__ Rathaus befindet sich ein__er__ alt__er__ Brunnen.
3. In dies_____ Gebäude gibt es ein elegant_____ Geschäft.
4. Monika hat ein__es__ hübsch__es__ und interessant__es__ Gesicht.
5. Ich habe mir ein_____ neu__er__ Pullover gekauft.
6. Ich möchte in ein__em__ klein__em__ Dorf in der Nähe ein__er__ groß__en__ Stadt wohnen.
7. Ein vorsichtig__e__ Autofahrer hat kein__e__ Unfälle.

III. Declension of adjectives not preceded by a der- or ein-word

Ich trinke gern dunkles Bier.
I like to drink dark beer.

In diesem Café erhält man guten Kuchen.
In this café you get good cake.

Haben Sie gute oder schlechte Nachrichten von Ihren Eltern erhalten?
Have you received good or bad news from your parents?

Er ist der Sohn reicher Eltern.
He is the son of rich parents.

In some sentence constructions no **der-** or **ein-**word is required in front of the attributive adjective. In that case the adjective takes the endings of the **der-**words, in order to show the gender and case of the noun it modifies.

Diese reichen Leute kümmern sich nicht um arme Leute.
[(der-word) **-en**]   [(no **der** word) **-e** like **die**]
These rich people don't worry about poor people.

An exception is the masculine and neuter genitive singular, where the ending **-en** is used instead of **-es**.[1]

Here finally is the so-called "strong" declension of adjectives.

	Singular		
	Masc.	**Fem.**	**Neut.**
nom.	gut**er** Kuchen	schwierig**e** Arbeit	frisch**es** Wasser
acc.	gut**en** Kuchen	schwierig**e** Arbeit	frisch**es** Wasser
dat.	gut**em** Kuchen	schwierig**er** Arbeit	frisch**em** Wasser
gen.	gut**en** Kuchens	schwierig**er** Arbeit	frisch**en** Wassers

	Plural
nom.	krank**e** Leute
acc.	krank**e** Leute
dat.	krank**en** Leuten
gen.	krank**er** Leute

---

[1] Nowadays the construction with a noun in the genitive modified by an adjective is becoming rare; instead, for instance, of **das Einatmen dicken Rauches ist gefährlich** (*the inhaling of dense smoke is dangerous*), one hears **das Einatmen von dickem Rauch ist gefährlich.**

CHECK YOUR COMPREHENSION

Fill in the blanks with the appropriate ending of the **der**-words, **ein**-words, and adjectives.

1. In dies_____ Restaurant erhält man heiß_____ Suppe und kalt _____ Bier.
2. Fritz, setz dich nicht mit schmutzig_____ Händen an d_____ Tisch!
3. Geh und wasch dir auch dein schmutzig_____ Gesicht.
4. Wir haben schlecht_____ Nachrichten von unser_____ Eltern erhalten.
5. Heute muß unser lieb_____ Freund abfahren.
6. Wir müssen frisch_____ Brot kaufen.
7. In deutsch_____ Städten sieht man oft alt_____ Rathäuser neben neu_____ Gebäuden.

Conversation

auf jeden Fall	*by all means; in any event*
Wie seh' ich aus?	*How do I look?*
einigermaßen akzeptabel	*fairly acceptable*
Wo denkst du hin?	{ *What do you mean?* / *Are you out of your mind?*
sich die Haare schneiden lassen	*to get a haircut*
bei kaltem (warmem) Wetter	*in cold (warm) weather*

DIE LANGEN HAARE

Frau Eichendorff ist eine berufstätige° Mutter. Ihr Sohn Jürgen, 16 Jahre alt, ist Schüler an einem städtischen Gymnasium.[1] Er zieht sich gerade um,° um zu einer kleinen Geburtstagsfeier° seines guten Freundes Dirk, Sohn reicher Leute, zu gehen.

working

is changing clothes
birthday party

[1]The **Gymnasium** corresponds to an American high school, plus two years that are roughly the equivalent of lower-division general education in an American college or university.

Jürgen   (*ruft vom oberen° Stock herunter*): Du, Mutti, was soll   *upper*
            ich denn anziehen?
Mutter   Auf jeden Fall ein frisches Hemd und die neue Krawatte.
Jürgen   Welche neue Krawatte? Ach so, die langweilige Krawatte,
            die° mir Onkel Emil geschenkt hat! Aber was für einen Anzug   *that*
            ziehe ich an?
Mutter   Den dunkelblauen° natürlich. Warum fragst du denn?   *dark blue*
            Vergiß auch nicht, frische passende° Socken anzuziehen.   *matching*

Nach kurzer Zeit kommt Jürgen die Treppe herunter.

Jürgen   So, wie seh' ich aus?
Mutter   Einigermaßen akzeptabel. Aber zieh den warmen Mantel
            an und setz dir eine Mütze auf! Bei diesem kalten Wetter!
Jürgen   Aber nein! Ich friere doch nicht. Und übrigens will ich nicht
            wie ein ambulanter Kleiderhaken° herumlaufen.   *mobile clothes hanger*
Mutter   Aber wart mal! Warum hast du dir die Haare nicht schnei-
            den lassen?
Jürgen   Wo denkst du hin? Bei kaltem Wetter halten° mich die lan-   *keep*
            gen Haare schön warm. Tschüß!

QUESTIONS ON THE CONVERSATION

1. An welchem Gymnasium ist Jürgen Schüler?
2. Warum zieht sich Jürgen gerade um?
3. Wessen (*whose*) Sohn ist Dirk?
4. Gefällt Jürgen die neue Krawatte?
5. Was für einen Anzug zieht Jürgen an?
6. Was fragt Jürgen, als er die Treppe herunterkommt?
7. Was antwortet ihm seine Mutter?
8. Warum will er den warmen Mantel nicht anziehen?
9. Warum ließ sich Jürgen nicht die Haare schneiden?

PERSONAL QUESTIONS

1. Was tragen Sie, wenn Sie eine sehr elegante Party besuchen?
2. Was tragen Sie bei kaltem Wetter? bei warmem Wetter?
3. Tragen Sie oft eine Mütze? Warum oder warum nicht?
4. Haben Sie lange oder kurze Haare? Lassen Sie sich oft die Haare schneiden?
   Sogar bei kaltem Wetter?

Practice

A. Substitute the items in parentheses for the noun in italics, and make the necessary changes in the adjective endings.

1. Wo ist der neue *Wagen?*
   (Geschäft / Fabrik / Anzug / Büro / Brunnen)

2. Vor vielen Jahren stand hier eine alte *Brücke.*
   (Haus / Brunnen / Kirche / Baum / Burg)

3. Jürgen, zieh doch deinen warmen *Mantel* an.
   (Jacke / Hemd / Anzug / Socken / Pullover)

B. Put sentences 1 and 2 of exercise A into the plural.

C. Replace the **der**-word by the word in parentheses and change the adjective ending where necessary.

1. Da ist das schöne Haus.   *(unser)*
2. Hast du den neuen Mantel gekauft?   *(ein)*
3. Wo befindet sich dieser große Parkplatz?   *(ein)*
4. Kennt er das städtische Gymnasium?   *(euer)*
5. Sie hat sich endlich von der gefährlichen Krankheit erholt.   *(ein)*

D. Eliminate the **der-** or **ein**-word in italics and adjust the ending of the adjective.

1. Hast du *dieses* kalte Bier getrunken?
2. Wir haben *die* schlechten Nachrichten erhalten.
3. Er hat sich *die* warmen Socken angezogen.
4. Sie ist die Tochter *dieser* reichen Leute.
5. Habt ihr *den* guten Kaffee gekauft?

E. Fill in the blanks with the appropriate ending of the **der**-words, **ein**-words, and adjectives. Use contractions where possible.

1. In dies_____ Stadt befindet sich ein_____ schön_____ Rathaus.
2. In d_____ Rheintal gibt es viel_____ Dörfer mit hübsch_____ Häusern und Kirchen.
3. Felix rief von d_____ ober_____ Stock herunter: „Gibt es heute ein_____ interessant_____ Film in d_____ Fernsehen?"
4. Von welch_____ groß_____ Gebäude redet ihr?
5. Du sollst dir ein_____ warm_____ Mantel anziehen.
6. Wo habt ihr unser_____ neu_____ Regenschirme hingestellt? Hier sind eur_____.

7. In d_____ Sommer trinke ich gern kalt_____ Wein von d_____ Weinbergen d_____ Rheintals.

8. Oskar, wasch dir doch dein_____ Gesicht und zieh dir dies_____ frisch_____ Hemd an!

9. Dies_____ Sportclub hat viel_____ Mitglieder; aber manch_____ sind kein gut_____ Athleten.

10. Zu lang_____ Ferien können langweilig werden und sind nicht immer gut für unser_____ Gesundheit.

11. Wir sind durch dunkl_____ Wälder und tief_____ Täler gegangen.

12. Ich konnte d_____ langweilig_____ Gespräch mein_____ Gäste nicht mehr zuhören.

F. Give the English equivalent.

1. Vor einigen Tagen habe ich mir einen neuen Anzug gekauft; er gefällt meiner Freundin sehr gut.

2. Seit mehreren Wochen trinkt sie nur noch warmen Tee, aber keinen Kaffee mehr. ~ anymore

3. Wem gehörten diese dunkelblaue Jacke und die rote (red) Mütze?

4. Wann willst du dir die Haare schneiden lassen?

5. Ach, Albert, wie siehst du denn aus? Wasch dir schnell dein Gesicht und die Hände und zieh dir ein anderes Hemd an!

6. Bei diesem kalten Wetter wirst du doch nicht ohne Mantel in die Stadt gehen! Wo denkst du denn hin?

aussehen—to look

Vocabulary development

A. Clothing

In Chapter 9 you learned the word for "suit," **der Anzug,** and "dress," **das Kleid.** Here are the words for other articles of clothing:

die Hose, -n	*trousers, pants*
die Jacke, -n	*jacket*
der Mantel, ¨	*overcoat*
das Hemd, -en	*shirt*
die Socke, -n	*sock*
der Schuh, -e	*shoe*

die Krawatte, -n	*tie*
der Rock, ⸚e	*skirt*
die Bluse, -n	*blouse*
die Weste, -n	*vest*
das Kopftuch, ⸚er	*scarf*
die Sandale, -n	*sandal*
der Pulli, -s } der Pullover, -	*sweater*

B. Colors

It's time to learn the German words for a few colors. Many of them can easily be recognized, since they have cognates in English. Here then are **die Farben** (*the colors*):

blau	*blue*	grün	*green*
blond	*blond*	rot	*red*
braun	*brown*	schwarz	*black*
gelb	*yellow*	weiß	*white*
grau	*gray*		
		bunt	*colorful*
		farbig	*(multi)colored*

One can shade the colors by adding either **hell** (*light, pale*) or **dunkel** (*dark*): **hellblau, dunkelgrün,** etc.

Hell and dunkel may of course be used independently, as in **helles Bier** or **dunkles Bier.**

Communicative exercises

A. Assume that your neighbor has had a little unexpected "windfall" of money. Ask him/her:

Was wirst du / ⎫
  werden Sie ⎬   **mit dem Geld tun?**
            ⎭

Have them answer with the following elements:

Ich werde mir	ein / neu / Wagen	kaufen.
	elegant / Stiefel	
	interessant / Bücher	
	ein / schön / Kleid	
	ein / warm / Mantel	
	ein / klein / Haus	
	ein / gut / Plattenspieler	
	teuer / Möbel	

B. You and your friend are preparing for a party tonight. Ask him/her:

Was ziehst du denn heute abend an?

Have them answer with:

Ich glaube, ich ziehe	der / blau / Anzug	an.
	und ein / weiß / Hemd	
	mein / neu / Jeans	
	die / schwarz / Stiefel	
	die / rot / Bluse	
	und ein / schön / Kopftuch	
	mein / alt / Kleid	
	die / neu / Schuhe	
	mein / grün / Pulli	
	und die / schwarz / Jacke	

C. Pretend you are in a family setting and ask your wife or husband: **Wo hast du mein . . . hingelegt?** and have her/him answer with: **Dein . . . ?** and an expression from the right:

Wo hast du	mein / schmutzig / Hose	hingelegt?	Deine . . . ?
	mein / rot / Bluse		Auf den Stuhl da
	mein / braun / Socken		Auf dein Bett
	sein / neu / Jacke		Auf sein Bett
	ihr / schön / Mantel		Auf ihr Bett
	mein / weiß / Hemd		

D. Ask your neighbor the following questions and have him/her answer with: **Wen? Nein, ich sehe ihn (sie, es,** etc.) **nicht.**

Siehst du	die Frau da mit	die / blond / Haare	Wen? . . .
	den Studenten mit	die / rot / Mütze	
	das Mädchen in	die / eng / Hose	
	das Fräulein mit	die / elegant / Stiefel	
	den Herrn mit	die / farbig / Krawatte	
	die Frau in	der / lang / Rock	
	das Mädchen mit	das / grün / Kopftuch	
	den Herrn in	der / grau / Anzug	

E. Ask a classmate the following questions and get an answer.

Welche Farbe hat /	dein Auto?	Er / Es ist . . .
haben	seine Schuhe?	Sie sind . . .
	dein neuer Pullover?	
	ihre Haare?	
	das Meer?	
	das Blut?	
	frischer Schnee?	

F. An old adage says **Kleider machen Leute**[1] (*Clothes make the man*). Do you believe that? Look at the picture below and describe what the people in them are wearing. What do you yourself prefer to wear when you go downtown, shopping, to a movie, a play, a concert, a party, a football game, etc.?

[1]This is also the title of a novella by the noted Swiss-German writer, Gottfried Keller (1819–90).

len° Armee anfangen?"°—„Deshalb bauen wir doch jetzt die großen Zivilschutzbunker".°8—„Das wird wohl nicht viel helfen."—„Sei doch nicht so pessimistisch!"—Lange reden wir nicht mehr. Man hört nur das Brummen° des Motors.

    In Zürich im Restaurant „Zum Rüden" gibt es viel Händedrücken,° Erzählen und ein gutes Essen mit Weißwein und Rotwein. Während des Gesprächs kommen wir auch auf den Verkehr zu sprechen. „Wir leben in einer verkehrten Welt", sagt ein alter Kamerad, „jetzt haben wir die schnellen Wagen, aber wegen des dichten Autoverkehrs braucht man eine Ewigkeit,° in die Stadtmitte zu fahren."—„Fahrt doch mit dem Fahrrad", sage ich, „dann werdet ihr auch nicht so viele Abgase° einatmen müssen."—„Was! Du meinst, daß wir unsere Fahrräder aus dem Keller° holen sollen? Wo denkst du hin? Erstens ist mein Drahtesel[9] verrostet,° zweitens will ich nicht in den Tramschienen[10] hinfallen und drittens ist im Krankenhaus° nicht genug Platz für die vielen Fahrradunfälle!"

    „Na", denke ich, „vielleicht sind nicht die Welt und der Verkehr verkehrt, sondern die Menschen."

conventional / here: do / civil defense shelters

roar(ing)

handshaking

eternity

exhaust fumes
cellar
rusted
hospital

·

CULTURAL NOTES

1. **Das Bundeshaus** is the Federal Building in Berne, where the Swiss Parliament meets.

2. The **Eurailpass** is a season ticket valid on most Continental European railways.

3. Swiss-German differs considerably in structure, vocabulary, and pronunciation from standard German. Moreover, there are many distinct dialects, which make the standardization of the spelling nearly impossible. But **Schwyzerdüütsch** for **Schweizerdeutsch** is a fairly accurate rendering of the pronunciation.

4. **Riegelhaus:** a Swiss expression denoting a type of half-timbered house.

5. The **Aare,** a tributary of the Rhine, winds through the city.

6. Basle dialect for **Salü, Robi!** (*hi, Bob*).

7. The official speed limit on freeways in Switzerland is 130 km (ca 80 miles); in West Germany this is the "recommended" limit (largely for energy conservation reasons).

8. For a conventional war, Switzerland has a high degree of military preparedness and, of late, has also developed an elaborate civil defense system. All able-bodied male citizens are subject to the draft (women may be drafted for auxiliary services).

9. **Drahtesel:** a colloquial expression for **Fahrrad,** meaning literally *wire-donkey.*

10. **Tramschienen** is Swiss and southern German for **Straßenbahnschienen** (*streetcar tracks*).

QUESTIONS

1. Wo steht Robert und wohin schaut er?
2. Was für Leute befinden sich heutzutage unter den Touristen in der Schweiz?
3. Was versuchen einige der jungen Leute zu tun?
4. Wie sind alle jungen Leute gekleidet?
5. Welche Dinge sind gleich geblieben?
6. Wer ist gerade angekommen?
7. Warum müssen sie sich beeilen?
8. Warum fragt Robert seinen Freund, ob sein Wagen einen Flugzeugmotor hat?
9. Wovon (*about what*) sprechen die beiden Freunde?
10. Was gibt es im Restaurant in Zürich?
11. Warum sagt ein alter Kamerad, daß wir in einer verkehrten Welt leben?
12. Warum will Roberts Freund sein Fahrrad nicht aus dem Keller holen?
13. Was denkt Robert?

Review

A. Answer the questions with the cues given in parentheses. Use the appropriate endings and the same tense as in the question.

EXAMPLE: Wen erwartet ihr heute abend?
　　　　　(erwarten / wir / Freund / unser / alt)
　　　　　Wir erwarten unseren alten Freund.

1. Wo wohnt Ihr Freund jetzt?
(Wohnen / er / seit / mehrere / Jahre / in / ein / groß / Hotel)

2. Wohin werden Sie in die Ferien fahren?
(machen / ich / eine   Reise / lang / durch / das   Rheintal / schön / und / der Norden / Deutschland)

3. Wo seid ihr gestern abend gewesen?
(gehen / wir / in / das Kino / und / sich ansehen / ein   Film / sehr interessant)

4. Was für ein Gesicht macht deine Freundin?
(machen / sie / auf / jeder Fall / kein / Gesicht / freundlich)

B. Answer the following questions with an attributive adjective.

EXAMPLES: **Was für eine Mütze trägt Peter?**
 Er trägt eine graue Mütze.

 Welchen Koffer soll ich mitnehmen?
 Nimm den kleinen Koffer mit!

1. Welcher Wagen gehört dir?
2. Welchen Pullover soll ich anziehen?
3. Welcher Mantel gefällt Ihnen?
4. Was für Geschichten hat er erzählt?
5. Was für eine Krawatte hat dir dein Onkel geschenkt?

C. Fill in the appropriate form of the **der-** and **ein-**words, adjectives, nouns, and pronouns suggested.

1. _____ gehören _____ _____ Socken? (*Wer, dies, grün*)
2. Was tragen _____ _____ Männer? (*manch, jung*)
3. In _____ _____ Straßen stehen _____ Autos. (*die, eng, viel*)
4. Für _____ _____ Moment dachte ich an _____ _____ Tochter. (*ein, kurz, sein, hübsch*)
5. Das war _____ _____ Vergnügen, sich mit _____ Freunden zu unterhalten. (*ein, groß, gut*)
6. Zieht _____ doch _____ _____ Pulli an! (*ihr, fam., ein, warm*)
7. Wo sind _____ _____ Hemden? (*das, frisch*)
8. Gefällt _____ _____ _____ Jacke? (*er, dies, neu*)

D. Fill in the appropriate form of the words given in English.

1. Seit _____ Jahren wohnt er allein in _____ Haus. (*many, his*)
2. In den _____ Monaten haben sich _____ Dinge verändert. (*last, many*)
3. Die _____ Männer von heute tragen keine _____ Krawatten. (*young, red*)
4. Hier kann man _____ Fleisch bekommen. (*good*)
5. Während der _____ Vorstellung schlief ich ein. (*boring*)
6. Die _____ Kleidung der _____ Leute gefällt mir. (*modern, young*)
7. Wir erinnern uns sehr gut an _____ _____ Eltern. (*his, dear*)
8. _____ _____ _____ Film muß man sich ansehen. (*Such, an interesting*)

E. Express in German.

1. The city traffic has become too dense, and too many people park their cars in the narrow streets.
2. Jürgen, why don't you put on a warm overcoat or at least the new jacket?
3. Be careful. Even on this new freeway you mustn't drive so fast.
4. In any event please get a haircut.
5. What do you mean? In this cold weather I won't walk around with short hair.
6. I don't like these new boots.
7. Where did you buy this elegant suit?

Guided composition

Describe some part of a city that you particularly like. Give one or two impressions of the people you see, what they look like, how they are dressed, and what they do there; what the traffic is like; whether there are many policemen around; whether the people drive carefully or not. What is the traffic like on the nearby freeways? How fast do people drive? How fast do you drive?

Chapter vocabulary

Nouns

die	Autobahn, -en	freeway
die	Bluse, -n	blouse
die	Farbe, -n	color
die	Geschichte, -n	history, story
die	Idee, -n	idea
die	Jacke, -n	jacket
die	Jugend	youth
der	Kamerad, -en	comrade
die	Kleidung	clothing
das	Kopftuch, ̈-er	scarf
der	Mantel, ̈	overcoat
die	Maschine, -n	machine
das	Meer, -e	sea
die	Mitte	middle
das	Musikinstrument, -e	musical instrument
die	Mütze, -n	cap
der	Pullover, -	sweater
der	Rock, ̈-e	skirt
der	Schüler, -	pupil
die	Socke, -n	sock
die	Sorge, -n	worry, care
	sich Sorgen machen (um + acc.)	to worry (about)
der	Sportwagen, -	sports car
der	Stiefel, -	boot
der	Stock, die Stockwerke	floor, story (of a building)

die	Terrasse, -n	terrace
der	Verkehr	traffic
der	Weg, -e	way, path
der	Zuhörer, -	listener

Verbs

sich (dat.) an·schauen	to look (at something)
sich an·ziehen, zog, angezogen	to dress, put on
sich (dat.) auf·setzen	to put on (a hat, etc.)
aus·sehen (sieht), sah, ausgesehen (+ adj.)	to look (healthy, etc.)
bauen	to build
sich beeilen	to hurry
erwarten	to expect
fliegen, flog, (ist) geflogen	to fly
frieren, fror, gefroren	to be cold
rufen, rief, gerufen	to call
schenken	to give (a gift)
schneiden, schnitt, geschnitten	to cut
tragen (trägt), trug, getragen	to wear (clothes); to carry
übernachten	to stay overnight
verändern	to change (something)
sich verändern	to change (be changed)
werfen (wirft), warf, geworfen	to throw

Other words

arm	poor
bequem	comfortable
braun	brown
breit	broad, wide
bunt	colorful
dicht	dense
drittens	in the third place
dunkel	dark
einigermaßen	somewhat, to some extent, fairly
elegant	elegant
eng	narrow
erstens	in the first place
farbig	(multi) colored
frisch	fresh
gekleidet (sein)	to be dressed
gemütlich	jolly, good-natured, cozy
gleich	(the) same
grau	gray
hell	light, pale (of color)
international	international
konservativ	conservative
kurz	short
langweilig	boring, dull
letzt-	last
reich	rich
rot	red
schwarz	black
städtisch	municipal
tief	deep
verkehrt	topsy-turvy
weiß	white
zweitens	in the second place

See lists of clothing and colors on pp. 243–244.

Mini-dialogues

Student(in) A   Was gibt's Neues?
           B   Nichts.
           A   Sollen wir heute abend tanzen gehen?
           B   Wo denn?
           A   Oh, es gibt mehrere gute Diskotheken in der Stadt.
           B   Sie sind wahrscheinlich sehr laut.
           A   Leise sind sie natürlich nicht. Aber viele der neuen Hits sind wirklich fantastisch.

           A   Magst du die moderne Popmusik?
           B   Ja, einige der neuen Hits sind wirklich sehr gut und auch von soziologischem Interesse.
           A   Sind nicht alle amerikanisch?
           B   Oh, nein! Einige kommen aus England und Frankreich und andere auch aus Deutschland.
           A   Gefallen dir die amerikanischen Hits?
           B   Ja! Die habe ich besonders gern.

A   What's new?
B   Nothing.
A   Shall we go dancing tonight?
B   Where?
A   Oh, there are several good discos in the city.
B   They are probably very loud.
A   Of course, they aren't quiet. But many of the new hits are really fantastic.

A   Do you like modern pop music?
B   Yes, some of the new hits are really very good and also have some sociological interest.
A   Aren't all of them American?
B   Oh, no. Some are from England and France and others are also from Germany.
A   Do you like the American hits?
B   Yes. I like them above all.

Grammar explanations

I. Attributive adjectives with numerical words

Im Rheinland gibt es **mehrere** bekannte Burgen.
In the Rhineland there are several well-known castles.

Diese Band spielt **viele** gute Schlager.
This band plays many good hit songs.

Alle neuen Studenten treffen sich heute abend in einer Diskothek.
All new students will meet tonight in a discotheque.

A. Andere (*other*), **einige** (*some, a number of*), **mehrere** (*several*), **viele** (*many*), and **wenige** (*few*) are numerical words that function as attributive adjectives and take *strong* adjective endings. Quite often they are followed by a descriptive attributive adjective. In that case, the descriptive adjective also takes the *strong endings.*

Natürlich haben **andere** große Städte auch Universitäten.	*Naturally other large cities also have universities.*
Kennst du **einige** junge Amerikanerinnen?	*Do you know some young American women?*
An diesem Stadttheater sind **mehrere** bekannte Schauspieler.	*In this municipal theater there are several well-known actors.*
Gibt es in Köln **viele** große Fabriken?	*Are there many large factories in Cologne?*
Nur **wenige** alte Leute gehen in Diskotheken.	*Only a few old people go to the discos.*

B. With **alle, beide,** and **solche,** however, a descriptive attributive adjective that follows takes the *weak* endings.

Alle neuen amerikanischen Studenten treffen sich heute abend.	*All new American students will meet tonight.*
Wo findet man **solche** guten Freunde?	*Where do you find such good friends?*

CHECK YOUR COMPREHENSION

Supply the appropriate adjective endings.

1. Die Studentinnen kennen auch ander__e__ englisch__e__ Zeitungen.
2. In der Stadtmitte befinden sich nur wenig__e__ grün__e__ Gärten.

in comparison with

3. Im Vergleich mit einig*en* alt*en* Gebäuden scheint das Rathaus neu zu sein.
4. Neben einig*en* schön*en* Brunnen sind große Parkplätze.
5. In der Einbahnstraße da drüben gibt es mehrer*e* interessant*e* Geschäfte.
6. Nicht all*en* neu*en* Anzüge sind bequem.
7. Hast du tatsächlich mit all*en* wichtig*en* Leuten gesprochen?
8. Er will beid*en* deutsch*en* Städte besuchen.

II. Participles used as adjectives

Endlich erhielten wir die **bestellten** Bücher.
Finally we received the books that we had ordered.

Die neue Band heißt „Die **singenden** Vampire".
The new band is called "The Singing Vampires."

In English and German there are two types of participles: the past participle and the present participle. Both may be used as adjectives.

A. Past participle

The formation of the past participle in German was discussed in Chapter 5. If used as an attributive adjective, it takes the usual adjectival endings already discussed.

Verschmutztes Wasser ist gefährlich.
(verschmutzen > verschmutzt)

Polluted water is dangerous.

Habt ihr das **verlorene Buch** wiedergefunden?
(verlieren > verloren)

Have you found the lost book again?

The past participle may also function as a predicate adjective.

Diese Bluse ist frisch **gewaschen.**

This blouse has just been washed.

B. Present participle

In German the present participle is formed by adding **-end** to the verb stem. The ending **-end** corresponds to the English *-ing*.[1]

---

[1]In English the present participle occurs most often in the progressive form of the verb: *They were laughing as I entered.* As explained in Chapter I, this formation is not possible in German.

fahrend = *moving* (a train, etc.)
fließend = *flowing*

If used as an attributive adjective, it also takes the usual adjectival endings.

Er ist auf den **fahrenden** Zug gesprungen.	*He jumped on the moving train.*
Dieses Zimmer hat **fließendes** Wasser.	*This room has running water.*

Quite often the German present participle must be translated into English as a relative clause.

Das *lachende* Mädchen da drüben ist meine Schwester.	*The girl over there who's laughing is my sister.*

At times, a present participle may also function as a predicate adjective.

Diese Limonade ist **erfrischend.**	*This lemonade is refreshing.*

CHECK YOUR COMPREHENSION

A. Fill in the past participle of the verb in parentheses.

1. Ich habe die ~~bestellten~~ [Pl.] Möbel erhalten. (*bestellen*)
2. Mit diesem ~~gemieteten~~ Auto hatten wir einen Unfall. (*mieten*)
3. Ich kann mich an diese _____ Gebäude nicht gewöhnen. (*restaurieren*) *restaurierten*
4. Hast du den _____ Brief erhalten? (*erwarten*) *erwarteten*

B. Form the present participle of the verb in parentheses and use it as an adjective.

1. Die Studentin sprang auf den _____ Bus. (*fahren*) *fahrenden*
2. Wo sind die _____ jungen Leute hingegangen? (*singen*) *singenden*
3. Kennst du das _____ Mädchen da drüben? (*lachen*) *lachende*
4. Wir mieteten ein Zimmer mit _____ Wasser. (*fließen*) *fließendem*

III. Adjectives used as nouns

Der Alte erinnert sich an viele Länder.
The old man remembers many countries.

Er ist **ein Bekannter** von mir.
He is an acquaintance of mine.

Wir wünschen euch **alles Gute.**
We wish you all the best (everything good).

Möchtest du **etwas Erfrischendes?**
Would you like something refreshing?

Bei den Müllers gibt's **nichts Neues.**
There's nothing new at the Müllers'.

In German, as in English, adjectives may be used as nouns. If an adjective functions as a noun it is capitalized, but it retains the appropriate ending of the attributive adjective. Its gender and number are those of the noun that it has absorbed.

Der alte Mann ist krank.   *The old man is sick.*

Der **Alte** ist krank.   *The old one is sick.*

Die kranke Frau ist noch jung.   *The sick woman is still young.*

Die **Kranke** ist noch jung.   *The sick one is still young.*

Adjectival nouns in the neuter refer most often to something abstract or general.

Das ist **das Gute** an diesem Fahrrad.   *That is the good thing about this bicycle.*

Neuter adjectival nouns occur frequently after **etwas, nichts, viel,** and **wenig.** After these words, adjectival nouns take the *strong* endings.

Er hat mir **etwas** Wichtiges geschrieben.   *He wrote me something important.*

Es gibt **nichts** Neues.   *There is nothing new.*

Sie hat uns **viel** Interessantes erzählt.   *She told us a lot of interesting things.*

Ihr habt sehr **wenig** Gutes über uns gesagt.   *You said very little good about us.*

When an adjectival noun follows **alles,** however, it takes the *weak* endings.

Ich wünsche euch **alles** Gute.   *I wish you all the best (everything good).*

Present and past participles may also function as adjectival nouns.

Ich möchte **etwas Erfrischendes** trinken.   *I would like to drink something refreshing.*

Sie ißt **nichts Gefrorenes.**[1]

She eats nothing frozen (or: no ice cream).

CHECK YOUR COMPREHENSION

A. Substitute the adjectival noun for the words in italics.

EXAMPLE: In dieser Stadt gibt es viele *arme Leute.*
　　　　In dieser Stadt gibt es viele Arme.

1. So wie es *die alten Leute* machten, so machen es *die jungen Leute.*
2. *Der kleine Junge* lief über die Straße.
3. *Die reichen Leute* machen sich keine Sorgen um *die armen Leute.*
4. *Der kranke Mann* lag im Bett.

B. Fill in the blanks with the adjectival nouns corresponding to the words in parentheses.

EXAMPLE: Ich weiß nichts _____. (new)
　　　　Ich weiß nichts Neues.

1. Er hat viel _Gutes_ getan. (good)
2. Das ist das _Schöne_ an meiner Arbeit. (nice)
3. Hier, trink etwas _____! (refreshing)   *ERFRISCHENDES*
4. Es gibt wenig _____ zu erzählen. (important)   *Wichtiges*
5. Sie wünschte uns alles _Gute_ zum neuen Jahr. (good)
6. Ich will nichts _____ tun. (unhealthy)   *Ungesundes*
7. Viktor möchte alles _____ lesen. (written)   *Geschriebene*

[handwritten annotations: GUT – good / Gutes – good things / She wished us all good / all the best / everything that has been written]

Conversation

---

befreundet sein	to be friends
Was gibt's Neues?	What's new?
das Übliche	the usual
Unglaublich!	Unbelievable!
Du mußt es ja wissen.	You should know

[1]In German, this is at times used specifically for "ice cream."

DIE LAUTE BAND

Jutta Jünger (22) ist Chemiestudentin in Köln. Hansjörg Braun (23) studiert Soziologie. Sie sind befreundet und treffen sich zufällig in der Stadt.

Jutta Hansjörg! Hansjörg! Hallo, Hansjörg! Hörst du mich denn nicht? Hansjörg!!!

Hansjörg Was? Wie bitte? Ach Jutta, du bist es! Guten Tag!

Jutta Wie geht es dir? Was gibt's Neues?

Hansjörg Nichts Neues. Das Übliche. Ich studiere und schreibe und bin wieder einmal mit einer Seminararbeit° verspätet.° Du kennst mich ja.   *seminar paper / late*

Jutta Aber wo kommst du denn jetzt her?

Hansjörg Wie bitte?

Jutta *(schreit)* Wo du jetzt herkommst? Aus der Uni-Bibliothek?

Wolf Biermann

Hansjörg	He? Ja, da aus der „Jimmy"-Diskothek. Da spielt jetzt eine ganz tolle Band—„Die singenden Vampire".
Jutta	Warum heißen sie nicht die „brüllenden° Vampire"? Du hörst ja fast nichts mehr.
Hansjörg	Auch gut. So höre ich nicht jeden Lärm. Übrigens singen die Vampire mehrere gute Schlager von soziologischem und politischem Interesse.
Jutta	Warum laden die Leute denn nicht einmal den Biermann[1] ein?
Hansjörg	Wie bitte? Du willst mich zum Bier einladen?
Jutta	Unglaublich! Aber komm! Wir trinken da drüben schnell etwas Erfrischendes. Das Schlucken° wird deinem Gehör gut tun.
Hansjörg	Was sagst du?

howling (glosses *brüllenden*)
swallowing (glosses *Schlucken*)

QUESTIONS ON THE CONVERSATION

1. Wo wohnen Jutta und Hansjörg?
2. Wo treffen sich die zwei zufällig?

[1]Wolf Biermann, born in 1936, is a poet and balladeer from the DDR. Having become embroiled with the East German regime, he was expelled from the DDR in 1977. He now lives in the BRD, where his songs and poems satirizing both East and West have earned him a large following.

3. Gibt es etwas Neues bei Hansjörg? Was hat er kürzlich getan?
4. Woher kommt er?
5. Wie heißt die fantastische Band?
6. Wie nennt Jutta die Band?
7. Warum kann Hansjörg nicht alles verstehen?
8. Warum findet Hansjörg einige Schlager dieser Band gut?
9. Was wird Hansjörgs Gehör gut tun?

DISKOTHEK
UNDERGROUND
44 Münster
Königsstr. 45
Geöffnet von 20.00 bis 3.00 Uhr

PERSONAL QUESTIONS

1. Gibt es in Ihrer Stadt eine Diskothek? Gehen Sie gern hin?
2. Was hast du gern, laute oder leise Musik?
3. Hört man in amerikanischen Diskotheken Schlager von soziologischem oder politischem Interesse? Welche zum Beispiel?

Practice

A. Substitute the adjectival noun for the word in italics.

1. Die *neue Professorin* ist wirklich populär.
2. Der Vater spielte mit der *kleinen Tochter*.
3. Da drüben ist der *alte Mann*.
4. Die Geschichte habe ich den *kleinen Kindern* erzählt.
5. Die *kranke Mutter* muß zu Hause bleiben.
6. In dieser Stadt wohnen nicht viele *reiche Leute*.

B. Supply the appropriate form of the past participle of the verb in parentheses.

1. Da drüben sind die _____ Kleider. (*bestellen*)
2. Der Professor zeigte mir den _____ Dom. (*restaurieren*)
3. Das _____ Programm ist hier. (*verändern*)
4. Wir trinken natürlich kein _____ Wasser. (*verschmutzen*)
5. Wir haben die _____ Schecks wieder gefunden. (*verlieren*)

C. Add the appropriate ending to the adjectival noun.

1. Während des Gesprächs erzählte sie uns nichts Interessant____.
2. Die Nachricht ist den Studenten nichts Neu____.
3. In der Zeitung lasen wir wenig Wichtig____.
4. Bier ist sicher etwas Erfrischend____.
5. Ich wünsche dir alles Gut____.
6. Von ihm hört man nie etwas Schlecht____.

D. Supply the inflected present participle of the verb in parentheses.

1. Der Autofahrer sah das _____ Kind nicht. (*spielen*)
2. Der Student sprang aus dem _____ Auto. (*fahren*)
3. Die _____ Studentin da drüben heißt Lotte. (*diskutieren*)
4. Der _____ Student da drüben ist mein Freund. (*lachen*)
5. Das _____ Kind läuft schnell nach Hause. (*frieren*)

E. Fill in the blanks with the appropriate adjective endings.

1. In mehrer _____ deutsch _____ Städten gibt es alte Brücken.
2. Einig _____ klein _____ Häuser sind noch nicht vermietet.
3. Natürlich gibt es viele groß _____ Geschäfte in Berlin.
4. Hast du all _____ neu _____ Filme von Fellini gesehen, Peter?
5. Ander _____ städtisch _____ Diskotheken haben gute Bands.
6. Zuviel erfrischend _____ Bier kann gefährlich werden.
7. Er kennt wenig _____ amerikanisch _____ Studenten.

Vocabulary development

A. *Freunde, befreundet,* or *Bekannte?*

Der Freund, -e, die Freundin, -nen, denote good friends who would in most cases use the **du**-form in addressing each other.

The adjective **befreundet** suggests being more than just chance acquaintances, *but not* intimate friends. People who are **befreundet** may use the **du**- or **Sie**-form among themselves, depending on their respective ages, their relationship, their agreed-upon preferences, etc.

Der, (die) Bekannte, -n (from **bekannt**) are mere acquaintances, often of a distant or superficial sort, who will always use the formal **Sie** in addressing each other. You may say:

Er ist **ein Bekannter** von mir.	*He is an acquaintance of mine.*
Sie ist **eine Bekannte** von mir.	*She is an acquaintance of mine.*

Note that the noun is derived from the (participial) adjective **bekannt** and, therefore, takes adjectival endings.

B. *hören, (sich) fühlen, riechen,* and *schmecken*

das Gehör	is obviously derived from **hören**. It denotes both the hearing mechanism and the sense of hearing.
das Gefühl	is derived from **fühlen** (*to feel*), and denotes many related things: the sense of touch; feeling; sentiment; emotion; etc.

The other nouns referring to the senses are:

der Geruch	from **riechen** (*to smell*), denoting the sense of smell or a smell.
der Geschmack	from **schmecken** (*to taste*), denoting the sense of taste, but also the taste of something, and to have (good) taste: **Sie hat Geschmack.** (*She has good taste.*) The verb **schmecken** is often heard at the table:

Wie schmeckt es?	*How does it taste?*
Es schmeckt sehr gut.	*It tastes very good.*

The sense of sight, however, is **das Sehvermögen** (*the ability to see*). **Das Gesicht,** also derived from **sehen,** denotes *the face.*

At this point, you might wish to learn and practice some words referring to parts of the human body. Easily recognized words are:

der Arm, -e	der Mund, ¨er
die Hand, ¨e	der Fuß, ¨e
der Finger, -	das Haar, -e
die Nase, -n	

Others:

der Körper, -	*body*	das Ohr, -en	*ear*
der Kopf, ¨e	*head*	der Bauch, ¨e	*stomach*
das Bein, -e	*leg*	die Brust, ¨e	*chest, breast*
das Auge, -n	*eye*	der Zahn, ¨e	*tooth*

Communicative exercises

A. Use the verbs **riechen, schmecken, sehen,** and **(sich) fühlen** about things you like or dislike. For example:

Ich rieche gern frischen Kaffee.
Mir schmeckte der Kuchen gut.
Ich habe gestern einen Film gesehen.
Seit Montag fühle ich mich wohl (or unwohl).

B. Describe a friend.

Er / sie hat blaue Augen.
Ihr / sein Haar ist grau.
Er / sie ist sehr schlank.

C. Name someone who is a friend of yours and some acquaintances. How long have you known these persons (remember, *seit* takes present tense!)? Do you use *du* or *Sie* among yourselves?

D. Begin a conversation with two or three classmates. Pretend you just came from a disco. Discuss your favorite songs, whether you like to dance, what songs you like to dance to, what bands you like especially, whether you like loud or soft music. Suggestions:

Wo ist die Diskothek?
Wieviel kostet ein Bier oder ein Glas Wein?
Wie schmeckt der Wein (das Bier)?
Tanzt du gern?
Oder ziehst du vor, der Musik nur zuzuhören?
Zu welchen Hits tanzt du besonders gern?

Reading

POPMUSIK[1]

Seit der Erfindung des Phonographen° durch Thomas Edison hat   *phonograph*
sich die Produktion von Schallplatten zu einem gigantischen internationalen Geschäft entwickelt. Die Bundesrepublik produziert
jährlich fast zweihundert Millionen Platten. Nur die USA und Japan

the growth

Response -ible

produzieren noch mehr Platten als Deutschland. Und wer ist für diese Entwicklung verantwortlich? Die Antwort ist einfach: die Jugendlichen[2] mit ihrer Popmusik.

„Popmusik" nennt man in den deutschsprechenden Ländern viele verschiedene Stile: Vom Jazz über den Rock 'n Roll bis zum Punkrock. Für die Jugend ist die Popmusik zum Ausdruck ihrer Weltanschauung° geworden. In Deutschland kaufen Jugendliche unter 25 Jahren fast neunzig Prozent aller neuen Platten. So kommt es, daß neunzig Prozent der verkauften Platten Popmusik und nur zehn Prozent klassische Musik bieten.° *perception of the world*

offer

Die deutsche Jugend von heute will aber nicht nur deutsche Popmusik hören. Sie möchte auch zu allen internationalen Schlagern tanzen, besonders am Wochenende in den Diskotheken. Und die deutsche Schallplattenindustrie hat ein sehr gutes Musikgehör: sie hört auf° die musikalischen Interessen der Jugend und produziert viele international bekannte Hits. Die Lizenzgebühren° sind klein im Vergleich zu dem Gewinn. Aber das Risiko ist jetzt groß wegen der vielen Raubpressungen.°

listens to
license fees

pirated record

Das Interesse der deutschen Jugend an internationalen Hits begann bald nach dem Zweiten Weltkrieg, denn man konnte wieder in andere europäische Länder reisen. Und man lernte Englisch! Schließlich kam die Invasion des Rock 'n Roll, der vielen großen Hits von Elvis Presley und mehrerer bekannter Gruppen, wie zum Beispiel der Beatles.

„Beat", wie man die amerikanische Rockmusik in Deutschland nennt, wurde zu einem eigentlichen Lebensstil. Er beeïnflußte° die Haartracht° der Jugendlichen, ihre Kleidung, ihre Freizeit. Und die Popsänger wurden zu Idolen.

    influenced
    hairdo

Inzwischen haben die Eltern mit diesem Lebensstil und der Ideologie der Jungen einige Kompromisse gemacht. Was sie aber kaum verstehen können, ist die Vorliebe° der Jugend für ohrenbetäubende° Musik. Das ist etwas anderes. Man kann die Ohren an neue Musik und einen neuen Rhythmus° gewöhnen, aber warum soll man dabei schwerhörig° werden?

    preference / deafening

    rhythm
    hard of hearing

Die Alten fragen sich, warum die Jugendlichen so laute Musik lieben und nicht leise Musik vorziehen. Wollen sie vielleicht die Leere° der modernen Zivilisation mit der lauten Musik ausfüllen?° Oder wollen sie den Lärm der modernen Zivilisation—des Stadt- und Flugverkehrs und der Industrie—durch laute Musik vergessen? Wer weiß? Niemand scheint die Antwort zu haben. Auf jeden Fall darf man sagen, daß das alte Sprichwort° „Wie die Alten sungen, so zwitschern° die Jungen"[3] auf dem Gebiet° des musikalischen Geschmacks nicht mehr so ganz wahr ist.

    emptiness
    fill

    proverb / chirp
    area

CULTURAL NOTES

1. **Popmusik, Hit, Punk,** and other linguistic imports denoting musical style such as **Beat, Rock 'n Roll,** or „**Country**" have become commonplace in Germany, even in the DDR.

2. **Die Jugendlichen** is used in the general sense of *young people*, whereas **die Jugend** means *youth*. **Der Junge** denotes *boy*; its plural is **die Jungen.**

3. Literally: *As the old ones sang, so do the young, that is, like father, like son.* (**Sungen,** an archaic form has been preserved in this old saying for the sake of the rhyme. **Sangen** is the correct modern form.)

QUESTIONS

1. Was war die Erfindung von Thomas Edison?
2. Was hat sich zu einem gigantischen Geschäft entwickelt?
3. Wieviele Schallplatten produziert die Bundesrepublik jährlich?
4. Wer ist für die Entwicklung in der Schallplattenindustrie verantwortlich?
5. Was nennt man in den deutschsprechenden Ländern „Popmusik"?
6. Wer kauft in Deutschland fast alle neuen Platten?
7. Was tut die deutsche Jugend am Wochenende?
8. Warum produziert die deutsche Schallplattenindustrie auch viele internationale Hits?
9. Wann begann das Interesse an internationalen Hits in Deutschland?
10. Warum liebt die Jugend die laute Musik und zieht nicht leise Musik vor?
11. Warum ist das alte Sprichwort nicht mehr so ganz wahr?

Review

A. Supply the appropriate adjective endings.

1. Heutzutage gibt es viel____ jung____ Leute, die kein____ passend____ Arbeit finden.
2. Wir machten d____ lang____ Reise mit einig____ gut____ Freunden.
3. Er kennt all____ neu____ Schlager.
4. Ich werde ander____ deutsch____ Bücher bestellen.
5. Ich schreibe nie solch____ lang____ Briefe.
6. In diesem Kino sieht man nur wenig____ alt____ Leute.
7. Wir finden beid____ neu____ Platten nicht.
8. In der Stadtmitte gibt es mehrer____ interessant____ Gebäude.

B. Supply the appropriate adjectival form of the past participle.

1. Monika fand die _____ Mütze wieder. (*verlieren*)
2. Ich kannte nicht alle _____ Gäste. (*einladen*)
3. Endlich erhielten wir die _____ Platten. (*bestellen*)

4. Die _____ Kleider gehören ihm. (*verschmutzen*)

5. Dieses _____ Buch war sehr teuer. (*illustrieren*)

6. Wo hast du den _____ Brief hingelegt? (*anfangen*)

C. Fill in the appropriate form of the present participle.

1. Der Tourist sprang aus dem _____ Zug. (*fahren*)

2. Peter kam _____ nach Hause zurück. (*frieren*)

3. Ich sehe _____ Menschen gern. (*lachen*)

4. Im Stadtpark sieht man viele _____ Kinder. (*spielen*)

5. Er sah die _____ Straßenbahn nicht. (*herankommen*)

6. Wir suchen ein Zimmer mit _____ Wasser. (*fließen*)

7. Ich kenne die _____ Studenten da drüben in der Ecke nicht. (*diskutieren*)

D. Answer the questions with the cues provided.

EXAMPLE: Was wünschen Sie einem guten Freund? (*alles / gut*) (*viel / gut*)
        Ich wünsche ihm alles Gute.
        Ich wünsche ihm viel Gutes.

1. Was gibt's heute bei Ihnen? (*nichts / neu*) (*wenig / interessant*)

2. Was sagt man über ihn? (*viel / schlecht*) (*nichts / gut*)

3. Was hat er Ihnen erzählt? (*wenig / unterhaltend*) (*viel / langweilig*)

4. Was kommt jetzt? (*etwas / erfrischend*)

E. Translate into German.

1. The old man (old one) doesn't like that loud band.

2. Many well-known books are not here.

3. When can we drink something refreshing?

4. Many young people of the Federal Republic of Germany like to listen to Western hits.
5. I know several popular professors.
6. The arriving train is full.
7. The polluted water of the river is dangerous for our health.
8. Some American hits express something sociological.
9. The old people (old ones) do not know why the young prefer to listen to loud music.

Die alten weißen nicht, warum die Jugend laute Musik aufhören vorzieht

Guided composition

Describe as exactly as you can the looks of your closest friend. Also include a description of your friend's clothing. What kind of music does your friend like? How long have you known each other?

Chapter vocabulary

Nouns

die	Band, -s	band
der	Bekannte, -n (ein Bekannter)	acquaintance
die	Chemie	chemistry
die	Diskothek, -en	disco
die	Entwicklung, -en	development
die	Erfindung, -en	invention
das	Gehör	sense of hearing
der	Geschmack, ⸚er	taste, sense of taste; good taste
der	Gewinn, -e	gain
die	Gruppe, -n	group
der	Hit, -s	hit
die	Ideologie, -n	ideology
das	Idol, -e	idol
das	Interesse, -n	interest
die	Invasion, -en	invasion
der	Jugendliche, -n (ein Jugendlicher)	the youth
der	Kompromiß, -sse	compromise
die	Musik	music
die	Produktion	production
das	Prozent, -e	per cent, percentage
das	Risiko, -s	risk
der	Sänger, -	singer, entertainer
der	Schlager, -	hit, popular song
der	Stil, -e	style
der	Verkauf, ⸚e	sale
das	Wochenende, -n	weekend

Verbs

befreundet sein mit	*to be friends with*
beginnen, begann, begonnen	*to begin*
ein·laden (lädt), lud, eingeladen	*to invite*
sich entwickeln	*to develop*
sich erfrischen	*to refresh*
sich (wohl, unwohl) fühlen	*to feel (well, unwell, or sick)*
fühlen	*to feel*
illustrieren	*to illustrate*
lachen	*to laugh*
lieben	*to love*
produzieren	*to produce*
riechen, roch, gerochen	*to smell*
schmecken	*to taste*
schreien, schrie, geschrien	*to scream, yell*
singen, sang, gesungen	*to sing*
tanzen	*to dance*
träumen	*to dream*
vor·ziehen, zog, vorgezogen	*to prefer*
zu·nehmen (nimmt), nahm, zugenommen	*to increase*
wünschen	*to wish*

Other words

amerikanisch	*American*
dabei	*in so doing*
gern: etwas gern haben	*to like something*
gigantisch	*gigantic*
klassisch	*classical*
laut	*loud*
leise	*silent, quiet*
musikalisch	*musical*
niemand	*nobody*
politisch	*political*
soziologisch	*sociological*
toll	*fabulous (slang), mad, crazy*
üblich	*usual*
unglaublich	*unbelievable*
verantwortlich	*responsible*
zufällig	*by coincidence, by chance*

See also the words for some of the senses and the parts of the body on p. 265.

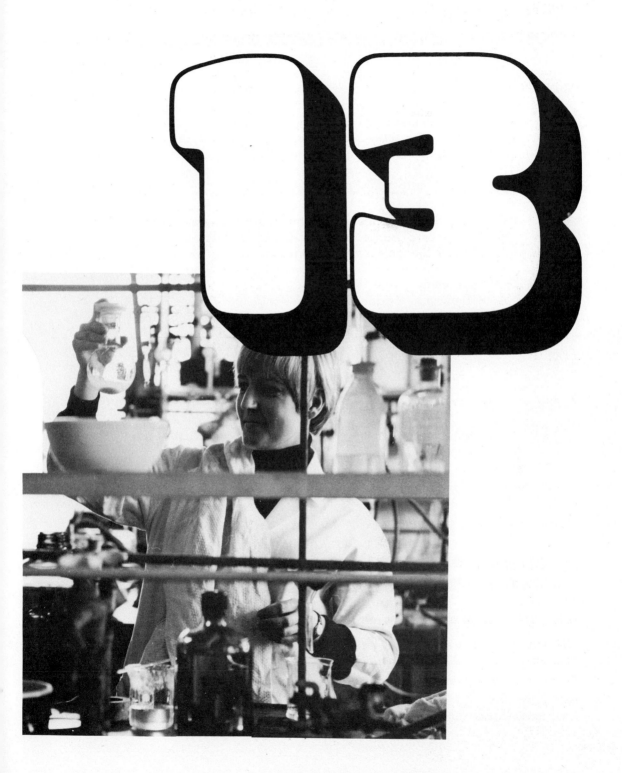

Mini-dialogues

Student(in) A Gehst du am Donnerstag in die Bibliothek?
B Nein. Ich gehe mittwochs hin.
A Wie lange bleibst du dort?
B Von sechs bis zehn Uhr abends. Für mich ist das die beste Zeit. Sollen wir einmal zusammen hingehen?
A Zu dumm! Ich kann nur donnerstags für zwei bis drei Stunden, mittwochs habe ich keine Zeit.

A Haben Sie den neuesten Film mit Jane Fonda gesehen?
B Allerdings! Er ist viel besser als ihr letzter Film.
A Möchten Sie ihn ein zweites Mal sehen?
B Ja, gern! Gute Filme sehe ich am liebsten zweimal oder noch öfter.
A Sollen wir heute abend um acht Uhr gehen?
B Abgemacht! Früher kann ich nicht, weil ich bis sechs Uhr arbeiten muß.

A Are you going to the library on Thursday?
B No. I go on Wednesdays.
A How long do you stay there?
B From six to ten in the evenings. That's the best time for me. Shall we go together some time?
A Too bad. I can only go on Thursdays for two to three hours, on Wednesdays I have no time.

A Did you see Jane Fonda's newest movie?
B I should say so! It is much better than her last film.
A Would you like to see it a second time?
B Very much so. I like to see good movies twice or even more often.
A Shall we go this evening at eight o'clock?
B Agreed. I can't go any earlier because I have to work until six o'clock.

Grammar explanations

I. Comparison of adjectives and adverbs

Paul fühlt sich nicht **so wohl, wie** er sagt.
Paul doesn't feel as well as he says.

Kuchen schmeckt **besser als** Brot.
Cake tastes better than bread.

Klara ist **die älteste** Studentin.
Klara is the oldest student.

Wenn er die Polizei sieht, fährt er am vorsichtigsten.
When he sees the police, he drives most carefully.

Je billiger, desto besser!
The cheaper, the better.

In German as in English, there are three degrees of comparison: the *positive*, the *comparative*, and the *superlative*. When used as attributive adjectives, all three degrees add adjective endings, as discussed in Chapter 11.

A. The positive

The positive represents the basic form of an adjective, as listed in the dictionary.

To indicate equality between two persons or items, the positive form of the predicate adjective or adverb is used with the particles **so** . . . **wie** (*as . . . as*).

Das Auto ist so alt wie das Fahrrad.	*The car is as old as the bicycle.*
Jutta schwimmt so gut wie Brigitte.	*Jutta swims as well as Brigitte.*

B. The comparative

The comparative is formed by adding the suffix **-er** to the adjective stem; it denotes a comparison between two unequal objects.

Attributive:

Jutta ist die schönere Frau.	*Jutta is the more beautiful woman.*
Hansjörg ist der intelligentere Junge.	*Hansjörg is the more intelligent youngster.*

The word **als** (*than*) is used with predicate adjectives and adverbs in the comparative form.

Predicate adjective/adverb:

als — then
(not when)

Peter ist kleiner als Jutta.	*Peter is shorter than Jutta.*
Unser Auto fährt schneller als eures.	*Our car goes faster than yours.*

In conjunction with the comparative, the word **immer** (*always*) suggests a progressive increase. Note the equivalent in English.

Die Filme werden immer schlechter.	*The movies are getting worse and worse.*

getting alway worse
worse & worse

Ich werde **immer vorsichtiger.**	*I'm becoming more and more cautious.*

Je . . . desto (*the . . . the*) expresses the interdependence of two comparatives.

Je mehr ich lese, **desto** weniger verstehe ich.	*The more I read, the less I understand.*

C. The superlative

The superlative is formed by adding the suffix **-st: das kleinste Haus.** However, **-est** is added after **-d, -t, -s, -ß, -sch, -x,** and **-z: das gesündeste Gemüse, die frischeste Milch.**

Attributive:

Jörg hat das **kleinste** Stück Kuchen.	*Jörg has the smallest piece of cake.*

When used as a predicate adjective or as an adverb, the superlative form occurs as the phrase **am . . . -sten.**

Predicate adjective/adverb:

Hier ist der Fluß **am tiefsten.**	*Here the river is deepest.*
Er spricht **am lautesten.**	*He speaks the loudest.*

There are some deviations from the above rules. In order to facilitate pronunciation:

(a) Adjectives with stems ending in **-e** merely add an **-r** in the comparative: **leise** (*quiet*) > **leiser.**

Hans sprach **leiser** als ich.	*Hans spoke more quietly than I.*

(b) Adjectives with stems ending in **-el** or **-er** drop the **-e-** in the comparative: **dunkel** > **dunkler; teuer** > **teurer.**

Unser Auto ist **teurer** als der Volkswagen.	*Our car is more expensive than the VW.*

In addition, most monosyllabic adjectives with the stem vowels **a, o,** or **u** form the *comparative* and *superlative* by adding an umlaut to the vowel. The following adjectives which you have studied follow this pattern:

Positive	Comparative	Superlative	
alt	älter	ältest-	am ältesten
arm	ärmer	ärmst-	am ärmsten

groß	größer	größt-	am größten[1]
jung	jünger	jüngst-	am jüngsten
kalt	kälter	kältest-	am kältesten
klug	klüger	klügst-	am klügsten
krank	kränker	kränkst-	am kränksten
kurz	kürzer	kürzest-	am kürzesten
lang	länger	längst-	am längsten
schwach	schwächer	schwächst-	am schwächsten
stark	stärker	stärkst-	am stärksten
warm	wärmer	wärmst-	am wärmsten

Fred ist der jüngere Bruder.   *Fred is the younger brother.*

Hilde ist die Jüngste[2] von uns.   *Hilde is the youngest of us.*

There are a number of common adjectives and adverbs that form irregular comparatives and superlatives.

Positive	*Comparative*	*Superlative*	
gut	**besser**	**best-**	**am besten**
hoh-/hoch (*high*)	**höher**	**höchst-**	**am höchsten**
nahe (*near*)	**näher**	**nächst-**	**am nächsten**
oft	**öfter**	**meist-**	**am meisten** (*most often*)
viel	**mehr**	**meist-**	**am meisten** (*the most*)

gern   *lieber*   *liebt*   *am liebsten*

Note that **hoch** is the predicate adjective and the adverb, while **hoh-** is the attributive adjective.

     Der Berg ist **hoch**.   *The mountain is high.*

     Das ist **hoch**interessant.   *That's extremely (highly) interesting.*

But:

     Dieser **hohe** Berg heißt das Matterhorn.   *This high mountain is called the Matterhorn.*

The irregular adverb **gern** adds the meaning *to like* to the verb; the comparative **lieber** adds the meaning *to prefer to*; the superlative **am liebsten** adds the meaning *to prefer to . . . most of all* or *to like to . . . best of all.*

Sie schreibt **gern** Briefe.   *She likes to write letters.*

---

[1]Note that this is a special superlative form (not **größest**).

[2]In statements like "She is the tallest, the youngest, etc. of us," one uses the superlative of the adjective as a noun: **. . . die Jüngste von uns.** Not: **Sie ist am jüngsten von uns.**

Er trinkt **lieber** Bier.   *He prefers to drink beer.*

Wir essen **am liebsten** Obst.   *We like to eat fruit best of all.*

CHECK YOUR COMPREHENSION

Supply the appropriate adjective or adverb in parentheses.

1. Ich verstehe Deutsch _____ Englisch.   (*as well as*)
2. Ich werde leider immer _____.   (*weaker*)
3. Er nahm natürlich das _____ Zimmer.   (*more expensive*)
4. Wenn die Tage _____ werden, kommt bald der Winter.   (*shorter*)
5. Der Bahnhof ist _____ als der Flugplatz.   (*nearer*)
6. Hier sind die Zigaretten _____.   (*cheapest*)
7. Das _____ Auto war der Mercedes 600.   (*biggest*)
8. Ihr seid heute _____ gekommen.   (*later*)
9. Je _____ er ißt, desto _____ wird er.   (*more / fatter*)

II. Past perfect tense

Wir **waren** gerade am Bahnhof **angekommen,** als der Zug abfuhr.
We had just arrived at the railroad station when the train departed.

Wir **hatten abgemacht,** uns um elf Uhr zu treffen.
We had agreed to meet at eleven o'clock.

The past perfect tense is formed with the *past tense* of the auxiliaries **haben** or **sein,** and the *past participle* of the principal verb.

With **haben**	*With* **sein**	*Past perfect* *tense*

Singular

ich **hatte** gesagt	ich **war** abgefahren
du **hattest** gesagt	du **warst** abgefahren
er ⎫	er ⎫
sie ⎬ **hatte** gesagt	sie ⎬ **war** abgefahren
es ⎭	es ⎭

Plural

wir **hatten** gesagt	wir **waren** abgefahren
ihr **hattet** gesagt	ihr **wart** abgefahren
sie **hatten** gesagt	sie **waren** abgefahren

Formal

Sie **hatten** gesagt	Sie **waren** abgefahren

This tense is used to indicate that one event or action (A) had already occurred when another event (B) took place in the past. If the other event is stated, it uses the simple past tense.

      (Event B)   *(Event A)*

(1) **Als Hans ankam, hatten wir den Kaffee schon getrunken.**
      When Hans arrived, we had already drunk the coffee.

      (Event A)   *(Event B)*

(2) **Nachdem wir gegessen hatten, fuhren wir nach Hause.**
      After we had eaten, we drove home.

In example 1, the drinking of the coffee had already been completed when Hans arrived. The entire occurrence—both the drinking of the coffee and the arrival of Hans—lies in the past. In example 2, the eating precedes the driving home.

CHECK YOUR COMPREHENSION

Supply the correct form of the past perfect tense, using the verbs in parentheses.

1. **Als ich ankam, _____ die Polizei schon _____.** *(abfahren)*

2. Sie _____ drei Jahre Deutsch _____, bevor sie nach Deutschland kam. (*studieren*)

3. Bevor es zu regnen begann, _____ die Sonne _____. (*scheinen*)

4. Wir gaben das Geld sofort aus, nachdem wir es vom Vater _____ _____. (*bekommen*)

5. Wir _____ ____, daß das Wetter besser wird, aber es schneite den ganzen Tag. (*hoffen*)

III. Numbers, dates, and expressions of time

Was geschah am Samstag, dem 20. November 1982?[1]
What happened on Saturday, November 20, 1982?

Um 20 Uhr beginnt der Film.
The movie starts at 8:00 p.m.

Um Viertel vor zwölf gehe ich zu Bett.
At a quarter to twelve I go to bed.

A. Numbers

There are two major groups of numbers: the *cardinal* and the *ordinal* numbers. *Cardinal* numbers were discussed in the introductory chapter. When cardinal numbers are used as nouns, they are always feminine.

Für mich ist **die Dreizehn** eine Glückszahl.	*For me, thirteen is a lucky number.*

Ordinal numbers refer to a specific number in a series and are declined like adjectives. They rarely occur without a preceding **der-** or **ein-**word.

Er trinkt schon die **dritte** Tasse Kaffee.	*He's already drinking his third cup of coffee.*
Ihr **zweiter** Mann heißt Eugen.	*Her second husband's name is Eugene.*

When written in figures, ordinal numbers are followed by a period.

Lincolns Geburtstag ist am **12.** Februar.	*Lincoln's birthday is on February twelfth.*

Ordinal numbers are formed by adding **-t** to the cardinal numbers up to nineteen, and **-st** to twenty and above, plus the adjective ending. Note the slight irregularities in **erste, dritte, siebte,** and **achte,** and the com-

---

[1]Read: **dem zwanzigsten November neunzehnhundertzweiundachtzig.**

pounds ending in these four ordinal numbers, such as **hunderterste**
(*hundred and first*), **hundertundsiebte** (*hundred and seventh*), etc.

---

1. der die } **erste** das	19. der die } neunzehnte das	*Ordinal* *numbers*
2. zweite	20. zwanzigste	
3. **dritte**	21. einundzwanzigste	
4. vierte	30. dreißigste	
5. fünfte	40. vierzigste	
6. sechste	50. fünfzigste	
7. **siebte**	60. sechzigste	
8. **achte**	70. siebzigste	
9. neunte	80. achtzigste	
10. zehnte	90. neunzigste	
11. elfte	100. (ein)hundertste	
12. zwölfte	101. (ein)hundert**erste**	
13. dreizehnte	200. zweihundertste	
14. vierzehnte	1 000. (ein)tausendste	
15. fünfzehnte	2 000. zweitausendste	
16. sechzehnte	1 000 000. millionste	
17. siebzehnte	2 000 000. zweimillionste	
18. achtzehnte		

Ordinal numbers can be used as nouns, in which case they follow the same rules as adjectives used as nouns (see Chapter 12) and are capitalized.

Heinrich der Achte hatte sechs Frauen.

Henry the Eighth had six wives.

CHECK YOUR COMPREHENSION

Write out the number in parentheses.

1. Das ist meine _____ Tasse Kaffee. *(1)*
2. _____ dieser beiden Fahrräder ist meins. *(1)*
3. Die _____ ist meine Glückszahl. *(7)*
4. Meine Tante raucht jetzt schon die _____ Zigarette. *(6)*
5. Ihren _____ Mann kenne ich nicht. *(3)*
6. Ich war nicht in der _____ Vorlesung. *(2)*
7. Zwischen dem _____ und dem _____ Schlager hat sie etwas Unbekanntes gespielt. *(4, 5)*
8. _____ ihrer Kinder sind verheiratet. *(3)*

B. Additional times of the day

In Chapter 8 (p. 166) you learned certain common expressions with **an:** **am Morgen** (*in the morning*), **am Nachmittag** (*in the afternoon*), **am Abend** (*in the evening*), **am Montag** (*on Monday*). Here are some additional times of day:

am Vormittag	*about ten A.M. to twelve noon*	der Vormittag, -e
zu Mittag	*at noon*	der Mittag, -e
in der Nacht	*during the night*	die Nacht, ̈e
um Mitternacht	*at midnight*	die Mitternacht, ̈e

Habitual or repetitious actions are expressed by the corresponding adverbs which end in **-s.** Remember that adverbs are not capitalized.

Elsa geht **vormittags** ins Büro, und **nachmittags** macht sie Einkäufe.

In the morning Elsa goes to the office, and in the afternoon she goes shopping.

In the same way adverbs can be formed with the days of the week:

Er fährt dienstags immer nach Köln.

On Tuesdays he always goes to Cologne.

CHECK YOUR COMPREHENSION

A. Answer each question with a sentence that includes a prepositional phrase expressing a time of day.

EXAMPLE: **Wann tanzen Sie gern?**
        Ich tanze gern am Abend.

1. Wann studieren Sie am liebsten?
2. Wann schlafen Sie am besten?
3. Wann machen Sie Einkäufe?
4. Wann hören Sie auf zu arbeiten?

5. Wann beginnt diese Vorlesung?
6. Wann trinken Sie morgens die erste Tasse Kaffee?

B. Replace the prepositional time phrases with their corresponding adverbs.

1. Am Vormittag gehe ich immer zur Universität.
2. Zu Mittag essen die Deutschen meistens sehr viel.
3. Am Abend sehe ich oft einen Film im Kino oder im Fernsehen.
4. In der Nacht arbeiten viele Leute.
5. Am Sonntag gehe ich oft zur Kirche.

C. Telling time

Telling time is based on a twenty-four hour clock in German; A.M. and P.M. are not used. The twenty-four hour clock is particularly used *in official announcements* like the news, and in programs, timetables, etc.

Es ist jetzt **18.55 Uhr.**	*It is now 6:55 P.M.*
(*Read:* Es ist jetzt achtzehn Uhr fünfundfünfzig.)	
Der Film beginnt **um 20 Uhr.**	*The movie starts at 8:00 P.M.*
Der Bus fährt **um 15.38 Uhr** ab.	*The bus leaves at 3:38 P.M.*

As in English, however, the twelve-hour clock is generally used *in conversation* to indicate both morning and afternoon. Sometimes an adverb is used to indicate A.M. and P.M.

Er fährt um neun Uhr **morgens** ab.	*He's leaving at nine o'clock in the morning.*
Sie kommt um sechs Uhr **abends** an.	*She'll arrive at six o'clock in the evening.*

German is similar to English in its use of **nach** and **vor** to indicate minutes past or before the hour.

Es ist zwanzig (Minuten) **nach** neun.	*It's twenty (minutes) after nine.*
Es ist zehn (Minuten) **vor** acht.	*It's ten (minutes) before eight.*

Fractions are more commonly used—for the twelve-hour clock only—to express the English *a quarter after, half past,* and *a quarter to.*

Es ist Viertel nach zwei.	*It's a quarter after two.*
Es ist Viertel vor eins.	*It's a quarter to one.*
Es ist dreiviertel vier.	*It's 3:45 (lit., three-quarters of the way to four).*
Es ist halb acht.	*It's 7:30 (lit., halfway to eight).*

Thus 7:45 P.M. can be expressed in all of the following ways:

Es ist fünfzehn Minuten vor acht.
Es ist sieben Uhr fünfundvierzig.
Es ist Viertel vor acht.
Es ist dreiviertel acht.
Es ist neunzehn Uhr fünfundvierzig.

CHECK YOUR COMPREHENSION

A. Read the following times as A.M. and P.M. times in German, using (a) the colloquial and (b) the official way, wherever possible.

1. Es ist fünf Uhr zwanzig.
2. Es ist 3 Uhr 38.
3. Mein Bus fährt um 9.29 Uhr.
4. Ich trinke meinen Kaffee immer um Viertel vor sechs.
5. Um halb acht höre ich meistens Nachrichten.
6. Es ist gerade viertel nach eins.

B. Read the following times as many ways as you can, in both the colloquial and the official ways.

1. 4:10 A.M.
2. 5:27 P.M.
3. 8:45 P.M.
4. 10:15 A.M.

D. Dates

Dates are always written in the order: day, month, year.

Peter ist **am 11. November 1957** geboren.	*Peter was born on November 11, 1957.*
Konrad Adenauer wurde **am 5. Januar 1876** geboren.	*Konrad Adenauer was born on January 5, 1876.*
Am 22. 3. 1832 starb Goethe in Weimar.	*On March 22, 1832, Goethe died in Weimar.*

Note that if a person is still alive the verb construction **ist geboren** has to be used, if the person is deceased the construction is **wurde geboren.**

It is not possible to say *in 1832* in German; say either **1832** or **im Jahr 1832.**

Goethe starb 1832.
Goethe starb im Jahr 1832.

When you ask for the date, you may say it in either of two ways:

Welches Datum haben wir heute? }
Der wievielte ist heute?   *What's the date today?*

E. Definite and indefinite time expressions

Certain time expressions are used without any preposition to specify when something happened or will happen. These must be specific enough to be located on the calendar or the clock. Such *definite* time expressions are in the accusative case.

Er ist **jeden Winter** in die Alpen gefahren.	*He went to the Alps every winter.*
Wir fahren **nächsten Montag** in Urlaub.	*We are going on vacation next Monday.*

The expressions **heute morgen** and **heute früh** (*this morning*), **gestern abend** (*last night*), **morgen nachmittag** (*tomorrow afternoon*), etc., are considered adverbs of time and therefore are not capitalized.

Other time expressions with no preposition refer to *indefinite time* and take the *genitive case*.

Eines Tages wird er zurückkommen.	*He'll come back someday.*
Eines Abends ging ich sehr früh zu Bett.	*One evening I went to bed quite early.*

CHECK YOUR COMPREHENSION

A. Supply the dates.

1. Mein Geburtstag ist am _____.
2. Vor drei Wochen war der _____.
3. George Washingtons Geburtstag ist am _____.
4. Welches Datum haben wir heute?
5. Wann sind Sie geboren? Und Ihre Brüder und Schwestern?

B. Fill in the time expressions as indicated in parentheses.

1. Wir fahren _____ in die Berge.   (*every summer*)
2. Sie geht fast _____ in ein Café.   (*every afternoon*)
3. Ich reise _____ in die Schweiz.   (*next Tuesday*)
4. _____ wird er ein bekannter Mann sein.   (*someday*)
5. Ich habe _____ einige Gäste eingeladen.   (*last week*)
6. _____ stand er sehr früh auf.   (*one morning*)

Conversation

außer Atem	*out of breath*
Zu dumm!	*Too bad! How dumb (of me)!*
Allerdings!	*Indeed! I should say so!*
Sei mir nicht böse!	*Don't be angry with me!*
Abgemacht!	*Agreed! It's a deal!*
Ehrlich?	*Really? Honestly?*

NACH DER VORLESUNG

Werner ist Physikstudent an einer deutschen Universität, und seine Freundin Helga studiert im vierten Semester Medizin. Beide sind 23 Jahre alt. Helga kommt ganz außer Atem in die Mensa.[1] Dort findet sie ihren Freund. Er sitzt halb träumend vor seinem Essen.

Helga	Werner, ach, da bist du ja!
Werner	Ja, natürlich. Wo sonst? Es ist doch schon . . . (*schaut auf seine Uhr*) . . . zwanzig nach zwölf und höchste Zeit zum Essen.
Helga	Aber wir hatten doch eine Verabredung, uns um Viertel vor zwölf vor dem Labor° zu treffen und in der Stadt zu essen.
Werner	Aber hatten wir das nicht für morgen abgemacht?
Helga	Nein, für heute.
Werner	Du, da habe ich mich tatsächlich geirrt. Zu dumm!
Helga	Allerdings!
Werner	Bitte, sei mir nicht böse. Setz dich doch hin. Ich habe schon für uns beide das Essen geholt.
Helga	Na gut, aber dann essen wir morgen in der Stadt. Unsere Seminare fangen doch erst nachmittags um halb fünf an.
Werner	Abgemacht! Aber weißt du, die Vorlesung von Frau Professor Schürmann heute morgen war fantastisch, klar und unterhaltend.

lab(oratory)

[1]**Die Mensa** is the student cafeteria at the university. The word is of Latin origin, meaning "table."

Helga   Ehrlich? Eine unterhaltende Mathematik-Vorlesung ist wirklich etwas Ungewöhnliches!

Werner   Aber die Schürmann hat wirklich Humor.

Helga   Werner, morgen komme ich am besten mit zur Vorlesung. Dann können wir zusammen in die Stadt fahren.

QUESTIONS ON THE CONVERSATION

1. Wer sind Werner und Helga? Was studieren sie?
2. Wo findet Helga ihren Freund Werner? Was tut er?
3. Wieviel Uhr ist es gerade?
4. Wo und wann wollten sich Werner und Helga treffen?
5. Wer hat sich geirrt?
6. Ist Helga ihrem Freund böse?
7. Wo will Helga morgen essen?
8. Welche Vorlesung findet Werner klar und unterhaltend?
9. Warum will Helga morgen mit zur Vorlesung kommen?

PERSONAL QUESTIONS

1. Irren Sie sich oft? Geben Sie ein Beispiel!
2. Wenn ein Freund (oder eine Freundin) zu einer Verabredung zu spät kommt, sind Sie ihm (oder ihr) böse? Was sagen Sie zu ihm (ihr)?
3. Wie finden Sie die Vorlesungen Ihrer Professoren? Sind sie meistens klar und unterhaltend, oder . . .?
4. Haben Ihre Professoren Humor? Glauben Sie, daß das wichtig ist? Warum oder warum nicht?

Practice

A. Fill in the appropriate comparative form of the adjectives or adverbs in parentheses.

1. Sind die Studenten an dieser Universität _____ oder _____ in Amerika? (*older / younger than*)
2. Finden Sie diese Vorlesung _____ und _____ die erste? (*clearer / more interesting than*)
3. Immer _____ Menschen sagen, daß die Luft immer _____ wird. (*more / dirtier*)
4. Ein _____ Land ist nicht immer _____ ein _____ Land. (*smaller / weaker than / larger*)

5. Die _____ Bands sind _____, aber manchmal _____ die _____ Bands. (*louder / crazier / more entertaining than / quieter*)

6. Fahren die Europäer im Stadtverkehr _____ oder _____ die Amerikaner? (*faster / slower than*)

B. Fill in the appropriate superlative form of the adjectives or adverbs in parentheses.

1. Wer am _____ studiert, verdient später am _____ Geld. (*lang / viel*)
2. Der Urlaub ist für uns die _____ aber auch die _____ Zeit des Jahres. (*schön / teuer*)
3. Am _____ fahre ich ins Rheintal. (*gern*)
4. Der _____ Berg in Deutschland ist die Zugspitze. (*hoch*)
5. Amerika ist eines der _____, _____ und _____ Länder der Welt. (*groß / stark / reich*)
6. Im Dezember sind die Tage am _____. (*kurz*)

C. Change the following sentences into the past perfect tense.

1. Der Kaffee sah gestern dunkler aus.
2. 1982 gab es in Deutschland viele Touristen.
3. Die Berge hatten viel mehr Regen, als ich dachte.
4. Bis zu seinem Unfall machte ihm das Skilaufen viel Spaß.
5. Sie wohnten drei Jahre in Marburg, bevor sie nach Basel kamen.
6. Der Bus fuhr einfach weiter, ohne auf mich zu warten.
7. Als er im Hotel ankam, war sein Gepäck schon da.
8. Weil das Wetter schön war, ging ich ohne Regenschirm in die Stadt.
9. Bevor er meine Schwester heiratete, wohnte er lange in Frankreich.
10. Sie fuhren schon ab, als ich anrief.

D. Give the English equivalent.

1. Können Sie mir bitte einen Scheck über DM 526, 72 wechseln?
2. Sind Sie älter oder jünger als 18 Jahre?
3. Geben Sie mehr als $225.00 für Ihre Wohnung aus?
4. Das Benzin ist schon wieder um 16% teurer geworden. Wieviel bezahlen Sie jetzt für Benzin?
5. Welcher Präsident der Vereinigten Staaten wurde am 22.2.1732 geboren?
6. Ich bin 1, 72 m groß. (m = Meter)

E. Write down and read aloud the exact time as shown on the **Weltzeituhr**, first assuming that the clock shows the A.M. time.

EXAMPLE: A.M. In Berlin ist es jetzt genau vierundzwanzig Uhr zwölf. (*official*)
Or: In Berlin ist es jetzt genau zwölf Minuten nach zwölf (mitternachts). (*colloquial*)
P.M. In Berlin ist es jetzt genau zwölf Uhr zwölf. (*official*)
Or: In Berlin ist es jetzt genau zwölf Minuten nach zwölf (mittags). (*colloquial*)

1. London (11:12)
2. New York (6:12)
3. Johannisburg (1:12)

4. Moskau (3:12)
5. Schanghai (8:12)
6. Sidney (9:12)

Then announce the official time, assuming that the clock shows the P.M. time.

Vocabulary development

A. *Sind Sie ledig, verheiratet oder geschieden?*

There are a number of words relating to marriage or getting married that you should learn.

heiraten = *to marry*

Er hat meine alte Freundin geheiratet.	*He has married my old girl friend.*

But (*to be*) *married* = **verheiratet sein:**

Er ist mit meiner alten Freundin verheiratet.	*He is married to my old girl friend.*

The opposite of **verheiratet** is **ledig** (*single*).

Er ist schon 36 Jahre alt und immer noch ledig.	*He is already 36 years old and still single.*

Die Hochzeit (literally, *high time!*) denotes all the celebrations and festivities connected with a wedding.

Wann werden die beiden Hochzeit feiern?	*When will the two of them celebrate their wedding?*

Die Trauung denotes the wedding—more specifically, the civil and/or church ceremony.

Die Ehe denotes *matrimony*—the state of being married.

geschieden = *divorced*
sich scheiden lassen von = *to get a divorce from*

Helmut hat sich von seiner zweiten Frau scheiden lassen.	*Helmut got a divorce from his second wife.*

B. Are you right or wrong?

In Chapter 7 you encountered the expression **recht haben** (*to be right*). The opposite would be **unrecht haben** (*to be wrong*). The verb **sich irren** means *to make a mistake, to be mistaken*.

Ich habe mich geirrt.	*I made a mistake.*
Da irren Sie sich!	*There you are mistaken.*

But if you make a trivial mistake, such as an error in spelling, the expression **einen Fehler machen** should be used:

Hier hast du einen kleinen Fehler gemacht.	*Here you made a small mistake.*

Communicative exercises

A. Student A makes the statements below to B, who counters with a comparative. Student C breaks in with a superlative.

Ich habe ein teures Auto.
Ich spreche sehr gut Deutsch.

Meine Freundin (mein Freund) ist intelligent.
Ich spiele gut Klavier.
Ich bin groß.
Wir haben weiße Zähne.
Ich habe elegante Stiefel.
Wir tragen moderne Kleider.
Im Winter ist unser Haus sehr warm.
Wir schlafen in bequemen Betten.

Now, invent some statements of your own.

B. Student A makes the statements below and B (more modest than B above!) counters by saying: . . . **(genau) so . . . wie . . .**

Ich bin müde.
Wir sind hungrig.
Ich laufe sehr schnell.
Ich kenne Rita (Hanspeter, etc.) sehr gut.
Mein Vater hat viel Geld.
Unser Wohnzimmer ist sehr groß.

C. One student asks the whole class the following questions. Who can answer the fastest in a correct sentence?

Wie heißt der höchste Berg der Welt? Europas? der USA?
Welches ist der kürzeste Tage im Jahr? der längste?
Welches ist der größte Staat der USA? der kleinste?
Welches ist der längste Fluß der Welt?
Welches Land hat die meisten Einwohner der Welt?
Welches ist die größte Stadt der Welt?

Now, ask: **Wer hat einen Fehler gemacht?** and make the corrections (**der höchste Berg Europas ist nicht . . . sondern . . . .** , etc.) and then invent some questions of your own.

D. Student A asks B the following questions. B answers and counters with: **Und du?** A replies.

Um wieviel Uhr gehst du zu Bett?
Wann stehst du auf? (*to get up*)
Um wieviel Uhr fängt die Deutschstunde (*German lesson*) an?
Um wieviel Uhr gehst du nach Hause?
Wieviele Stunden arbeitest du pro (*per*) Woche?
Gehst du jeden Tag in die Stadt arbeiten? Oder nur montags, mittwochs, etc.?
Wann bist du geboren?
Wie alt bist du jetzt auf den Monat genau (*to the month*)?
Heiratest du bald? Oder willst du lange ledig bleiben?
Wieviele Kinder möchtest du haben?

Now, formulate some questions of your own and address them to your neighbor.

E. Ask your neighbor what he/she usually does in the morning, at noon, in the afternoon, in the evening, at night, and at midnight. Then tell him/her what you generally do at these times.

Reading

EHE ODER PARTNERSCHAFT OHNE TRAUSCHEIN?° *partnership without marriage license*

   In den letzten zehn Jahren ist in der Bundesrepublik wie auch in der DDR die Zahl der Ehescheidungen bemerkenswert gestiegen. In den fünfziger Jahren° gab es in Deutschland als Resultat des Krieges *in the fifties* sehr hohe Ehescheidungsraten. Diese hohen Zahlen sind inzwischen wieder erreicht. Innerhalb von zwölf Jahren ist die Zahl der Ehescheidungen um fast 100 Prozent gestiegen. So gab es im Jahr 1975 in der Bundesrepublik allein 106 829 Ehescheidungen.

   Aber die Gründe für diese Entwicklung sind heute ganz anderer Art als nach dem Krieg, vor fünfundzwanzig oder dreißig Jahren. In Industriestaaten wie Deutschland ist die Frau heutzutage häufiger in einem Beruf tätig als früher. Viele Frauen sind durch ihren Beruf un-

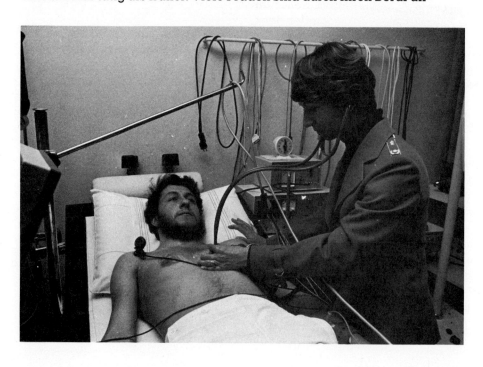

7. Welche schwierige Frage muß man in einer konventionellen oder unkonventionellen Ehe lösen?
8. Wofür sollen die Frauen, Ihrer Meinung nach (*in your opinion*), die besten Jahre ihres Lebens hergeben: für die Kinder und den Haushalt oder für einen Beruf?
9. Soll der Mann mehr im Haushalt mithelfen, so daß die Frau einen Beruf haben kann?
   a. *Für die Männer:* Werden Sie eines Tages eine solche Arbeitsteilung akzeptieren?   → Some day
   b. *Für die Frauen:* Gefällt Ihnen eine solche Arbeitsteilung?
10. Scheint die Gesellschaft in Amerika die Ehe ohne Trauschein zu akzeptieren?

Meiner Meinung nach —
in my opinion —

Review

A. Supply the appropriate comparative form by using the adjective or adverb in parentheses.

1. Mein Freund hatte das _____ Haus eigentlich nie gesehen.   (*schön*)
2. Je _____ Obst ich esse, desto _____ werde ich sein.   (*viel, gesund*)
3. Studenten sind viel _____, als man denkt.   (*aufmerksam*)
4. Vater ist _____, als wir wußten.   (*krank*)
5. Ich finde den Kuchen viel _____ als den Kaffee.   (*gut*)
6. Die _____ Kirche steht in der Stadtmitte.   (*alt*)
7. Thomas nimmt immer den _____ Zug.   (*spät*)
8. Es gibt immer _____ Parkplätze in dieser Stadt.   (*viel*)

B. Supply the appropriate superlative form by using the adjective or adverb in parentheses.

1. Der Dom in Köln ist nicht der _____ und auch nicht der _____ in Deutschland.   (*hoch / alt*)
2. Nach dem Abendessen gehe ich _____ ins Kino.   (*gern*)
3. Nächsten Samstag gehen wir zum Abendessen in das _____ Restaurant der Stadt. Leider ist es aber auch das _____.   (*gut / teuer*)
4. Die _____ Leute haben keine Ahnung, wie schön Skilaufen sein kann.   (*viele*)
5. Seine dritte Frau ist _____.   (*intelligent*)
6. Seit 12 Jahren haben wir jetzt die _____ Ehescheidungsrate.   (*hoch*)
7. Zum Glück war das _____ Buch _____.   (*dick / interessant*)

C. Tell someone the following story in the past perfect tense. Those verb forms which have to be changed are in italics.

DER UNFALL

Eines Tages—es *war* genau am 27. Februar dieses Jahres—*fuhr* ich mit meiner Freundin am späten Nachmittag auf der Autobahn in Richtung Regensburg. Es *schneite* den ganzen Tag. Das Autofahren war höchst gefährlich. Um etwa 17.30 Uhr *hielten* wir auf einem Parkplatz *an*, um zu Abend zu essen. Die frische Luft *machte* uns hungrig.

Plötzlich *hörten* wir einen furchtbaren Lärm. Es war ein Unfall: Ein Mercedes *ist* auf einen langsam fahrenden Bus *aufgefahren (to ram)*. Der Mercedes-Fahrer *versuchte* wahrscheinlich, den Bus zu überholen, aber das war in dem hohen Schnee nicht möglich. Der Autofahrer war schwer verletzt *(badly injured)*.

Wir liefen sofort zum nächsten Telefon und riefen die Polizei an. Zum Glück gibt es auf den deutschen Autobahnen alle 1000 Meter ein Autobahn-Telefon. Nachdem ein Rettungshubschrauber *(rescue helicopter)* ankam und den schwer verletzten Fahrer zum nächsten Krankenhaus *brachte*, fuhren wir weiter. Als wir endlich in Regensburg ankamen, waren wir sehr hungrig. Aber alle Restaurants *machten* schon *zu*.

D. Express in German.

1. Unfortunately, traveling from New York to London is becoming more and more expensive.
2. In my opinion, the fastest bicyclists are in France.
3. The air is best in the highest mountains.
4. German is her fifth language.
5. The most beautiful castles are in the oldest regions of France and Germany.
6. At eight o'clock in the morning he listens to the news.
7. This is not the most expensive car. There are even more expensive cars than this one.
8. Do you know George Orwell's book *1984*?
9. The number of divorces had climbed remarkably.
10. Often the worst problem has the simplest solution.
11. It had been her fourth accident this year.
12. Do you prefer to drink your coffee with or without sugar?
13. Someday the last shall be the first.

Guided composition

What are your plans for this week (month, summer, year, etc.)? Look at your calendar and write down in German when you plan to do what. For example, you might want to see a movie this week, or study for a class or pay the rent for your apartment.

Write down in German your activities in any given day, indicating the appropriate time. You may also wish to state how you intend to organize your daily work differently from now on.

Chapter vocabulary

Nouns

die	Art, -en	kind, sort
der	Atem	breath
der	Beruf, -e	profession
die	Beziehung, -en	relationship
die	Chance, -n	chance
die	Ehe, -n	marriage
die	Ehescheidung, -en	divorce
der	Fehler, -	mistake
die	Frage, -n	question
der	Geburtstag, -e	birthday
die	Gesellschaft, -en	society
das	Gesetz, -e	law
die	Glückszahl, -en	lucky number
der	Grund, ̈e	reason (for something)
der	Haushalt, -e	household
die	Hochzeit, -en	wedding
der	Humor	humor, sense of humor
der	Kapitalismus	capitalism
das	Krankenhaus, ̈er	hospital
die	Lösung, -en	solution
die	Meinung, -en	opinion
	meiner Meinung nach	in my opinion
der	Osten	east
der	Partner, -	partner
die	Rate, -n	rate
der	Sozialismus	socialism
die	Trauung, -en	wedding ceremony (civil or church)
die	Uhr, -en	clock, watch
	Wieviel Uhr ist es?	What time is it?
die	Vorlesung, -en	lecture
die	Zahl, -en	number

Verbs

ab·machen	to arrange, agree upon
auf·fahren (fährt), fuhr, (ist) aufgefahren	to ram
akzeptieren	to accept
feiern	to celebrate
heiraten	to marry
sich irren	to be mistaken, make a mistake
lösen	to solve
passen: zueinander passen	to be compatible, suit each other
scheiden, schied, geschieden	to divorce, separate
sterben (stirbt), starb, (ist) gestorben	to die
teilen	to share, divide
zurück·kehren, (ist) zurückgekehrt	to return

Other words

bemerkenswert	remarkable, noteworthy
böse (+ dat.)	angry (with)
dumm	stupid, dumb
ehrlich	honest
genau	exact
gering	insignificant, slight
geschieden	divorced
häufig	frequent
hoch, hoh-	high
hungrig	hungry
je . . . desto	the (more) . . . the (more)
klar	clear
konventionell	conventional
ledig	single (unmarried)
liberal	liberal
menschlich	human
nahe	near
sonst	otherwise, else
sozial	social
tätig	employed, occupied, active
unabhängig	independent
ungewöhnlich	unusual

See also the ordinal numbers and expressions of time on pp. 280–287.

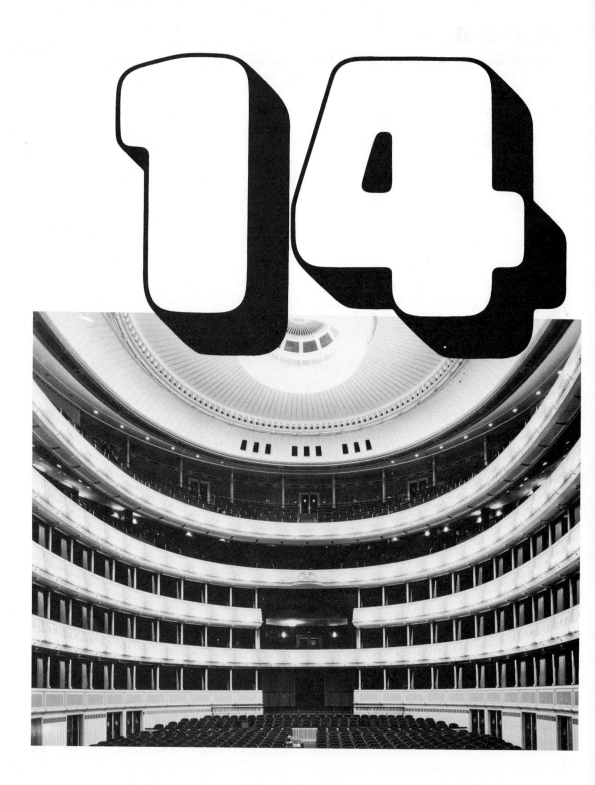

Mini-dialogues

Student(in) A Wie heißt der junge Mann, von dem du kürzlich gesprochen hast?

B Ich weiß nicht, wen du meinst.

A Den Psychologie-Studenten, den du beim Tanzen kennengelernt hast.

B Ach so. Wart mal, das ist Rudi Sellner. Warum fragst du?

A Ich habe ihn gestern abend in der Oper gesehen, aber konnte mich nicht mehr an seinen Namen erinnern.

B Er ist sehr nett, nicht wahr?

A Wo sind die Eintrittskarten, die ich dir vor einigen Tagen gegeben habe?

B Welche Eintrittskarten? Ich weiß nicht, wovon du sprichst.

A Na, die Eintrittskarten für das Konzert morgen abend.

B Ach ja. Ich glaube, die habe ich in das Buch gelegt, das auf meinem Tisch liegt.

A Weißt du, wann er ankommt?

B Heute abend. Das ist alles, was ich weiß.

A Hat er jemand, der ihn am Flughafen abholen wird?

B Oh ja, mach dir keine Sorgen! Seine Freundin.

A What's the name of the young fellow you recently talked about?

B I don't know who(m) you mean.

A The psychology student you got to know at the dance.

B Oh yes. Wait a minute. That's Rudi Sellner. Why do you ask?

A I saw him last night at the Opera but could not remember his name.

B He's very nice, isn't he?

A Where are the (admission) tickets I gave you a few days ago?

B Which tickets? I don't know what you are talking about.

A Well, the tickets for the concert tomorrow night.

B Oh well, of course. I believe I put them in the book that's lying there on my desk.

A Do you know when he'll arrive?

B Tonight. That's all I know.

A Does he have somebody who'll pick him up at the airport?

B Oh yes, don't worry! His girlfriend.

Grammar explanations

I. Relative pronouns

Dies ist der psychologische Test, den wir gestern besprochen haben.
This is the psychological test that we discussed yesterday.

Das alte Haus, in dem wir wohnen, gehört nicht uns.
The old house in which we live doesn't belong to us.

Der Psychologe, dessen Theorien ich nicht verstehe, ist sehr bekannt.
The psychologist whose theories I don't understand is very well known.

Die Kaiser Österreichs, die wir gestern im Seminar besprachen, waren sehr populär.
The emperors of Austria, whom we discussed yesterday in the seminar, were very popular.

A relative pronoun introduces a dependent clause, which relates to and further characterizes an element in the main clause.

The singer whom I heard is famous.

In this sentence the dependent clause *whom I heard*, introduced by the relative pronoun *whom*, relates to the singer and tells us something about him: he is not just a singer, but that particular singer *whom I heard*. The forms of relative pronouns in German are quite similar to those of the definite article **der, die, das.**

	Singular Masculine	Feminine	Neuter	Plural All genders	*Relative pronoun forms*
nom.	der	die	das	die	
acc.	den	die	das	die	
dat.	dem	der	dem	**denen**	
gen.	**dessen**	**deren**	**dessen**	**deren**	

In the preceding table, note that certain forms differ from those of the definite article: the genitive in all four instances, and the dative plural.

In German the relative clause is set off by commas. Since it is a dependent clause, the inflected verb stands at the end of the clause.

Wie heißt der Schlager, den man jetzt überall hört?   *What's the name of the song (that) one hears everywhere these days?*

The *gender* and *number* of the relative pronoun are determined by the noun to which the relative pronoun is related. The *case* of the relative pronoun depends on how it is used in its own clause. In the above example, the relative pronoun **den** functions as a direct object of the verb **hören** and is therefore in the accusative.

In English the relative pronoun may sometimes be omitted, as suggested in the above example. This omission is not possible in German.

Der Sänger, der kürzlich am Fernsehen sang, ist sehr bekannt.

masc. sing.   subj. (nominative)

The singer who sang on television recently is very famous.

Hier ist das Bild **des Politikers, den** ich kürzlich getroffen habe.

masc. sing.   dir. obj. (accusative)

Here's the picture of the politician whom I met recently.

Die Frau, mit **der** er tanzt, ist seine Freundin.

fem. sing.   obj. of mit (dative)

The woman he's dancing with (with whom he's dancing) is his friend.

Hier ist **das Bild, dessen** Bedeutung ich nicht interpretieren kann.

neuter sing.   genitive

Here's the picture whose meaning I can't interpret.

CHECK YOUR COMPREHENSION

Fill in the appropriate form of the relative pronoun.

Procedure: locate the antecedent, determine its gender and number; determine the role of the relative pronoun in its own clause and then choose the correct form.

1. Das ist das neue Haus, _____ ich letzte Woche gekauft habe.
2. Das ist übrigens der Professor, bei _____ ich studiere.
3. Nicht alle Studenten, _____ dieses Buch gelesen haben, konnten es verstehen.
4. Die Band, _____ Musik ich gehört habe, ist aus Berlin.
5. Die Professorin, von _____ ich viel gehört, aber von _____ ich noch nichts gelesen habe, ist in Amerika sehr bekannt.
6. Der Mercedes gehört zu den teuersten Wagen, _____ es gibt.
7. Das Kind, _____ wir geholfen hatten, war ganz außer Atem.
8. Es gibt viele Probleme, _____ Lösung nicht einfach ist.

II. Interrogatives introducing dependent clauses

Das Erste, **was** die Wiener wieder aufbauten, war die Staatsoper.
The first thing that the Viennese rebuilt was the Opera House.

Ich weiß nicht, mit **wem** sie tanzt.
I don't know with whom she's dancing (who she's dancing with).

Er weiß sicher, **wann** sie ankommen wird.
He must know when she'll arrive.

Peter erklärte, **warum** er gestern nicht hier war.
Peter explained why he wasn't here yesterday.

Wer viel Zeit hat, hat meistens kein Geld.
He who has lots of time usually has no money.

Interrogatives like **wann, warum, was, wer, wie, wieviel, wo, woher, wohin, wovon,** etc., often introduce a dependent clause (and therefore use dependent word order).

Ich weiß nicht, **wann** er ankommt.	*I don't know when he's arriving.*
Ich weiß, **wo** er ist.	*I know where he is.*
Wer weiß, **wieviel** dieses Buch kostet?	*Who knows how much this book costs?*
Sie wußten nicht, **woher** er kam.	*They didn't know where he was coming from.*

When so used, **wer** must be declined in the usual fashion.

Ich weiß nicht, **wer** dich angerufen hat.	*I don't know who called you.*
Sag mir, **wen** ich anrufen soll.	*Tell me whom I should call.*
Er wollte uns nicht sagen, mit **wem** er getanzt hat.	*He wouldn't tell us who(m) he danced with.*
Sag mir, **wessen**[1] Freund du bist, und ich sage dir, wer du bist.	*Tell me whose friend you are, and I'll tell you who you are.*

Especially in proverbs, **wer** and **was** often occur as relative pronouns that refer to no specific, identifiable noun. In this case they have the sense of *he who* or *whoever*, and *that which* or *whatever*.

Wer zuletzt lacht, lacht am besten.	*He who laughs last, laughs best.*
Was ich nicht weiß, macht mich nicht heiß.	*What I don't know doesn't bother me.*

[1]**Wessen** (*whose*) is the genitive form of **wer**. It can also be used as an interrogative, but in the spoken language it is not heard very often. **Wessen Buch ist das?** *Whose book is this?* Preferable in German: **Wem gehört dieses Buch?** *To whom does this book belong?*

Innenansicht des Stephandoms im Wien

Was must also be used as a relative pronoun to refer back to:

(a) a *neuter superlative adjective* (including expressions like **das Beste, das Erste, das Letzte,** etc.)

Das Beste, was er jetzt tun kann, ist nichts zu sagen.	*The best he can do now is to say nothing.*
Das Erste, was ich jetzt brauche, ist etwas zu essen.	*The first thing I need now is something to eat.*

(b) indefinite pronouns like **alles, etwas, nichts, viel, wenig,** etc.

Es gibt **nichts, was** er nicht weiß.	*There's nothing he doesn't know.*
Das ist **alles, was** sie sagte.	*That's all she said.*[1]

CHECK YOUR COMPREHENSION

A. Begin the following sentences with **Ich weiß nicht,** and make the appropriate changes.

[1]**Was** may also refer to the whole idea expressed in the preceding clause. **Sie lachte nur, was ihn sehr böse machte.** *She only laughed, which made him very angry.*

1. Wieviel Uhr ist es?
2. Warum ist er noch nicht hier?
3. Wem gehört das Bild?

4. Wann ist Helga zurückgekehrt?
5. Wer hat sich geirrt?

B. Fill in the appropriate form of the indefinite relative pronoun **wer** or **was.**

1. Es gibt nichts, _____ Franz nicht kann.
2. _____ soviel Geld hat wie er, braucht nicht mehr.
3. _____ ich nicht verstehen kann, ist der Schmutz in diesem Haus.
4. Das Letzte, _____ ich jetzt brauche, ist mehr Arbeit.
5. _____ dir das sagte, ist dumm.
6. Es gibt etwas, _____ ich noch nicht weiß.
7. _____ nicht für uns ist, ist gegen uns.
8. Das ist das Schönste, _____ ich je gesehen habe.

Conversation

das hat keine Eile	*no need to hurry*
einen Test machen	*to take an examination*
mir knurrt der Magen	*my stomach is growling*
zum Ausdruck kommen	*to be expressed*
Genau!	*Exactly!*
Im Moment kann ich nur an eines denken.	*At the moment I can think only of one thing.*

DER PSYCHOLOGE

Franz und Ferdi[1] sind Studenten an der Universität Wien.° Vienna
Franz ist im zweiten Semester Psychologie und Ferdi im ersten
Semester Germanistik. Sie wohnen zusammen in einer klei-
nen gemieteten Wohnung und sind auf dem Weg nach Hause
von der Universität.

Franz   Du, wir müssen uns beeilen.

---

[1]**Ferdi** is a nickname for **Ferdinand.** For many first names the nicknames used in
Austria may also end in **-l,** from **-lein,** as in **Franz > Franzl.** But nowadays this form
is heard more often in the countryside than in the city.

Universität Wien, Hauptportal

Ferdi   Warum denn?

Franz   Hast du's schon vergessen? Du hast mir doch versprochen, den psychologischen Test zu machen, den wir kürzlich im Seminar besprochen haben.

Ferdi   Ach so, ja. Aber das hat keine Eile. Ich will zuerst im Café da drüben etwas essen. Mir knurrt der Magen.

Franz   Gut! Aber dann schnell nach Hause!

(Sie setzen sich an einen Tisch auf dem Bürgersteig.)

Ferdi   Wie heißt der Test schon wieder, von dem du so begeistert
bist?

Franz   Es ist ein „Thematischer Apperzeptionstest".[2] Wir zeigen
dir einige Bilder, deren Bedeutung du interpretieren sollst.

Ferdi   Ach ja, ich verstehe. Dabei soll meine Persönlichkeit zum
Ausdruck kommen.   *Imagine, for example*

Franz   Allerdings. Stell dir zum Beispiel vor, auf einer Test-Karte
siehst du einen Mann, der träumend vor einem Bild steht.

Ferdi   Und ich soll dann sagen, was auf dem Bild ist und woran
der Mann denkt?

Franz   Genau!   *I'm sorry*

Ferdi   Es tut mir leid. Im Moment kann ich nur an eines denken:
auf dem Bild ist eine Sachertorte,[3] und der Mann denkt „Ich bin
aber wirklich sehr hungrig".

QUESTIONS ON THE CONVERSATION

1. Wo und was studieren Franz und Ferdi?

[2]In a "Thematic Apperception Test" the subject is usually given a series of pictures
showing human beings in various situations or predicaments. From the problems that
the subject reads into the picture the psychologist may draw some interesting, if not
wholly accurate, conclusions about the subject's personality.

[3]A rich chocolate cake with a layer of apricot jam, covered with chocolate frosting and
served with whipped cream, a well-known Viennese specialty.

2. Wieviele Semester haben Franz und Ferdi schon studiert?
3. Was hat Ferdi seinem Freund versprochen?
4. Was will Ferdi noch tun, bevor er nach Hause geht?
5. Wie heißt der Test, von dem Franz so begeistert ist?
6. Was soll Ferdi mit den Bildern des Tests machen? *tun*
7. Was ist auf der Test-Karte, die Franz beschreibt (*describes*)?
8. Was ist auf dem Bild, und was denkt der Mann, der träumend vor dem Bild steht?

PERSONAL QUESTIONS

1. Was halten Sie von diesem Test?
2. Haben Sie je einen solchen Test gemacht?
3. Glauben Sie, daß dabei Ihre Persönlichkeit zum Ausdruck kam?

[handwritten: halten von — Think about]

[handwritten: Was halten sie von dem Buch — What do you Think about The book.]

Practice

A. Fill in the indicated forms.

1. Ist Inge das Mädchen, *mit dem* _____ Heinz gearbeitet hat? (*with whom*)
2. Hast du das Buch schon gelesen, *das* du kürzlich gekauft hast? (*which*)
3. Dies ist mein Freund, *dessen* Vater in Hamburg wohnt. (*whose*)
4. Der Zug, *mit dem* ich nach Hamburg fuhr, kam 33 Minuten zu spät an. (*by which*)
5. Gehören Sie zu den Männern, *deren* Frauen nicht an die Emanzipation glauben? (*whose*)
6. Dies ist der Professor, *von dem* _____ ich am meisten gelernt habe. (*from whom*)
7. Der Tisch, *an dem* ich arbeite, ist aus dem 18. Jahrhundert. (*at which*)
8. Wie heißt die Universität, _____ Sie studieren? (*at which*)

[handwritten: can't use contractions for relative pronouns]

B. Fill in the appropriate form of **wer** or **was**.

1. _____ das sagt, weiß nicht, _____ er sagt.
2. _____ nicht weiß, _____ er tun soll, soll mich fragen.
3. _____ Deutsch gelernt hat, kann auch andere Sprachen lernen.
4. Mit _____ bist du nach Zürich gereist? Mit deinem Freund?
5. Ich weiß nicht, _____ er das Auto gegeben hat.
6. _____ hast du mitgebracht? Deine Freundin oder eine Kollegin?
7. _____ hast du mitgebracht? Bier oder Wein?
8. Von _____ hast du diese gute Nachricht gehört?
9. Bei _____ wohnen diese zwei Studenten?
10. Tun Sie das Beste, _____ Sie können.

C. Combine each pair of sentences by using the appropriate relative pronoun.

EXAMPLE: Was denkt der Mann? Er steht träumend vor einem Bild.
Was denkt der Mann, der träumend vor einem Bild steht?

1. Zeigen Sie mir den Anzug. Sie haben den Anzug gestern gekauft.
2. Endlich traf ich den Mann. Helga ist mit dem Mann verheiratet.
3. Das ist eine Studentin. Sie ist sehr gut in Deutsch.
4. Ich kenne jetzt die Leute. Du hast so oft von den Leuten gesprochen.
5. Wieviel kosteten die Blumen? Sie standen auf dem Tisch.
6. Ich kenne die Frau nicht. Dieser Student wohnt bei der Frau.
7. Wiederhole bitte das Wort. Du verstehst die Bedeutung dieses Wortes nicht.
8. Die Schlager sind aus dem Westen. Die Jugendlichen hören die Schlager am liebsten.

D. Express in German.

1. There is nothing he doesn't know.
2. All you said is correct.
3. What I like most is too expensive for me.
4. Who(m) are you talking about?
5. Tell me what he said about your friend.

E. Give the English equivalent.

1. Ich glaube nichts, was Willi uns erzählt hat.
2. Wer zur Universität geht, hat nicht viel Zeit zum Vergnügen.
3. Willst du wissen, wem dieser Wagen gehört?
4. Was du studiert hast, wirst du nie vergessen!
5. Ist das der Zug, mit dem Sie aus Heidelberg kamen?
6. Das Letzte, was er braucht, ist mehr Geld.

Vocabulary development

A. What is your profession?

Many names of professions are derived from the words denoting academic and other fields of endeavor; a suffix will do the trick. Note these corresponding suffixes:

The occupation	*The person*
-(log)ie	**-e**
-ik	**-er**
-t	**-ler**

die Psychologie	der Psychologe	*psychologist*
die Musik	der Musiker	*musician*
der Sport	der Sportler	*athlete*

The corresponding feminine forms (as you expected!) end in **-in:**

die Psychologin
die Musikerin
die Sportlerin

Now derive the names of the professions from the following disciplines and occupations:

die Kunst (*hint: add an umlaut*)	die Politik
die Biologie	die Meteorologie
die Archäologie	die Mathematik
die Geologie	die Physik

Of course not all names of professions are formed this way. For instance, there is **der Geschäftsmann** (*businessman*), whose plural you have already encountered—what is it? And if **der Arzt, ̈e** and **die Ärztin, -nen** mean *doctor*, what does **der Zahnarzt** (**der Augenarzt; der Hals-, Nasen-, Ohrenarzt**) mean?

B. *Stell dir das mal vor!* (Just imagine that!)

The verb **vor·stellen** has multiple uses. Its literal meaning is *to put in front of* (oneself), *to place before*, or *to put forward*.

Wenn man mit dem Flugzeug reist, muß man seine Uhr oft vorstellen. (*Opposite:* **nachstellen.**)

In a figurative sense it means *to introduce* one person to another—literally, *to place one before the other*.

Darf ich Ihnen meine Freundin vorstellen? Fräulein Kleinert, Herr Staiger.

After that the two persons introduced usually shake hands and say „**Angenehm!**" or „**Sehr erfreut!**" or „**Freut mich sehr!**"
When used as a reflexive, **sich vorstellen** means to imagine, with **sich** in the *dative* case.

Stell dir das mal vor!
Ich kann mir das nicht gut vorstellen.

The noun **die Vorstellung** is most often used in the sense of a stage performance:

Morgen gehen wir zu einer Theatervorstellung.

A synonym is **die Theateraufführung,** and a *première* is **eine Erstaufführung.**

Communicative exercises

A. Join items from both columns into plausible sentences, using the appropriate relative pronoun. Have one of your classmates answer your questions.

Kennst du die jungen Leute, mit	deren	du beim Tanz getroffen hast?
Hier ist ein Bild,	dem	Mann kürzlich gestorben ist.
Das ist der Professor, bei	denen	ich Psychologie studiere.
Das ist die junge Frau,	die	mir sehr gut gefällt.
Hier ist ein Kleid,	der	sie spricht?
Wo hast du die Eintrittskarte	das	ich heute gekauft habe?
hingelegt,	den	du diesen langen Brief
Was macht der junge Mann,	dessen	schreibst?
Wer ist die Freundin,		Bedeutung ich nicht
		interpretieren kann.

B. Ask your classmate the following questions and have them answer in a complete sentence, starting with: **Ich weiß nicht, . . .**

Wieviel haben diese Jeans gekostet?
Wen sollen wir anrufen?
Wem gehört dieses Gepäck?
Mit wem fährt er nach Hamburg?
Bei wem wohnt sie?
Warum hat er das gesagt?
Wann ist sie gestorben?
Was studiert sie?

C. Ask your classmate: **Was möchten Sie (möchtest du) gern werden?** and have him/her answer with the suggestions below (converting the word for the subject matter into that of its practitioner) or any other profession he/she may wish to learn:

Ich möchte am liebsten   Biologie   werden.
                                     Physik
                                     Musik
                                     Mathematik
                                     Politik
                                     Sport

D. Introduce two of your classmates to each other; have them go through the brief ceremony, including the handshake.

E. Ask your classmate whether he/she has ever taken a psychological test and have him/her answer. The following suggestions may help:

Questions:

Hast du je einen psychologischen Test gemacht?
Wo? Wann?

Answers:

ein schriftlicher Test
ein Interview
Fragen beantworten
Bilder oder Tintenkleckse (*inkblots*) interpretieren

F. Describe briefly what the two people in the picture below are doing.

Reading

WIENER BLUT[1]

Wer den Namen „Wien" hört, denkt wohl gleich an die Walzer von Johann Strauß,[2] wie zum Beispiel „An der schönen blauen Donau"° oder „Wiener Blut". Tatsächlich ist die Musik ein Teil der Kultur Wiens, den man nicht vergißt und der weit in die Geschichte der Stadt zurückgeht.

    Danube

Die größten Namen der deutschen Musik sind mit ihrer Geschichte eng verbunden. Haydn[3] war lange in Wien tätig und starb, als Napoleon im Jahre 1809 zum zweiten Mal mit seiner Armee die Stadt besetzte. Mozart[4] komponierte° in Wien einige seiner größten Werke und dirigierte° die Erstaufführung seiner Oper „Die Zauberflöte"° in einem Theater, das heute noch steht. Auch Beethoven[5] lebte lange in Wien. Drei seiner Symphonien erlebten da ihre Erstaufführung. Das Titelblatt° der bekannten dritten Symphonie, der „Eroica", enthielt eine Zueignung° Beethovens an Napoleon, die Beethoven allerdings später zerriß, nachdem er seine Begeisterung für den Kaiser verloren hatte.[6] Ungefähr zur gleichen Zeit war auch der junge Schubert[7] in Wien tätig, in dessen Musik sich die Seele Wiens und Österreichs vielleicht am besten ausdrückt. Auch am Anfang dieses Jahrhunderts war Wien wieder eine der führenden Städte Europas auf den meisten Gebieten der Musik.

    composed
conducted / "The Magic Flute"
title page
dedication

Am Ende des Krieges, im Jahr 1945, als ein großer Teil der Stadt zerstört war, waren die Staatsoper[8] und das Burgtheater[9] das Erste, was die Wiener wieder aufbauten. Und schlecht angezogene Wiener wanderten oft hungrig durch die halbdunklen Straßen, um sich ein Konzert oder eine Oper anzuhören° oder um ein Theaterstück zu sehen.

    listen to

Auch im tiefsten Unglück verliert der Wiener seinen Lebensmut nicht. Er hat diesen Mut in der Vergangenheit oft gezeigt. Im 16. und 17. Jahrhundert belagerten° die Türken° zweimal die Stadt; am Anfang des 19. Jahrhunderts besetzte sie Napoleon, und während des Zweiten Weltkrieges war es Hitlers Armee, die über die Stadt und das ganze Land herrschte.° Aber diese Katastrophen verstärkten nur den Lebensmut der Wiener. Nach der Belagerung° durch die Türken im Jahr 1683 schmolzen° die Wiener die Kanonen der Feinde in eine Glocke[10] um, die auch heute noch im bekannten Stephansdom[11] hängt und deren Klang an vergangenes° Unglück erinnert, aber gleichzeitig auch zu neuem Leben aufruft.°

    besieged / the Turks
ruled
siege
recast
past
inspires

Und das neue Leben zeigt sich überall. Neue Gebäude und Hochhäuser stehen neben alten Palästen, die man gleich nach dem Krieg wieder aufgebaut hatte. Eine Untergrundbahn windet sich un-

Die Wiener Staatsoper

Wiener Opernball

Beethovenhaus, Wien: Hof

ter der Stadt hindurch, und die Vereinten Nationen° haben in Wien
ein großes Verwaltungszentrum°12 gebaut.

    Auch im Bewußtsein° der Wiener sind Altes und Neues eng ver-
bunden. Viele denken noch gern und oft an die schöne Zeit von Franz
Joseph I.13 zurück, als Österreich im Zenith seiner Macht stand. Und
viele moderne Restaurants, Bars und Tanzlokale° sind in alten, im-
posanten Gebäuden untergebracht.° Fast möchte man sagen, daß

United Nations
administrative center
consciousness

dance bars
installed

Wien nach dem Krieg

Stephansdom

der Wiener von heute seine Unterhaltung im Schatten der Vergangenheit sucht. Und wie in der Vergangenheit hören die Theatervorstellungen und Konzerte um 22 Uhr auf. Ein Humorist sagte einmal, daß die Wiener genug Zeit zum Träumen haben wollen und daß Sigmund Freud,[14] dessen Theorie der Traumanalyse in der ganzen Welt bekannt ist, ein Wiener sein mußte. Auf jeden Fall ist der alte Schlager, in dem es heißt: „Wien, Wien, nur du allein, sollst stets° die Stadt meiner Träume sein", mehr als nur in einem Sinne° wahr.

forever

sense

CULTURAL NOTES

1. Literally, *Viennese blood.* It means the temper or disposition of the Viennese.

2. Johann Strauß the Younger (1825–99), probably the most famous waltz composer of all time.

3. Franz Joseph Haydn (1732–1809), noted for his symphonies, quartets, sonatas, etc.

4. Wolfgang Amadeus Mozart (1756–91) composed in all musical forms; especially famous are his quartets, concertos, symphonies, and operas.

5. Ludwig van Beethoven (1770–1827) is known for his symphonies, sonatas, concertos, and quartets.

6. A number of German writers and artists, such as Goethe and Beethoven, at first admired Napoleon for his military and political genius, and his imposition of greater political unity on Germany; but their enthusiasm soon began to fade.

7. Franz Schubert (1797–1828), the noted Austrian composer of quartets, symphonies, and songs.

8. The famous Opera House in Vienna. Built and rebuilt in complex early French Renaissance style, it somehow achieves a noble architectural harmony.

9. The National Theater, originally built in the nineteenth century in a kind of Neo-Renaissance style.

10. The bell is called **die Pummerin,** suggesting the deep sound it produces. For the Viennese it has perhaps the same significance as the Liberty Bell for the Americans. It was severely damaged during the Second World War, but was recast largely with the original material.

11. St. Stephen's Cathedral, a much-loved Viennese landmark begun in the twelfth century, rebuilt after a disastrous fire in the fourteenth, and expanded several times thereafter. It is an interesting blend of Romanesque, Gothic, and Renaissance architecture.

12. The so-called "UN-City," inaugurated in August 1980, is a mammoth complex on the left bank of the Danube containing the administrative

Das Geburtshaus Franz Schuberts, Wien

offices of many UN organizations. Vienna now rivals Geneva/Switzerland as a subsidiary seat of the UN.

13. Emperor of Austria from 1848 until his death in 1916, he enjoyed one of the longest reigns of any monarch in European history and became a symbol of Austrian unity.

14. Sigmund Freud (1856–1939), the Austrian psychiatrist whose theories of psychoanalysis have had a vast influence on psychology, anthropology, education, literature, and art.

QUESTIONS

1. An welche Walzer denkt man, wenn man den Namen Wien hört?
2. Welche Namen der Musik sind mit der Geschichte Wiens eng verbunden?
3. Wann besetzte Napoleon Wien zum zweiten Mal?
4. Welche Erstaufführung dirigierte Mozart in Wien?
5. Welche Symphonie enthielt eine Zueignung von Beethoven an Napoleon?
6. Warum zerriß Beethoven diese Zueignung später?
7. In wessen Musik drückt sich die Seele Wiens am besten aus?
8. Was bauten die Wiener nach dem Zweiten Weltkrieg sofort wieder auf?
9. Wer belagerte Wien im 16. und 17. Jahrhundert zweimal?
10. Woraus (out of what) hat man die Glocke im Stephansdom gemacht?
11. Wann stand Österreich im Zenith seiner Macht?
12. Welche Organisation hat in Wien ein großes Verwaltungsgebäude gebaut?
13. Wie heißt der Wiener, dessen Theorie der Traumanalyse in der ganzen Welt bekannt ist?

Review

A. Complete the following sentences with a relative pronoun and, in some cases, another word or phrase to make a personal statement.

EXAMPLE: _____ ist ein Staat, _____ ich gut kenne.
　　　　　Kalifornien ist ein Staat, den ich gut kenne.

1. _____ ist eine Stadt, _____ mir gefällt.
2. _____ ist ein Gebiet, _____ ich eines Tages besuchen will.
3. _____ ist ein Fluß, _____ ich nie gesehen habe.
4. Das Letzte, _____ ich von ihm erhielt, war _____.
5. _____ ist ein bekannter Mann, _____ sich sehr oft irrt.
6. _____ ist ein Land, _____ Sprache ich ein wenig verstehe.

7. _____ ist ein Beruf, _____ mir gefällt.
8. Das Erste, _____ ich morgens tue, ist _____.

B. Fill in the appropriate interrogative or relative pronoun.

1. Ich frage ihn, _____ ich ihm am besten helfen kann.   (*how*)
2. Das Fahrrad, _____ ich gekommen bin, ist furchtbar schmutzig.   (*with which*)
3. Das ist der Bus, _____ Sie am schnellsten zur Universität kommen.   (*by which*)
4. Es gibt niemand, _____ immer sagt, _____ er denkt.   (*who/what*)
5. Alles, _____ ich über Hans weiß, ist, daß er wirklich nett ist.   (*that*)
6. Sag mir, _____ du dein Geld verdienst.   (*how*)
7. _____ das sagt, hat eigentlich recht.   (*he who*)
8. Aber _____ Sprachen lernen will, muß das, _____ er gelernt hat, immer wiederholen, und das ist natürlich das, _____ wir hier tun.   (*he who/which/what*)
9. Sie möchte gern wissen, _____ du das gehört hast?   (*from whom*)
10. Wissen Sie, _____ Einwohner das kleine Land Österreich hat?   (*how many*)

C. Express in German.

1. Vienna is a lovely city whose soul Schubert expresses best.
2. The movie, which at first didn't sound very interesting, was really very good.
3. The first thing they did was to rebuild the theater.
4. Napoleon, who occupied Vienna twice, was Emperor of France.
5. What I know, I learned at home.
6. They never lose the courage that they have often shown in the past.
7. I don't know whom I should believe.
8. Ask him when the new subway will be ready.

Guided composition

Try to describe in a few sentences what you consider to be the prominent traits in the life-style of the citizens of your hometown or place of residence. How do they spend their free time? Do they go to movies? Is there a theater or concert hall in town? Are concerts and plays well attended? Are there many bars and discos? Or are the citizens more oriented toward the outdoors? Do they go hiking, jogging, swimming, skiing, etc.? Is there one cultural or recreational activity in your town that you consider to be outstanding?

You may also wish to state what your own preferred cultural activities are. What is your favorite music? Who is your favorite composer?

Chapter vocabulary

Nouns

die	Analyse, -n	*analysis*
die	Armee, -n	*army*
die	Aufführung, -en	*performance*
die	Bedeutung, -en	*meaning*
die	Begeisterung	*enthusiasm*
das	Bild, -er	*picture*
die	Eintrittskarte, -n	*(admission) ticket*
die	Erstaufführung, -en	*première*
der	Fall, ⁻e	*case*
	auf jeden Fall	*in any case*
der	Feind, -e	*enemy*
die	Glocke, -n	*bell*
der	Hals, ⁻e	*neck, throat*
der	Humorist, -en	*humorist*
das	Jahrhundert, -e	*century*
das	Kalifornien	*California*
die	Kanone, -n	*cannon*
die	Katastrophe, -n	*catastrophe*
der	Klecks, -e	*blot, spot*
das	Konzert, -e	*concert*
die	Macht, ⁻e	*power*
der	Magen, -	*stomach*
der	Mut	*courage*
die	Persönlichkeit, -en	*personality*
der	Psychologe, -n	*psychologist*
die	Psychologie	*psychology*
der	Schatten, -	*shadow, shade*
die	Seele, -n	*soul*
die	Symphonie, -n	*symphony*
der	Test, -s	*test*
die	Theorie, -n	*theory*
die	Tinte, -n	*ink*
der	Traum, ⁻e	*dream*
das	Unglück, -e	*misfortune, accident*

die	Untergrundbahn, -en	*subway*
die	Unterhaltung, -en	*entertainment, talk*
der	Walzer, -	*waltz*
der	Weg, -e	*way*
	auf dem Weg	*on the way*
das	Werk, -e	*work (of an author, composer, etc.)*
die	Wohnung, -en	*apartment*

Verbs

auf·bauen	*to rebuild, build up*
bauen	*to build*
besetzen	*to occupy*
besprechen (bespricht), besprach, besprochen	*to talk over, discuss*
führen	*to lead*
interpretieren	*to interpret*
knurren	*to growl*
sterben (stirbt), starb, (ist) gestorben	*to die*
verstärken	*to strengthen*
sich vor·stellen	*to imagine; introduce (see also pp. 311–312)*
wandern	*to wander; hike*
zerreißen, zerriß, zerrissen	*to tear up*
zerstören	*to destroy*

Other words

allerdings	*to be sure, indeed*
begeistert (von + dat.)	*enthusiastic (about)*
imposant	*imposing*
psychologisch	*psychological*
schriftlich	*written (test, etc.)*

See also the names of professions on pp. 310–311.

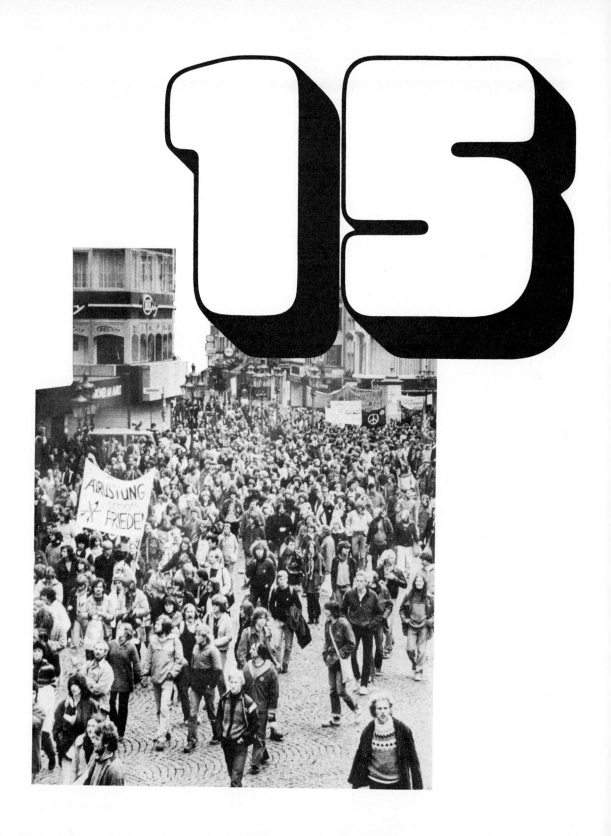

Mini-dialogues

A Wenn er doch nur angerufen hätte, dann wüßten wir, wann er zurückkommt.
B Ja! Das hätte er wirklich tun können!
A Wahrscheinlich ist er wieder in die Tanzbar gegangen.
B Wenn er in eine Tanzbar geht, vergißt er immer, wieviel Uhr es ist.
A Würdest du jeden Abend tanzen gehen?
B Natürlich nicht! Aber so ist Gerd nun einmal!

A Möchten Sie eine Tasse Kaffee?
B Nein danke! Ich hätte lieber etwas Orangensaft.
A Wenn ich Orangensaft hätte, könnten Sie gern etwas haben. Aber leider haben wir keinen im Haus. Wie wäre es mit einem Glas Bier?
B O, ja! Das wäre noch besser.
A Einen Moment, dann bringe ich Ihnen gleich ein Bier.

A If he had only called then we would know when he'll be back.
B Yes. He really could have done that.
A He probably went to a dance bar again.
B Whenever he goes to a dance bar he forgets what time it is.
A Would you go dancing every night?
B Of course not. But that's Gerd (for you)!

A Would you like a cup of coffee?
B No, thanks. I'd rather have some orange juice.
A With pleasure (you could have some), if I had some orange juice. But unfortunately we don't have any in the house. How about a glass of beer?
B Oh, yes. That would be even better.
A One moment, and I'll bring you a beer right away.

Grammar explanations

Wenn sie nur nicht so konservativ **wären!**
If only they weren't so conservative!

Wir **wünschten,** ihr **könntet** besser Deutsch sprechen.
We wish you could speak better German.

Wenn sie nur schon da gewesen **wären!**
If only they had already been there!

Hätte ich nur etwas mehr Geld **gehabt!**
If only I had had some more money!

Ich **hätte** einen Brief schreiben **sollen.**
I should have written a letter.

Würden Sie mir bitte das Buch **geben?**
Would you please give me the book?

Wir **würden** lieber hier **bleiben.**
We would rather stay here.

Wenn ich ihn **gekannt hätte, wäre** ich zu ihm **gegangen.**
If I had known him, I would have gone to him.

Ich **würde mich** nach dem Preis **erkundigen, wenn** ich an dem Auto interessiert **wäre.**
I would find out the price if I were interested in the car.

The general subjunctive

The subjunctive is a "mood" of the verb. In both German and English, the indicative mood is used to state facts and ask direct questions, while the imperative mood is used for commands. The *subjunctive* mood, however, has other uses: to express *wishes, requests,* and *hypothetical situations.*

1. Indicative:

Ich habe ihr einen langen Brief geschrieben.
I wrote her a long letter.

2. Imperative:

Schreib ihr doch einen Brief!
Do write her a letter!

3. Subjunctive:

Wenn ich den Brief doch schon geschrieben **hätte!**
If only I had already written the letter!

While the indicative has six tenses, the general subjunctive is limited to two: present and past.

A. Present subjunctive: formation

The present subjunctive is formed by adding the subjunctive personal endings to the past indicative stem (= the 2nd principal part).[1]
The personal endings of the subjunctive are:

	Singular		Plural	
1st person	ich	**-e**	wir	**-en**
2nd person	du	**-est**	ihr	**-et**
3rd person	er sie	**-e**	sie	**-en**
	es			
2nd formal	Sie	**-en**	Sie	**-en**

Notice that these endings are identical to the past indicative endings (without the **-t-** insert) for weak verbs.

In *strong verbs, irregular weak verbs* (like **bringen, denken, wissen, nennen, kennen**), and the *four modals* (**dürfen, können, mögen,** and **müssen**) the past indicative stem is umlauted.

	Past indicative	Present subjunctive
strong verbs	er fuhr	er **führe**
	du liefst	du **liefest**
irreg. weak verbs	ich brachte	ich **brächte**
	ihr wußtet	ihr **wüßtet**
modals	sie durfte	sie **dürfte**
	es konnte	es **könnte**
	ich mochte	ich **möchte**
	wir mußten	wir **müßten**

[1]Traditionally this subjunctive is referred to as Subjunctive II, because it is based on the second principal part of the verb. The "Indirect Discourse" subjunctive discussed in Chapter 18 is referred to as Subjunctive I, because it is based on the first principal part of the verb.

In the subjunctive, the auxiliary verbs **haben** and **sein** follow the same pattern.

haben (*past stem:* **hatt-**)		**sein** (*past stem:* **war-**)		*Present subjunctive:* **haben** *and* **sein**
ich **hätte**	wir **hätten**	ich **wäre**	wir **wären**	
du **hättest**	ihr **hättet**	du **wärest**	ihr **wäret**	
er **hätte**	sie **hätten**	er **wäre**	sie **wären**	
Sie **hätten**		Sie **wären**		

Weak verbs and the two modals **sollen** and **wollen** do *not* take an umlaut. Therefore, the forms of the present subjunctive are identical with the past indicative for these verbs.

Past indicative	Present subjunctive	*Present subjunctive: weak verbs, modals, with o-stem*
ich **lachte**	ich **lachte**	
du **solltest**	du **solltest**	
ihr **wolltet**	ihr **wolltet**	

CHECK YOUR COMPREHENSION

Restate in the present subjunctive.

1. sie fährt
2. er ist
3. ihr hattet
4. er kommt
5. ihr sollt
6. ich kann
7. Sie bringen
8. ihr schreibt
9. du liest
10. ich studiere

B. Past subjunctive: formation

The past subjunctive generally indicates an unreal or hypothetical action that could have occurred in the past but did not. As one might expect, the past subjunctive in German consists of the subjunctive form of the auxiliary **haben** or **sein** and the past participle of the principal verb.

Wir **hätten** gern **angerufen.**	*We would have liked to call.*
Er **wäre** lieber mit uns **gekommen.**	*He would have preferred to come with us.*

When a modal is used with another infinitive, the *double infinitive* construction (see chapter 8) is used.

Er **hätte** uns **helfen können.**	*He could have helped us.*

CHECK YOUR COMPREHENSION

Change the following sentences into the past.

1. Wenn er doch anriefe!
2. Sie käme lieber später.
3. Hätten Sie Lust, mit uns nach Nürnberg zu fahren?
4. Wer bliebe lieber in Österreich?
5. Wenn Sie nur nicht nach Rom führen!
6. Ihr solltet mehr essen!

C. *Würden* plus infinitive as an alternate construction in the present subjunctive: formation

Frequently, the present subjunctive of **werden** plus the infinitive are used as an alternative form for the present subjunctive, similar to *would* plus infinitive in English.

Subjunctive of the main verb	**würde** + *infinitive of the main verb*
Ich wünschte, er **käme** sofort.	Ich wünschte, er **würde** sofort **kommen.**
I wish he'd come at once.	
Wenn er doch nur **anriefe!**	Wenn er doch nur **anrufen würde!**
If he would only call.	

The present subjunctive of **werden** is as follows:

ich **würde**	wir **würden**	*Present subjunctive:* **werden**
du **würdest**	ihr **würdet**	
er **würde**	sie **würden**	
	Sie **würden**	

The **würde**-construction is *never* used with **haben, sein,** and the *modals,* or with the *past subjunctive* of any verbs.

Wenn ich nur mehr Zeit **hätte!**	*If only I had more time!*
Wenn sie nur schon hier **wäre!**	*If only she were here already!*
Wenn ich das nur **könnte!**	*If only I could do that!*
Ich **hätte** ihn **angerufen.**	*I would have called him.*
Er **wäre** wahrscheinlich **gekommen.**	*He probably would have come.*

CHECK YOUR COMPREHENSION

Express the following statements by using the **würde** + *infinitive* construction.

EXAMPLE: Sprechen Sie bitte langsamer!
          Würden Sie bitte langsamer sprechen?

1. Fahren Sie bitte nicht so schnell!
2. Ich lese das Buch nicht.
3. Helfen Sie dem Herrn da drüben!
4. Bringen Sie mir noch ein Glas Bier!
5. Das tue ich nicht gern.
6. Wenn sie doch nur käme!

D. Uses of the subjunctive

1. Contrary-to-fact statements

A conditional sentence consists of a clause containing a *condition* and a clause containing a *conclusion*. Since the condition is generally expressed with *if,* it is called the *if*-clause in English and the **wenn**-clause in German.

Some conditions are contrary to fact, while others are not.

Condition		*Conclusion*
not contrary to fact	If I have the book (and maybe I do or will),	I'll read it.
contrary to fact	If I had the book (but I don't),	I would read it.

In German as in English, if a condition is *not* contrary to fact, it is expressed with the indicative.

Wenn ich das Buch habe,	*If I have the book,*
lese ich es.	*I'll read it.*

However, if a statement *is* contrary to fact, it is expressed with the subjunctive in German.

Condition	Conclusion
Wenn ich das Buch hätte,	{ **läse ich es.** { **würde ich es lesen.**
If I had the book,	*I would read it.*
Wenn sie gekommen wäre,	**hätte ich mich gefreut.**
If she had come,	*I would have been happy.*

In the *conclusion* of a contrary-to-fact statement, the **würde**-construction for the present subjunctive is very common:[1]

Wenn ich das Buch hätte, würde ich es lesen.

(Remember, the **würde**-construction cannot be used with **haben, sein,** the modals, and the past subjunctive.)

	Condition	Conclusion	
present	**Wenn er mich anriefe,**	{ **ginge ich jetzt.** { **würde ich jetzt gehen.**	*present*
	If he called me,	*I would go now.*	
past	**Wenn er mich angerufen hätte,**	**wäre ich gegangen.**	*past*
	If he had called me,	*I would have gone.*	
past	*Wenn er mich* **angerufen hätte,**	{ **ginge ich jetzt.** { **würde ich jetzt gehen.**	*present*
	If he had called me,	*I would go now.*	

Note that the conclusion derived from a condition in the past may be either in the past or present, depending on the situation.

---

[1]In the *condition*, the straight subjunctive form is considered better. But nowadays the **würde**-construction is permissible, especially in spoken German.

Wenn er mir schriebe, } würde ich ihm gleich antworten.
Wenn er mir schreiben würde, }
If he wrote me, I would answer him immediately.

Either clause may be in first position in the sentence. Since **wenn** is a subordinating conjunction, dependent word order ("Verb-Last") is required in the *condition.*

Conclusion	Condition
Ich ginge jetzt,	**wenn** er mich **anriefe.**
I would go now	*if he called me.*

When the condition is at the beginning, the conclusion is in inverted (V-S) word order.

Condition	Conclusion
Wenn du willst,	**kannst du** jetzt gehen.
If you want,	*you may go now.*

The conjunction **wenn** may be omitted, in which case the condition is in the V-S order. The conclusion often starts with **so** or **dann.**

Hätte ich mehr Zeit, **(so)** würde ich mehr Bücher lesen.	*If I had more time, I'd read more books.*
Wäre sie hier, **(dann)** würden wir sofort einkaufen gehen.	*If she were here, we would go shopping right away.*

Note that in a dependent clause with a double infinitive construction, the auxiliary (**hätte**) precedes the double infinitive.

Wenn ich gestern meinen Wagen hätte fahren können, wäre ich natürlich gekommen.	*If I had been able to drive my car yesterday, naturally I would have come.*

CHECK YOUR COMPREHENSION

A. Change the following sentences into contrary-to-fact statements. Use the **würde**-construction wherever it is most appropriate.

1. Wenn du das tust, gebe ich dir zwanzig Mark.
2. Wenn sie keine Zeit haben, kommen sie bestimmt nicht.
3. Ich kaufe mir das Auto, wenn ich das Geld habe.
4. Wenn er mehr Zeit hat, macht er eine Reise.

5. Ihr kommt früher an, wenn ihr mit dem Zug fahrt.
6. Sind wir wirklich hungrig, dann essen wir etwas.
7. Wenn er diese Nachricht hört, freut er sich ganz sicher.
8. Wir kommen nicht zu spät, wenn wir uns beeilen.

B. Now change the sentences above into contrary-to-fact statements of the past.

_____

2. Other uses

As in English, the subjunctive is used to express *wishful thinking* and *polite requests:*

I wish you would stay a little longer.
Would you please let me know soon!

a. Wishful thinking

Wishful thinking is frequently expressed by an introductory clause with a subjunctive form of **wünschen.**

Ich **wünschte,** er **käme** sofort.	*I wish he would come at once.*
Wir **wünschten,** sie **hätte** uns schon **besucht.**	*We wish she had visited us already.*

Wishful thinking can also be expressed by a clause with **wenn** (*if*).

Wenn ich nur mehr Geld **hätte!**	*If only I had more money!*
Wenn er doch nur **angerufen hätte!**	*If only he had called!*

b. Polite requests

The subjunctive is used to make a request more polite.

Hätten Sie einen Moment Zeit?	*Would you have a moment?*
Könntest du mir bitte sagen, wo das Restaurant ist?	*Could you please tell me where the restaurant is?*

The **würde**-construction must be used in polite requests with all verbs except **haben, sein,** and the *modals.*

Würden Sie bitte etwas langsamer **sprechen?**	*Would you please speak more slowly?*
Würden Sie mir bitte **helfen?**	*Would you please help me?*

Würdest du ihm das bitte **erklären?**	*Would you please explain that to him?*

Many wishes and polite requests contain the adverbs **gern, lieber, am liebsten.**

Ich hätte **gern** das Stück Kuchen gegessen.	*I would have liked to eat that piece of cake.*
Möchten Sie **lieber** etwas Obst essen?	*Would you rather eat some fruit?*
Ich würde **am liebsten** Bier trinken.	*I would like to drink beer best of all.*

CHECK YOUR COMPREHENSION

A. Fill in the appropriate subjunctive forms, using the cues given in parentheses.

1. Wenn er doch zu Hause _____! (*bleiben*)
2. Ich _____, Karl _____ öfter. (*wünschen, schreiben*)
3. Wir _____, wir _____ mehr Zeit für dich. (*wünschen/haben*)
4. Wenn er das Bild nur _____! (*bringen*)
5. Verzeihung, _____ ich Sie bitten, Ihre Zigarre nicht hier zu rauchen? (*dürfen*)
6. _____ Sie mir bitte sagen, wie spät es ist? (*können*)

B. Now use the **würde**-construction for sentences 1 and 4.

Conversation

Mir brummt der Kopf.	*I am totally confused.*
Fabelhaft!	*Fantastic!*
Stell dich doch nicht so an!	*Don't make such a fuss!*
Hör dir das mal an!	*Just listen to that!*
Er macht sich über mich lustig.	*He is making fun of me.*
Daß ich nicht lache!	*Don't make me laugh!*

Was ist (denn schon wieder) los? $\Big\{$ *What's the matter (again)?*
What's this all about (again)?

DAS ABITUR[1]

Anita, Anton und Wolfgang sind drei Oberprimaner,[2] die vor
dem Abitur stehen.° Seit fast drei Monaten studieren sie drei-   are about to take
mal in der Woche zusammen, um sich auf die Prüfung vor-
zubereiten. Eines Abends unterhalten sie sich während einer
kurzen Pause.

Anton   Hört mal! Mir brummt der Kopf. Das war ein ganz ge-
     meines° mathematisches Problem, das wir da gelöst haben.   mean
Wolfgang   Du solltest sagen: „das Anita für uns gelöst hat."
Anton   Allerdings. Wenn wir nur das Abitur zusammen als eine
     Gruppe machen dürften, dann würden wir ganz großartig
     abschneiden!°   pass
Anita   Fabelhafte Idee! Dann würde ich die Mathematik

[1]The **Abitur** is a stiff general examination that lasts several days and covers all core
subjects (mathematics, science, languages, German literature, etc.) taught in the Gymnasium over nine years. It is a prerequisite for admission to a university. Because of
overcrowded facilities, only students with high passing grades have a chance to be
accepted at a university. The so-called *Numerus Clausus* (Latin for "closed number")
sets an upper limit to the number of admissions authorized in many academic
disciplines.

[2]**Oberprimaner** are students in the last year of the Gymnasium.

Friedrich von Schiller

übernehmen° und Anton könnte für uns den englischen Aufsatz   *take on*
schreiben.

Wolfgang   Und ich?

Anton   Stell dich doch nicht so an! Du kennst doch die deutsche
Literatur vorwärts und rückwärts.

Wolfgang   Ja, ja. Aber ich möchte lieber mein eigenes Gedicht
schreiben, als ein abgedroschenes Zitat° aus einem Schiller[3]-   *hackneyed quote*
Gedicht kommentieren.

Anton   Ha, ha! Sein eigenes Gedicht! Hör dir das mal an, Anita!
Die Lehrer würden ihm sicher für sein Gedicht den Nobel-Preis
verleihen.°   *to confer*

Wolfgang   Anita, siehst du, jetzt macht er sich schon wieder über
mich lustig. Anton, du hast leider keine Phantasie.

Anton   „Phantasie"! Daß ich nicht lache!

Wolfgang   Und wenn die Lehrer etwas mehr poetischen Sinn hätten,
dann würden sie unserem eigenen Denken und Fühlen etwas
mehr Raum lassen.

Anita   Was ist denn los? Streitet euch doch nicht schon wieder. Wir
können alle den Streß fast nicht mehr aushalten. Wie wär's,   — How about
wenn wir nachher alle in unsere Tanzbar gehen würden?

Wolfgang   Tolle Idee!

Anton   Los! Worauf warten wir noch?

[3]Though recognized as the greatest classical dramatist in German literature, **Friedrich
Schiller** (1759–1805) also wrote historic treatises, philosophic essays, and poems, often
of a didactic nature.

QUESTIONS ON THE CONVERSATION

1. Warum studieren die drei Oberprimaner seit drei Monaten dreimal in der Woche zusammen?
2. Wovon brummt Anton der Kopf?
3. Wer hat das mathematische Problem gelöst?
4. Wer von den drei Oberprimanern kann einen Englischaufsatz am besten schreiben?
5. Was möchte Wolfgang am liebsten tun?
6. Warum streiten sich Wolfgang und Anton?
7. Wohin will Anita gehen, wenn sie mit dem Studieren fertig ist?
8. Wie findet Wolfgang die Idee, in die Tanzbar zu gehen?

PERSONAL QUESTIONS

1. Brummt Ihnen auch manchmal der Kopf, wenn Sie studieren? Warum?
2. Wenn Sie Abitur machen müßten, welche Prüfung würden Sie dann am liebsten machen—in Mathematik, in Literatur oder in Physik? Warum?
3. Möchten Sie Ihr eigenes Denken und Fühlen in einer Prüfung ausdrücken? Haben Sie das schon einmal getan?
4. Gibt es etwas, was Sie besonders gut können? Was zum Beispiel?
5. Schreiben Sie gern Ihre eigenen Gedichte, oder kommentieren Sie lieber ein Gedicht?

Practice

A. Put the sentences into the subjunctive, then into the substitute construction (**würde** + *infinitive*), by using the phrase **Ich wünschte, . . .**

1. Meine Freundin löst dieses mathematische Problem für mich.
2. Der Busfahrer fährt jetzt etwas schneller.
3. Sie bringen mir bessere Nachrichten.
4. Er spricht etwas lauter.
5. Ihr streitet euch nicht jeden Tag.
6. Du hast mehr Glück.
7. Wir gehen auf dem Heimweg in unser Café.
8. Mein Freund mietet das Zimmer in unserem Haus.
9. Du kommst nicht immer zu spät.
10. Die Studenten halten den Streß besser aus.

B. Using the **würde**-construction for the subjunctive, express the request more politely.

1. Geben Sie mir bitte die Zeitung!
2. Setzen Sie sich bitte da drüben an den Tisch!
3. Fahren Sie bitte weiter!
4. Bringen Sie mir bitte noch ein Bier!
5. Mach bitte das Fenster zu!
6. Kommt bitte sofort nach Hause!
7. Geht bitte einen Moment hinaus!

C. Change the following statements into contrary-to-fact statements.

1. Wenn das wahr ist, haben wir keine Chance.
2. Wenn Sie genug Zeit haben, studieren Sie auch Deutsch?
3. Wenn er das tut, weiß ich es auch.
4. Wenn das Buch zu teuer ist, kaufen wir es bestimmt nicht.
5. Ist er durstig, dann trinkt er ein Glas Wasser.
6. Wenn es möglich ist, fliege ich gern im Herbst nach Deutschland.
7. Wenn wir ein Haus kaufen, haben wir mehr Platz als jetzt.

D. Now change the sentences in exercise C into contrary-to-fact statements of the past.

E. Give the English equivalent.

1. Ich würde lieber zu Hause bleiben.
2. Könnten Sie mir bitte das Buch da drüben geben?
3. Wenn er nicht bald kommt, gehe ich nach Hause!
4. Wenn er doch nur nicht so schnell spräche!
5. Ich wünschte, ich würde die deutsche Literatur etwas besser kennen.
6. Wenn er mehr Zeit gehabt hätte, wäre er sicher gekommen.
7. Wenn doch meine Seminararbeit endlich fertig wäre!
8. Wenn Brigitte nicht hier gewesen wäre, hätten wir sie vielleicht vergessen.

Vocabulary development

A. *Was ist los?* (What's going on? What's the matter?)

The particle **los** is a kind of "free agent" in German grammar since it adapts easily to its "free" grammatical environment. Its basic meaning is something like *loose, free, -less,* (meaning *without,* as in *senseless*).

As an *adverb* it occurs in some frequently used colloquial expressions:

Was ist los?	*What's the matter?*
Los!	*Let's go!*
Der Teufel ist los!	*All hell's broken loose.*
Es muß etwas los sein!	*Something must be going on.*

It also occurs as a *separable prefix* with several verbs:

los·fahren   *to depart*

Fahrt mal los!
Get going!

los·gehen   *to begin, get under way*

Es geht bald los.
Things will soon get going.
Nun geht's los!
Now things are moving!

los·lassen   *to let loose, let go*

Laß doch deinen Hund mal los!
Unleash your dog, will you!

los·machen   *to loosen, disengage, get away from*

Ich kann mich von ihm nicht losmachen.
I can't get away from him.

As a *suffix* it combines with many nouns to form *adjectives:*

die Arbeit	arbeitslos	*out of work*
der Atem	atemlos	*out of breath*
das Ende	endlos	*endless*
das Herz	herzlos	*heartless*
die Kinder (*pl.*)	kinderlos	*childless*
die Ruhe	ruhelos	*restless*

B. Be careful when you make a promise (*das Versprechen*)

Versprechen (from **sprechen**) means *to promise:*

Sie hat mir **versprochen,** ihm zu helfen.

She promised me to help him.

Vielversprechend means *very promising:*

Die Entwicklung ist **vielver-sprechend.**

The development is very promising.

But the reflexive **sich versprechen** means *to make a slip of the tongue, to say something wrong.* Therefore: **Wenn Sie etwas versprechen, versprechen Sie sich nicht!**

Communicative exercises

A. Ask your classmate: **Was ist bei dir (Ihnen) zu Hause los?** and have him/her answer. Suggestions:

Skiurlaub vorbereiten; (der Bruder, die Schwester) auf ein Examen vorbereiten; (eine Schwester, ein Bruder) sich verheiraten; (die Eltern) sich scheiden lassen; einen Unfall haben; krank sein; (ein Onkel, eine Tante, der Großvater, etc.) sterben; den ganzen Tag im Garten arbeiten; (ein Freund aus Deutschland, aus der Schweiz, etc.) auf Besuch (*for a visit*) kommen; (der Vater, die Mutter, der Bruder) arbeitslos

B. Ask your classmate: **Wem hast du kürzlich etwas versprochen und was?** and have him/her answer. Suggestions:

ins Kino, Theater, zum Tanzen, in ein Restaurant gehen; zusammen auf Ferien gehen; zusammen wohnen; bei einem mathematischen Problem helfen; (sie, ihn) heiraten; (für sie, ihn) ein Gedicht schreiben; oft während der Ferien anrufen

C. Ask someone in your class whether he or she would like to:

drink a cup of coffee; smoke a cigarette; study in Vienna; go shopping; play the guitar
Now tell him/her what you yourself prefer to do.

D. With several classmates engage in a discussion. Suggested questions:

Do you often study for an exam with a friend or friends? Which subjects do you study? What kinds of tests would you prefer? Would you rather write an essay or composition (**der Aufsatz**) at home or answer questions in class? Would you rather have a long exam at the end of a term (**das Semester, das Quartal**), or a series of short tests during the term? What assignments would you give, if you were the instructor? Perhaps you have some ideas about improving education in general. What would you do? Express two or three ideas: **Wenn ich Professor wäre, würde ich . . .** Then describe your habitual place of study; if you don't particularly like it, describe in what kind of environment you would most like to study.

Reading

STUDENTENPROBLEME

Sabine und Stefan sind gute Freunde, die wegen des Numerus Clausus an verschiedenen Universitäten studieren müssen.[1] Sie schreiben sich ziemlich oft.

München, den 5. November

Lieber Stefan:

Nun sind es schon drei Wochen, seitdem ich hier in München mein Winter-Semester begonnen habe. Wenn ich nicht schon so sehr mit meinem Medizinstudium beschäftigt wäre, hätte ich sehr wahrscheinlich Heimweh. Denn so gute Freunde wie Dich, Hans-Peter und Annegret werde ich wohl hier nicht so schnell finden. Ich wünschte, es wäre schon Weihnachten, dann könnten wir alle zusammen wieder Skilaufen gehen. Du hast doch unsere Verabredung nicht vergessen, oder? Der Winter ist ja dieses Jahr vielversprechend. Kürzlich habe ich in der Zeitung gelesen, daß in den Bayrischen Alpen° schon tiefer Schnee liegt. *Bavarian Alps*

Du hast wohl auch gehört, daß die meisten Studenten hier wieder einmal streiken. Es hat bei den Germanisten und Juristen[2] begonnen, denn die leiden an einer ganz großen Berufsangst[3] und sagen, daß sie für die Arbeitslosigkeit studieren. Es ist auch verständlich. Die beiden Disziplinen° sind einfach überbelegt.° Man müßte entweder weniger Studenten zulassen oder mehr Stellen schaffen. Aber wie? *disciplines / over-enrolled*

Dann sind die meisten Studenten auch mit der Bafög[4]-Erhöhung° nicht zufrieden. Wenn sie anständig° leben wollten, brauchten sie wenigstens 700 Mark im Monat, sagen sie. Fast hätten auch die Medizinstudenten mitgemacht, wenn sie nicht so konservativ wären, heißt es in der Studentenzeitung. Das stimmt aber nicht ganz. Erstens *increase* *decently*

erhält nur ein Drittel der Medizinstudenten Bafög, und zweitens,
wenn wir zu häufig abwesend sind, erhalten wir keine Zulassung
mehr° zu weiteren Pflichtseminaren.° Und dann ist es praktisch mit
dem Medizinstudium aus!° Wer ist da konservativ, die Studenten oder
die Professoren?

    Jetzt muß ich wieder zu einer Anatomie-Vorlesung rennen. Mehr
später. Ich freue mich schon auf den Skiurlaub.

we won't be admitted /
  required seminars
it is finished

Gruß und Kuß,

Deine Sabine

Marburg, den 11. November

Liebe Sabine,

Natürlich habe ich unsere Pläne für den Skiurlaub nicht vergessen. Wenn er nur schon da wäre! Der Gedanke an unseren Urlaub macht mir das Wintersemester etwas erträglicher.° Ob Annegret und Hans-Peter mitkommen wollen, ist noch nicht ganz sicher. (In letzter Zeit streiten sie sich sehr oft!) Wenn nicht, müßten wir eben allein gehen. Um so besser!

    more bearable

Auch hier wird der Studentenstreik wohl bald anfangen. Und ich werde mitmachen müssen. Du weißt doch, daß ich einer der armen Jura°-Studenten bin, die für die Arbeitslosigkeit studieren und Bafög erhalten, weil sie keine wohlhabenden° Eltern haben. Du scheinst, das vergessen zu haben. Oder glaubst Du, daß ich einer der Glücklichen sein werde, die nach dem Studium eine Stelle finden? Hoffen wir das Beste! Vielleicht könntest Du nach Deinem Studium mit der finanziellen Hilfe Deines Vaters eine Klinik eröffnen, und ich würde Dein juristischer Berater° werden. Dann würden wir beide reich! Aber ich will nicht zynisch° werden und verspreche Dir, während der Ferien von meinen Berufsaussichten° nicht zu sprechen. Es ist ohnehin° noch zu früh.

    law
    well-to-do

    legal counsel
    cynical
    job prospects / anyway

Aber es wäre großartig, wenn Du hier in Marburg studieren könntest. Dann würden wir manchmal über unsere Zukunft offen reden, nicht wahr? Hast Du übrigens gehört, daß Studenten anfangen, für Geld Studienplätze° zu wechseln?[5] Ich könnte hier vielleicht je-

    openings for study

mand finden, der mit Dir den Platz wechseln möchte. Ich weiß nicht, ob solch ein Wechsel° legal ist. Ich würde mich aber natürlich sofort erkundigen,° wenn Du interessiert wärest. Du wärst dann mein erster „Rechtsfall".°

exchange
inquire
legal case

Bis bald. Der Skiurlaub wird toll werden, das verspreche ich Dir.

Dein Stefan

CULTURAL NOTES

1. In Dortmund there is a central clearing house for student admissions; under the *Numerus Clausus* provisions, students in certain fields (medicine, etc.) are assigned to universities and have little choice in the matter.

2. Germanists and jurists—here, students of Germanic languages, literatures, and linguistics, and law students.

3. Fear of not finding a job. In the BRD as elsewhere, the job prospects of many academic professions are not very rosy these days. Many prospective students have therefore opted for a practical trade. But even apprenticeship positions are difficult to find, since there are so many applicants.

4. Abbreviation for **Bundesausbildungsförderungsgesetz** (ouch!)—the federal law for higher education. Students whose parents' income is below a certain level are eligible for a monthly stipend of 550 Marks if they live at home or 630 Marks if they live elsewhere, even during the long summer recess. Almost half of all students in institutions of higher learning in the BRD receive such aid, which might ultimately be converted to loan programs.

5. For personal or academic reasons, students are placing ads in daily papers and student publications in order to trade places; money is sometimes involved. Thus medical student A in Munich may pay medical student B in Marburg to take A's place in Munich, while A goes to study in Marburg.

QUESTIONS

1. Wann hat Sabines Winter-Semester in München begonnen?
2. Hat sie Heimweh? Warum oder warum nicht?
3. Was für eine Verabredung haben Sabine und Stefan für die Weihnachtsferien?
4. Warum streiken die Studenten an Sabines Universität?
5. Haben die Medizinstudenten während des Studentenstreiks mitgemacht? Warum oder warum nicht?
6. Warum werden Annegret und Hans-Peter vielleicht nicht zum Skilaufen mitkommen?
7. Was studiert Stefan, und was sind seine Berufsaussichten?
8. Was wäre nach Stefans Meinung großartig?

Review

A. Answer the following questions with the appropriate **würde**-construction where applicable.

Was würden Sie tun, wenn . . .

1. Ihre Freundin oder Ihr Freund Sie um Geld bäte?
2. es so stark schneite, daß Sie das Haus nicht verlassen könnten?
3. Sie einen Autounfall gehabt hätten und der andere Autofahrer den Unfallort verlassen hätte?
4. Sie plötzlich $20,000 gewännen?
5. Sie drei Wochen kostenlos Urlaub machen dürften? Würden Sie dann am liebsten nach Jamaika, Hawaii, Japan, Deutschland, Österreich oder in die Schweiz fliegen?
6. Sie wohnen könnten, wo Sie wollten? Wohnten Sie dann am liebsten in Los Angeles, New York, New Orleans, San Franzisko, Boston oder in Vancouver, B.C.?
7. Sie mit einem Freund ausgehen könnten? Gingen Sie am liebsten ins Kino, ins Theater, in die Oper, in den Stadtpark oder in ein französisches Restaurant?

B. Put the following sentences in the present subjunctive.

1. Wenn ich so lange in anderen Ländern gewohnt hätte wie du, hätte ich oft Heimweh gehabt.
2. Wenn das Wetter besser gewesen wäre, wären wir vielleicht schwimmen gegangen. — *gehen, ging, gegangen*
3. Wenn er nicht so konservativ gewesen wäre, hätte er vielleicht mitgemacht.
4. Hätte der Bus hier angehalten, dann wäre ich hier ausgestiegen.
5. Wenn er mehr Zeit gehabt hätte, hätte er vielleicht den Streß besser ausgehalten.
6. Hättest du auf mich gehört, so hättest du eine Stelle gefunden.
7. Wenn ihr euch nicht so oft gestritten hättet, hättet ihr das Problem schneller gelöst.
8. Ich hätte dich öfter angerufen, wenn ich nicht so sehr mit meinen Kursen beschäftigt gewesen wäre.
9. Hättest du ihm mehr Geld gegeben, so wäre er doch nicht zufrieden gewesen. *satisfied (at peace)*

C. Express the following requests more politely by using the **würde**-construction.

1. Bezahlen Sie bitte das Bier.
2. Raucht bitte nicht im Schlafzimmer.
3. Ruf mich bitte nicht immer so spät an.
4. Trinken Sie bitte Ihren Kaffee.
5. Fahren Sie bitte nicht, wenn Sie Alkohol getrunken haben.
6. Öffne bitte der Frau die Tür.

D. Express in German.

1. Would you call me tomorrow, please?
2. If I couldn't drive, I would have to walk (go on foot).
3. If I were Peter, I would definitely buy the car.
4. Would you please speak a little louder?
5. I wish we could live in Munich.
6. If only it weren't so terribly expensive!
7. If I had money, I would give you some.
8. If only I had more time!

Guided composition

Write about a student problem in the United States. Also discuss employment prospects after completion of a university education. Mention what conditions you would like to change. Use the subjunctive and the **würde**-construction throughout where appropriate.

Chapter vocabulary

Nouns

das	Abitur	*final examination covering all secondary-school studies*
die	Angst, ̈e	*fear*
die	Arbeitslosigkeit	*unemployment*
der	Aufsatz, ̈e	*written composition*
das	Drittel, -	*third*
der	Gedanke, -n	*thought*
das	Gedicht, -e	*poem*
der	Heimweg, -e	*way (or return) home*
	auf dem Heimweg	*on the way home*
das	Heimweh	*homesickness*
	Heimweh haben	*to be homesick*
der	Kuß, ̈sse	*kiss*
der	Lehrer, -	*teacher*
die	Medizin	*medicine*
die	Phantasie	*imagination*
der	Preis, -e	*prize*
die	Prüfung, -en	*examination*
das	Semester, -	*semester*
die	Stelle, -n	*position, job*
der	Streik, -s	*strike*
der	Streß	*stress*
das	Studium, die Studien	*study*
das	Weihnachten	*Christmas*
	Fröhliche Weihnachten! (*pl.*)	*Merry Christmas!*

Verbs

aus·halten (hält), hielt, ausgehalten	to endure, bear, stand
kommentieren	to comment on
leiden, litt, gelitten	to suffer
sich lustig machen über (+ acc.)	to poke fun at
mit·machen	to go along (with something)
rennen, rannte, ist gerannt	to run
schaffen	to create
streiken	to strike
sich streiten, stritt, gestritten	to quarrel
versprechen (verspricht), versprach, versprochen (+ dat.)	to promise
vor·bereiten (auf + acc.)	to prepare (for)
zu·lassen (läßt), ließ, zugelassen	to admit

Other words

abwesend	absent
beschäftigt	busy
eigen	own
entweder . . . oder	either . . . or
fabelhaft	fabulous
fertig	complete; ready
finanziell	financial
glücklich	happy, lucky
großartig	magnificent
konservativ	conservative
kostenlos	free of charge
legal	legal
nachher	later
nötig	necessary
etwas nötig haben	to need something
poetisch	poetic
praktisch	practical
rückwärts	backward
um so besser!	so much the better!
verschieden	different
verständlich	understandable
vielversprechend	very promising
vorwärts	forward
ziemlich	rather
zufrieden (mit + dat.)	satisfied (with)

ACHTUNG
Sie verlassen jetzt
West-Berlin

Mini-dialogues

A (*Aus seinem Wagen*) Hallo, Fritz, worauf wartest du?
B Auf den Bus.
A Da kannst du aber lange warten. Wo willst du denn hin?
B Zum Kudamm.
A Steig ein! Ich fahre auch dorthin.
B Sehr nett von dir. Vielen Dank.

A Woran denkst du?
B An all die Dinge, die ich noch zu tun habe.
A Denk doch nicht immer daran, tu eines nach dem andern!
B Das ist leichter gesagt als getan.

A Worüber sprecht ihr?
B Über die Sommerferien.
A Ja, ja, ich freue mich auch schon darauf.
B Gott sei Dank ist das Semester bald zu Ende.
A Wohin fahrt ihr in den Ferien?
B Das wissen wir noch nicht.

A (*From his car*) Hello, Fritz, what are you waiting for?
B For the bus.
A You could be waiting a long time. Where do you want to go?
B To the Kudamm.
A Hop in! I'm going there too.
B Nice of you. Many thanks.

A What are you thinking about?
B About all the things I still have to do.
A Don't think about them all the time, do one after the other.
B That's easier said than done.

A What are you talking about?
B About summer vacation.
A Oh yes, I'm looking forward to it, too.
B Thank heaven, the semester will soon be over.
A Where are you going on your vacation?
B We don't know yet.

Grammar explanations

I. *Da-* and *wo-* compounds

Darauf war ich nicht vorbereitet.
I was not prepared for that.

Ich bat sie **darum,** doch mitzukommen.
I asked her to come along.

Worauf wartest du?
What are you waiting for?

Woran erinnert dich das?
What does that remind you of?

Wie heißt der Stadtteil, **worin** wir uns befinden?
What's the name of the part of town we're in?

Wo kommt ihr **her?**
Where are you coming from?

In German, pronouns or interrogatives following a preposition may refer to persons.

Ich käme gern **mit ihr.**	*I would like to go with her.*
Wissen Sie, **von wem** er den Brief erhalten hat?	*Do you know from whom he received the letter?*

But the pronoun or the interrogative word may also refer to an inanimate object or an idea. In that case, the pronoun or question word is replaced by a compound, which cannot be used in reference to a person.

A. *Da-* compounds

In a statement, the pronoun that would normally follow a preposition is replaced by a **da**-compound: **da** + preposition, or if the preposition begins with a vowel, **dar** + preposition.

Wir experimentieren **mit dem Motor.**	*We're experimenting with the motor.*
Wir experimentieren **damit.**	*We're experimenting with it.*
Peter spricht **über ein mathematisches Problem.**	*Peter is talking about a mathematical problem.*
Peter spricht **darüber.**	*Peter is talking about it.*

Prepositions governing the genitive, and the prepositions **außer, bis, ohne,** and **seit,** do *not* form **da**-compounds.

If the object of a preposition is an infinitive phrase or a whole clause, that phrase or clause is anticipated by a **da**-compound before the preposition.

Er denkt nicht **daran**, das Buch zu lesen.	*He doesn't consider reading the book.*
Ich glaube nicht **daran**, daß sie noch lebt.	*I don't believe that she is still alive.*

B. *Wo*-compounds

In a question, the interrogative word **was**, when following a preposition, is replaced by a **wo**-compound: **wo** + preposition, or if the preposition begins with a vowel, **wor** + preposition.

Heidi erzählt **von der Reise**.	*Heidi is telling about the trip.*
Wovon erzählt Heidi?	*What is Heidi telling about?*
Karl sitzt **auf dem Stuhl**.	*Karl is sitting on the chair.*
Worauf sitzt Karl?	*What is Karl sitting on?*

The **wo**-compound may also be used as a *relative pronoun*.

Hier ist das Zimmer, **worin** (= in dem) er gestorben ist.	*Here is the room in which he died.*
Ich lese das Buch, **wovon** (= von dem) sie gesprochen hat.	*I am reading the book she talked about.*

Here the use of the **wo**-compound is optional. (Nowadays, many German speakers no longer use the **wo**-compound as a relative pronoun.)

If the preceding idea is not identified, the **wo**-compound *must* be used:

Ich weiß nicht, **wovon** (*not* von was) sie sprechen.	*I don't know what they are talking about.*

Note that with verbs of motion—especially **fahren**, **gehen**, and **kommen**—the directional compounds **dahin, dorthin, daher, dorther;** in questions, **wohin**, and **woher** are used, rather than **da**- and **wo**-compounds.

Woher kommst du?	*Where are you coming from?*
Ich komme gerade aus dem Theater.	*I'm just coming from the theater.*
Kommst du auch aus dem Theater?	*Are you, too, coming from the theater?*
Ja, ich komme auch **daher**.	*Yes, I'm coming from there, too.*
Wohin gehst du?	*Where are you going?*
Ich gehe ins Kino.	*I'm going to the movies.*
Gehst du auch **dahin**?	*Are you going there, too?*
Ja, natürlich.	*Yes, of course.*

Remember that **wohin** and **woher** are often split.

Wo gehst (fährst) du **hin?**	*Where are you going?*
Wo kommt ihr **her?**	*Where do you come from?*

CHECK YOUR COMPREHENSION

A. Substitute a **da**-compound for the prepositional phrase in the sentence.

EXAMPLE: Wir sprechen über den Unfall.
      Wir sprechen darüber.

1. Er denkt an die Geburtstagsfeier.
2. Birgit versteht etwas von Soziologie.
3. Wir antworten nicht auf die Frage.
4. Sie helfen ihr bei der Arbeit.
5. Gleich gehen wir zum Bahnhof.
6. Wir kommen gerade von der Universität.

B. Using a **wo**-compound, ask questions to which the following statements are answers.

EXAMPLE: Ich denke an die Reise.
      Woran denkst du?

1. Sie weiß nichts über den Unfall.
2. Morgen fliegen wir nach Hamburg.
3. Klaus spricht von dem Film.
4. Peter arbeitet an einem mathematischen Problem.
5. Ich fahre mit Ingeborgs Wagen.
6. Er hat sie an ihre Verabredung erinnert.

C. Replace the relative pronoun by a **wo**-compound.

1. Hast du das Buch schon gelesen, *über das* der Professor gestern sprach?
2. Ich kenne den Ort nicht, *von dem* er so begeistert ist.
3. Hier ist das Auto, *mit dem* wir einen Unfall hatten.
4. Zeigen Sie mir das Haus, *in dem* Sie wohnten.

II. Future perfect tense

Was werden die Leute wohl **gedacht haben?**
What must the people have thought?

Darüber **werden** die meisten Autofahrer sicher **gelacht haben.**
Most of the drivers probably laughed about it.

The future perfect tense is formed with the present tense of **werden,** the past participle of the principal verb, plus **haben** or **sein.** Literally, it expresses the conclusion of an action in the future, but is rarely used in that sense.

Bis heute abend werde ich diesen langen Brief **geschrieben haben.**	*By tonight I will have written this long letter.*
Ich hoffe, daß **sie** bis morgen **abgereist sein werden.**	*I hope they will have departed by tomorrow.*

It occurs more frequently with words such as **wohl** and **sicher** to express *past* or *future probability*, which in English is most often rendered with *must, probably,* or *I guess.*

Bis morgen werde ich das Buch **wohl gelesen haben.**	*By tomorrow I'll probably have read the book.*
Sie wird **sicher hungrig gewesen sein.**	*She must have been hungry.*

CHECK YOUR COMPREHENSION

Translate the following sentences into idiomatic English.

1. **Er wird wohl nicht daran gedacht haben.**
2. **Sie wird sicher böse gewesen sein.**
3. **Er wird wohl kaum davon gehört haben.**
4. **Bis morgen abend werde ich die Seminararbeit geschrieben haben.**

Conversation

Ach, ich Idiot!	*How stupid of me!* / *Oh, what a dummy I am!*
Prima!	*Great!*
Das trifft sich gut.	*That's fortunate, lucky.*
Sind Ihre Papiere in Ordnung?	*Are your papers in order?*

Ich kenne mich aus.	*I know the ropes.*
Auch uns geht es so.	*We feel the same way.*

DER AUTOSTOP

Ray ist ein amerikanischer Student deutscher Abstammung,° der an der Freien Universität in Berlin studiert. Er steht am Stadtrand° West-Berlins in der Nähe der Berliner Mauer an einem Übergangspunkt° in die DDR. Er hält einen Pappdeckel° in den Händen, worauf er „Nach Hamburg" geschrieben hat. Monika und Freddy nähern sich in einem Opel und halten an.

descent

city limits

transit point / piece of cardboard

Monika   (*aus dem Wagen*) Hallo, worauf warten Sie?

Ray   Worauf ich warte? Auf eine freundliche Seele, die mich nach Hamburg mitnimmt.

Monika   Nach Hamburg? Aber was steht denn da auf Ihrem Pappdeckel?

Ray   Was darauf steht? „Nach Hamburg", natürlich.

Freddy   Aber sehen Sie sich den Deckel doch mal von vorne an!

Ray   (*lacht*) Ach, ich Idiot. Ich hatte den Deckel auf den Kopf gestellt. Darüber werden die meisten Autofahrer wohl so gelacht haben, als sie mich sahen. Aber keiner wollte anhalten.

Freddy   Aber steigen Sie doch ein! Wir fahren nämlich nach Hamburg.

Ray   (*steigt ein*) Prima! Das trifft sich gut. Vielen Dank.

Monika   (*im Auto*) Sind Ihre Papiere in Ordnung für den Grenzübergang?°   *der Ausweise —ID*

border crossing

Ray   Oh ja. Ich kenne mich aus. Ich reise ziemlich oft in die Bundesrepublik.

Monika   So, warum?

Ray   Berlin gefällt mir ja gut. Aber manchmal muß ich einfach raus.° Man fühlt sich so eingesperrt.   *raus = heraus*

Monika   Allerdings. Uns geht es auch so.

QUESTIONS ON THE CONVERSATION

1. Welcher Abstammung ist Ray?
2. Wo befindet sich Ray gerade?
3. Was hält Ray in der Hand?
4. Was für einen Wagen fahren Monika und Freddy?
5. Wohin will Ray?
6. Warum konnte man Rays Pappdeckel nicht lesen?
7. Warum fährt Ray oft in die Bundesrepublik?

PERSONAL QUESTIONS

1. Sind Sie jemals per Autostop gereist? Im welchem Land? Und wohin? Hatten Sie Glück, oder mußten Sie oft lange warten?
2. Was für einen Wagen fahren Sie? Sind Sie zufrieden damit, oder würden Sie einen anderen kaufen, wenn Sie genug Geld hätten? Warum?
3. Wenn Sie einen Anhalter (*hitchhiker*) sähen, würden Sie ihn in Ihrem Wagen mitnehmen? Warum oder warum nicht?

Practice

A. Substitute a **da**-compound for the prepositional phrase.

1. Ursula schreibt Frau Schmidt über ihr Problem.
2. Ihre Antwort auf dieses Problem ist fabelhaft.
3. Das Mädchen denkt nur an ihre Arbeit.
4. Wir warten schon eine halbe Stunde auf eine Auskunft.
5. Ich spreche nicht gern über Politik.
6. Wir hören uns die Nachrichten über den Unfall an.
7. Morgen beginnen die Studenten mit der Prüfung.
8. Er will wieder eine Vorlesung über Physik halten.
9. Helga bittet um eine zweite Tasse Kaffee.
10. Die Europäer erinnern sich noch sehr gut an den letzten Weltkrieg.

B. Using a **wo**-compound, ask questions to which the following statements are answers.

EXAMPLE: Ich spreche von meinem Studium.
          Wovon sprichst du?

1. Ich weiß nichts über die Industrie in Amerika.
2. Die Touristen reden alle über die hohen Preise.
3. Frau Hagen wartet auf Nachricht.
4. Meine Freundin fährt gern mit meinem Fahrrad.
5. Gisela liest viel über Theater und Oper.
6. Ich trinke auf seine Gesundheit.
7. Wir halten nichts von diesem Gasthaus.
8. Sie versuchen alles mit Geld zu erreichen.
9. Helmut interessiert sich gar nicht für Geschichte.
10. Klaus kümmert sich um die Reise.

C. Fill in the appropriate relative pronoun, then substitute a **wo**-compound where possible.

1. Ist dies das Gedicht, über _____ du einen Test schreiben mußtest?
2. Wer ist die Frau, von _____ er so oft spricht?
3. Hier ist das neue Haus, in _____ unsere Eltern jetzt wohnen.
4. Was ist das für eine Krankheit, an _____ ihr Vater gestorben ist?
5. Wie heißt der Herr, mit _____ ihr eine Verabredung habt?

D. Substitute a directional compound (**dahin** or **dorthin, daher** or **dorther**) for the prepositional phrase, then rephrase as a question.

EXAMPLE: Morgen fahre ich nach Berlin.
          Ich fahre dorthin. Wohin fahre ich?

1. Ursula geht jeden Tag ins Kino.
2. Das Taxi kommt gerade vom Flugplatz.
3. Du fährst zum Bahnhof.
4. Wir gehen zu Fuß in die Stadt.
5. Ich komme gerade aus dem Theater.
6. Sie gehen zum Abendessen ins Restaurant „Goldene Stadt".

E. Adding the expression of probability in parentheses, put each sentence into the future perfect tense, then translate.

EXAMPLE: Sie ist durstig. *(wohl)*
          Sie wird wohl durstig gewesen sein.

1. Er hat nicht daran gedacht. *(sicher)*
2. Sie ist krank. *(wohl)*
3. Sie fahren gleich in die Stadt. *(wohl)*
4. Er hat sehr viel zu tun gehabt. *(wohl)*
5. Du hast von meinem Unfall gehört. *(sicher)*

F. Give the English equivalent.

1. Darüber weiß ich nicht viel.
2. Wo kommt sie her?
3. Sie sagt, daß sie nie darüber spricht.
4. Er wird wohl nicht sehr gesund gewesen sein.
5. Worüber hat euch Erna erzählt?
6. Er arbeitet schon lange daran.
7. Ich habe nichts dagegen.
8. Sie bat ihn darum, ihr nicht mehr zu schreiben.

Vocabulary development

Reflexive changes in some verbs

A. You know the verb **treffen,** *to meet.*

Ich habe sie gestern im Theater getroffen.	*I met her yesterday in the theater.*

It may also be used as a *reflexive verb.*

Wir haben **uns** vor Jahren einmal **getroffen.**	*We met once years ago.*

The impersonal idiom **das trifft sich gut** is a derivative of **sich treffen,** meaning *that's lucky, fortunate.*

Ich fahre nach Berlin.	*I'm driving to Berlin.*
Das trifft sich gut.	*That's lucky.*
Ich fahre auch dahin.	*I'm also going there.*

B. Kennen, *to know something* or *someone,* gives rise to **sich aus·kennen in** = *to be well versed in.*

Ich kenne mich in diesen Dingen aus.	*I know these matters well.*
Er **kennt sich in** dieser Stadt **aus.**	*He knows his way around in this city.*

C. Fühlen is often used reflexively with *an adjective.*

Er fühlt sich nicht **wohl.**	*He isn't feeling well.*
Sie fühlt sich **allein** und **verlassen.**	*She is feeling alone and abandoned.*

Hier fühlt man sich etwas **eingesperrt.**	*Here you feel a little hemmed in.*

Communicative exercises

A. Student A asks student B one of the following questions. Student B answers in the affirmative or negative with a **da**-compound, wherever possible.

Hast du deinen Eltern über deinen Unfall geschrieben?   Ja, ich habe ihnen . . .

Bist du auf die Prüfung vorbereitet?   Nein, ich habe . . .

Wartest du auf Sabine?

Habt ihr schon an eure Ferien gedacht?

Hast du sehr viel für diese neuen Jeans bezahlt?

Haben Sie schon etwas von dem neuen Theaterstück
gehört?

Bist du gestern mit Claudia ins Kino gegangen?

Bist du schon mit dem neuen Audi 5000 gefahren?

Hast du dich schon nach dem Preis dieses eleganten
Wagens erkundigt?

Denken sie oft an ihre Freunde in Ost-Berlin?

Weißt du, was man unter diesem Ausdruck versteht?

Hast du Herrn Steiner für die Einladung gedankt?

B. Student A makes a statement. Student B doesn't fully understand and asks A what was said or done. (Use **wo**-compounds wherever possible.)

Paul hat die ganze Zeit über seine eigenen   . . . hat Paul gesprochen?
Schwierigkeiten gesprochen.

Theo fährt morgen nach Hamburg.

Wir mußten lange auf Nachricht von ihm warten.

Wir redeten lange über unsere alten Schul-
kameraden.

Als ich ihn traf, kam er gerade aus Ost-Berlin.

Sie kennt sich in diesen Dingen sehr gut aus.

Ich kann leider nichts für diese armen Leute tun.

Er hat nichts gegen diesen Plan.

Wir fahren immer mit dem Bus.

Ich erinnere mich sehr gut an diesen Film.

C. Address questions to your classmates by using the following expressions in any combinations that make sense and have them answer in the affirmative or negative.

EXAMPLE: sich erinnern an   diese Prüfung
Erinnerst du dich an diese Prüfung? Ja, ich erinnere mich sehr gut daran.

denken an	die Reise
sprechen über	die Einladung
hören von	der Unfall
fahren mit	das Auto
danken für	die Ferien
sich erkundigen nach	die Freunde
warten auf	der Urlaub
arbeiten an	die Schwester
sich freuen auf	das mathematische Problem
erzählen von	der Preis des Wagens
	der Zug aus Hamburg
	die Zukunft

D. Two students play the roles of two friends meeting unexpectedly in town. A asks B what he/she is waiting for, where he/she is coming from and where he/she is going. B asks whether A has heard of the recent marriage of a mutual friend and whether he/she has received an invitation to the wedding reception. They decide they will go there together. One invites the other for a cup of coffee after they have finished their errands and they agree on where to meet.

Reading

EINDRÜCKE BEI EINEM BESUCH IN OST-BERLIN

Die Formalitäten am Checkpoint Charlie[1] dauern fast vierzig Minuten. Paßkontrolle, Geldwechsel, Ausfüllen von Formularen. Als ich wieder in meinem Wagen sitze, fragt mich ein Vopo:[2] „Haben Sie Zeitungen oder Bücher bei sich?" Darauf war ich nicht vorbereitet. Er öffnet alle Autotüren, schaut auf die Sitze und darunter. Auch muß ich ihm den Inhalt meiner Mappe zeigen. Endlich öffnet man mir die Schranke,° und ich bin in Ost-Berlin, die „Mauer"[3] liegt hinter mir.

Hier gibt es vorerst fast keinen Verkehr. Nach dem großen Straßenlärm auf der anderen Seite ist die Stille° fast willkommen. Ich fahre nach links und dann an einem Grashügel vorbei. Darunter liegt der Bunker, worin Hitler Selbstmord beging.°[4] „Ironie der Geschichte," denke ich, das ganze Dritte Reich[5] auf einen Grashügel zusammengeschrumpft°!

Aber weiter! Da vorne komme ich zur berühmten Allee „Unter den

"Checkpoint Charlie"

Linden".° Hier werde ich den Wagen mal parken und zu Fuß gehen. *"Under the Linden Trees"*
Eine schöne Allee mit ihren zwei Reihen von Bäumen in der Mitte;
dazwischen, im Schatten der Bäume, der Fußgängerweg und daneben, auf beiden Seiten, die Straße und der Bürgersteig! Das ist der
Ort, an dem sich ein großer Teil des kulturellen Lebens besonders
des Zweiten und Dritten Reiches abspielte.° Und einige Monumente *took place* sich abspielen
dieser Epochen in Deutschlands Geschichte sind immer noch da: die   *Continues*
Staatsbibliothek, die Humboldt-Universität,[6] etwas weiter unten der
Berliner Dom.[7]   *somewhat further down*

Wohin laufen denn die vielen Leute? Ach, Wachablösung° am   *changing of the guards*
„Mahnmal für die Opfer des Faschismus."[8] Soldaten im Stahlhelm,°   *(steel) helmet*
mit aufgezogenem Bajonett,° im Stechschritt.°   *drawn bayonets / goose stepping*

Ich glaube, ich gehe lieber in die andere Richtung. Da ist der weite   *believe*
Platz, in dessen Mitte das imposante „Brandenburger Tor" steht. Un-   *Tor- goal (in sports)*
ter dem Tor geht ein braun-rot uniformierter russischer Soldat auf und
ab.

Ich denke an ein Gespräch, das ich vor zwei Jahren mit einem Stu-   *before*
denten in Weimar hatte, der nicht gern Russisch lernte.[9] „Aber die
Russen sind doch Eure Freunde," sagte ich. „Unsere Brüder," antwortete er kurz, „Freunde kann man sich aussuchen."

Jetzt aber wieder zu „Unter den Linden" zurück, an der Deutschen

Brandenburger Tor. Dahinten: Unter den Linden

Staatsoper vorbei, zum Marx-Engels-Platz. Da steht ein neues Gebäude, die „Volkskammer",° worin das Parlament der DDR[10] zusammenkommt. Es ist ein großer Glaspalast, den man abends „von innen° illuminiert", lese ich in meinem Führer.° Ein langhaariger Junge, der neben mir steht, sagt: „Wir nennen das Ding ,das größte Lampengeschäft° in der DDR'," lacht und verschwindet.

lit., People's Chamber

from within / here: guide book

electric lighting store

Alexander-Platz

Der Fernsehturm

Kaiser-Wilhelm-Gedächtniskirche

Bald komme ich zum Alexander-Platz, einem offenen, schönen Platz, umgeben° von offiziellen Gebäuden, Geschäften und langen Reihen von hohen Wohnhäusern, worin viele Funktionäre° der DDR wohnen. Da steht auch das moderne Wahrzeichen von Ost-Berlin, der Fernsehturm.[11] Weit oben am Turm, in einer großen Glaskugel, die sich langsam dreht, befindet sich ein Restaurant. Die Kugel reflektiert oft die Abendsonne wie ein großes goldenes Kreuz.° Die West-Berliner nennen das Phänomen° lachend: „Die Rache des Vatikans°".[12]

surrounded
government employees

das Zeichen

golden cross
phenomenon / "The Revenge of the Vatican"

Auf beiden Seiten der Mauer haben die Berliner ihren bekannten Witz° und Humor nicht verloren!

wit

Jetzt sitze ich in einer Piano-Bar des neuen „Palasthotels"[13] auf der Karl-Liebknecht-Straße, nicht weit von „Unter den Linden". Das Hotel ist ganz im westlichen Stil eingerichtet.° Im Parterre[14] gibt es zum Beispiel eine „Boutique für die Dame", worin man Christian-Dior-Produkte kaufen kann. In zwölf verschiedenen Restaurants und Bars kann der Gast speisen und trinken, wovon allerdings sechs den Bürgern reserviert sind, die etwas „gleicher"° sind als die andern. Da kann man nur mit „harter West-Währung"°, also nicht mit DDR-Mark, bezahlen.[15] Aber auch westliche Kredit-Karten sind willkommen.

arranged

"equaller"
hard Western currency

Ich unterhalte mich mit einem Ingenieur, der sich an meinen Tisch gesetzt hat. „Hören Sie die verschiedenen Sprachen?" fragt er. „Wissen Sie, die Rumänen,° Bulgaren,° Ungarn° kommen auf Urlaub nach Ost-Berlin, weil ihnen die Stadt viel Neues, Westliches bietet. Ost-Berlin ist das Schaufenster des Ostens geworden." Wir sprechen noch lange über Ost und West. Aber um elf Uhr muß ich mich verabschieden, denn mein Visum ist nur bis Mitternacht gültig.[16] Wir schütteln uns die Hände, und er sagt: „Vielleicht treffen wir uns einmal wieder . . . hoffentlich im Westen."[17]

Rumanians / Bulgarians / Hungarians

Checkpoint Charlie liegt wieder hinter mir. Da vorne ist der Kudamm. Ein interessanter Tag, denke ich, und fast scheint mir, daß der ausgebrannte° Turm der Gedächtniskirche[18] gedankenvoll° auf die geteilte° Stadt heruntersieht.

burnt-out / thoughtfully
divided

CULTURAL NOTES

1. The point of entry to East Berlin for non-German nationals.

2. Abbreviation for **Volkspolizist,** a member of the **Volkspolizei,** the East-German state police force.

3. The Berlin Wall was erected in August 1961 to stop the massive outflow of refugees from the DDR to the West.

4. Now a mere grassy knoll, the bunker in which Hitler died is close to the Berlin Wall.

5. The "Third Empire," the Nazis' dramatic name for their state (1933–45),

was in fact taken from the title of a book published in 1923 by Arthur Moeller van den Bruck (1876–1925), a cultural critic whom the Nazis denied as a precursor. The First Reich was the Holy Roman Empire (of the German Nation), which Napoleon ended by force in 1806; the Second Reich (1871–1918) was the new empire created by the policies of Bismarck.

6. Originally the University of Berlin, founded in 1810, later renamed by the East-German regime for the university's founder, Alexander von Humboldt.

7. Severely damaged during the war, the Berlin Cathedral is only now being rebuilt (with some financial assistance from the BRD).

8. The "Commemorative Monument to the Victims of Fascism and Militarism."

9. Russian is a required subject in the public schools of the DDR.

10. The **Volkskammer** consists of 500 members, most of them belonging to the SED (**Sozialistische Einheitspartei** [= *Unity Party*] **Deutschlands**). The real political power resides in the **Staatsrat,** whose chairman is the president of the country. There is also a **Ministerrat,** a cabinet, directly responsible to the **Staatsrat** and indirectly to the **Volkskammer.**

11. The Television Tower was the East German regime's first great prestige project. Approximately 1200 feet high, it dominates the Berlin landscape. Since it had to be erected on Berlin's sandy soil, the tower represents a great engineering feat and is seen by many East Germans as a symbol of their capital.

12. Though the Christian churches are not suppressed in the DDR, they are certainly not furthered by the Socialist state!

13. Opened in 1980.

14. *Parterre* (French) or **Erdgeschoß:** in continental Europe the first floor of a building. „**Erster Stock**" in Germany = *second floor* in America!

15. This is a new feature in the chain of "Intershops" established by the regime many years ago. Though railing against "bourgeois consumerism," the government needed freely convertible currency. In the "Intershops" one can buy imported coffee, cosmetics, jeans, all sorts of "luxury" items, even automobiles, if one can pay in the hard currency of the West.

16. The most common tourist visa to East Berlin is valid only for one day. For a longer stay in East Berlin and/or the rest of the country, the visa formalities (including travel and hotel arrangements) are more complicated.

17. It is under highly exceptional and stringent circumstances that a DDR-citizen is permitted to travel outside the Soviet Bloc countries. However, retired people may leave the country or freely travel in the West.

18. The **Kaiser-Wilhelm-Gedächtniskirche,** whose blackened main tower has been left as a war memorial. It and the modern church now built beside it are known simply as the *Memorial Church* (**Gedächtniskirche**)— a symbol of Berlin's indomitable will to live even in the midst of rubble, as it had to do for a long time after the war.

QUESTIONS

1. Worauf war der Besucher nicht vorbereitet?
2. Was mußte er dem Vopo zeigen?
3. Was liegt unter dem Grashügel?
4. Wo parkt der Besucher seinen Wagen?
5. Wohin laufen die Leute?
6. Worunter steht ein russischer Soldat?
7. Woran denkt der Besucher?
8. Wie nennt der Junge die „Volkskammer"?
9. Auf welchem Platz steht der Fernsehturm?
10. Für wen sind einige Restaurants und Bars im Palasthotel reserviert?
11. Mit wem unterhält sich der Besucher?
12. Worüber unterhalten sich die beiden?

Review

A. Replace the **da-** compound by a prepositional phrase that includes the words in parentheses.

1. Wir wohnen direkt daneben.   (*factory*)
2. Du wirst hoffentlich bald darüber erzählen.   (*your trip*)
3. Hat er wirklich nichts davon gegessen?   (*this meat*)

1 Bornholmer Strasse
2 Chausseestrasse
3 Invalidenstrasse
4 Friedrichstrasse
5 Heinrich Heine Strasse
6 Oberbaumbrücke
7 Sonnenallee

4. Sie hatten schon davon gehört.   (*the wedding*)   *die Hochzeit*
5. Wir wollen jetzt nicht darüber sprechen.   (*the accident*)

B. Replace the expressions in italics with a **da**-compound.

1. *Mit diesem Buch* kann er viel Geld verdienen.
2. Leider fing er wieder an, *von seiner Krankheit* zu reden.
3. *An diesem Sport* gefällt mir sehr wenig.
4. Sie lachen nur *über meine Probleme*.
5. Ursula versteht *vom Bergsteigen* mehr als ich.

dienen – serve
der Diener – servant
die Dienst – service
verdienen – earn
(deserve)

C. Answer the questions by using the words in parentheses.

1. Wovon hat er dir erzählt?   (*his many journeys*)
2. Woran arbeitest du?   (*a mathematical problem*)
3. Wozu habt ihr keine Zeit?   (*to converse with visitors*)
4. Wonach erkundigt er sich?   (*the price of the car*)
5. Worauf freuen Sie sich schon?   (*my summer vacation*)

Er habt keine Zeit, sich mit den Besuchern zu unterhalten

to look forward to

D. Ask the questions with a **wo**-compound that would yield the following answers.

1. Ich glaube nicht an diese Theorie.
2. Sie freut sich auf das Wiedersehen mit ihrem Freund.
3. Er sprach lange über seine Zukunftspläne.
4. Alle Leute laufen zum Alexanderplatz.
5. Wir haben kein Geld für unseren Urlaub.

E. Express in German.

bitten

1. We cannot talk about it now.
2. What were the children playing with?
3. I don't know what he is writing about.
4. She must have been very angry.
5. What is he working on now?
6. She asked me never to write her again.
7. I know my way around in this town.
8. Where are you coming from?
9. I don't feel too well.
10. I no longer remember that.

nicht mehr

Guided composition

Write a short monologue on the thoughts and impressions that you had when driving into a new city or country. Describe some of the architectural features or public monuments that impressed you most. You may also report conversations you had with strangers or friends. Use **da**- and **wo**-compounds whenever possible.

Chapter vocabulary

Nouns

die	Abendsonne	*evening sun*
die	Allee, -n	*avenue*
der	Anhalter, -	*hitchhiker*
der	Autostop, -s	*hitchhiking*
die	Autotür, -en	*car door*
der	Besuch, -e	*visit*
der	Besucher, -	*visitor*
die	Boutique, -n	*boutique*
der	Bunker, -	*shelter*
der	Deckel, -	*lid, cover*
die	Einladung, -en	*invitation*
die	Epoche, -n	*epoch*
das	Erdgeschoß, -sse	*first floor*
der	Fernsehturm, ̈e	*TV tower*
die	Formalität, -en	*formality*
der	Führer, -	*leader, guide*
der	Fußgängerweg, -e	*sidewalk*
die	Geschichte	*history*
die	Glaskugel, -n	*glass ball*
der	Glaspalast, ̈e	*glass palace*
der	Grashügel, -	*grass hill*
der	Idiot, -en	*idiot*
der	Ingenieur, -e	*engineer*
der	Inhalt, -e	*contents*
die	Kreditkarte, -n	*credit card*
das	Mahnmal, -e	*monument*
die	Mappe, -n	*folder*
die	Mauer, -n	*wall*
das	Monument, -e	*monument*
das	Opfer, -	*victim*
die	Ordnung, -en	*order*
	in Ordnung sein	*to be OK*
der	Osten	*east*
die	Papiere (pl.)	*documents*
das	Parterre	*first floor*
die	Paßkontrolle, -n	*passport control*
das	Reich, -e	*empire*
die	Reihe, -n	*series, row*
(das)	Russisch	*Russian*
das	Schaufenster, -	*display window*
die	Schranke, -n	*barrier*
die	Schwierigkeit, -en	*difficulty*
die	Seite, -n	*side*
der	Selbstmord, -e	*suicide*
der	Soldat, -en	*soldier*
die	Sommerferien (pl.)	*summer vacation*
der	Stadtteil, -e	*city district*
der	Straßenlärm	*street noise*
das	Tor, -e	*gate*
der	Turm, ̈e	*tower*
das	Visum, Visa	*visa*
die	Wachablösung, -en	*change of the guard*
das	Wahrzeichen, -	*landmark*
das	Wohnhaus, ̈er	*home, house*
der	Zukunftsplan, ̈e	*plan for the future*

Verbs

sich aus·kennen, kannte, ausgekannt	*to know one's way around*
(sich) aus·suchen	*to select*
(sich) drehen	*to turn*
ein·richten	*to furnish*
ein·sperren	*to lock in*
experimentieren	*to experiment*
herunter·sehen (sieht), sah, heruntergesehen	*to look down*
illuminieren	*to illuminate*
sich nähern	*to approach*
reflektieren	*to reflect*
reservieren	*to reserve*
schütteln	*to shake*
speisen	*to dine*
stellen; auf den Kopf—	*to put; to turn upside down*
sich treffen (trifft), traf, getroffen	*to meet*
das trifft sich gut	*that's lucky*
verabschieden	*to say good-bye*
verschwinden, verschwand, (ist) verschwunden	*to disappear*
verstehen von	*to understand about*
verstehen unter	*to mean by*
vorbereiten	*to prepare*

Other words _____

aufgezogen	*drawn (bayonet)*	gültig (sein)	*valid*
berühmt	*famous*	langhaarig	*long-haired*
dagegen	*however*	kulturell	*cultural*
daher	*therefore; from there*	offiziell	*official*
dahin	*there (to)*	prima	*great*
dorther	*from there*	uniformiert	*uniformed*
dorthin	*there (to)*	vorerst	*first of all*
golden	*golden*	westlich	*western*
Gott sei Dank!	*thank heaven*	willkommen	*welcome*
		wonach	*according to which*
		wozu	*why, what for*

Mini-dialogues

A Wo gehst du hin?
B Zu einem Essen im Hotel „Vier Jahreszeiten".[1]
A Was, im Hotel „Vier Jahreszeiten"? Wo hast du denn so viel Geld her?
B Ich bin von den Eltern meiner Freundin eingeladen worden.
A Toll! Dahin möchte ich auch einmal eingeladen werden.

A Hier darf nicht geraucht werden.
B Tatsächlich? Hier darf man nicht rauchen? Warum denn nicht?
A Das ist doch ein öffentliches Gebäude.
B Na und?
A Bei uns in Amerika ist nach einem neuen Gesetz das Rauchen in
öffentlichen Gebäuden verboten.

A Habt ihr euch gestern bei der Party gut unterhalten?
B Und wie! Es wurde viel gegessen und getrunken.
A Und getanzt wurde nicht?
B Oh doch! Aber stell nicht so viele Fragen. Ich habe einen
scheußlichen Kater.

A Where are you going?
B To dinner in the Hotel "Vier Jahreszeiten."[1]
A What, in the Hotel "Vier Jahreszeiten?" Where
did you get all that money from?
B I've been invited by my girl friend's parents.
A Terrific! I'd like to be invited there sometime
myself.

A Smoking is not allowed here.
B Really? You're not allowed to smoke here? Why
not?
A This is a public building.
B So what?
A Here in America, according to a new law,
smoking is prohibited in public buildings.

A Did you have a good time at the party last
night?
B And how! There was a lot to eat and drink.
A And there was no dancing?
B Of course there was. But don't ask so many
questions. I have a terrible hangover.

*Hofbräuhaus in
München*

[1]"The Four Seasons," a well-known and luxurious hotel and restaurant in Munich.

Grammar explanations

Passive voice

München **wird** manchmal „die heimliche Haupstadt der Bundesrepublik" **genannt.**
Munich is sometimes called the "secret capital of the Federal Republic."

Ich **wurde** von weinenden Kindern *geweckt.*
I was awakened by crying children.

Die gute Luft **ist** von der Industrie **verschmutzt worden.**
The good air has been polluted by industry.

Berlin **wurde** durch den Krieg **zerstört.**
Berlin was destroyed by the war.

Die berühmte Bierstube in München **kann** heute noch **besichtigt werden.**
The famous beer hall in Munich can be visited to this day.

Du **mußt** in eine bessere Laune **versetzt werden.**
You need to be cheered up.

Hier **wird** nicht **getanzt!**
No dancing here!

Es **wurde** viel **erzählt** und **gelacht.**
There was much talk and laughter.

A. Formation

The passive in English is formed with the auxiliary *to be* and the past participle of the principal verb.

The "Oktoberfest" is celebrated every year in the early fall.
The letter was (being) written by Karl.

In German the passive voice is formed by using the conjugated form of the auxiliary **werden** and the *past participle* of the principal verb. The passive voice can be formed in all six tenses merely by conjugating the auxiliary **werden.**

Pres.:	Der Brief **wird** von Karl **geschrieben.**	*The letter is (being) written by Karl.*
Past:	Der Brief **wurde** von Karl **geschrieben.**	*The letter was (being) written by Karl.*
Pres. perf.:	Der Brief **ist** von Karl **geschrieben worden.**	*The letter has been written by Karl.*
Past perf.:	Der Brief **war** von Karl **geschrieben worden.**	*The letter had been written by Karl.*
Future:	Der Brief **wird** von Karl **geschrieben werden.**	*The letter will be written by Karl.*
Fut. perf.:	Der Brief **wird** von Karl **geschrieben worden sein.**[1]	*The letter will have been written by Karl.*

In the *perfect tenses*, note that the past participle of the auxiliary **werden** drops the **ge-: worden;** this form occurs only in the passive and only in these tenses. Also note that the auxiliary of **werden** is **sein.**

CHECK YOUR COMPREHENSION

Put the following verbs into the passive voice, using the indicated subject and tense.

EXAMPLE: Ich / aufhalten (*present perfect*)
     Ich bin aufgehalten worden.

  1. Sie (*3rd sing.*) / erkennen (*past*)   2. Die Frage / entscheiden (*future*)

---

[1]In the passive, the future perfect is rarely used. It is listed here for the sake of completing the paradigm.

3. Das Problem / lösen (*present perfect*)
4. Das Theater / aufbauen (*present*)
5. Die Städte / besetzen (*past perfect*)

6. Die Dörfer / zerstören (*future*)
7. Diese Mauer / verstärken (*present perfect*)
8. Ein Walzer / spielen (*past*)

B. Usage

The passive voice is used when the subject does not perform the action, but is *acted upon*.

Die Stadt München wird jedes Jahr von vielen Touristen besucht.	*The city of Munich is visited by many tourists every year.*

Since the focus of a sentence is usually on the subject, the passive voice allows the speaker to emphasize the receiver, rather than the performer, of the action. Compare the above sentence with its equivalent in the active voice:

Viele Touristen besuchen jedes Jahr die Stadt München.	*Many tourists visit the city of Munich every year.*

Here the emphasis is on **viele Touristen.**

In the passive voice the performer of the action (or "agent") may therefore be omitted:

Sie wird jeden Tag am Bahnhof (von ihrem Mann) abgeholt.	*Every day she is picked up at the railway station (by her husband).*

If the "agent" is mentioned, a preposition must be used:

von (+dat.!) is the most frequent and occurs with a *personal agent.*
durch (+acc.!) is used with an *impersonal force.*
mit (+dat.!) is used when the agent is an *instrument.*

Sie wird jeden Tag von ihm abgeholt.	*She is picked up by him every day.*
Dresden wurde durch den Krieg zerstört.	*Dresden was destroyed by the war.*
Dieser Brief ist mit einem Computer geschrieben worden.	*This letter was written with a computer.*

Notice the structural changes as a sentence is converted from the active into the passive voice.

Active

Subject = Performer   Direct Object = Receiver

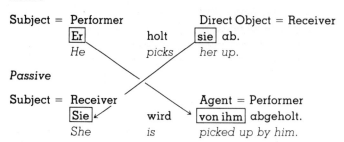

Er   holt   sie ab.
He   picks   her up.

Passive

Subject = Receiver   Agent = Performer

Sie   wird   von ihm abgeholt.
She   is   picked up by him.

In dependent ("Verb Last") word order, be careful to put the conjugated auxiliary at the end of the clause!

Ich glaube nicht, daß er am Flugplatz abgeholt **wird**.

Wir glauben nicht, daß er am Flugplatz abgeholt worden **ist**.

CHECK YOUR COMPREHENSION

A. Form the passive voice in the tense indicated in parentheses.

1. Er _____ lange _____. (*aufhalten, present perfect*)
2. Der Schauspieler _____ sofort vom Publikum _____. (*erkennen, past*)
3. Wir _____ am Bahnhof _____. (*abholen, future*)
4. Dieser junge Professor _____ oft für einen Studenten _____. (*halten, present*)
5. Das Problem _____ endlich _____. (*lösen, present perfect*)
6. Ein Teil der Kirche _____ während des Krieges _____. (*zerstören, past perfect*)
7. Nach dem Krieg _____ sie wieder _____. (*aufbauen, past*)
8. Ich glaube kaum, daß er von ihnen _____. (*einladen, present & present perfect*)

B. Fill in the blanks with the appropriate preposition.

1. Dieser Brief ist sicher _____ ihr geschrieben worden.
2. Dieses Gasthaus wurde vor einem Jahr _____ ein Feuer zerstört.
3. Ich wurde am Flugplatz _____ einer Limousine abgeholt.
4. Er wurde _____ ihren Eltern eingeladen.

C. Change the following sentences from the active to the passive voice.

1. Sie hat dieses Gedicht sehr gut interpretiert.
2. Er ruft sie jeden Tag an.
3. Die Professoren haben das Problem sehr lange besprochen.
4. Sie hatte ihn gleich erkannt.

C. Passive voice with modal auxiliaries

A sentence in the passive voice may contain a modal auxiliary, especially in the present and the simple past. In that case the word order is: conjugated form of the modal + past participle of the principal verb + infinitive of **werden.**

Hilde **möchte** am Flugplatz **abgeholt werden.**	*Hilde would like to be picked up at the airport.*

CHECK YOUR COMPREHENSION

Form a sentence in the passive voice with the modal indicated in parentheses.

EXAMPLE: Er zeigte dieses Bild nicht.   (*dürfen*)
   Dieses Bild durfte von ihm nicht gezeigt werden.

1. Mit der finanziellen Hilfe seines Vaters eröffnete er eine Klinik.   (*können*)
2. Ingeborg interpretiert ein bekanntes Gedicht von Schiller.   (*sollen*)
3. Was für Theorien studiert ihr bei Professor Weimann?   (*müssen*)
4. Wir besprachen dieses Problem nicht.   (*können*)

D. Special problems with the passive in German

In English the indirect object in the active voice can be made into the subject of the passive voice.

Indirect object	*Subject*
They told *him* the truth.	*He* was told the truth.

In German this is not possible. The direct object of the active voice is always used as the subject in the passive voice. The indirect object remains in the dative case.

Man sagte **ihm** die Wahrheit.	*They told him the truth.*
Die Wahrheit wurde **ihm** gesagt.	*He was told the truth.* *(The truth was told to him.)*

For the sake of emphasis, the indirect object may move to first position in the sentence.

Ihm wurde die Wahrheit gesagt.   *They told him the truth.*

However, it is possible to use the impersonal **es** as a subject, especially with verbs that govern the dative:

Es ist **ihm** gesagt worden, daß er   *He was told that he was wrong.*
unrecht hatte.

At times **es** is used, even where there is a noun that could serve as a passive subject:

Es wurde **ein alter Film** gezeigt   *An old film was (being) shown.*
(= Ein alter Film wurde gezeigt.)

Or where there is no ostensible subject:

Es wurde getanzt.   *There was dancing.*

If there is another expression in first position such as an adverb of time or in a question, **es** cannot be used.

Gestern wurde ihm gesagt, daß . . .   *Yesterday he was told that . . .*

Während des Fluges wurde ein alter   *During the flight an old movie was*
Film gezeigt.   *being shown.*

Wurde ein alter Film gezeigt?   *Did they show an old movie?*

Ist ihm gesagt worden, daß . . .?   *Was he told that . . .?*

Wurde getanzt?   *Was there dancing?*

Notice that in the active voice the indefinite **man** would be used.

Man sagte ihm gestern, daß . . .   *They told him yesterday that . . .*

Während des Fluges zeigte **man**   *During the flight they showed an*
einen alten Film.   *old movie*

Zeigte **man** einen alten Film?   *Did they show an old movie?*

Hat **man** ihm gesagt, daß . . .?   *Did they tell him that . . .?*

Tanzte man?   *Did they dance?*

The passive voice of some verbs, such as **arbeiten** and **lachen,** which do not normally govern an accusative object, may express an activity as such. This leads to a characteristically German construction that cannot be translated directly.

Hier wird gearbeitet.   ⎫   *There is work going on here.*
Es wird hier gearbeitet.   ⎭   *(Lit.: Here is being worked.)*

Es wurde viel gelacht.   *There was much laughing.*
                                                    (Lit.: It was being laughed a lot.)

CHECK YOUR COMPREHENSION

A. Put the following sentences into the passive voice, first without **es** and then with it.

1. Man machte ihm klar, daß . . .
2. Man versprach uns nichts.
3. Man wird Ihnen nicht danken.

B. Translate the following sentences into English.

1. Es wurde getrunken.
2. Was wird hier vorbereitet?
3. Hier wird nicht getanzt.
4. Ist viel geredet und gelacht worden?

Conversation

das Übliche	*the usual*
(jemand) in eine bessere Laune versetzen	*to cheer (someone) up*
Reg dich nicht auf!	*Don't get excited!*
Prost! Zum Wohl!	*Cheers! To your health!*

DIE MAß BIER[1]

Josef, der in New York bei einer deutschen Firma arbeitet, ist gerade in seiner Heimatstadt München gelandet und trifft sich mit seinem alten Freund Franz im Flughafen-Restaurant.

Franz   Hast du einen angenehmen Flug über den Atlantik gehabt?

pleasant

Josef   Das Übliche. Es wurde gegessen und getrunken und irgendein Film gezeigt, der mich aber nicht interessiert hat.

Franz   Hast du dich auch etwas ausruhen können?

Josef   Nein, dieses Mal nicht. Ich wurde immer wieder von einem weinenden Kind und einigen laut sprechenden Passagieren aufgeweckt.

Franz   Du mußt dich eben heute nacht von der Zeitumstellung° erholen.

jetlag

Josef   Das werde ich auf jeden Fall tun.

Franz   Aber zuerst mußt du in eine bessere Laune versetzt werden. (*Zur Kellnerin*): Zwei Maß, bitte!

(Die Kellnerin bringt zwei riesige Krüge Bier.)

Franz   Sieh dir mal diese Maß an!

Josef   Wieso denn?

[1]In Munich and most parts of Bavaria **die Maß,** denoting a *tankard* or *stein*, is used in the feminine. **Das Maß,** however, means *measure, size, dimension*, etc.

Hofbräuhaus in München

Franz   Zwei oder drei Zentimeter Schaum! Man spricht hier vom „großen Betrug im Krug" und sagt, die Maß sollte um zwei oder drei Zentimeter vergrößert werden. Oder mehr Bier und weniger Schaum.[2]

Josef   Reg dich nicht auf und trink doch. Jetzt mußt du in eine bessere Laune versetzt werden.

Franz & Josef (zueinander)   Prost! Prost! Zum Wohl!

QUESTIONS ON THE CONVERSATION

1. Bei was für einer Firma arbeitet Josef in New York?
2. Wo ist er gerade gelandet?
3. Mit wem trifft er sich?
4. Was wurde während des Fluges getan?
5. Von wem wurde Josef immer wieder aufgeweckt?
6. Womit soll Josef in eine bessere Laune versetzt werden?
7. Worüber regt sich Franz auf?
8. Wer muß jetzt in eine bessere Laune versetzt werden?

PERSONAL QUESTIONS

1. Fliegen Sie gern?
2. Sind Sie schon einmal über den Atlantik oder den Pazifik geflogen? Wohin?
3. Was tun Sie während eines Fluges?

[2]Some time ago, a large number of beer-drinking enthusiasts in Munich formed an association, the **"Verein gegen betrügerisches Einschenken"** (*Association against Fraudulent Drafting*) to reduce the amount of foam served in a stein of beer!

Practice

A. Change the following sentences from the active to the passive voice. Watch the change in the subject (the performer of the action), and be careful of the verb tense.

EXAMPLE: Die Passagiere haben Josef aufgeweckt.
Josef ist von den Passagieren aufgeweckt worden.

1. Der Feind hat einen großen Teil der Stadt zerstört.
2. Er hat uns an den Stadtrand geführt.
3. Während des Fluges aß man wenig und trank viel.
4. Der Wecker weckt mich jeden Morgen um sechs Uhr.
5. Das Feuer zerstörte ein großes Geschäftshaus.
6. Meine Freunde holen mich am Flugplatz ab.
7. Hier darf man nicht rauchen.
8. Ich weiß nicht, ob man ihn eingeladen hat.
9. Man öffnet das Museum schon sehr früh.
10. Man spielte einen bekannten Walzer.
11. Wir glauben, daß man diese Katastrophe nicht so bald vergessen wird.
12. Herr und Frau Kunz haben mich gestern zum Konzert eingeladen.
13. Er hat den Brief zerrissen.
14. Man wird dieses Lied zu Weihnachten singen.
15. Diese Touristen brachten nur wenig Gepäck mit.

B. Using the impersonal construction, change each sentence into the passive voice.

EXAMPLES: Man sagte uns, daß wir hier bleiben können.
Uns wurde gesagt, daß wir hier bleiben können.

Man arbeitet hier viel.
Hier wird viel gearbeitet.

1. Man sagte mir, heute ist ein Feiertag.
2. Man antwortete ihm nicht auf seine Frage.
3. Man tanzte den ganzen Abend.
4. Man redet sehr viel über uns.
5. Man arbeitet hier sehr schwer.

C. Put the following sentences into the active voice.

1. Es wurde uns nichts darüber gesagt.
2. Wann wird uns das Mittagessen gebracht werden?
3. Ist sie schon angerufen worden?
4. Er wurde vom Publikum nicht gut verstanden.
5. Darf hier geraucht werden?

D. Give the English equivalent.

1. Dieses mathematische Problem wurde von den meisten Studenten nicht gut verstanden.
2. Diese Platte wird sehr oft gespielt.
3. Darüber wird sehr viel geredet.
4. Diese Kirche ist durch Feuer zerstört worden.
5. Es wurde ihm von niemand geholfen.
6. Dieses Dokument soll von uns unterschrieben werden.
7. Während des Fluges wurde viel gegessen und wenig geschlafen.
8. Diese Briefe sind mit einem Computer geschrieben worden.

Vocabulary development

A. *Maß halten ist gut!* (To know one's bounds is good.)

Das Maß has many uses and meanings. Fundamentally it means *measure, measurement, size, dimension, gauge;* also *proportion* and *moderation.*

Some examples:

in hohem Maße	*to a high degree*
in großem Maße	*to a large extent*
in gewissem Maße	*to a certain extent*
in vollem Maße	*amply, completely*

(Notice that in these set expressions the old dative ending **-e** is retained.)
You will also find **das Maß** in some idioms such as:

Das Maß ist voll.	*My patience is exhausted.*
Das geht über alle Maßen.[1]	*That exceeds all bounds.*
Das Maß vollmachen.	*Fill the cup to the brim.*

What then is ein **Anzug nach Maß?** And what is the meaning of: **Halte Maß in allen Dingen!**

The adjective derived from **Maß** is **mäßig,** *moderate:* its antonym **maßlos,** *immoderate.*

[1] An old plural form.

Er ist ein mäßiger Trinker.   *He is a moderate drinker.*

   Mittelmäßig means *average* or *mediocre*.

Jakob ist ein mittelmäßiger Student.   *Jacob is an average (or: mediocre)*
                                               student.

   Regelmäßig means *regularly*. The ad for a German schnaps reads:

„Trink ihn mäßig, aber regelmäßig."   *"Drink it moderately but regularly."*

B. *aufwachen or (auf)wecken?*

   The verb **auf·wachen** means to *awaken, wake up (oneself)*. The verb
auf·wecken, however, means *to wake somebody else up.*

Um wieviel Uhr wachst du auf?   *At what time do you wake up?*

Wachen Sie immer selber auf, oder   *Do you wake up by yourself, or do*
müssen Sie geweckt werden?   *you have to be awakened?*

Haben Sie einen Wecker?   *Do you have an alarm clock?*

   The past participle of **auf·wecken, aufgeweckt,** used as an adjective,
means *alert, lively.*

Sie ist ein **aufgewecktes** Mädchen.   *She is a lively girl.*

Communicative exercises

A. Ask your classmates the following questions and have them give answers in
the passive voice. Choose answers from the suggestions on the right, or think of
other appropriate responses.

Wer singt dieses Lied?   Dieses Lied wird von . . .
Wer hat diese Frage gestellt?   der große Lärm
Wer muß diesen Brief unterschreiben?   mein reicher Freund
Was hat ihn in eine schlechte Laune versetzt?   ein Bekannter
Wer hat diesen eleganten Wagen gekauft?   eine bekannte Rockgruppe
Wer wird sie am Flugplatz abholen?   ein aufmerksamer Student
Wer weckt dich jeden Morgen?   sie und ich
Wer hat euch zum Konzert eingeladen?   Herr und Frau Schlesinger
                                            meine Eltern

B. Student A makes the statement on the left. Student B utters his/her disbelief, starting the sentence with **tatsächlich** (= *possible*) and then using the **man**-construction.

Hier darf nicht geraucht werden.   Tatsächlich, man darf . . .
Das Auto ist schon gewaschen worden.
Er ist mit einer Limousine am Flugplatz abgeholt
    worden.
Hier wird nur am Sonnabend getanzt.
Dieses Problem ist nie diskutiert worden.
Mir wurde dieses Dokument nicht gezeigt.
Es wird hier keine Auskunft gegeben.
Das Oktoberfest wird schon im September gefeiert.

C. Student A asks student B the following questions. B answers and then asks **Und du?** eliciting a reply from A.

Um wieviel Uhr wachst du während der Woche auf? Und am Sonntag?
Mußt du immer geweckt werden? Von wem oder womit?
Um wieviel Uhr willst du nach einer langen Party geweckt werden?
Schläfst du manchmal bei den Vorlesungen an der Universität ein?
Von wem wirst du dann geweckt?
Glaubst du, daß du ein guter oder mittelmäßiger Student bist?
Bist du ein mäßiger oder regelmäßiger Trinker? Raucher?
Versuchst du, in allen Dingen Maß zu halten?

D. Student A asks student B what people do during a long flight:
Was tut man während eines langen Fluges?
Student B answers, using as many impersonal passive forms as possible:
Es wird . . . etc.

Reading

MÜNCHEN UND DAS OKTOBERFEST

    München wird manchmal „die heimliche Hauptstadt der Bundesrepublik" genannt, denn sie hat jene Eigenschaften, die oft mit einer Hauptstadt verbunden werden. Sie hat ein reges kulturelles Leben—viele Theater, Museen, Bibliotheken, Orchester und heutzutage auch Filmproduktionsgesellschaften°—und viele schöne Paläste und Kirchen, in denen die großen Baustile der Vergangenheit, zum Beispiel der Barock, das Rokoko oder der Neo-Klassizismus,[1] großartig verwirklicht° worden sind. Sie hat aber auch schöne Parks und viel

film production companies

realized

„saubere" Industrie, durch die die gute Luft, die von den Alpen her-
unterweht,° nicht zu sehr verschmutzt wird. Die Alpen liegen nur un-   *blows down*
gefähr 45 Kilometer außerhalb der Stadt und können an schönen
Tagen von den Türmen der bekannten Frauenkirche[2] gesehen werden.

Im Jahr 1972 wurden in München die Olympischen Spiele ausgetragen, wofür ein großer Teil der Stadt restauriert wurde. Auch wurden ein großes, modernes Stadion gebaut und eine Untergrundbahn,
durch die der Straßenverkehr sehr erleichtert worden ist. Nach Berlin
und Hamburg ist jetzt München die drittgrößte Stadt in der Bundesrepublik und wird jedes Jahr von mehr Touristen als die meisten anderen Städte Deutschlands besucht.

München hat eine Geschichte, die bis ins Mittelalter zurückgeht.
In der neuesten Geschichte wird die Stadt oft auch als Ausgangs-
punkt° der Nazi-Bewegung genannt, denn im Jahre 1923 fand da der   *starting point*
Hitler-Putsch[3] in einer Bierhalle statt, die heute noch besichtigt werden kann. Aber trotz dieses schwarzen Blattes° in ihrer Geschichte   *leaf, page*
hat die Stadt nach dem Krieg ihre frühere „Gemütlichkeit" wiedergefunden. Bezeichnend für diese Gemütlichkeit ist das Oktoberfest,
wofür München in der ganzen Welt bekannt geworden ist.

Das Oktoberfest beginnt Mitte September und hört Anfang Oktober
auf. Es wurde zum ersten Mal im Jahr 1810 gefeiert. Es ist eine Art

Frauenkirche in München

Jahrmarkt, an dem sich das ganze Volk über zwei Wochen lang
großartig unterhält. Es gibt Umzüge durch die ganze Stadt, zu denen
die meisten Gegenden Deutschlands und viele andere Länder Europas, zum Beispiel Österreich, die Schweiz oder Italien, ihre folk-
loristischen° Gruppen senden.

　folkloric

Von manchen dieser Gruppen werden auch Vorstellungen gegeben. Volkstänze werden von den vielen „Dirndln und Buam"[4] auf-
geführt, und natürlich werden auch viele Volkslieder gesungen. Und
auf der „Wies'n"[5] gibt es Schaubuden° und Verkaufsstände.° Es wird
viel getanzt und noch viel mehr getrunken. Münchner Bier, natürlich,
denn das Oktoberfest wird besonders von den weltbekannten Braue-
reien Münchens organisiert und unterstützt. Das Fest wird in einer
großen Halle vom Oberbürgermeister° der Stadt eröffnet. Er zapft ein
großes Faß° Bier an und erklärt „o'zapft is!"[6] Und dann geht es los!

　booths for games /
　vending stands

　Lord Mayor
　barrel

Wer einmal erfahren will, was die Worte des alten Volksliedes
„Trink, trink, Brüderlein,° trink, lasse die Sorgen zu Haus" bedeuten,
der muß einmal nach München zum Oktoberfest gehen. Man kann da
tatsächlich für kurze Zeit seine Sorgen vergessen. Es kann aber auch
sein, daß man am Tag nach dem Fest mit einem großen Kater aufwacht.

　little brother

Mit freundlichen Grüßen
With kind regards
Avec nos compliments

Landeshauptstadt München, Fremdenverkehrsamt
Munich Tourist Office
Office du Tourisme de Munich

Rindermarkt 5, D-8000 München 2
Tel. (089) 2 39 11, Telex 05-24 801 frast d

CULTURAL NOTES

1. Baroque, rococo, neoclassicism: important architectural styles.

2. A cathedral built in the fifteenth century, whose massive cupola-capped towers are conspicuous landmarks of Munich.

3. A revolt staged on November 8, 1923, by Hitler and his Nazi followers, which failed. But within ten years the Nazis came to power in Germany.

4. **Dirndln** (also **Dirndls**), sing. **Dirndl**, is a dialect term, used especially in Bavaria and Austria, for girl or young woman. **Buam** is an approximation of the Bavarian pronunciation of **Buben**, here meaning *young men*.

5. Bavarian for **Wiese**, a big open space (i.e., meadow) where the fair is held.

6. Bavarian for „**Es ist angezapft!**" *It (the barrel) has been tapped!*

QUESTIONS

1. Warum wird München manchmal „die heimliche Hauptstadt der Bundesrepublik" genannt?
2. Was hat München an kulturellen Dingen zu bieten?
3. Warum ist die Luft in München so gut?
4. Wie weit entfernt sind die Alpen von München?
5. Welches sind die zwei größten Städte der Bundesrepublik?
6. Wie weit geht die Geschichte Münchens zurück?
7. Wann beginnt das Oktoberfest, und wann hört es auf?
8. Wer organisiert und unterstützt das Oktoberfest?

Review

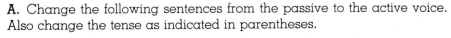

A. Change the following sentences from the passive to the active voice. Also change the tense as indicated in parentheses.

1. Auf seiner Reise ist er von vielen Autofahrern mitgenommen worden. (*past*)
2. Von den Studenten wurden verschiedene Theorien zur Psychologie diskutiert. (*present perfect*)
3. Das Medizinstudium ist von Renate im Herbst begonnen worden. (*present*)
4. Die finanzielle Hilfe für das Studium wird vom Staat organisiert. (*past perfect*)
5. Dieses Buch ist sicher nicht von ihm geschrieben worden. (*past*)
6. Diese Vorlesung muß von uns natürlich besprochen werden. (*past*)
7. Die größten Namen der Musik werden oft mit der Geschichte Wiens verbunden. (*present perfect*)
8. Während des Krieges wurde ein großer Teil dieser Stadt von Napoleons Armeen zerstört. (*past perfect*)
9. Mir ist gestern von meinem Arzt ein psychologischer Test gegeben worden. (*past*)
10. Die Sachertorte ist von uns sofort gegessen worden. (*present*)
11. Diese Ehe mußte als ein großes Risiko betrachtet werden. (*present*)
12. Von den Männern muß im Haushalt mehr getan werden. (*past*)

B. Complete the following passive sentences with the cue in parentheses.

1. Im Kriegsfall _____ die Barrieren auf der Autobahn _____ _____. (*can be removed*)
2. Glaubst du, daß in den USA _____ langsamer als in Europa _____? (*one drives*)
3. München _____ als die heimliche Hauptstadt der Bundesrepublik _____ _____. (*can be considered*)
4. Das Rathaus _____ vor vielen Jahren _____ _____. (*was destroyed*)
5. Hitlers Bierhalle _____ heute noch _____ _____. (*can be seen*)
6. Die Vergangenheit _____ manchmal durch die Augen der Gegenwart _____ _____. (*has to be understood*)
7. Man sagt, daß das Theater vom Film und Fernsehen _____ _____ _____. (*has been replaced*)
8. Es _____ _____ _____, daß England auf eine lange Tradition zurückschauen kann. (*has to be recognized*)
9. Auf diesem Fest _____ viele Volkslieder _____. (*were sung*)
10. Während der Pause _____ Sekt _____ und Kuchen _____. (*is being drunk, eaten*)

C. Express in German.

1. The air in Munich is not being polluted by industry.

2. May one smoke here?
3. In the year 1936 the Olympic Games were held in Berlin.
4. During the war many famous theaters, museums, and libraries were destroyed.
5. This city is being visited by many tourists every year.
6. The city of Munich has become famous for its „Oktoberfest."
7. Performances were given by many groups.
8. The Olympic Games are organized and supported by almost all countries.
9. I don't want to be awakened by crying children.
10. She needed to be cheered up.

Guided composition

Describe what people in your town or region do at a local festival, such as a county or state fair. Are there parades? Who participates (**teilnehmen an** + *dat.*)? Is there a lot of dancing, drinking, eating? Are there special performances given by certain groups?

Chapter vocabulary

Nouns

der	Atlantik	*Atlantic Ocean*
der	Baustil, -e	*architecture*
der	Betrug	*fraud*
die	Bierhalle, -n	*beer hall*
die	Brauerei, -en	*brewery*
der	Bube, -n	*boy*
der	Computer, -	*computer*
das	Dokument, -e	*document*
die	Eigenschaft, -en	*quality*
das	Einschenken	*drafting (beer, etc.)*
der	Feiertag, -e	*holiday*
das	Fest -e	*festival*
die	Firma, Firmen	*company*
die	Gegend, -en	*area*
die	Gemütlichkeit	*coziness*
das	Geschäftshaus, ̈er	*business building*
die	Hauptstadt, ̈e	*capital*
die	Heimatstadt, ̈e	*home town*
der	Jahrmarkt, ̈e	*fair*
der	Kater, -	*hangover (slang); (tom) cat*
die	Kellnerin, -nen	*waitress*
der	Krug, ̈e	*mug*
die	Laune, -n	*temper, mood*
die	Limousine, -n	*limousine*
das	Maß, -e	*measurement, measure; moderation*
das	Orchester, -	*orchestra*

der	Passagier, -e	passenger
der	Pazifik	Pacific Ocean
der	Putsch, -e	putsch
die	Rockgruppe, -n	rock group
das	Rokoko	rococo
der	Schaum	foam
der	Schnaps, ⁻e	schnaps
das	Spiel, -e	game
das	Stadion, Stadien	stadium
der	Trinker, -	drinker
der	Umzug, ⁻e	parade
die	Untergrundbahn, -en	subway
der	Verein, -e	club
das	Volkslied, -er	folksong
der	Volkstanz, ⁻e	folkdance
der	Wecker, -	alarm clock
die	Wiese, -n	meadow
das	Wohl	welfare, well-being
	Zum Wohl!	cheers!
der	Zentimeter, -	centimeter

Verbs

an·zapfen	to tap
auf·führen	to perform, stage
auf·halten, (hält), hielt, aufgehalten	to stay
sich auf·regen	to get upset
auf·wachen, (ist) aufgewacht	to wake up
auf·wecken	to wake s.o. up
sich aus·ruhen	to rest
aus·tragen (ein Spiel), (trägt), trug, ausgetragen	to carry out; to hold (games)
besichtigen	to visit
ein·schenken	to pour, draft (beer)
entscheiden, entschied, entschieden	to decide

erfahren (erfährt), erfuhr, erfahren	to learn, get to know
erleichtern	to relieve
eröffnen	to open
klar·machen	to make clear
organisieren	to organize
senden	to send
statt·finden, fand, stattgefunden	to take place
stellen; eine Frage stellen	to ask a question
verbieten, verbot, verboten	to forbid
vergrößern	to enlarge
versetzen; in gute Laune versetzen	to put someone in a good mood
wecken	to wake up (someone)
weinen	to cry

Other words

aufgeweckt	alert, lively
betrügerisch	deceitful
bezeichnend	significant
drittgrößter, -e, -es	third biggest
folkloristisch	
gewiß	certain
heimlich	secret
mäßig	moderate
maßlos	immoderate
mittelmäßig	mediocre, average
öffentlich	public
Prost!	cheers!
rege	active
regelmäßig	regular
riesig	huge
scheußlich	dreadful
wieso	why
weltbekannt	world-famous

Mini-dialogues

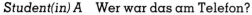

Student(in) A Wer war das am Telefon?

B Renate. Sie sagt, daß sie heute abend nicht mit uns ausgehen könne.

A Was ist denn wieder los?

B Sie hätte schon lange eine andere Verabredung.

A Warum hat sie uns das nicht früher wissen lassen?

B Sie hätte es ganz vergessen, behauptet sie.

A Was machen wir denn jetzt mit ihrer Eintrittskarte?

B Nichts! Sie sagte, sie würde uns das Geld so bald wie möglich zurückgeben.

A Who was that on the phone?
B Renate. She says that she cannot go out with us tonight.
A What's the matter again?
B (She says) she has had another engagement for some time.
A Why didn't she let us know earlier?
B She had completely forgotten it, she maintains.
A But what are we going to do now with her ticket?
B Nothing! She said she would give us the money back as soon as possible.

Grammar explanations

The subjunctive in indirect discourse

Peter sagte, daß er nichts von Rockkonzerten halte / hielte.
Peter said that he didn't think much of rock concerts.

Anita sagt, daß sie morgen zu Hause seien / wären.
Anita says that they'll be home tomorrow.

Sie erzählte uns, daß sie in einem teuren Restaurant gegessen habe / hätte.
She told us that she had eaten in an expensive restaurant.

Sie versprach, sie werde / würde später kommen.
She promised she would come later.

Heinz sagte, daß er sich nicht an das Wetter gewöhnen könne / könnte.
Heinz said that he couldn't get used to the weather.

Sag deinem Bruder, er **solle** / **sollte** einmal mit uns ausgehen.
Tell your brother he should go out with us sometime.

Hilde fragte, wo der Bahnhof sei / wäre.
Hilde asked where the railraod station was.

Er erkundigte sich, ob ich etwas gelernt habe / hätte.
He inquired whether I had learned anything.

A. Formation

In indirect discourse the "Special Subjunctive"[1] may be used. It is formed by adding to the *infinitive stem* (= the first principal part of the verb) the subjunctive endings.

		Singular	Plural	
1st person	ich	-e	wir	-en
2nd person	du	**-est**	ihr	**-et**
	er			
3rd person	sie	**-e**	sie	-en
	es			
2nd formal	Sie	-en	Sie	-en

Special subjunctive endings

Compare the special subjunctive with the present indicative forms:

	kommen		**laufen**		
	Subjunctive	Indicative	Subjunctive	Indicative	
ich	komme	(komme)	laufe	(laufe)	
du	komm**est**	(kommst)	l**au**f**est**	(läufst)	
er					
sie	komm**e**	(kommt)	l**au**f**e**	(läuft)	
es					
wir	kommen	(kommen)	laufen	(laufen)	
ihr	komm**et**	(kommt)	lauf**et**	(läuft)	
sie	kommen	(kommen)	laufen	(laufen)	
Sie	kommen	(kommen)	laufen	(laufen)	

Special subjunctive: **kommen** *and* **laufen**

[1]Some grammarians call this "Subjunctive I," because it is based on the first principal part of the verb.

	lesen		haben		Special subjunctive: **lesen** and **haben**
	Subjunctive	Indicative	Subjunctive	Indicative	
ich	lese	(lese)	habe	(habe)	
du	lesest	(liest)	habest	(hast)	
er sie es	lese	(liest)	habe	(hat)	
wir	lesen	(lesen)	haben	(haben)	
ihr	leset	(lest)	habet	(habt)	
sie	lesen	(lesen)	haben	(haben)	
Sie	lesen	(lesen)	haben	(haben)	

Notice that the umlaut variation in the 2nd and 3rd persons singular is not carried over from the indicative to the subjunctive.

There is only one exception to the rule for forming the special subjunctive: **sein.**

		Special subjunctive: **sein**
ich	sei	
du	seist	
er sie es	sei	
wir	seien	
ihr	seiet	
sie	seien	
Sie	seien	

B. Usage

There are two ways of reporting what someone has said.

One can quote directly (=direct discourse):

Er sagte: „Ich verstehe nichts von Psychologie."[1]	He said, "I don't know anything about psychology."

One can quote indirectly (=indirect discourse), which is far more common:

Er sagte, er **verstehe** nichts von Psychologie.	He said he knew nothing about psychology.

Most often we report the words of others rather than our own. Result: a

[1]Note the differences in *punctuation:* in English, a comma setting off the quote; in German, a colon and lowering of first quotation mark.

statement made in the 1st person (by someone else) must be reported (by us) in the 3rd person.

Direct discourse	*Indirect discourse*
"I am sick."	He said he was sick.
"We are sick."	They said they were sick.

The special subjunctive is used for indirect discourse largely in a somewhat *formal style*. This means that in converting a direct into an indirect quote we change the mood of the verb from indicative to subjunctive.

Time	Direct Discourse	Indirect Discourse	Tenses of subjunctive in indirect discourse
Statement in the *present*	„Ich bin krank." „Ich habe genug Geld."	Er sagt, er **sei** krank. Er sagt, er **habe** genug Geld.	
past	„Ich war krank." „Ich hatte genug Geld."	Er sagt, er **sei** krank **gewesen.** Er sagt, er **habe** genug Geld **gehabt.**	
future	„Ich werde krank sein." „Ich werde genug Geld haben."	Er sagt, er **werde** krank **sein.** Er sagt, er **werde** genug Geld **haben.**	

Two points must be noted:

a) The opening clause for the indirect quote can be in any tense without affecting the quote itself.

Er sagt Er sagte Er hat gesagt Er hatte gesagt Er wird sagen	}	er **sei** krank. er **sei** krank **gewesen.** er **werde** krank **sein.**

b) There is only one past tense in the subjunctive. Statements made in any of the three past tenses in the indicative are reported with that one subjunctive past.

Direct		*Indirect*
„Ich hatte genug Geld." „Ich habe genug Geld gehabt." „Ich hatte genug Geld gehabt."	}	Er sagt, er **habe** genug Geld **gehabt.**

In English, notice the change to the past tense when the direct statement was made in the present tense.

"I *am* disappointed."   She said that she *was* disappointed.

When the direct statement is in the past tense, the indirect statement is also in a tense of the past.

"I *was* disappointed."   She said she *was* disappointed

or: she *had been* disappointed (somewhat stilted)

If the direct statement is in the future tense, English also requires the subjunctive mood in the indirect statement.

"I *will be* disappointed."   She said she *would be* disappointed.

CHECK YOUR COMPREHENSION

A. Form the special subjunctive.

1. Gerd sagt, sie _____ erst später _____.   (*abfahren*)
2. Er sagte, er _____ sofort.   (*kommen*)
3. Fritz hat geschrieben, er _____ letzte Woche krank geworden.   (*sein*)
4. Karin erzählte uns, daß du ihn gut _____.   (*kennen*)

B. Put each sentence into special subjunctive by using the opening phrase, **Sie sagt, . . .**

1. „Karl bleibt hier."
2. „Monika ist nach Frankfurt gefahren."
3. „Willi hat das Buch noch nicht gelesen."
4. „Das Wetter ist heute furchtbar."

___

C. Special problems with the subjunctive in indirect discourse.[1]

Nowadays in conversation most Germans use the general subjunctive in indirect discourse (with the exception of **sein**).

Er sagt, er hätte genug Geld.
But: **Sie sagte, sie sei krank.**

___

[1]The special subjunctive occurs also in the third-person singular in certain idiomatic exhortations:

So sei es!   *So be it!*
Gott sei Dank!   *Thank God!*
Es werde Licht!   *Let there be light!*

To an extent this is due to the fact that in the following instances, the present indicative is identical with the indirect discourse subjunctive.

		Indicative	Special subjunctive
1st sing.	ich	komme	komme
1st pl.	wir	kommen	kommen
3rd pl.	sie	kommen	kommen
Formal	Sie	kommen	kommen

So, if one wishes to make sure that the indirect quote is understood as a subjunctive, then it is possible to substitute the general subjunctive:

Sie schrieben, daß sie um 4 Uhr   *They wrote that they would arrive*
ankämen (*instead of* **ankommen**).   *at four.*

In conversation, there is even a tendency to do away with the subjunctive in indirect discourse altogether.

Er sagte, daß sie um sechs Uhr   *He said she'd arrive at five.*
ankommt.

As you can see, in this area of grammar, conversational style is very much in flux.[1]

Notice also that the indirect discourse is often introduced with **daß,** which requires dependent ("Verb Last") word order.

Er sagt, daß er krank sei.   *He says (that) he's sick.*

When **daß** is omitted, the clause reverts to regular (S-V) word order.

Er sagt, er sei krank.   *He says (that) he's sick.*

CHECK YOUR COMPREHENSION

In the following sentences, use the subjunctive form that does not coincide with the form of the indicative.

1. Er sagt, sie (*pl.*) _____ bald zurück. (*kommen*)
2. Klara erzählt uns, daß ihre Eltern noch eine Woche hier _____. (*bleiben*)

[1]There are indeed situations where the use of the subjunctive is not recommended. The subjunctive relieves the reporter, so to speak, of the responsibility for the veracity of the statement he reports. But when I repeat my own words, I probably do not wish to cast doubt on them, especially if I wish to stress the factual nature of my statement: *Ich sagte ihm, daß ich nicht krank* **bin.** Or when a statement is readily verifiable: **„Ich bin da". > Er sagt(e), er ist da.**

3. Fritz sagt, sie (*pl.*) _____ uns heute _____. (*anrufen*)
4. Sie behaupten, daß sie nichts darüber _____. (*wissen*)
5. Seine Eltern schrieben, sie _____ es bei uns nicht länger _____. (*aushalten*)
6. Er erzählte, daß alle sehr gelitten _____. (*haben*)

D. The modals and *wissen* in the special subjunctive

These verbs follow the regular pattern of derivation for the special subjunctive (infinitive stem + subjunctive endings).

	dürfen	können	mögen	müssen	sollen	wollen	wissen	*Special subjunctive of modals and* **wissen**
ich	dürfe	könne	möge	müsse	solle	wolle	wisse	
du	dürfest	könnest	mögest	müssest	sollest	wollest	wissest	
er sie es	dürfe	könne	möge	müsse	solle	wolle	wisse	
wir	dürfen	können	mögen	müssen	sollen	wollen	wissen	
ihr	dürfet	könnet	möget	müsset	sollet	wollet	wisset	
sie	dürfen	können	mögen	müssen	sollen	wollen	wissen	
Sie	dürfen	können	mögen	müssen	sollen	wollen	wissen	

With these verbs, the special subjunctive is used most often in the *singular*, while the general subjunctive is preferred in the *plural*.

Er sagte, du dürfest mit uns ausgehen.

He said you could go out with us.

Er sagte, wir dürften mit euch ausgehen.

He said we could go out with you.

CHECK YOUR COMPREHENSION

Supply the appropriate subjunctive form.

1. Franz sagte, er _____ lieber hier bleiben. (*wollen*)
2. Fräulein Müller sagt, daß sie mich nicht verstehen _____. (*können*)
3. Meine Eltern sagten, daß sie mir einen Brief schreiben _____. (*wollen*)

4. Er erzählte uns, daß er darüber nichts _____. (*wissen*)
5. Wir glaubten, daß sie (*pl.*) heute nicht arbeiten _____. (*müssen*)
6. Wir sagten, wir _____ alles. (*wissen*)

E. Imperatives and questions in indirect discourse

If the direct discourse contains an imperative, it is converted into indirect discourse with the aid of the modals **sollen** or **müssen.**

Direct discourse	*Indirect discourse*
„Geh nach Hause!"	Sie sagte, ich **solle** nach Hause **gehen.**[1]
"Go home!"	*She said that I ought to go home.*

Questions *without* an interrogative word are rendered into indirect discourse with the help of the conjunction **ob** (*if, whether*). If there *is* an interrogative word, that word introduces the indirect clause.

Direct discourse	*Indirect discourse*
„Kommt dein Vater?"	Er fragte mich, **ob** mein Vater komme / käme.
"Is your father coming?"	*He asked me if my father was coming.*
„Wann kommt dein Vater?"	Er fragte mich, **wann** mein Vater komme / käme.
"When is your father coming?"	*He asked me when my father was coming.*

Notice that **ob** and **wann** are subordinating conjunctions, therefore requiring dependent ("Verb-Last") word order.

CHECK YOUR COMPREHENSION

Change the following sentences into indirect discourse.

1. Hans sagt: „Komm sofort hierher!"
2. Sie sagte: „Hört auf zu reden!"
3. Sie fragt: „Wieviel Uhr ist es?"
4. Wir fragten sie: „Kommt ihr morgen zu uns?"

---

[1]Since even in the indicative **sollen** contains a hypothetical element, it would be acceptable to say: *Sie sagte, ich* **soll** *nach Hause gehen.*

F. *Werden* or *würden?*

As illustrated in the table on p. 392, a direct discourse statement in the future tense will be rendered in indirect discourse with the subjunctive forms of **werden.**

Direct discourse	*Indirect discourse*
„Ich werde nicht zu spät kommen."	Er versprach, daß er nicht zu spät kommen **werde.**
"I won't come too late."	*He promised he wouldn't come too late.*

The **würde**-form may be substituted.

Er versprach, daß er nicht zu spät kommen würde.	*He promised that he wouldn't come too late.*

Often the **würde**-form is used, even if the direct discourse statement is in the present (by analogy with the **würde**-substitute in the general subjunctive).

Direct discourse	*Indirect discourse*
„Er schreibt nicht gern."	Sie behauptet, er **würde** nicht gern **schreiben.**
"He doesn't like to write."	*She claims that he doesn't like to write.*

As is to be expected, with **sein** and the **modals,** the **würde**-construction is *never* used in the indirect discourse.

„Er ist krank."	Sie schreiben, er **sei** / **wäre** krank.
"He is sick."	*They wrote that he was sick.*
„Er kann noch nicht arbeiten."	Sie schrieben, daß er noch nicht arbeiten **könne** / **könnte.**
"He still can't work."	*They wrote that he still couldn't work.*

CHECK YOUR COMPREHENSION

Put each sentence into indirect discourse with the **würde**-form by using the opening phrase, **Sie sagten, . . .**

1. „Wir werden mitkommen."
2. „Er wird wohl zu Hause bleiben."
3. „Sie liest gern."
4. „Wir geben ihnen den Schlüssel."
5. „Ihr findet das Hotel schon."

Conversation

Ich könnte das nicht!	*I couldn't do that!*
Blödsinn!	*Nonsense!*
Das hätte ich von ihm (ihr, usw.) nicht erwartet.	*I wouldn't have expected that of him (her, etc.).*
Gib doch nicht so an!	*Don't be so conceited!*

DER KRIMINAL-SCHRIFTSTELLER°

mystery writer

*Eine Gruppe junger Leute geht zu einem Rockkonzert.
Aber Gerds Bruder Franz geht nicht mit.*

Anita   Gerd, wo ist denn dein Bruder? Kommt er nicht mit?

Gerd   Er sagt, er wolle zu Hause bleiben, da er von Rockkonzerten
nicht viel halte.

Hilde   Er liest sicher wieder einen langen Roman. Ich könnte das
nicht!

Gerd   Blödsinn! Er will sich einen Krimi im Fernsehen ansehen.

Berthold   Was, dein Bruder? Das hätte ich von ihm nicht erwartet.

Gerd   Oh ja! Er behauptet, daß man dabei etwas vom wirklichen Leben lernen könne.

Hilde   Ha, Anita, hast du das gehört? Gerd, sag doch deinem Bruder, er solle mal mit uns ausgehen, dann würde er etwas vom wirklichen Leben lernen!

Berthold   Ach, Hilde, gib doch nicht so an!

Gerd   Übrigens sagt Franz, er wolle selber Kriminal-Schriftsteller werden. Man könne damit sehr viel Geld verdienen.

Anita   Er denkt ans Geld? Was macht er übrigens mit seiner Eintrittskarte?

Gerd   Er hat sie mir gegeben und gesagt, ich solle sie am Eingang zum doppelten Preis verkaufen.

Berthold   Aha! Wer hat gesagt, Franz verstehe nichts vom wirklichen Leben?

QUESTIONS ON THE CONVERSATION

1. Wohin will die Gruppe junger Leute gehen?
2. Warum will Franz nicht mitgehen?
3. Warum sagt Gerd, Franz würde zu Hause bleiben?
4. Was glaubt Hilde, was Franz tut?

ERLESENE VERBRECHEN UND MAKELLOSE MORDE

19.45 Ein Detektiv

Der Detektiv Tyree (Georg Thomalla) wird engagiert, um ein Treffen zwischen Mr. Dean (Peter Weck) und einem Mann zu arrangieren, der angeblich vor 20 Jahren Deans Frau umbrachte. Tyree kommt aber der Verdacht, daß der Unbekannte einen Auftraggeber für den Mord hatte. Hat Mr. Dean den Mörder gedungen?

5. Warum hat Berthold nicht erwartet, daß Franz sich einen Krimi im Fernsehen ansehen würde?
6. Was behauptet Franz von Krimis im Fernsehen?
7. Warum sagt Hilde, Franz solle mal mit ihnen kommen?
8. Was sagt Franz, was er einmal werden wolle?
9. Was hat Franz mit seiner Eintrittskarte getan?

PERSONAL QUESTIONS

1. Glauben Sie, daß Franz recht hat, wenn er sagt, daß man von Krimis etwas über das wirkliche Leben lernen kann?
2. Gehst du lieber zu einem Rockkonzert, oder siehst du dir lieber zu Hause ein Fernsehprogramm an? Warum?
3. Lesen Sie oft lange Romane?
4. Welche Kriminal-Schriftsteller kennen Sie?

Practice

A. Put the sentences into direct discourse.

EXAMPLE: Sie sagte, sie sei immer zu Hause.
        „Ich bin immer zu Hause."

1. Sie hatte gesagt, die Polizei sei da gewesen.
2. Er sagte, er sei müde.
3. Sie sagte, sie habe ein neues Klavier gekauft.
4. Sie sagten, sie hätten nichts gehört.
5. Ihr sagtet, wir kämen zu spät.
6. Du sagtest, du werdest morgen abfahren.
7. Er hat gesagt, Sie seien sehr krank.
8. Sie wird sagen, das habe sie schon gewußt.
9. Ich sagte, das Wetter sei nicht sehr schön.
10. Wir sagten, daß er ein neues Auto habe.

B. Put the sentences into indirect discourse by using the opening phrase, Er sagte, . . .

1. „Franz kann nicht mitgehen."
2. „Franz will zu Hause bleiben, da er von Rockkonzerten nichts hält."
3. „Franz wird wieder einen langen Roman lesen."
4. „Wir sehen uns keinen Film im Fernsehen an."
5. „Das habe ich nicht von euch erwartet."
6. „Franz will nicht Schriftsteller werden."
7. „Denkt nicht schon wieder ans Geld!"

8. „Sie haben uns die Eintrittskarte gegeben."

9. „Franz versteht etwas vom wirklichen Leben."

C. Put the questions into indirect discourse by using the opening phrase, **Er fragte mich / uns, . . .**

EXAMPLES: „Gehen Sie zu einem Rockkonzert?"
      Er fragte mich, ob ich zu einem Rockkonzert ginge.

      „Warum sind Sie müde?"
      Er fragte uns, warum wir müde seien.

1. „Hast du einen Moment Zeit?"
2. „Haben Sie eine Zigarette für mich?"
3. „Bist du gleich fertig?"
4. „Kann man hier die Medizin bekommen?"
5. „Was ist denn los?"
6. „Was tun die Passagiere?"
7. „Warum ist alles so teuer?"
8. „Lesen Sie gern?"
9. „Von wem wissen Sie das?"
10. „Willst du auch die Hauptstadt besichtigen?"
11. „Geht es Ihnen gut?"
12. „Wird hier getanzt?"
13. „Um wieviel Uhr wachen Sie meistens auf?"
14. „Hat dein Freund schon geschrieben?"
15. „Wie spät ist es?"
16. „Wo wohnen Sie?"
17. „Wann findet das Konzert statt?"
18. „Wozu studieren Sie Deutsch?"
19. „Warum weint das Kind?"
20. „Darf ich Sie zu einer Tasse Kaffee einladen?"

D. Put the command into indirect discourse by using the opening phrase, **Sie sagt, . . .** and the correct form of **sollen.** Do not use the conjunction **daß.**

EXAMPLE: „Wecke mich früh auf!"
      Sie sagt, ich solle sie früh aufwecken.

1. „Komm doch mit zum Konzert!"
2. „Geh sofort nach Hause!"
3. „Setzen Sie sich!"
4. „Sprecht etwas langsamer!"
5. „Warten Sie einen Moment!"
6. „Kauf ein paar Brötchen!"
7. „Streitet euch nicht!"
8. „Schreib mir mal!"
9. „Fahrt doch in Urlaub!"
10. „Stell dich nicht so an!"

E. Give the German equivalent.

1. Gerd asks where his brother is.
2. Franz said he didn't want to come along.
3. Anita asked what time it was.
4. They said he was reading a novel.
5. We asked where they lived.
6. Ray wanted to know what was going on.
7. She said that Ingrid knew German literature backwards and forwards.
8. Peter said that he would rather write his own poem than interpret one by Schiller.
9. He asked me what I was waiting for.
10. She asked me where I was now.

Vocabulary development

Aus·gehen, aus·führen, and *aus·kommen*

The expression **aus·gehen mit (jemand)** means *to go out with (somebody).*

Ich gehe heute abend mit Hildegard aus.   *Tonight I'll go out with Hildegard.*

The expression **aus·führen** means *to take out somebody.*

Peter hat Inge gestern zum ersten Mal ausgeführt.   *Peter took out Inge yesterday for the first time.*

But **aus·kommen mit** means *to get along with somebody.*

Kommen sie gut miteinander aus?   *Are they getting along well together?*

Communicative exercises

Form a group of three students. Student A asks student B a question. B answers. Student C pretends not to have understood and asks A what B had said (**Was hat er/sie gesagt?**) A repeats B's statement in the indirect discourse, starting with **Er/sie sagt(e), . . .**
Suggestions for the initial questions:

Wo bist du gestern hingegangen?
Mit wem bist du gestern ausgegangen?
Hat dir das Rockkonzert gefallen?
Wen hat Peter gestern abend ausgeführt?
Welchen Film habt ihr euch angesehen?
Wie hat euch der Film gefallen?
Was machst du am Wochenende? Während der Ferien?
Etc.

Reading

DAS PUBLIKUM SPIELT JAMES BOND

Man hört oft, daß das Fernsehen das Publikum in einen passiven Zustand des Sehens und Nicht-Denkens versetze. Es wird auch gesagt, daß viel, was im Fernsehen gezeigt wird, das Publikum nur aufrege und nicht belehre. Oder es wird darauf aufmerksam gemacht, daß den Kindern und Schülern im Fernsehen ein schlechtes Beispiel des menschlichen Lebens gegeben werde und daß sie durch das viele Fernsehen von ihren Studien abgehalten° würden. Einige Pessimisten sagen sogar voraus, daß zukünftige Generationen große Augen wie Nachteulen° und kleine Ohren haben würden, weil ihnen durch die laute Musik, der sie täglich zuhören, das Gehör beeinträchtigt° werde. Es kann natürlich nicht verneint werden, daß in solchen Behauptungen ein Kern° von Wahrheit enthalten ist.

kept away from
night owls
impaired
grain

Aber auf der anderen Seite muß doch auch gesagt werden, daß viele Kritiker das Problem des Fernsehens übertreiben. Das deutsche Fernsehen bietet auch viel Interessantes, zum Beispiel Sendungen über fremde Länder, über Politik, Medizin, die neuesten Entdeckungen in den Wissenschaften oder auch Gespräche über wichtige Tagesprobleme. Außerdem muß hervorgehoben werden, daß das Fernsehen in Deutschland mit seinen drei Programmen[1] staatliche Subventionen erhält, so daß die Werbung auf ein Minimum reduziert worden ist und die Sendungen nicht immer unterbrochen werden. Die Werbung ist auf° eine halbe Stunde pro Tag beschränkt.°[2] So ist

to / restricted

Aktenzeichen:
XY ... ungelöst
Die Kriminalpolizei
bittet um Mithilfe
Freitag, 20.15 Uhr

es nicht erstaunlich, daß viele Besucher, die aus Deutschland nach
den USA kommen, sagen, sie könnten sich nie an die vielen Unterbrechungen der Sendungen im amerikanischen Fernsehen gewöhnen.

Natürlich gibt es im deutschen Fernsehen auch viele Unterhaltungssendungen mit Shows, Quizzes und Krimis, die bei der großen
Masse beliebt sind, weil man eben nach anstrengender° Arbeit die   *strenuous*
Probleme des Tages vergessen will. Viele Krimis kommen aus den
USA, zum Beispiel die Serie „Die Straßen von San Franzisko". Neben
den typischen Fernsehfilmen gibt es im Fernsehen aber auch eigent-
liche Spielfilme,[3] wie sie in den Kinos gezeigt werden. Das sind oft
gute Filme, die einen oder mehrere Oscars erhalten haben. Sehr populär sind natürlich auch die Sportsendungen im Fernsehen, besonders Fußball.[4] Nie sind die Straßen im ganzen Land so leer wie bei
großen Fußballspielen, weil dann fast jeder vor dem Fernsehapparat
sitzt. Ein Journalist aus den USA hat einmal bemerkt, er hätte während
eines Fußballspiels, das im Fernsehen gezeigt wurde, den Eindruck
gehabt, die ganze Bevölkerung° sei an einem Virus erkrankt° und läge   *population / fallen ill*
zu Hause im Bett.

Eine Serie, die schon seit zehn Jahren läuft, ist besonders beliebt.
Sie heißt „Aktenzeichen XY—ungelöst".[5] In dieser Sendung werden
Szenen aus Kriminalfällen gespielt, die bis zur Stunde noch nicht auf-

geklärt worden sind. Nur authentische Fälle werden gezeigt. Und die Kripo[6] gibt Erklärungen. In einem Fall zum Beispiel wurde hervorgehoben, daß ein abgebrochenes Blatt° einer Hauspflanze° ein wichtiger Beweis für einen Mord sei. In einem anderen Fall wurden Bilder von einem Bankraub° gezeigt und das Publikum gewarnt, daß die Täter Waffen trügen und gefährlich seien. Die Zuschauer können während der Sendung die Fernsehstudios über Verdächte° telefonisch informieren, worauf die Kripo sofort solchen Tips nachgeht. Auf diese Weise wurden in den letzten Jahren viele schwierige Kriminalfälle aufgeklärt. Die Serie ist besonders wirkungsvoll,° weil fast alle deutschsprachigen Länder[7]—die Bundesrepublik, Österreich und die Schweiz—daran teilnehmen. Ein Zyniker° schrieb darüber in einer bekannten Tageszeitung, daß die Zuschauer des deutschsprachigen Fernsehens alle gern James Bond spielen möchten. Aber warum denn auch nicht, wenn dadurch der Justiz geholfen werden kann?

broken-off leaf / house plant

bank robbery

suspicions

effective

cynic

CULTURAL NOTES

1. **Programme** here means *channels*. There are only three channels, all public, for the whole of the **Bundesrepublik.** Channels I and II are the most popular. Channel II is for local telecasts. TV is supported primarily by the monthly fees that owners of TV sets must pay and by special subsidies for the arts from the Culture Ministry of each state **(Bundesland).** The management of the TV channels is the responsibility of public radio commissions. The federal government takes no direct interest in TV matters (since such direct involvement might infringe upon the freedom of the medium).

2. Commercials are televised for about half an hour of the broadcast day, which varies from channel to channel, even day to day.

3. One usually distinguishes between films made specially for TV **(Fernsehfilme)** and movies broadcast on TV **(Spielfilme).**

4. **Fußball:** *soccer.* American "football" is not well known in Europe.

5. Criminal Dossier XY—Unsolved.

6. **Kripo:** abbreviation for **Kriminalpolizei** (*detective squad*).

7. The series is not carried on the **DDR**-channels.

QUESTIONS

1. Was hört man oft über das Fernsehen?
2. Warum kann man im deutschen Fernsehen die Werbung auf ein Minimum reduzieren?

3. Was für Unterhaltungssendungen gibt es im deutschen Fernsehen?
4. Was für Filme werden im Fernsehen gezeigt?
5. Wann sind in der BRD und anderen Ländern die Straßen fast leer?
6. Welche Kriminalserie ist in der BRD besonders beliebt?
7. In welchen anderen Ländern wird diese Serie auch gezeigt?
8. Warum ist diese Serie nicht nur interessant, sondern auch wichtig?

Review

A. Put the sentences into indirect discourse by using an appropriate opening phrase such as **sie fragt, er behauptete, sie fragten,** etc.

1. „Das Fernsehen bietet viel Interessantes."
2. „Geh doch einmal mit mir aus! Wir werden gut miteinander auskommen."
3. „Das Fernsehen gibt den Kindern keine guten Beispiele des menschlichen Lebens."
4. „Viele Kritiker haben das Problem des Fernsehens übertrieben."
5. „Ich konnte mich nicht an die vielen Unterbrechungen der Sendungen gewöhnen."
6. „Nie sind die Straßen so leer wie bei großen Fußballspielen."
7. „Werden nur authentische Kriminalfälle gezeigt?"
8. „Ist das ein wichtiger Beweis für diesen Mord?"
9. „Habt ihr an dieser Sendung von ‚Aktenzeichen XY' teilgenommen?"

B. In each passage change the direct statements into indirect discourse.

ÄRGER° MIT DER HAUSWIRTIN°

Heute morgen sagte meine Hauswirtin zu mir: „Herr Fischer, Sie hatten gestern abend Damenbesuch.° Das wünsche ich nicht. Das wissen Sie doch." Ich antwortete: „Frau Neubauer, es tut mir leid, aber das ist wirklich meine Sache.° Ich bezahle meine Miete,° sogar eine sehr hohe Miete, für mein Studentenzimmer, und da kann ich einladen, wen ich will." Meine Hauswirtin war ärgerlich° über diese Antwort und sagte: „Sie, junger Mann, hören Sie mal. Vielleicht verstehen Sie etwas von Musik oder was Sie studieren, aber von einer Hausordnung° verstehen Sie offensichtlich° nichts! Ich erwarte, daß Sie auf Ihrem Zimmer keinen Damenbesuch empfangen. Basta!"° Ich war wütend° und sagte: „Das ist Diskriminierung! Das ist unsozial!

dispute / landlady

a visit from a lady

concern / rent

annoyed

house rules / obviously
Enough!
furious

Ich habe mit jener Studentin nur für das Examen gelernt, und das ist
ja wohl nicht verboten!" „So, fürs Examen gelernt haben Sie", sagte
sie. „Kein Student lernt am Samstagabend mit einer Dame für ein
Examen!" Ich sagte: „Dann müssen Sie Ihre Vorstellungen° über Stu-   *ideas*
denten von heute revidieren!"°   *revise*

DIE VERFOLGUNG°   *pursuit*

Fräulein Bänziger sieht sich immer die Fernsehsendung „Aktenzeichen XY—ungelöst" an. Eines Tages glaubt sie, einen Verbrecher,
dessen Bild im Fernsehen gezeigt wurde, zu sehen, gerade als er in
eine Limousine einsteigt. Später erzählt sie einer Freundin, was
geschah:

Ich sprang in ein Taxi und sagte zum Taxifahrer: „Bitte, folgen Sie
der schwarzen Limousine da drüben!" Der Taxifahrer wollte wissen:
„Warum soll ich dem Auto folgen? Sind Sie denn von der Kriminalpolizei?" Ich antwortete: „Fragen Sie nicht soviel! Fahren Sie lieber
etwas schneller, sonst verlieren wir den Wagen aus den Augen." Er
sagte: „Furchtbares Wetter haben wir heute. Der Regen will überhaupt nicht aufhören." Ich sagte: „Passen Sie auf, Mann! Der schwarze
Wagen ist gerade links abgebogen.° Fahren Sie schneller!" Er sagte: *turned*
„Es tut mir leid, mein Fräulein, aber ich muß die Straßenbahn zuerst
vorbeifahren lassen." Ich sagte ärgerlich: „Der Gangster ist uns entkommen.° Fahren Sie mich nach Hause!"   *escaped*

DER AUGENZEUGE°   *eye witness*

Herr Beckmann, Copilot einer DC-10, war Augenzeuge einer Flugzeugentführung.° Er mußte die Kriminalpolizei genau darüber infor-   *airplane hijacking*
mieren, was geschehen war. Er erzählte:

Plötzlich stand ein Mann im Cockpit mit einer Handgranate in der
Hand und sagte: „Tun Sie, was ich sage. Dann passiert nichts. Fliegen Sie sofort nach Havanna!" Der Chefpilot sagte: „Das ist unmöglich!

Soviel Benzin haben wir nicht." Daraufhin sagte der Luftpirat: „Ich habe gesagt, fliegen Sie nach Kuba! Sonst wird dieses kleine runde Ding explodieren." Der Chefpilot sagte: „Sehen Sie doch selbst! Wir haben nur noch 800 Liter Benzin. Damit kommen wir bestenfalls noch bis Atlanta." Der Luftpirat fluchte° wie verrückt° und sagte schließ-   *swore / crazy*
lich: „Okay. Landen Sie in Atlanta und tanken Sie voll! Sagen Sie dem Tower, daß ich die Maschine in die Luft jage,° wenn die Polizei   *blow up*
auf uns schießt."° Ich zeigte dem Luftpiraten die Flugkarte und sagte: *shoots*
„Sehen Sie, wir sind jetzt hier. In einer halben Stunde . . ." In diesem Moment schlug° unsere Stewardeß den Mann mit einem Karate-Schlag°   *felled / chop*
nieder.

Guided composition

Give a short description of the TV programs that you like best. Also state what some of your family or friends think and say about these programs. In so doing, use indirect discourse.

Chapter vocabulary

Nouns _____

das	Aktenzeichen, -	*reference number*
der	Beweis, -e	*evidence*
der	Blödsinn	*nonsense*
der	Chefpilot, -en	*chief pilot*
das	Cockpit, -s	*cockpit*
der	Copilot, -en	*co-pilot*
der	Direktor, -en	*boss; chairman*
die	Diskriminierung, -en	*discrimination*
der	Eingang, ⸚e	*entrance*
die	Entdeckung, -en	*discovery*
die	Erklärung, -en	*explanation*
das	Examen, -	*examination*

das	Fernsehstudio, -s	*TV studio*
die	Flugkarte, -n	*flight ticket*
das	Fußballspiel, -e	*soccer game*
die	Generation, -en	*generation*
die	Handgranate, -n	*hand grenade*
die	Justiz	*justice*
der	Karate-Schlag, ⸚e	*karate blow*
der	Kriminalfall, ⸚e	*criminal case*
die	Kriminalpolizei	*criminal investigation police*
der	Kritiker, -	*critic*
der	Luftpirat, -en	*hijacker*
die	Masse, -n	*crowd*
das	Minimum	*minimum*
der	Mord, -e	*murder*

das	Programm, -e	program
das	Rockkonzert, -e	rock concert
der	Roman, -e	novel
die	Sendung, -en	broadcast
die	Serie, -n	series
der	Spielfilm, -e	movie
die	Sportsendung, -en	sport show
die	Stewardeß, -dessen	stewardess
die	Szene, -n	scene
der	Tip, -s	hint
der	Zustand, ⸚e	condition

Verbs

an·geben (gibt), gab, angegeben	to give; declare
auf·klären	to clear
aus·führen	to do, execute
aus·kommen, kam, (ist) ausgekommen	to get along (with)
behaupten	to state
belehren	to inform, instruct
bemerken	to remark
bieten, bot, geboten	to offer
empfangen (empfängt), empfing, empfangen	to receive
explodieren	to explode
hervor·heben, hob, hervorgehoben	to stress
nach·gehen, ging, (ist) nachgegangen	to follow
reduzieren	to reduce
sich streiten, stritt, gestritten	to quarrel

tanken	to fill up (gasoline)
teil·nehmen an (+ *dat.*) (nimmt), nahm, teilgenommen	to participate
übertreiben, übertrieb, übertrieben	to exaggerate
unterbrechen (unterbricht), unterbrach, unterbrochen	to interrupt
verkaufen	to sell
verneinen	to negate
versetzen	to put
voraus·sagen	to predict
vorbei·fahren (fährt), fuhr (ist) vorbeigefahren	to pass
warnen	to warn
zwingen, zwang, gezwungen	to force

Other words

authentisch	authentic
bestenfalls	at best
doppelt	double
eigentlich	actual
erstaunlich	amazing
leer	empty
passiv	passive
telefonisch	by telephone
typisch	typical
ungelöst	unsolved
unsozial	unsocial
zukünftig	future

APPENDIX

Supplementary Guide to Pronunciation

Since the standards of pronunciation for English and German differ widely, it is essential that you develop proper speaking habits from the very beginning. This can best be accomplished by carefully listening to and closely imitating your instructor and the voices on the tapes of the Lab program. The following nevertheless gives some practical phonetic guidelines for speaking German.

As a rule, in the German language sounds are much more concise and forceful than the gliding sound patterns characteristic of the English spoken in the United States, and in pronunciation the tongue and lips are slightly more forward.

The German vowel system

In German, there are long and short single vowel sounds (including umlauted vowels, or umlauts)—also known as monophthongs—and diphthongs, sounds that contract two different vowels. In contrast to English, German vowels are predominantly of a single vowel quality: they do not glide, as so frequently is the case in English, but rather hold their pitch.

The following table roughly represents German vowel sounds, and wherever possible attempts to give an English sound that resembles its German counterpart. Keep in mind, however, that the English sounds are only approximations of the German, and are similar in sound only and not in length.

VOWEL SOUND	LONG			SHORT	
	ENGLISH	GERMAN		ENGLISH	GERMAN
a	[a:] *father*	Name	[a]	bl*u*nt	gen*a*nnt
e	[e:] Santa F*e*	Tee	[ɛ]	m*e*t	w*e*nn
-e(-)	[ə] —	—		*a*go	b*i*tte
-er	[ə] —	—		moth*er*	Arbeit*er*
i	[i:] m*e*	Vieh	[i]	*i*t	b*i*tte
o	[o:] d*ou*gh	Lohn	[ɔ]	cl*o*th	k*o*mmen
u	[u:] s*oo*n	tun	[u]	b*oo*k	*u*nd
ä	[ɛ:] f*ai*r	Fähre	[ɛ]	m*e*n	M*ä*nner
ö	[ø:] —	König	[œ]	—	k*ö*nnen
ü	[y:] —	fühlen	[y]	—	f*ü*llen
au	[ao] n*ow*	Frau		—	—
ei, ai	[ai] m*i*ne	mein		—	—
eu, äu	[ɔy] *joy*	heulen		—	—

A vowel is always *long* if it

1. stands at the end of a syllable: ge-ben
2. is followed by an **h**: sah
3. is followed by an **ß** plus an **e**: Grüße
4. is doubled (only possible with **a**, **e**, and **o**): Tee
5. is an **i** followed by an **e**: sie

A vowel is always *short* if it is followed by a double consonant: kom-men. A vowel is usually short if it is followed by two or more different consonants, not including **h**: Stadt. However, neither long nor short vowels are always predictable by the spelling of a word.

The following English vowel phonemes do not occur in German:

1. the short *a* as in "mat"
2. the long gliding *a* as in "male," "fail"
3. the long gliding *o* as in "go," "bloat," "globe," and "snow"

The a

The German **a** resembles the English *a* as in "father" (long) or *u* as in "bl*u*nt" (short).

LONG		SHORT	
Kahn	Samen	kann	sammeln
Name	Haar	genannt	lang
Schal		Schall	

The e

The German **e** slightly resembles pronunciation of the *e* in "Santa Fe" (long) or the English *e* as in "met" (short).

LONG		SHORT	
wen	Tee	wenn	Tennis
wer	sehen	Herr	setzen
stehen		Student	

The unstressed e and er

The unstressed **e** usually occurs at the end of a word or syllable, as in **-en** or **-te**, and in the prefixes **be-** and **ge-**. It resembles the English *a* as in "ago." The unstressed **er** occurs at the end of many words. It vaguely resembles the British *er* as in "mother." Many Americans find it difficult to distinguish between these two sounds, but the difference can be critical. Therefore it is particularly important that you listen closely to your instructor and the tapes of the Lab program.

diese	Begriff	dieser	leider
fahren	rauchte	Fahrer	Raucher
bitte		bitter	

The i

The German **i** resembles the English *e* as in "me" (long) or *i* as in "it" (short).

LONG		SHORT	
bieten	Miene	bitten	Minne
Schiefer	Sieb	Schiff	Sippe
ihren		irren	

The **o**

The German **o** slightly resembles the English *o* as in "dough" (long) or "cloth" (short).

LONG		SHORT	
Kohle	Ton	kommen	Tonne
Sohn	Lohn	Sonne	von
Boot		Bock	

The **u**

The German **u** resembles the English *oo* as in "soon" (long) or "book" (short).

LONG		SHORT	
Mut	Buch	Mutter	Bucht
tun	Luke	und	Lust
Schuh		Schutz	

The **ä**

The umlaut **ä** quite frequently resembles the German *e* and slightly approximates the English *ai* as in "fair" (long) or *e* as in "men" (short). For practice, say an open "a" as in "father," hold the lips in that position, and lift the tongue to say "e."

LONG		SHORT	
Gespräch	Fähre	Schwäche	ändern
Mädchen	Gerät	Männer	hätte
nämlich		Klänge	

Note the difference between **a** and **ä**.

LONG		SHORT	
Name	nämlich	Mann	Männer
Sprache	spräche	lang	Länge

The **ö**

The umlaut **ö** is a sound that cannot be compared to any English sound. Listen closely to your instructor and the tapes of the Lab program.

LONG		SHORT	
König	schön	können	nördlich
Höhle	rötlich	Hölle	rösten
Öl		öffnen	

Note the difference between **o** and **ö**.

LONG		SHORT	
schon	schön	kommen	können
hohe	Höhe	offen	öffnen

The **ü**

The umlaut **ü** is a sound that cannot be compared to any English sound. Listen closely to your instructor and the tapes.

LONG		SHORT	
fühlen	Mühle	füllen	Müller
grüßen	glühen	küssen	Glück
für		füttern	

Note the difference between **i**, **u**, and **ü**.

LONG		SHORT	
vier	Kultur	Mitte	Kuß
fuhren	führen	Mutter	Mütter
Tier	Tür	Kissen	küssen

Generally, the English vowels are evenly balanced in the mouth. If the tongue is forward and high, the lips are pulled back: "pl*ea*se." When the tongue is pulled back, the lips are pushed forward: "b*oa*t." This is not the case with the German **ö** and **ü**. The German **ö** is produced with the tongue in position for an *e* as in the English "bed," and the lips forward for an *o* as in "hope." Similarly for the **ü**: the tongue is forward for an *ee* as in "meet," and the lips are also forward for an *oo* as in "soon." With the lips and tongue both forward, one can enunciate the German **ö** and **ü**. There is a slight difference other than the length between short **ö** and **ü** and long **ö** and **ü**: for the short vowels, the tongue is not quite so far forward.

The **au**

The German diphthong **au** resembles the English *ow* as in "now," but the shift from one vowel to the other is done rapidly in German.

Frau	glauben
Aufschrift	auch
Raum	

The **ei** *and* **ai**

The German diphthong **ei** or **ai** resembles the English *i* as in "mine."

mein	arbeiten
nein	gleich
Mai	

Note the difference between the diphthong **ei** as in English "high" and the combination **ie** as in English "he."

Wein	Wien
arbeiten	bieten
heiraten	hier
Bein	Bier
sein	sieben

The **eu** *and* **äu**

The German diphthong **eu** or **äu** resembles the English *oi* as in "joy."

heulen	Fräulein
Deutschland	Häuser
Freund	

The glottal stop

In German words or syllables that begin with a vowel, the flow of air is halted instantaneously just prior to articulation, and then released suddenly. This phenomenon is called the "glottal stop." Thus you would say **im Áugenblick** and not **imaugenblick.** Compare

veréisen	verreisen
veréngen	verrenken
eréignen	erreichen

Study the following statements.

1. Ein altes Auto ist oft unsicher.   *An old car is often unsafe.*
2. Er ist ungeheuer beeindruckt.   *He is tremendously impressed.*
3. Dein englischer Plattenspieler ist ausgezeichnet.   *Your English record player is excellent.*

The German consonant system

Many German consonants differ from English only in their more precise and forceful pronunciation. Only those consonants that require particular attention because of basic differences are discussed here.

The following English consonant phonemes do not occur in German:

1. the soft *g* or *j* as in "gentle," "rage," "ledger," and "jot"
2. the *l* as in "loan," "ball," and "tailor"
3. the *r* as in "riot," "berry," "clear," and "harm"
4. the *th* as in "the," "leather," and "bath"
5. the *w* as in "wood" and "where"

The **ch**

For Americans, the back and the front **ch** sounds are quite difficult to master, therefore listen closely to your instructor and the tapes of the Lab program. The back **ch**, so called because it is produced in the back of the mouth, is preceded by an **a, o, u,** or **au**; the front **ch**, produced in the front, is preceded by any letter other than **a, o, u, au,** or **s.** The front **ch** (**ich**) is quite like the English *h* in "huge," "Hughes," or a whispered "he."

BACK		FRONT	
nach	schwach	nicht	Schwäche
noch	auch	schlecht	Architekt
Koch		Köche	

When the **ch** is part of the **-chen** suffix, it is pronounced like the front **ch.**

Mädchen
Häuschen

Be careful not to use a **k** sound for the **ch.** Compare:

Acker	acht
Flak	flach
Lack	lachen
Fleck	Fläche
flicken	Pflicht

If a **ch** is followed by an **s** it is pronounced like the English *x*.

sechs	Sachsen
Lachs	wechseln
wachsen	

The l *and* r

For Americans, the German **l** and **r** are quite difficult to pronounce. Listen closely to your instructor and the tapes.

The German **l** is produced by pushing the tip of the flat tongue against the back of the upper teeth and the front part of the palate. There are two ways to pronounce the **r** in German, the commonly used uvular **r**, which is a gargling sound produced in the back of the throat, and the regional trilled **r**, produced in the front of the mouth.

	l		r
ENGLISH	GERMAN	ENGLISH	GERMAN
*l*and	Land	*r*ight	*r*ichtig
*l*iterature	Literatur	*r*ule	Regel
ba*ll*	Ball	cor*r*ect	kor*r*ekt
tunne*l*	Tunnel	ar*r*ogant	ar*r*ogant
a*l*so	also	pai*r*	Paa*r*

Final **r** is pronounced like the unstressed **er** discussed earlier.

wir	Rohr
der	Bar
pur	

The s, ß, ss, sch, sp, *and* st

If a single **s** is followed by a vowel, it is voiced—that is, it is pronounced like the English *z* as in "zoo." If, however, the **s** stands at the end of a word or if it is doubled, it is voiceless—that is, it is pronounced like the English *s* as in "son."

VOICED	VOICELESS
sagen	bis
sein	besser
gesund	Glas
Physik	wissen
besitzen	verlassen

The double **s** is expressed by the voiceless letter **ß** if

1. the preceding vowel is long: Gruß, grüßen
2. it appears at the end of a word: Kuß
3. it is followed by a **t**: vergißt

The German **sch** is pronounced like the English *sh* as in "shall."

schwimmen	Entschluß
schicken	Bu**sch**
be**sch**ädigen	

The German **sp** and **st,** if they appear at the beginning of a word or an independent component of a word, are pronounced like the English *sh* plus *t* or *p* respectively. Otherwise they are pronounced as in the English "spoon" or "stood."

sh + p/t		**sp/st**	
sprechen	Stand	Wespe	fast
Beispiel	bestellen	Aspekt	gestern
Studium		Fenster	

The **z** *and* **tz**

The German **z** and **tz** are both pronounced like the English *ts* as in "nuts."

Zucker	Blitz
Medizin	jetzt
kurz	

The **w, f, ph,** *and* **v**

The German **w** is pronounced like the English *v* as in "visit." The German **f** and **ph** are pronounced like the English *f* as in "fellow."

Wein	fahren
wollen	Fernseher
schwer	Physik
einwerfen	Pamphlet
langweilig	Philosoph

The German **v** is pronounced like the English *f* as in "fellow." In some words of foreign origin, however, the German **v** is pronounced like the English *v* as in "visit."

f SOUND		**v** SOUND	
Vater	Volk	Vanille	Universität
vergessen	völlig	Vase	Offensive
wieviel		Villa	

The **b, d,** *and* **g**

If **b, d,** or **g** stands at the beginning of a word or syllable, it is pronounced just like the English "boy," "dog," or "girl." Whenever these letters are at the end of a word or syllable, or are followed by **t** or **s**, they are pronounced like *p, t,* and *k* respectively as in "pig," "toy," or "kid."

FRONT **b**	END **b/p**	FRONT **d**	END **d/t**	FRONT **g**	END **g/k**
lieben	lieb	deutsch	Land	Geburt	Tag
aber	ab	dann	und	vergessen	Flug
verboten	Urlaub	drinnen	Sand	Gold	fliegt
Bus	lebt	gedient	verwandt	gibt	lügt
Band	Krebs	Gedanke	(Bads)	egal	(Schlags)

The **ig** *and* **ng**

If **ig** occurs at the end of a word or syllable or in front of a consonant, it is pronounced like the German **ich**. The German **ng** is pronounced like the English *ng* as in "singer."

hungrig	bringen
langweilig	gingen
wenig	hängen
Ewigkeit	Wohnung
Heiligtum	Heizung

The **pf, ps,** *and* **kn**

Both consonants are pronounced in the **pf, ps,** and **kn** combinations.

Pfeffer	**Ps**ychologie	**Kn**ie
Pfosten	**Ps**eudonym	**Kn**opf
Pflicht	**Ps**alm	**Kn**abe
A**pf**el	**ps**t!	**kn**urren
To**pf**	Ra**ps**	ge**kn**ackt

Additional guidelines

Some additional guidelines for proper German pronunciation that may be helpful include the following.

1. The German **j** is pronounced like the English *y* as in "young."

   jetzt   **j**ung   **J**ugend

2. The German **y** is pronounced like the German **ü.**

   Ph**y**sik   S**y**stem   Ps**y**chiatrie

3. The **ck** is pronounced like *k,* and the preceding vowel is always short.

   E**ck**e   Sa**ck**   Gepä**ck**

4. The German **qu** is pronounced like the English *k* plus *v.*

   Qualität   **qu**er   **Qu**ark

5. The ending **-tion** is pronounced *tsion,* with two distinct vowel sounds, the second one long.

   Na**tion**   Sensa**tion**   Reak**tion**

Word stress and sentence intonation

Aside from learning these phonetic guidelines, you will need to pay close attention to word stress and the intonation of the sentence.

Word stress in German is relatively simple. Most non-compound words put the stress on the first syllable or stem syllable: **mórgen, géstern, stéhen, Besúcher, Gespräch.** If the word is of non-German origin, this rule frequently does not apply: **Studént, Literatúr, Physík, Natión, Philosóph.** In compound words the stress lies on the first word or first stem syllable: **Aúfschrift, Déutschland, Férnseher, Gepäckträger, Verkéhrsunfall.** However, these rules do not always apply, so listen closely to your instructor and the tapes.

Sentence intonation is much more difficult. It is directly related to the syntax of the sentence. In an affirmative statement, for instance, the intonation is quite different from that in a question. Compare the intonation of the following sentences.

Karl geht in die Schule.   Geht Karl in die Schule?

Wohin geht Karl?

In addition, the stress of an individual word can change the meaning of a sentence significantly. There is a great difference between **Karl géht in die Schule** and **Karl geht in die Schúle.** In the first sentence we are told Karl *walks* to school, he does not drive. In the second sentence we learn that Karl goes to *school* and not anywhere else. Again, listen very carefully to your instructor and the tapes of the Lab program whenever new syntactical constructions are introduced, in order to learn the intonation properly.

After learning all the German sounds and stress patterns, practice saying the following sentences.

Wann kam Tante Anna?	*When did Aunt Anna come?*
Nach dem Tee gehen Peter und Werner an den See.	*After tea(time) Peter and Werner go to the lake.*
Liebe Lili, willst du wissen, wie ich dich liebe?	*Dear Lili, do you want to know how much I love you?*
Bitte, gib dem Klavierspieler noch ein Bier!	*Please give the piano player another beer.*
Mein Sohn, dort oben ist das Telefon.	*My son, the telephone is up there.*
Morgenstund hat Gold im Mund.	*The early bird catches the worm.*
Nach dem Essen sollst du ruhen oder tausend Schritte tun.	*After dinner you should rest or go for a short walk (lit. do a thousand paces).*
Unser Koch kocht auch gut nach einem Kochbuch.	*Our cook also cooks well by following a cookbook.*
Zehn Zigeuner ziehen zehn Zentner Zuckerrüben.	*Ten gypsies are pulling ten hundredweights of sugar beets.*

Translations of Conversations

Colloquial language cannot be translated literally. The English below is the colloquial equivalent of the German conversations; it does not attempt to translate word for word.

Chapter 1: A Piece of Information

JUDY Good morning. I'm looking for the Institute of German Language and Literature.
MR. KELLER Adenauer Street number one. It's right over there.—Are you from the United States?
JUDY Yes, I'm from Buffalo, New York. My name is Judy Miller.
MR. KELLER And now you're studying here in Germany?
JUDY Yes, I'm studying German and sociology.
MR. KELLER That's interesting.
JUDY I'm looking for a book by Kafka.
MR. KELLER What's the name of the book?
JUDY *Amerika*. I hope it's here.
MR. KELLER I'm not sure. The card catalogue is right over there.
JUDY Thank you for the information. Good-bye.
MR. KELLER You're welcome. Good-bye, Miss Miller. Good luck!

Chapter 2: On the Phone

KLAUS Schönberg speaking.
MONIKA Klaus, this is Monika. Excuse me, do you have a moment?
KLAUS Of course! Why?
MONIKA We have a record player now. It's brand new.
KLAUS Really? Great!
MONIKA It sounds simply fantastic! Do you perhaps have a record by Peter Alexander?
KLAUS Unfortunately, I have no record by Alexander, but I have a few jazz records, for instance by Louis Armstrong.
MONIKA Great! Do you know the record "Please, with Whipped Cream" by Udo Jürgens?
KLAUS No, is it a new one?
MONIKA No, it's not new, but I really like the record.
KLAUS Wonderful! I'll be right over. So long, Monika.
MONIKA So long, Klaus. See you soon.

Chapter 3: Bus or Taxi?

Berlin-Tegel Airport, Berlin. Robert has just arrived in West Berlin. He picks up his luggage and leaves the terminal. Outside, taxis are waiting. He asks a taxi driver for information.

ROBERT Good morning. Excuse me, is there a bus from here to the Kurfürstendamm?
TAXI DRIVER Not directly from here. But do you see the bus stop over there? Take bus number eight!

A bus number eight is just leaving.

ROBERT How often does the bus to the Kurfürstendamm run?
TAXI DRIVER Just a moment. I believe, every fifteen minutes.
ROBERT Really?
TAXI DRIVER But take a taxi! Hop in!
ROBERT Thank you. I'm not in a hurry and I don't have enough money for a taxi. Thanks for the information.
TAXI DRIVER You're welcome.

After fifteen minutes a bus number eight arrives and Robert boards it.

ROBERT   Are you going to the Kurfürstendamm?

BUS DRIVER   No, no. Get off quickly and take bus number fifteen.—(*To the passengers*) Get in please. Move on! Move to the rear, please!

The bus driver shuts the door.

ROBERT (*to himself*)   Next time, I'll take a taxi.

Chapter 4: The Student Room

Heinz lives in Cologne but is studying in Marburg. He is looking for a room. He reads the newspaper and then goes to a rental agency. There he talks with Miss Schell.

MISS SCHELL   Good morning. May I help you?

HEINZ   I'm a student here in Marburg and I'm looking for a room.

MISS SCHELL   How much can you pay per month?

HEINZ   About two hundred marks per month.

MISS SCHELL   One moment, please. Why don't you take a room right by the University? It costs two hundred and forty a month, heat included.

HEINZ   That's not particularly cheap. Does that include cooking facilities?

MISS SCHELL   Yes, I'm sure.

HEINZ   Does the room have a shower or a bath?

MISS SCHELL   No, but it has a wash basin.

HEINZ   And what about the toilet?

MISS SCHELL   It's right by the room.

HEINZ   Not bad! What's the address, please?

MISS SCHELL   Mrs. Becker, Lindenstraße five. Near Hindenburg Square.

HEINZ   Thank you! How much do I owe you?

MISS SCHELL   Eight marks. (*She brings the student a form.*) Please sign this form and give it to Mrs. Becker. (*Heinz signs and pays.*)

HEINZ   Many thanks! Good-bye!

Heinz goes home.

Chapter 5: In Court

DISTRICT ATTORNEY   Now please tell us, Mr. Steinhoff, how did the accident happen?

STEINHOFF   Well, I went to a party at the home of some friends.

D.A.   What did you drink?

STEINHOFF   We drank wine, beer, and orange juice.

D.A.   I see. And naturally you drank orange juice.

STEINHOFF   I think so.

D.A.   How is that? I don't understand. The police stopped you and took a blood test.

STEINHOFF   That's right.

D.A.   Did you really drink only orange juice?

STEINHOFF   Perhaps somebody mixed in some vodka, but I didn't notice anything.

D.A.   Mr. Steinhoff, have you forgotten already? You damaged public property!

STEINHOFF   Oh, you mean the tree?

D.A.   Yes, how did that happen?

STEINHOFF   A Porsche passed me and I immediately turned to the right.

D.A.   And there was a tree there?

STEINHOFF   Yes, unfortunately.

D.A.   And you didn't see it?

STEINHOFF   No, unfortunately not.

D.A.   Why not, Mr. Steinhoff?

STEINHOFF   I have no idea.

D.A.   Then I'll give you the answer. Unfortunately, you had too much orange juice in your blood.

Chapter 6: The Parking Ticket

George and Sybil had a date for nine a.m. in a stand-up coffee bar. George is fifteen minutes late.

SYBIL Here you are at last! Where have you been?

GEORGE Hi, Sybil. I'm sorry. I really meant to be on time.

SYBIL What happened this time?

GEORGE I looked for a parking place and couldn't find one.

SYBIL That's nothing new.

GEORGE Finally I parked the car on the sidewalk in front of the bakery.

SYBIL Go on.

GEORGE I was just about to get out when a cop came along. "You can't park here. Drive on," he said.

SYBIL But you know you can't park there.

GEORGE "Only for a few minutes," I begged him. But the guy showed no pity and was about to give me a ticket.

SYBIL But why did you want to go to the bakery?

GEORGE Well, I was supposed to bring some rolls.

SYBIL And where are they?

GEORGE The rolls? Oh no! I forgot all about them!

Chapter 7: The Vacation Trip

Jutta and Kurt have been married for fifteen years and have two children, Walter, 12, and Claudia, 10. They are making plans for the family vacation. They would like to take a vacation trip with the children.

JUTTA Listen, Kurt, we must make plans now for our vacation.

KURT (*reading the newspaper*) There's ample time for that.

JUTTA Not at all. In two months you'll have your vacation.

KURT (*drops the newspaper*) Agreed. But where shall we go? Unfortunately, we have hardly any money left for a vacation.

JUTTA Well, we certainly can't stay at home. The children, for instance, would like to see the South of France.

KURT What, the South of France? That's too expensive. Why don't we drive up to the North Sea, perhaps to Westerland?

JUTTA But you know very well that traveling within Germany isn't cheap either. Besides, it'll probably be raining up there again.

KURT Then we'll take umbrellas instead of bathing suits.

JUTTA Don't be so cynical. After all, we must do something for the children.

KURT Of course. But during our vacation I'd like to have some rest. Southern France is so far away and driving is so tiring.

JUTTA Well after all, I can drive too, can't I? So how do you feel about Southern France?

Chapter 8: Looking for the University

Fritz and Rudi, two friends, arrive in a Volkswagen in Münster, Westphalia, coming from Bielefeld. They are heading toward the railroad station. They stop on a street and ask a pedestrian for information.

FRITZ Excuse me, how do we get from here to the University?

PEDESTRIAN To the University? That's very simple. Do you see the fountain up ahead at the end of the parking lot?

FRITZ Oh, yes.

PEDESTRIAN There you turn immediately to the right and keep going until you get to the Klosterstraße.

FRITZ You mean right up there ahead, behind the fountain?

PEDESTRIAN Hm, yes. But be careful! At the Klosterstraße you must turn to the left.

RUDI (*studying a city map*) Will we pass the cathedral?

PEDESTRIAN No, the cathedral is straight ahead. But that way is no good. It's a pedestrian mall.

FRITZ But at the Klosterstraße we turn to the left?

PEDESTRIAN You'll have to. You'll see, it's a one-way street. After that you'll come to an intersection.

FRITZ All right.

PEDESTRIAN But after the intersection you drive on to the end of the Schützenstraße.

FRITZ And then?

PEDESTRIAN Then you better ask someone else.

FRITZ Thanks a lot.

PEDESTRIAN You're welcome.

FRITZ *(to Rudi)* Hey, did he say go to the right or straight ahead up at the corner?

RUDI I haven't the slightest idea. Go straight ahead. Don't worry, we'll find the University. They say it's a palace.

Chapter 9: Should We Go to the Movies?

Heinz is a film enthusiast. He calls up his friend Karl Zimmermann, and tries to convince him to go to a movie that night.

KARL Zimmermann speaking.

HEINZ Hi, Karl. This is Heinz. So you're home at last. I called you an hour ago, but didn't get an answer.

KARL Well, I was at Professor Dietrich's seminar. Toward the end he let a student go on talking, though we were all practically asleep.

HEINZ That's nothing new. When I was in his seminar a year ago, that happened every week. But listen, do you feel like going to the movies?

KARL Of course I do, but I've got a date already.

HEINZ Don't kid me! You've absolutely got to see the Fassbinder film at the Odeon if you're really interested in the art of the film.

KARL That's all fine and dandy, but I can't be in two places at the same time.

HEINZ Right! So I'll pick you up as soon as you've eaten. Okay?

KARL But Heinz, tonight I'm seeing *Faust* with Irene. Do you understand?

HEINZ Why didn't you say so in the first place?

KARL Because you keep right on talking.

HEINZ Okay, have fun! Then I'll go to the movie without you.

Chapter 10: The Rate of Exchange

Mr. and Mrs. Kohler, German Americans, are on a vacation trip through their old homeland. They flew from Chicago to Frankfurt two days ago and meanwhile have rested up from their flight. They enter the breakfast room of their hotel and sit down at a table. They have just ordered their breakfast and begin to talk.

MRS. K. Look, someone left his newspaper.

MR. K. I don't think so. It must belong to the hotel. Do you see the papers on the table over there? They are there for the guests.

MRS. K. Of course. I've got to get used to the customs over here again.

MR. K. Just a moment. I'll get myself the *Frankfurter Allgemeine.* Which newspaper would you like to look at?

MRS. K. The *Süddeutsche,* please. We must by all means look up the exchange rate of the dollar.

Mr. Kohler goes to the table and comes back with both newspapers.

MR. K. I hope the rate hasn't dropped any more. Unfortunately for us Americans, the Economic Miracle has its dark side.

MRS. K Fantastic! It says here: "Dollar recovers on the Frankfurt Exchange."

MR. K Good. We'll go to the bank as soon as we've finished eating, and change a few more traveler's checks.

One hour later in front of the bank.

MRS. K. How many marks have we gained now for two hundred dollars, in comparison with yesterday's rate of exhange?

MR. K. Just a minute! I'm computing it. Good grief! Five whole marks! That may be just enough for the taxi back to the hotel.

Chapter 11: Long Hair

Mrs. Eichendorff is a working mother. Her son Jürgen, aged 16, is a pupil at the municipal Gymnasium. He is changing clothes to go to a small birthday party for his good friend Dirk, the son of rich parents.

JÜRGEN *(calling from upstairs)* Hey, Mom, what should I wear?

MOTHER By all means, a clean shirt and your new tie.

JÜRGEN Which new tie? Oh, that boring tie that Uncle Emil gave me! But what suit should I wear?

MOTHER The dark blue one, of course. Why do you even ask? And don't forget to put on clean socks that match.

After a short while Jürgen comes downstairs.

JÜRGEN How do I look?

MOTHER Fairly acceptable. But put on your warm overcoat and a hat. It's cold out.

JÜRGEN No, no—I won't be cold. And anyway, I don't want to go walking around like a mobile clothes hanger.

MOTHER Wait a minute! Why didn't you get a haircut?

JÜRGEN Are you kidding? In cold weather my long hair keeps me nice and warm. See you!

Chapter 12: The Discothèque

Jutta Jünger (22) is a chemistry student in Cologne. Hansjörg Brau (23) studies sociology. They are friends and happen to meet downtown.

JUTTA Hansjörg! Hansjörg! Hello, Hansjörg! Can't you hear me? Hansjörg!!!

HANSJÖRG What? How's that? Oh Jutta, it's you—hello!

JUTTA How are you? What's new?

HANSJÖRG Nothing new—the usual. I'm reading and writing; and I'm late again with a seminar paper. You know how I am.

JUTTA But where are you coming from now?

HANSJÖRG Pardon?

JUTTA *(shouting)* Where are you coming from? From the university library?

HANSJÖRG What? Yes, from the Jimmy Discothèque. There's a great band playing there now—"The Singing Vampires."

JUTTA Why aren't they called the "Howling Vampires"? You can hardly hear any more.

HANSJÖRG So what? That way I won't hear every noise. By the way, the Vampires sing many good hits about social and political concerns.

JUTTA Why don't they ever invite Biermann?

HANSJÖRG What's that? You want to invite me for a beer?

JUTTA Unbelievable! Let's go! We'll drink something refreshing over there. Swallowing will do your hearing some good.

HANSJÖRG What did you say?

Chapter 13: After the Lecture

Werner is a physics student at a German university, and his friend Helga is in the fourth semester of medicine. Both are 23 years old. Helga arrives in the student cafeteria out of breath. There she finds her friend. He is sitting in front of his meal, half dreaming.

HELGA Werner, so there you are!

WERNER Yes, of course. Where else? It's already—*(looks at his watch)*—twenty after twelve and high time we had lunch.

HELGA   But we had agreed to meet at a quarter to twelve in front of the lab building, and to eat downtown.

WERNER   But hadn't we agreed on that for tomorrow?

HELGA   No, for today.

WERNER   Then I've sure made a mistake. How dumb of me!

HELGA   I should say so!

WERNER   Please don't be angry with me. Sit down. I already got lunch for both of us.

HELGA   Okay, but we'll eat downtown tomorrow. Our seminars don't start until 4:30 p.m. anyway.

WERNER   Agreed. But you know, the lecture by Professor Schürmann this morning was fabulous—clear and entertaining.

HELGA   Really? An entertaining math lecture certainly is something unusual.

WERNER   But Professor Schürmann really has a good sense of humor.

HELGA   Then I'd better come with you to the lecture tomorrow. Then we can go downtown together.

Chapter 14: The Psychologist

Franz and Ferdi are students at the University of Vienna. Franz is in the second semester of psychology and Ferdi in the first semester of German studies. They live in a small rented apartment and are on their way home from the university.

FRANZ   We must hurry.

FERDI   Why?

FRANZ   Have you forgotten already? You promised to take the psychological test we recently discussed in our seminar.

FERDI   Oh yes. But no need to hurry. I first want to eat something in the café over there. My stomach is growling.

FRANZ   Okay. But after that we'll hurry home.

They sit down at a sidewalk table in front of the café.

FERDI   What's the name of the test again you're so excited about?

FRANZ   It's a "Thematic Apperception Test." We show you a few pictures and you have to interpret their meaning.

FERDI   Of course, I understand. In the process my personality is supposed to express itself.

FRANZ   That's right. Imagine: on a test-card you see a man who stands in front of a picture, dreaming.

FERDI   And I'm supposed to say then what's in the picture and what the man is thinking about?

FRANZ   Exactly.

FERDI   I'm sorry. Right now I can think only of one thing: in the picture there's a Sachertorte and the man is thinking: "Boy, am I hungry!"

Chapter 15: The Abitur

Anita, Anton, and Wolfgang are three last-year students at the Gymnasium who are about to take the Abitur exam. For almost three months they have been studying together three times a week to prepare for the exam. One evening they talk with one another during a break.

ANTON   Listen, my head's pounding. That was a really mean math problem we solved.

WOLFGANG   You should say, "that Anita solved for us."

ANTON   True. If we could only take the Abitur together as a group, then we'd pass with flying colors.

ANITA   A fantastic idea! Then I would take on the math, and Anton could write the English composition for us.

WOLFGANG   And me?

ANTON   Don't make a fuss! You know German literature backwards and forwards.

WOLFGANG   Maybe. But I'd rather write my own poem than comment on a hackneyed quote out of a Schiller poem.

ANTON   Ha, ha—his own poem! Listen to that, Anita! The teachers would certainly confer the Nobel Prize on him for his poem.

WOLFGANG You see, Anita, he's laughing at me again! Anton, unfortunately you have no imagination.
ANTON "Imagination"! Don't make me laugh!
WOLFGANG If the teachers had more poetic sensitivity, they'd leave more room for our own thoughts and feelings.
ANITA What's going on? Don't start quarreling again already. None of us can take any more stress. Why don't we go to our discothèque afterward?
WOLFGANG Great idea!
ANTON Let's go! What are we waiting for?

Chapter 16: Hitchhiking

Ray is an American student of German descent, studying at the Free University of Berlin. He is standing at the city limits of West Berlin near the Berlin Wall, at an exit leading to the DDR. In his hands he holds a piece of cardboard on which he has written "To Hamburg." Monika and Freddy approach in an Opel and stop in front of him.

MONIKA *(leaning out of the car)* Hello. What are you waiting for?
RAY What am I waiting for? A friendly soul who'll take me to Hamburg.
MONIKA To Hamburg? But what's written on that piece of cardboard of yours?
RAY What's written on it? "To Hamburg," of course.
FREDDY But look at the sign from the front!
RAY *(laughing)* Oh, how dumb of me! I had it upside down. Most of the drivers must have laughed about it when they saw me. But nobody was willing to stop.
FREDDY As it happens, we're driving to Hamburg.
RAY *(gets into the car)* Great! That's lucky. Thanks!
MONIKA *(in the car)* Are your papers in order for crossing the border?
RAY Oh yes, I know the ropes. I travel quite often to the Federal Republic.
MONIKA Why?
RAY I like Berlin well enough. But once in a while I have to get out. One feels so locked in.
MONIKA Really. We feel the same way.

Chapter 17: The Stein of Beer

Joseph, who works for a German firm in New York, just landed in his home town of Munich and meets his old friend Franz in the airport restaurant.

FRANZ Did you have a pleasant flight over the Atlantic?
JOSEPH The usual. People ate and drank a lot and they showed a film that didn't interest me.
FRANZ Could you rest a little?
JOSEPH Not this time. I was always awakened by a crying child or a few noisy passengers.
FRANZ Well, you'll have to recover from your jet lag tonight.
JOSEPH By all means.
FRANZ But first you need to be cheered up. *(To the waitress)* Two steins, please.

The waitress brings two enormous mugs of beer.

FRANZ Look at this stein of beer!
JOSEPH What's the matter?
FRANZ Two or three centimeters of foam. Hereabouts they're talking about the "big fraud in the pitcher" and they say the stein should be increased by two or three centimeters. Or more beer and less foam.
JOSEPH Don't get excited and do have a drink. Now *you* need cheering up.
FRANZ & JOSEPH *(to each other)* Cheers! Cheers! To your health!

Chapter 18: The Mystery Writer

A group of young people are going to a rock concert. But Gerd's brother Franz doesn't want to go with them.

ANITA Gerd, where's your brother? Isn't he coming with us?
GERD He says he wants to stay home because he doesn't think much of rock concerts.

HILDEGARD He's probably reading a long novel again. I couldn't do that.

GERD Nonsense! He wants to see a detective story on TV.

BERTHOLD What, your brother? I wouldn't have expected that of him.

GERD Oh yes! He claims that one learns something about real life from them.

HILDEGARD Anita, did you hear that? Gerd, tell your brother he ought to come with us sometime—*then* he'd learn something about real life!

BERTHOLD Hilda, don't be so conceited!

GERD By the way, Franz says he wants to become a mystery writer himself. He says there's a lot of money in it.

ANITA He's thinking of money! Incidentally, what's he doing with his ticket?

GERD He gave it to me and told me to sell it at the entrance for double its price.

BERTHOLD Ha! Who said that Franz doesn't know anything about real life!

1st principal part		*2nd principal part*	*3rd principal part*
INFINITIVE	PRESENT	PAST	PAST PARTICIPLE
messen (*to measure*)	mißt	maß	gemessen
mißlingen (*to fail*)		mißlang	ist mißlungen
nehmen (*to take*)	nimmt	nahm	genommen
pfeifen (*to whistle*)		pfiff	gepfiffen
raten (*to advise, guess*)	rät	riet	geraten
reiben (*to rub*)		rieb	gerieben
reißen (*to tear*)		riß	ist gerissen
reiten (*to ride*)		ritt	ist geritten
riechen (*to smell*)		roch	gerochen
ringen (*to wrestle*)		rang	gerungen
rufen (*to call*)		rief	gerufen
saufen (*to drink; used of animals*)	säuft	soff	gesoffen
saugen (*to suck*)		sog	gesogen
schaffen (*to create*)		schuf	geschaffen
scheinen (*to seem, shine*)		schien	geschienen
schieben (*to push*)		schob	geschoben
schießen (*to shoot*)		schoß	geschossen
schlafen (*to sleep*)	schläft	schlief	geschlafen
schlagen (*to beat*)	schlägt	schlug	geschlagen
schleichen (*to sneak*)		schlich	ist geschlichen
schließen (*to close*)		schloß	geschlossen
schmeißen (*to fling*)		schmiß	geschmissen
schmelzen (*to melt*)	schmilzt	schmolz	ist geschmolzen
schneiden (*to cut*)		schnitt	geschnitten
schreiben (*to write*)		schrieb	geschrieben
schreien (*to cry*)		schrie	geschrien
schweigen (*to be silent*)		schwieg	geschwiegen
schwimmen (*to swim*)		schwamm	ist geschwommen
schwören (*to swear an oath*)		schwur	geschworen
sehen (*to see*)	sieht	sah	gesehen
sein (*to be*)	ist	war	ist gewesen
singen (*to sing*)		sang	gesungen
sinken (*to sink*)		sank	ist gesunken
sitzen (*to sit*)		saß	gesessen
spinnen (*to spin*)		spann	gesponnen
sprechen (*to speak*)	spricht	sprach	gesprochen
sprießen (*to sprout*)		sproß	ist gesprossen
springen (*to jump*)		sprang	ist gesprungen
stechen (*to sting*)	sticht	stach	gestochen
stehen (*to stand*)		stand	gestanden
stehlen (*to steal*)	stiehlt	stahl	gestohlen
steigen (*to climb*)		stieg	ist gestiegen
sterben (*to die*)	stirbt	starb	ist gestorben
stinken (*to stink*)		stank	gestunken

1st principal part		2nd principal part	3rd principal part
INFINITIVE	*PRESENT*	*PAST*	*PAST PARTICIPLE*
stoßen (*to push*)	stößt	stieß	gestoßen
streichen (*to stroke, spread*)		strich	gestrichen
streiten (*to quarrel*)		stritt	gestritten
tragen (*to carry*)	trägt	trug	getragen
treffen (*to hit, meet*)	trifft	traf	getroffen
treiben (*to drive*)		trieb	getrieben
treten (*to step, kick*)	tritt	trat	getreten
trinken (*to drink; used of humans*)		trank	getrunken
tun (*to do*)		tat	getan
verbergen (*to hide*)	verbirgt	verbarg	verborgen
verderben (*to spoil*)	verdirbt	verdarb	verdorben
vergessen (*to forget*)	vergißt	vergaß	vergessen
verlieren (*to lose*)		verlor	verloren
verschwinden (*to disappear*)		verschwand	ist verschwunden
verzeihen (*to forgive*)		verzieh	verziehen
wachsen (*to grow*)	wächst	wuchs	ist gewachsen
waschen (*to wash*)	wäscht	wusch	gewaschen
werben (*to advertise*)	wirbt	warb	geworben
werden (*to become*)	wird	wurde	ist geworden
werfen (*to throw*)	wirft	warf	geworfen
wiegen (*to weigh*)		wog	gewogen
winden (*to wind*)		wand	gewunden
zwingen (*to compel*)		zwang	gezwungen

Irregular weak verbs and modals

brennen (*to burn*)		brannte	gebrannt
bringen (*to bring*)		brachte	gebracht
denken (*to think*)		dachte	gedacht
dürfen (*to be allowed to*)	darf	durfte	gedurft
haben (*to have*)	hat	hatte	gehabt
kennen (*to know*)		kannte	gekannt
können (*to be able to*)	kann	konnte	gekonnt
mögen (*to like to*)	mag	mochte	gemocht
müssen (*to have to*)	muß	mußte	gemußt
nennen (*to name*)		nannte	genannt
rennen (*to run*)		rannte	ist gerannt

1st principal part		*2nd principal part*	*3rd principal part*
INFINITIVE	PRESENT	PAST	PAST PARTICIPLE
sollen (*to ought to*)	soll	sollte	gesollt
wenden (*to turn*)		wandte (wendete)	gewandt (gewendet)
wissen (*to know*)	weiß	wußte	gewußt
wollen (*to want to*)	will	wollte	gewollt

Common Units of Measurement

Measures and weights

1 ounce = 28 grams
1 pint *or* 16 oz. = 0.47 liter
1 quart *or* 2 pts. = 0.95 liter
1 pound *or* 16 oz. = 0.45 kilogram
1 ton *or* 2,200 lbs. = 1,000
  kilograms
1 hundredweight *or* 100 lbs. = 45
  kilograms

1 inch = 2.5 centimeters
1 cubic inch = 16 cubic centimeters
1 foot *or* 12 inches = 0.3 meter
1 yard *or* 3 feet = 0.9 meter
1 mile = 1,609 meters *or* 1.6
  kilometers
1 square mile = 2.6 square
  kilometers

Maße und Gewichte

¼ Liter = 8.45 ounces *or* 0.53 pint
½ Liter = 16.9 ounces *or* 1.06 pints
1 Liter = 2.1 pints *or* 1.06 quarts *or*
  0.26 gallon
1 Hektoliter = 210 pints *or* 106
  quarts *or* 26 gallons
1 Pfund *or* 500 g *or* ½ Kilo = 1.1
  pounds
1 Kilogramm (Kilo) *or* 1,000 g *or* 2
  Pfd = 2.2 pounds
1 Zentner *or* 100 Pfd *or* 50 kg = 110
  pounds *or* 1.1 hundredweight

1 Tonne *or* 1,000 kg = 2,200 pounds
  or 1.1 tons
1 Zentimeter *or* 10 mm = 0.4 inch
1 Kubikzentimeter = 0.06 cubic
  inch
1 Meter *or* 100 cm = 39.5 inches *or*
  3.3 feet *or* 1.1 yards
1 Kilometer *or* 1,000 m = 1,100
  yards *or* 0.62 mile
1 Quadratmeter = 10.8 square feet
  or 1.2 square yards

VERGLEICHS-
THERMOMETER

CENTIGRADE   FAHRENHEIT

DIE THERMOMETER

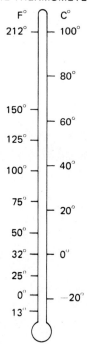

F°		C°
212°		100°
		80°
150°		60°
125°		
100°		40°
75°		20°
50°		
32°		0°
25°		
0°		—20°
13°		

$$°C = \frac{10°(F - 32)}{18} \qquad °F = \frac{18°C}{10} + 32$$

DIE ENTFERNUNG

Meilen

| 25 | | 50 | 62 | 75 | | 100 | | 125 |

| 20 | 40 | 60 | 80 | 100 | 120 | 140 | 160 | 180 | 200 |

Kilometer

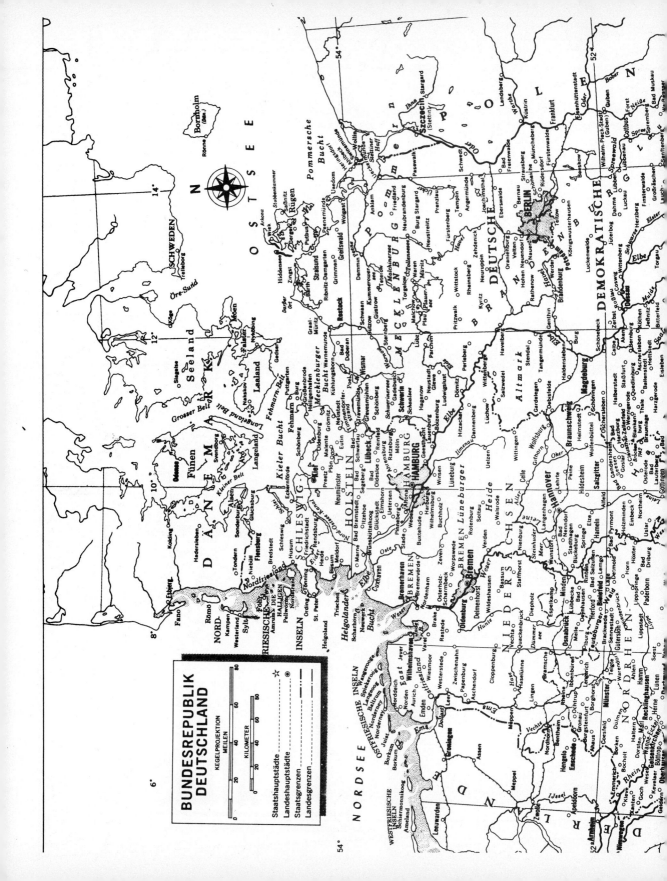

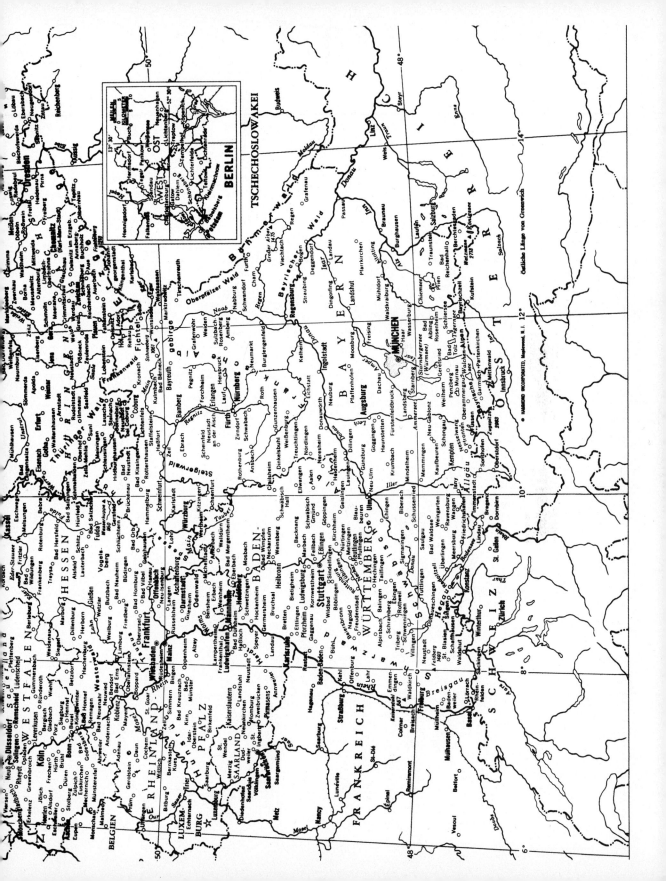

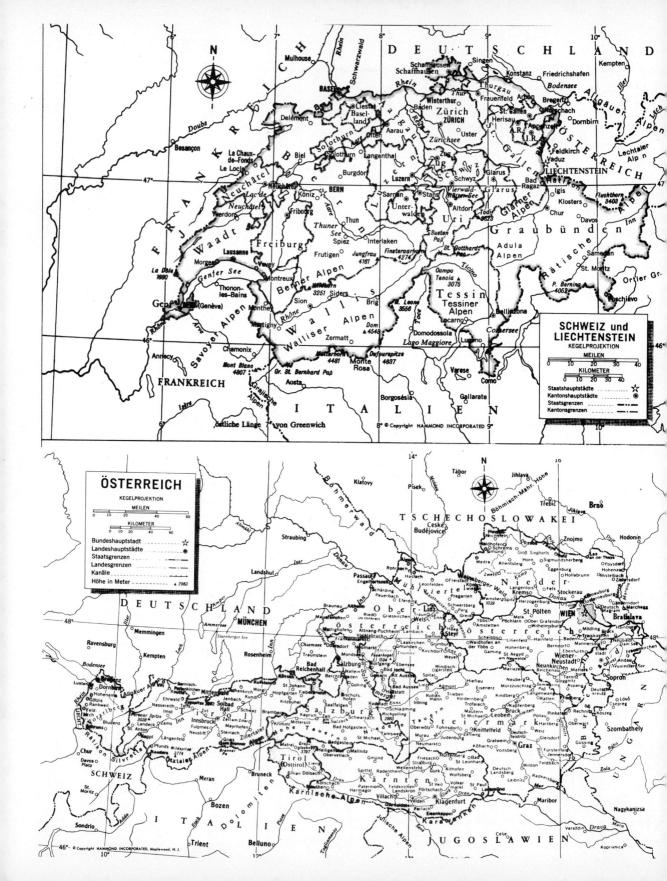

GERMAN-ENGLISH VOCABULARY

A

ab·biegen, bog ab, ist abgebogen, 18 to turn off

ab·brechen (bricht ab), brach ab, abgebrochen, 18 to break off

der Abend, -e, IC evening; Guten Abend!, IC Good evening!

das Abendessen, -, 4 dinner

abends, 13 in the evening

die Abendsonne, 16 evening sun

aber, 2 but

ab·fahren (fährt ab), fuhr ab, ist abgefahren, 3 to take off, leave

das Abgas, -e, 11 exhaust

abgedroschen, 15 hackneyed

ab·halten (hält ab), hielt ab, abgehalten, 18 to prevent, keep away

die Abhebegeschwindigkeit, 11 lift-off speed

ab·holen, 9 to pick up

das Abitur, 15 final examination (comparable to graduation from junior college)

ab·machen, 13 to agree upon

ab·reisen, 10 to leave

ab·schneiden, schnitt ab, abgeschnitten, 15 to come off (well / badly)

sich ab·spielen, 16 to take place, happen

die Abstammung, 16 origin, descent

ab·stürzen, ist abgestürzt, 8 to fall down, crash

das Abwasser, , 6 waste water, sewage

abwesend, 15 absent

acht, IC eight

achtzehn, IC eighteen

achtzig, IC eighty

die Adresse, -n, 4 address

die Ahnung, -en, 5 idea

die Akte, -n, 10 file

das Aktenzeichen, -, 18 file number

akzeptabel, 11 acceptable

akzeptieren, 13 to accept

der Alkohol, 2 alcohol

alle, 2/3 all

die Allee, -n, 10 avenue

allein, 7 alone

allerdings, 11 however

alles, 3 everything; alles schön und gut, 9 that's all fine and dandy

der Alltag, 7 workday

die Alpen (pl.), 7 the Alps

als, 5/7 as; than

als, 9 when

also, 7 i.e.; I mean

alt, 2 old

die Altstadt, 10 old town

ambulant, 11 ambulant, mobile

das Amerika, 1 America

der Amerikaner, -, 1 American

die Amerikanerin, -nen, 1 American woman

amerikanisch, 12 American

an, 8 at, on

die Analyse, -n, 14 analysis

die Anatomie, 15 anatomy

anderer, 2 other

die **Anerkennung, -en,** 13 recógnition

der **Anfang, ⸚e,** 5 beginning

an·fangen (fängt an), fing an, angefangen, 10 to begin, start

an·geben (gibt an), gab an, angegeben, 18 to be conceited, show off

angenehm, 14 comfortable

an·greifen, griff an, angegriffen, 11 to attack

die **Angst, ⸚e,** 15 fear

an·halten (hält an), hielt an, angehalten, 3 to stop

der **Anhalter, -,** 16 hitchhiker

an·hören, 14 to listen to

an·kommen, kam an, ist angekommen, 3 to arrive

an·kündigen, 6 to announce

an·nehmen (nimmt an), nahm an, angenommen, 10 to accept; assume

an·passen, 18 to adapt, accommodate

an·rufen, rief an, angerufen, 5 to call, phone

sich **an·schauen,** 11 to look at; to watch

sich **an·sehen (sieht an), sah an, angesehen,** 8 to look at; to watch

anständig, 15 decent

anstatt, 7 instead of

sich **an·stellen,** 15 to make a fuss

anstrengend, 18 strenuous

die **Antwort, -en,** 5 answer

antworten, 7 to answer, reply

an·zapfen, 17 to tap

sich **an·ziehen, zog an, angezogen,** 9 to put on, dress

der **Anzug, ⸚e,** 9 suit

der **April, IC** April

die **Arbeit, -en,** 5 work

arbeiten, 1 to work

arbeitslos, 15 unemployed

die **Arbeitslosigkeit,** 15 unemployment

die **Arbeitsteilung,** 13 division of labor

die **Arbeitszeit, -en,** 7 working hours

die **Archäologie,** 14 archaeology

der **Ärger,** 18 annoyance; anger

ärgerlich, 18 angry; annoying

das **Argument, -e,** 8 argument

die **Arkade, -n,** 11 arcade

arm, 11 poor

der **Arm, -e,** 12 arm

die **Armee, -n,** 11 army

die **Art, -en,** 13 kind

der **Arzt, ⸚e,** 14 physician

die **Ärztin, -nen,** 14 female physician

der **Atem,** 13 breath; **außer Atem sein,** 13 to be out of breath

atemlos, 15 breathless

der **Athlet, -en,** 8 athlete

der **Atlantik,** 17 Atlantic Ocean

der **Atomkrieg, -e,** 11 nuclear war

auch, 2 also

auf, 3 on

auf·bauen, 14 to establish, build up

auf·fahren (fährt auf), fuhr auf, ist aufgefahren, 13 to ram

auf·führen, 17 to perform

die **Aufführung, -en,** 14 performance

die **Aufgabe, -n,** 15 task

auf·geben (gibt auf), gab auf, aufgegeben, 8 to give up

aufgeweckt, 17 alert

aufgezogen, 16 drawn (bayonet)

auf·halten (hält auf), hielt auf, aufgehalten, 17 to stop

auf·heben, hob auf, aufgehoben, 10 to lift

auf·hören, 9 to end, stop

auf·kaufen, 7 to buy up

auf·klären, 18 to clear up

auf·machen, 8 to open

aufmerksam, 6 alert, attentive

auf·passen, 8 to watch out

sich **auf·regen,** 17 to get excited, upset

auf·rufen, rief auf, aufgerufen, 14 to call up

der **Aufsatz, ⸚e,** 15 essay, composition

auf·schauen, 10 to look up

sich **auf·setzen,** 11 to put on

auf·stehen, stand auf, ist aufgestanden, 13 to get up

auf·steigen, stieg auf, ist aufgestiegen, 3 to climb up

auf·wachen, ist aufgewacht, 17 to wake up

auf·wecken, 17 to wake up, awaken someone

das **Auge, -n,** 9 eye

der **Augenarzt, ⸚e,** 14 ophthalmologist

der **Augenzeuge, -n,** 18 eyewitness

der **August, IC** August

aus, 1 out of, from

aus·brennen, brannte aus, ist ausgebrannt, 16 to burn out

der **Ausdruck, ⸚e,** 9 expression

aus·drücken, 9 to express

aus·führen, 18 to do; to take someone out

aus·füllen, 12 to fill out

aus·geben (gibt aus), gab aus, ausgegeben, 9 to spend

aus·gehen, ging aus, ist ausgegangen, 7 to go out

aus·halten (hält aus), hielt aus, ausgehalten, 15 to endure, stand something

sich **aus·kennen, kannte sich aus, ausgekannt,** 16 to know something well

aus·kommen, kam aus, ist ausgekommen, 18 to get along with

die **Auskunft, ⸚e,** 1 information

aus·rechnen, 10 to calculate

sich **aus·ruhen,** 17 to rest

aus·schlafen (schläft aus), schlief aus, ausgeschlafen, 9 to sleep in

aus·sehen (sieht aus), sah aus, ausgesehen, 11 to look

außer, 4 except

außerdem, 5 besides

außerhalb, 7 outside

aus·steigen, stieg aus, ist ausgestiegen, 3 to get off

aus·suchen, 16   to select, choose

aus·tragen (trägt aus), trug aus, ausgetragen, 17   to carry out;   **ein Spiel [Spiele] austragen,** 17   to hold games [sport]

authentisch, 18   authentic

das   Auto, -s, 3   car

das   Autofahren, 7   driving

der   Autofahrer, -, 5   driver

der   Automat, -en, 2   automat

der   Autostop, 16   hitchhiking

die   Autotür, -en, 16   car door

der   Autoverkehr, 11   car traffic

B

die   Bäckerei, -en, 6   bakery

das   Bad, ˝er, 4   bathroom; bath

die   Badehose, -n, 7   bathing suit

das   Badezimmer, -, 4   bathroom

der   Bahnhof, ˝e, 4   railroad station

die   Bahnhofshalle, -n, 8   hall of a railroad station

das   Bajonett, -e, 16   bayonet

bald, 4   soon

die   Band, -s, 12   band, musical group

die   Bank, -en, 10   bank

das   Bankett, -e, 10   banquet

das   Bankgebäude, -, 10   bank building

der   Bankraub, 18   bank robbery

die   Bar, -s, 14   bar

die   Barriere, -n, 11   barrier

das   Barock, 4   baroque

Basta! (*Italian*), 18   Enough!

der   Bauch, ˝e, 12   belly

bauen, 11   to build

der   Baum, ˝e, 5   tree

der   Baustil, -e, 17   architecture

beantworten, 14   to answer

bedeuten, 4   to mean

die   Bedeutung, -en, 14   meaning

sich   beeilen, 11   to hurry

beeindrucken, 9   to impress

beeinflussen, 12   to influence

beeinträchtigen, 18   to impair

sich   befinden, befand, befunden, 10   to be

befreien, 7   to liberate

befreundet sein, 12   to be a friend of

begehen, beging, begangen, 16   to commit

begeistert, 14   enthusiastic

die   Begeisterung, 14   enthusiasm

beginnen, begann, begonnen, 9   to begin

begrüßen, 4   to greet, to salute

behaupten, 18   to assert, state

die   Behauptung, -en, 18   assertion

bei, 4   at

beide, 10   both

das   Bein, -e, 12   leg

das   Beispiel, -e, 2   example: **zum Beispiel,** 2   for example

bekannt, 6   famous

der   Bekannte, -n, 12   acquaintance

bekommen, bekam, bekommen, 5   to get, receive

beladen (sein), 10   (to be) loaded

belagern, 14   to besiege

die   Belagerung, -en, 14   siege

belehren, 18   to instruct

beliebt, 7   popular

bemerkenswert, 13   remarkable

bemerken, 18   to notice, mention

die   Bemerkung, -en, 17   remark

das   Benzin, 6   gasoline

bequem, 11   comfortable

der   Berater, -, 15   consultant

der   Berg, -e, 8   mountain

das   Bergsteigen, 8   mountaineering

der   Bergsteiger, -, 8   mountaineer

der   Bericht, -e, 6   report

der   Beruf, -e, 13   profession

die   Berufsangst, 15   fear of not finding a job

die   Berufsaussicht, -en, 15   job prospects

berufstätig, 11   working

berühmt, 16   famous

beschädigen, 5   to damage

beschäftigen, 9   to engage, occupy

die   Beschäftigung, -en, 7   occupation

beschränken, 18   to limit

beschreiben, beschrieb, beschrieben, 14   to describe

besetzen, 14   to occupy

besichtigen, 17   to inspect, see

der   Besitzer, -, 4   owner

besonders, 2   especially

besprechen (bespricht), besprach, besprochen, 14   to discuss

besser, 5   better

bestellen, 3   to order

bestenfalls, 18   at best

bester, 9   best

bestimmt, 15   certain

der   Besuch, -e, 16   visit

besuchen, 5   to visit

der   Besucher, -, 16   visitor

betrachten, 9   to look at

der   Betrug, 17   fraud

betrügerisch, 17   deceitful

das   Bett, -en, 4   bed

die   Bevölkerung, 18   population

bevor, 8   before

bewegen, 8   to move

die   Bewegung, -en, 8   motion

der   Beweis, -e, 18   proof, evidence

bewölkt, 7   cloudy

das   Bewußtsein, 14   consciousness

bezahlen, 4   to pay

bezeichnend, 17   significant

die   Beziehung, -en, 13   relation

der   Bezug, 6   reference; **mit Bezug auf,** 6   in reference to

die   Bibliothek, -en, 1   library

das   Bier, -e, 2   beer

die   Bierhalle, -n, 17   beer hall

bieten, bot, geboten, 18   to offer

das   Bild, -er, 7   picture

billig, 4   cheap, inexpensive

binden, band, gebunden, 13   to tie

die   Biologie, 14   biology

bis, 2   until; **bis gleich!,** 2   see you later!

bitte, IC   please; **Bitte sehr?,** 4   May I help you?; **Bitte** schön!, 8 You're welcome!

bitten um, bat, gebeten, 3 to ask for

das **Blatt, ̈er,** 17 leaf

blau, 11 blue

bleiben, blieb, ist geblieben, 5 to stay, remain

blitzen, 7 to flash (lightning); **Es blitzt.,** 7 It's lightning.

der **Blödsinn,** 17 nonsense

blond, 11 blond

die **Blume, -n,** 7 flower

die **Bluse, -n,** 11 blouse

das **Blut,** 5 blood

die **Blutprobe, -n,** 5 blood test

der **Boden, ̈,** 7 bottom

die **Börse, -n,** 10 stock market

böse, 13 angry; **Sei mir nicht böse!,** 13 Don't be angry with me!

die **Boutique, -n,** 16 boutique

der **Brauch, ̈e,** 10 custom

brauchen, 8 to need

die **Brauerei, -en,** 17 brewery

braun, 11 brown

breit, 11 wide

brennen, brannte, gebrannt, 5 to burn

der **Brief, -e,** 4 letter

bringen, brachte, gebracht, 4 to bring

das **Brot, -e,** 4 bread

das **Brötchen, -,** 4 roll

die **Brücke, -n,** 10 bridge

der **Bruder, ̈,** 8 brother

das **Brüderlein, -,** 17 little brother

brüllen, 12 to howl, roar

brummen, 11/15 to roar, buzz

der **Brunnen, -,** 8 well, fountain

die **Brust, ̈e,** 12 breast

der **Bube, -n,** 17 boy

das **Buch, ̈er,** 1 book

der **Bulgare, -n,** 16 Bulgarian

das **Bundeshaus,** 11 House of Parliament (Switzerland)

das **Bundesland, ̈er,** 9 Federal State

die **Bundesrepublik,** 6 Federal Republic

der **Bunker, -,** 16 shelter

bunt, 11 multicolored, colorful

die **Burg, -en,** 10 castle

der **Bürgersteig, -e,** 3 sidewalk

das **Büro, -s,** 8 office

der **Bus, -se,** 3 bus

der **Busfahrer, -,** 3 bus driver

die **Bus-Haltestelle, -n,** 3 bus stop

C

das **Café, -s,** 3 café

die **Chance, -n,** 13 chance

der **Chefpilot, -en,** 18 chief pilot

die **Chemie,** 12 chemistry

die **Chemikalie, -n,** 7 chemical

der **Club, -s,** 8 club

das **Cockpit, -s,** 18 cockpit

der **Computer, -,** 17 computer

der **Copilot, -en,** 18 co-pilot

D

da, 1 there; **da drüben,** 1 over there; **da** (conj.), 6 since, as; **da vorne,** 18 over there

dabei, 12 in so doing

dadurch, 13 by that

dagegen, 16 against it; however

daher, 16 from there; that's why

dahin, 16 there(to)

die **Dame, -n,** 14 lady

der **Damenbesuch, -e,** 18 lady visitor

damit, 16 with it; so that

der **Dampf, ̈e,** 7 steam

daneben, 16 beside(s)

der **Dank,** 3 thanks; **Vielen Dank!,** 3 Thank you very much.

danke, IC thank you; **Danke sehr!,** 4 Thank you.

danken (+ dat.), 10 to thank

dann, 3 then

daran, 16 of it

darauf, 16 on it

daraufhin, 18 thereupon

darüber, 16 about it; over it

darum, 16 around it; therefore

das, 3 that

daß (conj.), 9 that

das **Datum, Daten,** 13 date

dauern, 10 to last

die **Daunendecke, -n,** 3 eiderdown

davon, 16 by it, from it

dazu, 16 to that

dazwischen, 16 between it

der **Deckel, -,** 16 lid

dein, 10 your

denken, dachte, gedacht, 3 to think

denn (conj.), 4 for, because

denn (particle), 5 actually

deplaciert, 11 out of place

deshalb, 5 therefore

deutsch, 1 German

das **Deutsch,** 1 German language

der **Deutschamerikaner, -,** 10 German American

der **Deutsche, -n,** 1 German citizen

die **Deutsche, -n,** 1 German woman

das **Deutschbuch, ̈er,** 3 German textbook

das **Deutschland,** 1 Germany

deutschsprechend, 12 German-speaking

die **Deutschstunde, -n,** 13 German class

der **Dezember, IC** December

dicht, 11 dense

dick, 8 fat, heavy

dieser, 7 this

der **Dienstag, -e, IC** Tuesday

dienstags, 13 on Tuesdays

das **Ding, -e,** 2 thing

direkt, 3 direct

der **Direktor, -en,** 18 boss, director

dirigieren, 14 to conduct

die **Diskothek, -en,** 12 discotheque

die **Diskriminierung, -en,** 18 discrimination

diskutieren, 1 to discuss

die **Disziplin,** 15 discipline

doch, 3 yet

das **Dokument, -e,** 17 document

der **Dom, -e,** 8 cathedral

donnern, 7 to thunder

der **Donnerstag, -e, IC** Thursday

donnerstags, 13 on Thursdays

das **Doppelbett, -en,** 4   double bed

doppelt, 18   double

das **Dorf, ̈er,** 10   village

dort, 3   there

dorther, 16   from there

dorthin, 16   there (to)

dorthinten, 16   back there

der **Drahtesel, -,** 11   bike (*lit.;* wire donkey)

draußen, 3   outdoors, outside

sich **drehen,** 16   to turn

drei, IC   three

dreimal, 3   three times

dreißig, IC   thirty

dreizehn, IC   thirteen

das **Drittel, -,** 15   third

drittens, 11   thirdly

drittgrößter, 17   third biggest

drücken, 9   to press

du, 1   you

dumm, 13   stupid

dunkel, 11   dark

durch, 7   through

durchschauen, 10   to look through

dürfen (darf), durfte, gedurft, 6   to be allowed to

durstig, 9   thirsty

die **Dusche, -n,** 4   shower

die **Dynamik,** 10   dynamics

E

eben, 18   just

ebenso, 9   also

die **Ecke, -n,** 4   corner

die **Ehe, -n,** 13   marriage

eine Ehe schließen   to get married

die **Ehescheidung, -en,** 13   divorce

die **Ehescheidungsrate, -n,** 13   divorce rate

das **Ehescheidungsgesetz, -e,** 13   divorce law

ehrlich, 13   honest, frank

das **Ei, -er,** 4   egg

eigener, 15   own

die **Eigenschaft, -en,** 17   characteristic, quality

eigentlich, 2   actual

das **Eigentum,** 9   property

die **Eile,** 3   hurry; **in Eile sein,** 3

to be in a hurry; **Das hat keine Eile.,** 14   There is no hurry

ein paar, 2   a few

ein·atmen, 8   to breathe in

die **Einbahnstraße, -n,** 8   one-way street

der **Eindruck, ̈e,** 9   impression

einer, 10   someone, one

einfach, 8   simple

der **Eingang, ̈e,** 18   entrance

ein·gehen, ging ein, ist eingegangen, 13   to enter

einige, 6   some, a few

einigermaßen, 11   somehow

der **Einkauf, ̈e,** 8   shopping

ein·kaufen, 10   to shop

ein·laden (lädt ein), lud ein, eingeladen, 12   to invite

die **Einladung, -en,** 16   invitation

einmal, 3   sometime; once

ein·richten, 8   to furnish

eins, IC   one

ein·schenken, 17   to fill

ein·schlafen (schläft ein), schlief ein, ist eingeschlafen, 9   to fall asleep

ein·sperren, 16   to imprison

ein·steigen, stieg ein, ist eingestiegen, 3   to get in

die **Eintrittskarte, -n,** 14   [admission] ticket

der **Einwohner, -,** 7   inhabitant

einverstanden, 9   agreed

elegant, 11   elegant

elf, IC   eleven

die **Elite,** 9   elite

die **Eltern,** 8   parents

die **Emanzipation,** 9   emancipation

empfangen (empfängt), empfing, empfangen, 18   to receive

das **Ende, -n,** 8   end

endlich, 3   finally; **endlich einmal,** 5   finally

endlos, 15   endless

eng, 11   narrow

engagieren, 9   to engage

das **England,** 1   England

der **Engländer, -,** 1   Englishman

die **Engländerin, -nen,** 1   Englishwoman

das **Englisch,** 1,   English

die **Entdeckung, -en,** 18   discovery

entfernen, 11   to remove

enthalten (enthält), enthielt, enthalten, 14   to contain

entkommen, entkam, ist entkommen, 18   to escape

entscheiden, entschied, entschieden, 17   to decide

entweder . . . oder, 15   either . . . or

sich **entwickeln,** 12   to develop

die **Entwicklung, -en,** 12   development

die **Epoche, -n,** 16   epoch

er, 1   he

das **Erdgeschoß, -sse,** 16   ground floor

erfahren (erfährt), erfuhr, erfahren, 17   to experience; learn

die **Erfindung, -en,** 12   invention

erfreut, 14   pleased

erfrischen, 8   to refresh

erfrischend, 12   refreshing

erhalten (erhält), erhielt, erhalten, 5   to receive

sich **erheben, erhob, erhoben,** 10   to rise

die **Erhöhung, -en,** 15   rise

sich **erholen (von + *dat.*),** 10   to recover

erinnern (an + *acc.*), 10   to remind (of)

sich **erinnern (an + *acc.*),** 10   to remember

erkennen, erkannte, erkannt, 5   to recognize

erklären, 14   to explain; declare

die **Erklärung, -en,** 18   explanation

erkranken, ist erkrankt, 18   to get sick

sich **erkundigen (nach),** 10   to inquire

erleben, 10   to experience

erleichtern, 17   to relieve

eröffnen, 15   to open

ernst, 9   serious

erreichen, 6/8   to accomplish; reach

ersetzen, 9   to replace

erst, 9   only

die **Erstaufführung, -en, 14** première

erstaunlich, 18 amazing, remarkable

der **Erste, -n, 14** first one

erstens, 11 first of all

erster, 9 first

erträglich, 15 bearable

erwarten, 11 to expect

erzählen, 5 to tell

die **Erziehung, 13** education

es, IC it

essen (ißt), aß, gegessen, 3 to eat

das **Essen, -, 4** dinner, meal

das **Eßzimmer, -, 10** dining room

die **Etage, -n, 4** floor

etwas, 5 something

euer, eure, euer, 10 your

das **Europa, 4** Europe

der **Europäer, -, 7** European

europäisch, 12 European (*adj.*)

die **Ewigkeit, 11** eternity

das **Examen, -, 18** examination

experimentieren, 16 to experiment

explodieren, ist explodiert, 18 to explode

exportieren, 11 to export

F

fabelhaft, 15 fabulous

die **Fabrik, -en, 10** factory

fahren (fährt), fuhr, ist gefahren, 3 to drive

der **Fahrer, -, 6** driver

das **Fahrrad, ̈er, 6** bicycle

der **Fahrradweg, -e, 6** bicycle path

der **Fahrradunfall, ̈e, 11** bicycle accident

die **Fahrt, -en, 6** trip

der **Faktor, -en, 9** factor

der **Fall, ̈e, 11** case

fallen (fällt), fiel, ist gefallen, 10 to fall

fallen lassen, 7 to drop

falls, 9 in case

die **Familie, -n, 7** family

der **Fan, -s 9** fan, admirer

fantastisch, 2 fantastic

die **Farbe, -n, 9** color

farbig, 11 colorful

der **Faschismus, 16** fascism

das **Faß, ̈sser, 17** barrel

fast, 1 almost

faul, 8 lazy

der **Februar, IC** February

der **Fehler, -, 13** mistake, error

feiern, 13 to celebrate

der **Feiertag, -e, 17** holiday

der **Feind, -e, 14** enemy

der **Felsen, -, 10** rock

das **Fenster, -, 4** window

der **Fernsehapparat, -e, 8** television set

das **Fernsehen, 7** television

der **Fernsehfilm, -e, 9** television film

das **Fernsehprogramm, -e, 10** television program

die **Fernsehsendung, -en, 18** television show

das **Fernsehstudio, -s, 18** television studio

der **Fernsehturm, ̈e, 16** television tower

die **Ferien, 7** holidays, vacation

die **Ferienreise, -n, 6** vacation trip

fertig, 15 ready, finished

das **Fest, -e, 17** festival

die **Festung, -en, 4** fortress

das **Feuer, -, 3** fire

der **Feuerwehrwagen, -, 3** fire truck

der **Film, -e, 9** movie

die **Filmkunst, 9** art of making films

die **Filmproduktionsgesellschaft, -en, 17** film production company

der **Filmproduzent, -en, 9** film producer

der **Filter, -, 2** filter

die **Finanz, 10** finance

finanziell, 15 financial

das **Finanzzentrum, -zentren, 10** center of finance

finden, fand, gefunden, 1 to find

der **Finger, -, 12** finger

die **Firma, Firmen, 17** company

der **Fisch, -e, 4** fish

das **Fleisch, 4** meat

fliegen, flog, ist geflogen, 11 to fly

fließen, floß, ist geflossen, 6 to flow

fließend, 12 fluent

fluchen, 18 to swear

der **Flug, ̈e, 7** flight

die **Flugkarte, -n, 18** flight ticket; air map

der **Flugplatz, ̈e, 3** airport

der **Flugverkehr, 12** air traffic

das **Flugzeug, -e, 10** airplane

die **Flugzeugentführung, -en, 18** hijacking

der **Flugzeugmotor, -en, 11** airplane engine

der **Fluß, ̈sse, 6** river

folgen (+ *dat.*), ist gefolgt, 10 to follow

folkloristisch, 17 folkloristic

fördern, 9 to support

die **Form, -en, 9** form, shape

die **Formalität, -en, 16** formality

das **Formular, -e, 4** form sheet

das **Foyer, -s, 9** foyer, entrance hall

der **Frachter, -, 10** freighter

die **Frage, -n, 13** question

fragen, 3 to ask

fragen nach, 4 to ask for; inquire about

das **Frankreich, 1** France

das **Französisch, 6** French language

der **Franzose, -n, 1** Frenchman

die **Französin, -nen, 1** French woman

die **Frau, -en, 1** woman

das **Fräulein, -s, 1** Miss

frei, 3 free

der **Freitag, -e, IC** Friday

die **Freizeit, 7** spare time; leisure

die **Freizeitbeschäftigung, -en, 7** spare time activity, hobby

der **Freizeit-Gärtner, -, 7** hobby gardener

fremd, 18 strange

sich **freuen (über + *acc.*), 10** to be happy about

Freut mich sehr!, 14 Glad to meet you!

der **Freund, -e, 2** friend

die **Freundin, -nen, 2** (girl)-friend

freundlich, 16 friendly, kind

frieren, fror, gefroren, 7 to freeze; be cold; **es friert, 7** it is freezing frisch, 11 fresh

der Frost, 7 frost

früh, 3 early; morgen früh, 3 tomorrow morning

früher, 11 formerly

der Frühling, IC spring

das Frühstück, 4 breakfast

das Frühstückszimmer, -, 10 breakfast room, nook

sich fühlen (wohl, unwohl), 13 to feel (well, sick)

führen, 14 to guide

der Führer, -, 16 guide; leader

fünf, IC five

fünfzehn, IC fifteen

fünfzig, IC fifty

der Funktionär, -e, 16 functionary, official

für, 1 for

furchtbar, 5 dreadful

der Fuß, ¨sse, 8 foot; zu Fuß, 8 on foot

der Fußball, ¨e, 2 soccer (ball)

das Fußballspiel, -e, 18 soccer game

der Fußgänger, -, 8 pedestrian

der Fußgängerweg, -e, 16 sidewalk

die Fußgängerzone, -n, 8 pedestrian mall

die Fußwanderung, -en, 8 hike

G

ganz, 2/7 quite; whole

ganz recht, 9 quite right

der Garten, ¨, 4 garden

der Gartenbau, 7 gardening

der Gärtner, -, 7 gardener

der Gast, ¨e, 10 guest

das Gasthaus, ¨er, 4 inn

das Gebäude, -, 10 building

geben (gibt), gab, gegeben, 4 to give; es gibt, 4 there is (are)

das Gebiet, -e, 10 area

geboren, 13 born

das Geburtshaus, ¨er, 4 house of birth

der Geburtstag, -e, 13 birthday

die Geburtstagsfeier, -n, 11 birthday party

der Gedanke, -n, 15 thought

gedankenvoll, 16 thoughtful

das Gedicht, -e, 15 poem

gefährlich, 2 dangerous

gefallen (+ dat.) (gefällt), gefiel, gefallen, 10 to please; to like

das Gefühl, -e, 9 feeling

gegen, 6 against

die Gegend, -en, 17 area

die Gegenwart, 10 present

gehen, ging, ist gegangen, 3/8 to go; walk

die Gehirnerschütterung, -en, 5 concussion (of the brain)

das Gehör, 12 hearing

gehören (+ dat.), 10 to belong

gekleidet, 11 dressed

gelb, 11 yellow

das Geld, -er, 3 money

der Geldwechsel, 16 money exchange

gelingen (+ dat.), gelang, ist gelungen, 10 to succeed

gemein, 15 mean, nasty

das Gemüse, -, 4 vegetable

der Gemüsegarten, ¨, 7 vegetable garden

gemütlich, 11 cozy

die Gemütlichkeit, 17 coziness

genau, 13 exact, precise

die Generation, -en, 18 generation

genug, 3 enough

genügen (+ dat.), 10 to suffice

die Geologie, 14 geology

das Gepäck, 3 baggage, luggage

gerade, 3 just (now, then)

geradeaus, 8 straight ahead

das Gericht, -e, 5 court

gering, 13 little

der Germanist, -en, 15 German scholar

die Germanistik, 1 German studies

gern, 2/5 gladly; to like to

der Geruch, ¨e, 12 smell

das Geschäft, -e, 10 business; store

die Geschäftsentwicklung, -en, 12 business development

das Geschäftshaus, ¨er, 17 business building

die Geschäftsleute (pl.), 10 businessmen

der Geschäftsmann, 14 businessman

das Geschehen, 9 event

geschehen (geschieht), geschah, ist geschehen, 9 to happen, occur

die Geschichte, -n, 10 story

die Geschichte, 16 history

geschieden, 13 divorced

der Geschmack, ¨er, 12 taste

die Gesellschaft, -en, 7/13 company; society

das Gesetz, -e, 13 law

das Gesicht, -er, 10 face

das Gespräch, -e, 9 conversation, talk

gestern, IC yesterday; gestern abend, 5 last night

gestorben, 8 died

gesund, 2 healthy

die Gesundheit, 2 health

geteilt, 13 divided

der Gewinn, -e, 12 gain, profit

gewinnen, gewann, gewonnen, 10 to gain; win

gewiß, 17 certain

sich gewöhnen an (+ acc.), 10 to get accustomed to

gigantisch, 12 gigantic

der Gipfel, -, 8 top, peak

die Gitarre, -n, 2 guitar

das Glas, ¨er, 7 glass

die Glaskugel, -n, 16 glass globe

der Glaspalast, ¨e, 16 glass palace

glauben, 2 to believe

gleich, 1/11 right away; same; Bis gleich!, 2 See you later!

gleich bleiben, 11 to remain even

gleichzeitig, 9 simultaneous

die Glocke, -n, 14 bell

das Glück, 1 luck; Glück haben, 1 to be lucky; Viel Glück!, 1 Good luck!

glücklich, 15 happy

der Glückliche, -n, 15 happy one

die Glückszahl, -en, 13 lucky number

das Gold, 6 gold

golden, 16 golden

der   **Gott, ⸚er, 9**   god;   **Gott sei Dank!, 16**   Thank God!

der   **Grashügel, -, 16**   grass hill, knoll

grau, 11   gray

der   **Grenzübergang, ⸚e, 16**   border crossing

groß, 4   great, big

großartig, 15   great

die   **Großmutter, ⸚, 8**   grandmother

der   **Großvater, ⸚, 8**   grandfather

grün, 11   green

der   **Grund, ⸚e, 13**   reason

die   **Gruppe, -n, 7**   group

der   **Gruß, ⸚e, 5**   greeting

grüßen, 5   to greet

gültig, 16   valid

gut (besser, am besten), IC   good

die   **Güte, 10**   goodness;   **Meine Güte! 10**   My goodness!

das   **Gymnasium, Gymnasien, 11**   high school

H

das   **Haar, -e, 10**   hair

die   **Haartracht, -en, 12**   hairdo

haben (hat), hatte, gehabt, 1/2   to have

halb (neun), IC   half (past eight)

halbdunkel, 14   half dark

die   **Halle, -n, 3**   hall

hallo, 9   hello

der   **Hals, ⸚e, 12**   neck

halt!, 3   stop!

halten (hält), hielt, gehalten, 3   to hold; stop

halten von (hält von), hielt von, gehalten von, 7   to think of

die   **Haltestelle, -n, 3**   stop

die   **Hand, ⸚e, 9**   hand

der   **Handball, 2**   handball

das   **Händedrücken, 11**   shaking of hands

die   **Handgranate, -n, 18**   hand grenade

häufig, 13   frequently

die   **Hauptstadt, ⸚e, 17**   capital city

das   **Haus, ⸚er, 3**   house;   **nach Hause, 4**   home;   **zu Hause, 4**   at home

das   **Häusermeer, 11**   sea of houses

der   **Haushalt, -e, 13**   household

die   **Hausordnung, -en, 18**   house rules

die   **Hauspflanze, -n, 18**   house plant

die   **Hauswirtin, -nen, 18**   landlady

heben, hob, gehoben, 10   to lift

die   **Heimat, 10**   homeland

die   **Heimatstadt, ⸚e, 17**   home town

heimlich, 17   secret

der   **Heimweg, -e, 15**   way home

das   **Heimweh, 15**   homesickness

heiraten, 13   to marry

heiß, IC   hot

heißen, hieß, geheißen, 1   to be called;   **es heißt da, 1**   it says there

die   **Heizung, -en, 4**   furnace

helfen (hilft), half, geholfen, 8   to help

hell(blau), 11   light (blue)

das   **Hemd, -en, 11**   shirt

herab·kommen, kam herab, ist herabgekommen, 11   to come down

heran·kommen, kam heran, ist herangekommen, 3   to approach

herauf·kommen, kam herauf, ist heraufgekommen, 3   to come up

heraus·finden, fand heraus, herausgefunden, 13   to find out

der   **Herbst, IC**   autumn, fall

herein·bringen, brachte herein, hereingebracht, 5   to bring in

herein·kommen, kam herein, ist hereingekommen, 3   to come in

herein·lassen (läßt herein), ließ herein, hereingelassen, 3   to let in

her·geben (gibt her), gab her, hergegeben, 13   to give away

her·kommen, kam her, ist hergekommen, 12   to come from

der   **Herr, -en, 1**   gentleman

herrschen, 14   to govern

herum·laufen (läuft herum), lief herum, ist herumgelaufen, 11   to run around

herum·steigen, stieg herum, ist herumgestiegen, 8   to climb around

herunter·kommen, kam herunter, ist heruntergekommen, 3   to come down

herunter·laufen (läuft herunter), lief herunter, ist heruntergelaufen, 11   to run down

herunter·rufen, rief herunter, heruntergerufen, 11   to shout down, to call down

herunter·sehen (sieht herunter), sah herunter, heruntergesehen, 16   to look down

herunter·wehen, 17   to blow down

hervor·heben, hob hervor, hervorgehoben, 18   to point out

das   **Herz, -en, 15**   heart

herzlich, 5   cordial

herzlos, 15   heartless

heute, IC   today;   **heute abend, 1**   tonight

heutzutage, 5   nowadays

hier, 1   here

die   **Hilfe, 15**   help

der   **Himmel, 7**   sky

hinab·fahren (fährt hinab), fuhr hinab, ist hinabgefahren, 10   to drive down

hinab·schauen, 11   to look down

hinauf·fahren (fährt hinauf), fuhr hinauf, ist hinaufgefahren, 10   to drive up

hinauf·gehen, ging hinauf, ist hinaufgegangen, 3   to go up

hinaus·gehen, ging hinaus, ist hinausgegangen, 15   to walk out

das   **Hindernis, -se, 8**   obstacle

hinein·fahren (fährt hinein),

fuhr hinein, ist hineingefahren, 6 to drive into

hinein·gehen, ging hinein, ist hineingegangen, 3 to walk in

hinein·lassen (läßt hinein), ließ hinein, hineingelassen, 3 to let in

hinein·mischen, 5 to mix in

hin·fallen (fällt hin), fiel hin, ist hingefallen, 5 to fall down

hin·fahren (fährt hin), fuhr hin, ist hingefahren, 3 to drive there

hin·gehen, ging hin, ist hingegangen, 6 to walk there

hin·legen, 11 to lay down

sich hin·setzen, 13 to sit down

hin·stellen, 10 to put down

hinter, 8 behind

hinunter·gehen, ging hinunter, ist hinuntergegangen, 3 to go down

hinunter·sehen (sieht hinunter), sah hinunter, hinuntergesehen, 8 to look down

der Hit, -s, 12 hit

das Hobby, -s, 7 hobby

der Hobby-Raum, ⸚e, 7 hobby room

hoch, 13 high

die Hochburg, -en, 10 stronghold

das Hochhaus, ⸚er, 10 skyscraper

die Hochzeit, -en, 13 wedding

hoffen, 1 to hope

hoffentlich, 5 hopefully

holen, 9 to fetch, pick up

das Holland, 6 Holland

hören, 3 to hear, listen

hören auf (+ acc.), 8 to listen to

der Horizont, -e, 10 horizon

die Hose, -n, 11 pants, trousers

das Hotel, -s, 3 hotel

hübsch, 4 pretty

der Hügel, -, 10 hill

der Humor, 13 humor

der Humorist, -en, 11 humorist

der Hund, -e, 15 dog

hundert, IC hundred

hungrig, 13 hungry

I

ich, 1 I

die Idee, -n, 11 idea

die Ideologie, -n, 12 ideology

der Idiot, -en, 16 idiot

das Idol, -e, 12 idol

ihr, Ihr, 1 you

ihr, ihre, ihr, 10 her

Ihr, Ihre, Ihr, 10 your

illuminieren, 16 to illuminate

illustrieren, 12 to illustrate

immer, 2 always

immer noch, 6 still

importieren, 11 to import

imposant, 14 impressive

in, in

die Industrie, -n, 6 industry

das Industrieprodukt, -e, 10 industrial product

der Industriestaat, -en, 13 industrial country

die Inflation, -en, 7 inflation

informieren, 1/10 to inform

der Ingenieur, -e, 16 engineer

der Inhalt, -e, 16 contents

innen, 16 within; von innen, 16 from within

innerhalb, 7 within

der Intellekt, 9 intellect

intelligent, 13 intelligent

interessant, 1 interesting

das Interesse, -n, 12 interest

interessiert, 9 interested

international, 11 international

die Interpretation, -en, 9 interpretation

interpretieren, 14 to interpret

intervenieren, 7 to intervene

das Interview, -s, 14 interview

das Institut, -e, 1 institute

das Instrument, -e, 2 instrument

die Invasion, -en, 12 invasion

inzwischen, 10 meanwhile

die Ironie, 16 irony

sich irren, 13 to err

der Irrtum, ⸚er, 13 error

das Italien, 7 Italy

J

ja, 1/6, 11 yes

die Jacke, -n, 11 jacket

jagen, 18 to hunt; in die Luft jagen, 18 to blow up

das Jahr, -e, 4 year

das Jahrhundert, -e, 10 century

jährlich, 4 annual

der Jahrmarkt, ⸚e, 17 annual fair

der Januar, IC January

das Japan, 12 Japan

je, 14 ever

je ... desto, 13 the ... the

die Jeans, 11 (always plural) jeans

jeder, 9/10 every; each; either

jemals, 8 ever

jemand, 5 somebody

jemand anders, 8 someone else

jener, 18 that

jetzt, 1 now

der Journalist, -en, 6 journalist, reporter

die Jugend, 11 youth

die Jugendherberge, -n, 11 youth hostel

der Jugendliche, -n, 12 youth; young man (woman)

das Jugoslawien, 7 Yugoslavia

der Juli, IC July

jung, 1 young

der Junge, -n, 4 boy

der Juni, IC June

der Jura-Student, -en, 15 law student

der Jurist, -en, 15 lawyer

juristisch, 15 judicial

die Justiz, 18 justice (administration of)

K

der Kaffee, 2 coffee

die Kaffee-Bar, -s, 6 coffee bar

der Kaiser, -, 10 emperor

das Kalifornien, 14 California

kalt, IC cold

der Kamerad, -en, 11 fellow

der Kamin, -e, 10 chimney; fireplace

das Kanada, 1 Canada

der Kanadier, -, 1 Canadian

der **Kanal, ̈-e, 10** canal
die **Kanone, -n, 14** canon
der **Kapitalismus, 13** capitalism
der **Karate-Schlag, ̈-e, 18** karate chop
die **Karte, -n, 2** card
die **Kartoffel, -n, 4** potato
der **Katalog, -e, 1** catalogue
die **Katastrophe, -n, 14** catastrophe
der **Kater, 17** hangover
kaufen, 2 to buy
kaum, 5 hardly
kein, 2 no, not any
der **Keller, -, 11** basement, cellar
die **Kellnerin, -nen, 17** waitress
kennen, kannte, gekannt, 2 to know
der **Kerl, -e, 6** guy
der **Kern, -e, 18** core
das **Kernkraftwerk, -e, 10** nuclear power plant
das **Kind, -er, 1** child
die **Kindererziehung, 13** education of children
kinderlos, 15 childless
das **Kino, -s, 9** cinema
der **Kiosk, -e, 3** kiosk
die **Kirche, -n, 4** church
der **Klang, ̈-e, 2** sound
klar, 14 clear
klar·machen, 17 to make clear
die **Klasse, -n, 1** class
klassisch, 12 classical
das **Klavier, -e, 2** piano
der **Klecks, -e, 14** spot
das **Kleid, -er, 9** dress
der **Kleiderhaken, -, 11** hanger
die **Kleidung, 11** clothing
klein, 10 small, little
die **Klinik, -en, 15** clinic
klug, 1 clever
knurren, 14 to growl
die **Kochgelegenheit, -en, 4** cooking facility
der **Koffer, -, 4** suitcase
die **Kohle, -n, 10** coal
der **Kollege, -n, 10** colleague
kommen, kam, ist gekommen, 1 to come
kommentieren, 15 to comment
komponieren, 14 to compose

der **Kompromiß, -sse, 12** compromise
können (kann), konnte, gekonnt, 6 to be able to; can
konservativ, 11 conservative
die **Kontrolle, -n, 3** control
konventionell, 11 conventional
das **Konzert, -e, 14** concert
der **Kopf, ̈-e, 12** head
das **Kopftuch, ̈-er, 11** head scarf
der **Körper, -, 12** body
die **Körperbewegung, -en, 8** exercise
kosten, 4 to cost
kostenlos, 15 free (of charge)
krank, 2 sick
das **Krankenhaus, ̈-er, 13** hospital
die **Krankheit, -en, 7** sickness
die **Krawatte, -n, 11** tie
die **Kreditkarte, -n, 16** credit card
das **Kreuz, -e, 16** cross
die **Kreuzung, -en, 8** crossroad, intersection
kriecherisch, 9 fawning
der **Krieg, -e, 6** war
der **Kriegsfall, ̈-e, 11** case of war
der **Krimi, -s, 9** mystery novel, detective story
der **Kriminalfall, ̈-e, 18** criminal case
die **Kriminalpolizei, 18** detective force
der **Kritiker, -, 18** critic
der **Krug, ̈-e, 17** mug, stein
der **Kuchen, -, 3** cake
die **Kultur, -en, 9** culture
kulturell, 16 cultural
das **Kulturprogramm, -e, 9** cultural program
sich **kümmern um (+ acc.) 10** to care for
die **Kunst, ̈-e, 9** art
die **Kunstform, -en, 9** form of art
der **Kurs, -e, 7/9** course; rate
kurz, 5 short
kürzlich, 5 recently
die **Kusine, -n, 18** female cousin
der **Kuß, ̈-sse, 15** kiss

L

das **Labor, -s, 13** laboratory
lachen, 11 to laugh
das **Lampengeschäft, -e, 16** electric lighting store
das **Land, ̈-er, 7** country
landen, 17 to land
die **Landschaft, -en, 10** landscape
lang, 1 long
lange, 1 for a long time
langhaarig, 16 long-haired
langsam, 3 slow
langweilig, 11 boring
der **Lärm, 8** noise
lassen (läßt), ließ, gelassen, 3 to let
laufen (läuft), lief, ist gelaufen, 3 to run
die **Laune, -n, 17** mood
laut, 4 loud
das **Leben, 7** life; **am Leben, 8** alive
leben, 11 to live
der **Lebensmut, 14** vital energy
der **Lebensstil, -e, 12** life style
ledig, 13 single
leer, 18 empty
die **Leere, 12** void
legal, 15 legal
legen, 10 to lay, put
der **Lehrer, -, 15** teacher
lehrhaft, 9 didactic
die **Leibesübung, -en, 8** physical exercise
leicht, 9 easy, light
leid tun (+ dat.), 5 to feel sorry for
leiden, (an + acc.), 15 to suffer (from)
leider, 2 unfortunately
leise, 12 quiet
lernen, 5 to learn
lesen (liest), las, gelesen, 3 to read
letzter, 8 last
die **Leute (pl.), 7** people
liberal, 13 liberal
das **Licht, -er, 9** light
lieb, 5 dear
lieben, 12 to love
lieber rather
das **Lied, -er, 17** song
liegen (liegt), lag, gelegen, 4 to lie

die **Limonade,** 12 lemonade
die **Limousine, -n,** 17 limousine
links, 3 left; **nach links,** 3
to the left
die **Literatur, -en,** 1 literature
die **Lizenzgebühr, -en,** 12
license fee
los sein, 15 to be going on
lösen, 13 to solve
**los·fahren (fährt los), fuhr los,
ist losgefahren,** 8 to
depart, leave
**los·gehen, ging los, ist
losgegangen,** 15 to leave;
to start; **Es geht los!,** 11
It's starting!
**los·lassen (läßt los), ließ los,
losgelassen,** 15 to let go
los·machen, 15 to loosen
die **Lösung, -en,** 7 solution
die **Luft,** 6 air
der **Luftpirat, -en,** 18 hijacker
die **Luftverschmutzung,** 9 air
pollution
die **Lust, ⁻e,** 9 desire, delight;
Lust haben, 9 to like to
sich **lustig machen über** (+ *acc.*),
15 to make fun of

M

machen, 3/5 to make, do
die **Macht, ⁻e,** 14 power
das **Mädchen, -,** 1 girl
der **Magen., ⁻,** 14 stomach; **Mir
knurrt der Magen.,** 14 I
am terribly hungry
das **Mahnmal, -e,** 16 monument
der **Mai, IC** May
der **Makel, -,** 13 blot, flaw
das **Mal, -e,** 3 time; **das
nächste Mal,** 3 next time
mal, 3 sometime; **Moment
mal!,** 3 Just a moment!
man, 6 one, someone, they
mancher, 10 many a
manchmal, 2 sometimes
der **Mann, ⁻er,** 1 man
die **Mannschaft, -en,** 8 team
der **Mantel, ⁻,** 11 coat
die **Mappe, -n,** 16 folder
die **Mark, -,** 4 the mark
(German currency)
das **Marschlied, -er,** 12
marching song

der **März, IC** March
die **Maschine, -n,** 11 machine
die **Masern** (*pl.*), 5 measles
die **Maß, -,** 17 stein
das **Maß, -e,** 17 measure
die **Masse, -n,** 18 mass, crowd
mäßig, 17 moderate
maßlos, 17 immoderate
die **Mathematik,** 14 mathematics
mathematisch, 15
mathematical
die **Mauer, -n,** 16 wall
die **Medizin,** 13 medicine
der **Medizinstudent, -en,** 15
medical student
das **Medizinstudium,** 15 medical
studies
das **Meer, -e,** 7 sea
mehr, 6/7 more
mehrere, 10 several
die **Meile, -n,** 11 mile
mein, meine, mein, 10 my
meinen, 5/6 to think; to
mean
die **Meinung, -en,** 13 opinion
die **meisten,** 13 most
meistens, 2 usually
die **Mensa, -s,** 13 student
cafeteria
der **Mensch, -en,** 2 man, human
being
menschlich, 13 human
merken, 5 to notice
die **Meteorologie,** 14
metereology
das/der **Meter, -,** 13 meter
die **Miete, -n,** 18 rent
mieten, 7 to rent
die **Milch,** 4 milk
die **Million, -en, IC** million
das **Minimum,** 18 minimum
die **Minute, -n,** 3 minute
mit, 2 with
**mit·bringen, brachte mit,
mitgebracht,** 6 to bring
along
**mit·fahren (fährt mit), fuhr
mit, ist mitgefahren,** 3 to
go with
das **Mitglied, -er,** 8 member
**mit·helfen (hilft mit), half mit,
mitgeholfen,** 13 to assist
**mit·kommen, kam mit, ist
mitgekommen,** 3 to come
along

mit·machen, 15 to
participate
**mit·nehmen (nimmt mit),
nahm mit, mitgenommen,** 3
to take along
der **Mittag, -e,** 4 noon
das **Mittagessen, -,** 4 lunch
die **Mitte,** 11 middle
das **Mittelalter,** 10 Middle Ages
mittelmäßig, 17 mediocre
die **Mitternacht,** 13 midnight
der **Mittwoch, -e, IC**
Wednesday
mittwochs, 13 on Wednesday
das **Möbel, -,** (*usu. pl.*), 5
furniture
modern, 7 modern
**mögen (mag), mochte,
gemocht,** 6 to like
something
möchten, mochte, gemocht,
4 to want to, would like to
möglich, 3 possible
die **Möglichkeit, -en,** 8
possibility
der **Moment, -e,** 2 moment;
Moment bitte!, 4 Just a
moment, please!; **Moment
mal!,** 3 Just a moment!
der **Monat, -e,** 4 month
monatlich, 4 monthly
der **Montag, -e, IC** Monday
das **Monument, -e,** 16
monument
die **Moral,** 6 moral
der **Mord, -e,** 18 murder
der **Morgen, -, IC** morning;
Guten Morgen!, IC Good
morning!
morgen, IC tomorrow
morgens, 6 in the morning
der **Motor, -en,** 11 engine
müde, 7 tired
der **Mund, ⁻er,** 12 mouth
die **Münze, -n,** 11 coin
das **Museum, Museen,** 8 museum
die **Musik,** 12 music
musikalisch, 12 musical
der **Musiker, -,** 14 musician
das **Musikgehör,** 12 musical ear
das **Musikinstrument, -e,** 11
musical instrument
**müssen (muß), mußte,
gemußt,** 6 to have to,
must

der Mut, 14 courage
die Mutter, ̈, 8 mother
die Mutti, -s, 11 Mom
die Mütze, -n, 11 cap

N

na schön, 3 well then
nach, IC after; Viertel
  nach (neun), IC a quarter
  past (nine)
nach, 3 to
nachdem, 9 after
nach·denken, dachte nach,
  nachgedacht, 13 to think
  about
nachher, 15 later, afterward
nach·gehen, ging nach, ist
  nachgegangen, 18 to go
  after, follow
der Nachmittag, -e, 8 afternoon
nachmittags, 13 in the
  afternoon
die Nachricht, -en, 5 message
nächster, 3 next; das
  nächste Mal, 3 next time
die Nacht, ̈e, 13 night; in der
  Nacht, 8 at night
die Nachteule, -n, 18 night owl
nahe, 13 near, close
die Nähe, 10 proximity
sich nähern, 16 to approach
der Name, -n, 2 name
naß, 3 wet
die Nase, -n, 12 nose
die Nation, -en, 8 nation
dic Natur, 8 nature
natürlich, 2 naturally, of
  course
neben, 8 beside(s)
der Neffe, -n, 8 nephew
nehmen (nimmt), nahm,
  genommen, 3 to take
nein, 1 no
nennen, nannte, genannt, 10
  to call
nett, 5 nice, kind
neu, 2 new
neun, IC nine
neunzehn, IC nineteen
neunzig, IC ninety
nicht, 1 not; nicht mehr, 6
  no longer; nicht schlecht,

  4 not bad; Nicht wahr?,
  7 Isn't it? etc.
die Nichte, -n, 8 niece
der Nicht-Gärtner, -, 7 non-
  gardener
nichts, 4 nothing
nie, 5 never
nieder·schlagen (schlägt
  nieder), schlug nieder,
  niedergeschlagen, 18 to
  knock down
niemand, 12 nobody
der Nobelpreis, -e, 15 Nobel
  Prize
noch, 3 still
noch ein, 5 another
noch nicht, 5 not yet
Norddeutschland, 7 North
  Germany
der Norden, 10 north
die Nordsee, 7 North Sea
nötig, 6 necessary; etwas
  nötig haben, 6 to need
  something
der November, IC November
null, IC zero
die Nummer, -n, 3 number
nun, 10 now; well
nur, 5 only

O

ob, 9 whether
oben, 7 above; upstairs;
  da oben, 7 up there
der Oberbürgermeister, -, 17
  mayor
oberer, 11 upper
der Oberprimaner, -, 15 senior
  student (in a Gymnasium)
das Obst, 4 fruit
obwohl, 9 although
oder, IC or
offen, 9 open
offen·lassen, 9 to leave
  open
offensichtlich, 18 obviously
öffentlich, 17 public
offiziell, 16 official
öffnen, 1 to open
oft, 3 often
ohne, 2 without
ohnehin, 15 anyway
das Ohr, -en, 12 ear

ohrenbetäubend, 12
  deafening, earsplitting
der Oktober, IC October
der Onkel, -, 8 uncle
die Oper, -n, 6 opera
das Opfer, -, 16 victim
der Optimist, -en, 7 optimist
der Orangensaft, ̈e, 5 orange
  juice
das Orchester, -, 17 orchestra
die Ordnung, -en, 16 order; in
  Ordnung sein, 17 to be
  okay
organisieren, 17 to organize
der Ort, -e, 9 place
der Osten, 16 east
das Österreich, 1 Austria
der Österreicher, -, 1 Austrian
  citizen
das Osteuropa, 13 Eastern
  Europe

P

die Packung, -en, 2 pack, box
der Palast, ̈e, 8 palace
das Pamphlet, -e, 11 pamphlet
die Papiere (pl.), 16 documents
der Pappdeckel, -, 16
  cardboard
der Park, -s, 7 park
parken, 6 to park
der Parkplatz, ̈e, 6 parking lot
das Parlament, -e, 16 parliament
die Partei, -en, 8 party
das Parterre, 16 ground floor
der Partner, -, 13 partner
die Partnerschaft, -en, 13
  partnership
die Party, -s, 5 party
der Passagier, -e, 3 passenger
passend, 11 suitable
passieren, 5 to happen,
  occur
passiv, 18 passive
die Paßkontrolle, -n, 16
  passport control
der Pazifik, 17 Pacific Ocean
die Pause, -n, 9 pause,
  intermission
die Person, -en, 7 person
die Persönlichkeit, -en, 14
  personality
der Pessimist, -en, 7 pessimist

pessimistisch, 11
pessimistic

der **Pfad, -e,** 8 path, trail

die **Pfeife, -n,** 2 pipe

pflanzen, 7 to plant

das **Pflichtseminar, -e,** 15
obligatory course

das **Phänomen, -e,** 16
phenomenon

die **Phantasie, -n,** 15 fancy,
imagination

der **Phonograph, -en,** 12
phonograph

photographieren, 7 to
photograph

die **Physik,** 13 physics

der **Plan, ¨e,** 7 plan

die **Platte, -n,** 2 record

der **Plattenspieler, -,** 2 record
player

der **Platz, ¨e,** 3 place; seat;
Platz nehmen, 3 to take a
seat

plötzlich, 3 suddenly

poetisch, 15 poetical

die **Politik,** 1 politics

der **Politiker, -,** 12 politician

politisch, 12 political

der **Politsong, -s,** 12 political
song

die **Polizei,** 3 police

der **Polizist, -en,** 6 policeman

die **Popmusik,** 12 pop music

populär, 6 popular

die **Popularität,** 7 popularity

das **Postamt, ¨er,** 8 post office

praktisch, 15 practical

der **Präsident, -en,** 4 president

der **Preis, -e,** 15 prize
einen Preis verleihen, 15 to
award a prize

die **Presse,** 8 press

prima, 2 fine

der **Privatgarten, ¨,** 7 private
garden

die **Privatleute,** (*pl.*), 7 private
people

pro, 4 per

das **Problem, -e,** 2 problem

die **Produktion, -en,** 12
production

produzieren, 12 to produce

der **Professor, -en,** 9 professor

das **Programm, -e,** 1/18 program

Prost!, 17 Cheers!

protestieren, 3 to protest

das **Prozent, -e,** 12 percent

die **Prüfung, -en,** 15
examination

der **Psychologe, -n,** 14
psychologist

die **Psychologie,** 14 psychology

psychologisch, 14
psychological

das **Publikum,** 6 public,
audience

der **Pulli, -s,** 11 sweater

der **Pullover, -,** 11 sweater

pünktlich, 6 on time

der **Putsch, -e,** 17 putsch,
armed rebellion, riot

Q

die **Qualität, -en,** 7 quality

das **Quartal, -e,** 15 quarter
(year)

das **Quiz, -,** 9 quiz

R

die **Rache,** 16 revenge

das **Rad, ¨er,** 6 bicycle; wheel

**rad·fahren (fährt Rad), fuhr
Rad, ist radgefahren,** 6 to
bike

der **Radfahrer, -,** 6 cyclist

die **Randgruppe, -n,** 9 marginal
group; minority, faction

die **Rate, -n,** 13 payment

das **Rathaus, ¨er,** 10 city hall

die **Raubpressung, -en,** 12
pirated record

der **Rauch,** 3 smoke

rauchen, 2 to smoke

der **Raucher, -,** 17 smoker

der **Raum, ¨e,** 1 room

raus, 16 out

recht haben, 7 to be right

rechts, 3 right

der **Rechtsfall, ¨e,** 15 law case

reden, 3 to talk

reduzieren, 18 to reduce

reflektieren, 16 to reflect

rege, 17 active

regelmäßig, 17 regular

der **Regen,** 5 rain

der **Regenschirm, -e,** 7
umbrella

die **Regierung, -en,** 7
government

regnen, IC to rain; **es
regnet, IC** it's raining

reich, 11 rich

das **Reich, -e,** 16 empire

die **Reihe, -n,** 16 series; row

der **Reinfall, ¨e,** 6 bad luck;
disappointment

die **Reise, -n,** 6 journey

das **Reisebüro, -s,** 7 travel office

reisen, 4 to travel

der **Reisescheck, -s,** 10
traveler's check

rennen, rannte, ist gerannt,
15 to run

die **Renovierung, -en,** 7
renovation

die **Reparatur, -en,** 7 repair

reservieren, 16 to reserve

das **Restaurant, -s,** 9 restaurant

restaurieren, 10 to restore

das **Resultat, -e,** 5 result

der **Rettungshubschrauber, -,** 13
rescue helicopter

der **Rettungswagen, -,** 13
ambulance

revidieren, 18 to revise

der **Rhein,** 6 Rhine

der **Rheinfall, ¨e,** 6 Rhine falls

richtig, 5 right, correct

die **Richtung, -en,** 8 direction

riechen, roch, gerochen, 12
to smell

der **Riese, -n,** 10 giant

riesig, 17 huge

das **Risiko, -ken,** 12 risk

der **Rhythmus, Rhythmen,** 12
rhythm

der **Rock, ¨e,** 11 skirt

die **Rockgruppe, -n,** 17 rock
group

das **Rockkonzert, -e,** 18 rock
concert

das **Rokoko,** 17 rococo

der **Roman, -e,** 18 novel

rot, 11 red

der **Rotwein, -e,** 11 red wine

die **Routine,** 7 routine

der **Rücken, -,** 12 back

rückwärts, 15 backwards

rufen, rief, gerufen, 11 to call

die **Ruhe, 7** rest; silence
ruhelos, 15 restless
der **Rumäne, -n, 16** Rumanian
rund, 18 round
der **Russe, -n, 1** Russian man
die **Russin, -nen, 1** Russian
woman
das **Russisch, 16** Russian
language
das **Rußland, 1** Russia

S

der **Saal, Säle, 9** hall
die **Sache, -n, 18** matter
sagen, 1 to say
die **Sahne, 2** cream
der **Salat, -e, 4** salad; lettuce
der **Samstag, -e, IC** Saturday
die **Sandale, -n, 11** sandal
der **Sänger, -, 12** singer
satirisch, 6 satirical
säubern, 6 to clean
schade, 9 unfortunate;
sorry; too bad
**schaffen, schuf, geschaffen,
15** to create
die **Schallplattenindustrie, 12**
record industry
der **Schatten, -, 14** shadow
die **Schattenseite, -n, 10** seamy
side
schauen, 10 to look
die **Schaubude, -n, 17** show-
booth
das **Schaufenster, -, 16** display
window
der **Schaum, 17** foam
der **Schauspieler, -, 9** actor
der **Scheck, -s, 10** check
**scheiden, schied, ist
geschieden, 13** to
divorce; **sich scheiden
lassen, 13** to get a divorce
**scheinen, schien,
geschienen, 5/7** to seem;
to shine
schenken, 11 to give,
present
scheußlich, 17 dreadful
**schießen, schoß,
geschossen, 18** to shoot
das **Schild, -er, 4** sign
**schlafen (schläft), schlief,
geschlafen, 9** to sleep

das **Schlafzimmer, -, 5** bedroom
der **Schlag, ∹e, 18** chop, hit,
stroke
der **Schlager, -, 12** hit (musical)
schlank, 8 slender
schlecht, IC bad
schließlich, 6 finally
das **Schloß, ∹sser, 4** castle
der **Schloßgarten, ∹, 8** castle
garden
der **Schloßplatz, ∹e, 8** courtyard
der **Schluck, -e, 9** sip
schlucken, 12 to swallow
der **Schluß, ∹sse, 9** end;
conclusion
zum Schluß, 9 at the end
der **Schlüssel, -, 4** key
schmecken, 12 to taste
der **Schmutz, 6** dirt
schmutzig, 6 dirty
der **Schnaps, ∹e, 17** schnaps
das **Schneckentempo, 11** snail's
pace
der **Schnee, 7** snow
**schneiden, schnitt,
geschnitten, 11** to cut
schneien, IC to snow
schnell, 3 quick, fast
schon, 5 already
schön, IC beautiful
die **Schranke, -n, 16** barrier
der **Schrebergarten ∹, 7** hobby
garden
**schreiben, schrieb,
geschrieben, 5** to write
**schreien, schrie, geschrien,
12** to cry, shout, scream
schriftlich, 14 in writing
der **Schriftsteller, -, 18** writer
der **Schuh, -e, 11** shoe
der **Schüler, -, 11** pupil
der **Schulkamerad, -en, 11**
schoolmate
schütteln, 16 to shake
schwach, 9 weak
die **Schwäche, -n, 2** weakness
schwarz, 11 black
die **Schweiz, 1** Switzerland
der **Schweizer, -, 1** Swiss citizen
schwerhörig, 12 hard of
hearing
die **Schwester, -n, 8** sister
schwierig, 7 difficult
die **Schwierigkeit, -en, 16**
difficulty

**schwimmen, schwamm, ist
geschwommen, 8** to swim
sechs, IC six
sechzehn, IC sixteen
sechzig, IC sixty
der **See, -, 6** lake
die **Seele, -n, 14** soul
sehen (sieht), sah, gesehen, 3
to see
das **Sehvermögen, 12** sight
sehr, 2 very
**sein (ist), war, ist gewesen,
1/5** to be
sein, seine, sein, 2/10 his
seit, 3 since
seitdem, 9 since
die **Seite, -n, 16** side
der **Sekt, 9** champagne
(German)
selber, 9 oneself
selbst, 7 oneself
der **Selbstmord, -e, 16** suicide
selbstsicher, 9 self-
confident
das **Semester, -, 13** semester
das **Seminar, -e, 9** course
die **Seminararbeit, -en, 12** term
paper
senden, 17 to send
die **Sendung, -en, 18** shipment;
broadcast
der **September, IC** September
die **Serie, -n, 18** series
der **Sessel, -, 4** armchair
sich **setzen, 10** to sit down
die **Show, -s, 9** show
sich, 3 oneself
sicher, 1 certain, sure
sie/Sie, 1 she; they; you
(*formal*)
sieben, IC seven
siebzehn, IC seventeen
siebzig, IC seventy
singen, sang, gesungen, 12
to sing
der **Sinn, 14** sense
die **Sirene, -n, 3** siren
die **Situationskomödie, -n, 9**
situation comedy
der **Sitz, -e, 16** seat
sitzen, saß, gesessen, 8 to
sit
die **Skiferien (*pl.*), 15** skiing
vacation
das **Skilaufen, 5** skiing

der **Skiurlaub,** 15 skiing vacation
so, 1/6/9 so
so ... wie, 2/5 as ... as
so daß, 9 so that
sobald, 9 as soon as
die **Socke, -n,** 11 sock
sofort, 4 at once, right away
sogar, 6 even
der **Sohn, ⸚e,** 8 son
solange, 9 as long as
solcher, 9 such
der **Soldat, -en,** 16 soldier
sollen, 6 ought to, shall
der **Sommer, -, IC** summer
die **Sommerferien** (*pl.*), 16 summer vacation
der **Sonnabend, -e, IC** Saturday
sondern, 9 but
die **Sonne,** 5 sun
der **Sonntag, -e, IC** Sunday
sonst, 5 otherwise
sooft, 9 as often as
die **Sorge, -n,** 11 sorrow; care
soviel, 4 as much as
sozial, 13 social
der **Sozialismus,** 13 socialism
die **Soziologie,** 1 sociology
soziologisch, 12 sociological
das **Spanien,** 7 Spain
der **Spaß, ⸚e,** 6 fun
spät, 3 late
speisen, 16 to dine
speziell, 6 special
das **Spiel, -e,** 17 game
spielen, 2 to play
der **Spielfilm, -e,** 18 movie
der **Sport,** 8 sport
Sport treiben, trieb, getrieben, 8 to be active in sports
der **Sportclub, -s,** 8 sports club
der **Sportler, -,** 14 athlete
die **Sportsendung, -en,** 18 sports broadcast
der **Sportwagen, -,** 11 sports car
die **Sprache, -n,** 1 language
sprechen (spricht), sprach, gesprochen, 3 to speak
der **Sprecher, -,** 2 speaker
das **Sprichwort, ⸚er,** 12 proverb
springen, sprang, ist gesprungen, 8 to jump
der **Staat, -en,** 7 state
der **Staatsanwalt, ⸚e,** 5 public prosecutor

das **Staatseigentum,** 5 public property
die **Staatsoper, -n,** 14 state opera
das **Staatstheater, -,** 9 state theater
das **Stadion, Stadien,** 17 stadium
die **Stadt, ⸚e,** 4 city
städtisch, 11 urban
das **Stadtleben,** 8 urban life
der **Stadtmensch, -en,** 8 city dweller
die **Stadtmitte,** 4 city center
der **Stadtpark, -s,** 7 city park
der **Stadtplan, ⸚e,** 8 city map
der **Stadtrand, ⸚er,** 16 suburban area
das **Stadttheater, -,** 9 municipal theater
der **Stadtteil, -e,** 16 city district
der **Stadtverkehr,** 11 city traffic
der **Stahlhelm, -e,** 16 steel helmet
stark, 9 strong
die **Statistik, -en,** 7 statistics
statt, 7 instead
statt zu (+ *inf.*), 8 instead of
statt·finden, fand statt, stattgefunden, 17 to take place
der **Stechschritt, -e,** 16 goose step
das **Steckenpferd, -e,** 7 hobby
stehen, stand, gestanden, 3 to stand **hier steht,** 9 it says here
steigen, stieg, ist gestiegen, 8 to climb; to increase
die **Stelle, -n,** 15 place; position
stellen, 4 to put; **auf den Kopf stellen,** 16 to put something upside down; **eine Frage stellen,** 17 to ask a question
sterben (stirbt), starb, ist gestorben, 13 to die
stets, 14 always
die **Steuer, -n,** 7 tax
die **Stewardess, -en,** 18 stewardess
der **Stiefel, -,** 11 boot
der **Stil, -e,** 12 style
still, 10 quiet
die **Stille,** 16 silence
stimmen, 7 to be right; **es**

stimmt, 7 that's right; **Stimmt!,** 11 Quite right!
stimmen für, 13 to vote for
der **Stock, Stockwerke** (*pl.*), 11 floor, story (building)
das **Strafmandat, -e,** 6 traffic ticket
die **Straße, -n,** 1 street
die **Straßenbahn, -en,** 4 streetcar
die **Straßenbahnschiene, -n,** 11 streetcar track
die **Straßenecke, -n,** 8 street corner
der **Straßenlärm,** 16 street noise
der **Streik, -s,** 15 strike
streiken, 15 to strike
sich **streiten, stritt, gestritten,** 15 to quarrel
der **Stress,** 15 stress
das **Stück, -e,** 3 piece
der **Student, -en,** 1 student
das **Studentenparlament, -e,** 1 student council
das **Studentenproblem, -e,** 15 student problem
der **Studentenstreik, -s,** 15 student strike
die **Studentenzeitung, -en,** 15 student newspaper
das **Studentenzimmer, -,** 4 student room
die **Studentin, -nen,** 1 (female) student
der **Studienplatz, ⸚e,** 15 college or university (where one is applying or has been admitted)
studieren, 1 to study
das **Studium, -ien,** 15 study
der **Stuhl, ⸚e,** 4 chair
die **Stunde, -n,** 1 hour
stündlich, 4 by the hour; every hour
die **Subvention, -en,** 9 subsidy
die **Suche,** 8 search
suchen, 1 to search, look for
der **Süden,** 7 south
das **Südfrankreich,** 7 Southern France
die **Suppe, -n,** 4 soup
die **Symphonie, -n,** 14 symphony
die **Szene, -n,** 18 scene

T

der **Tag, -e, IC**   day;   **Guten Tag!, IC**   Hello!

die **Tageszeitung, -en, 18**   daily newspaper

täglich, 4   daily

das **Tal, ¨er, 10**   valley

tanken, 18   to fill with gas

die **Tante, -n, 8**   aunt

der **Tanz, ¨e, 14**   dance

die **Tanzbar, -s, 11**   discotheque

tanzen, 5   to dance

das **Tanzlokal, -e, 14**   dance hall, dance bar

die **Tasse, -n, 3**   cup

der **Täter, -, 18**   suspect

tätig, 13   active

tatsächlich, 6   indeed

tausend, IC   thousand

das **Taxi, -s** or **Taxen, 3**   taxi

der **Taxifahrer, -, 3**   taxi driver

der **Tee, -s, 3**   tea

der **Teil, -e, 9**   part

sich **etwas teilen, 13**   to share something

teil·nehmen (nimmt teil), nahm teil, teilgenommen, 18   to participate

das **Telefon, -e, 2**   telephone

telefonisch, 18   by telephone

das **Tennis, 2**   tennis

die **Terrasse, 11**   terrace

der **Test, -s, 14**   test

die **Test-Karte, -n, 14**   test card

teuer, 4   expensive

der **Teufel, -, 9**   devil;   **Zum Teufel noch mal!, 9**   For heaven's sake!

das **Theater, -, 9**   theater

die **Theateraufführung, -en, 14**   theater performance

der **Theatersaal, -säle, 9**   theater auditorium

das **Theaterstück, -e, 9**   drama

das **Thema, Themen, 9**   theme, topic

thematisch, 14   thematic

die **Theorie, -n, 14**   theory

tief, 9   deep

die **Tinte, 14**   ink

der **Tintenklecks, -e, 14**   ink blot

der **Tip, -s, 18**   hint

der **Tisch, -e, 4**   table

das **Titelblatt, ¨er, 14**   front page

die **Tochter, ¨, 8**   daughter

die **Toilette, -n, 4**   toilet, restroom

toll, 2   great

das **Tor, -e, 16**   gate; goal

der **Tourist, -en, 4**   tourist

die **Tradition -en, 9**   tradition

tragen (trägt), trug, getragen, 11   to carry

die **Tramschiene, -n, 11**   streetcar track

der **Traum, ¨e, 10**   dream

träumen, 12   to dream

die **Traumlandschaft, -en, 10**   dream landscape

der **Trauschein, -e, 13**   marriage certificate

die **Trauung, -en, 13**   wedding

treffen (trifft), traf, getroffen, 5   to hit

sich **treffen (trifft sich), traf sich, getroffen, 16**   to meet;   **Das trifft sich gut., 16**   That's a fortunate coincidence.

die **Treppe, -n, 3**   stairs, stairway

trinken, trank, getrunken, 2   to drink

der **Trinker, -, 17**   drinker

(sich) **trimmen, 8**   to work out

trotz, 7   in spite of

trotzdem, 2   still; nevertheless

Tschüß!, 2   Bye-bye!

tun, tat, getan, 5   to do;   **leid tun, (+ *dat.*) 5**   to be sorry

die **Tür, -en, 1**   door

der **Türke, -n, 14**   Turk

der **Turm, ¨e, 16**   tower

turnen, 8   to do gymnastics

die **Turnübung, -en, 8**   gymnastic exercise

typisch, 18   typical

U

üben, 8   to practice

über, 1/8   over; about

überall, 6   everywhere

überbelegt, 15   over-enrolled

der **Übergangspunkt, -e 6**   transit point

überhaupt, 10   at all; on the whole

überholen, 5   to pass

übermorgen, 10   day after tomorrow

übernachten, 11   to spend a night

übernehmen (übernimmt), übernahm, übernommen, 15   to take over

überreden, 9   to persuade, to talk someone into

überschattet, 10   overshadowed

übertreiben, übertrieb, übertrieben, 18   to exaggerate

die **Übertreibung, -en, 9**   exaggeration

üblich, 12   usual

das **Übliche, 12**   the usual

übrigens, 11   by the way

die **Übung, -en, 8**   exercise

die **Uhr, -en, IC**   clock; watch; o'clock   **Wieviel Uhr ist es?, IC**   What time is it?

um, 3/7   at; around;   **um die Ecke, 7**   around the corner;   **um fünf Uhr, 3**   at five o'clock

um so besser, 15   all the better

um zu, 8   in order to

die **Umfrage, -n, 13**   poll (opinion)

umgeben, 16   surrounded

der **Umrechnungskurs, -e, 10**   rate of exchange

um·schmelzen (schmilzt um), schmolz um, umgeschmolzen, 14   to remelt

um·wandeln, 7   to change

um·wechseln, 10   to exchange

sich **um·ziehen, zog um, umgezogen, 11**   to change clothes

der **Umzug, ¨e, 17**   parade

unabhängig, 13   independent

unbedingt, 9   necessarily

das **Unbekannte, 13**   the unknown

und, IC   and

unerbittlich, 6   inexorable

der   Unfall, ̈-e, 5   accident

die   Unfallstelle, -n, 13   place of accident

der   Ungar, -n, 16   Hungarian

ungefähr, 4   about, approximately

ungelöst, 18   unsolved

ungesund, 2   unhealthy

ungewöhnlich, 13   unusual

unglaublich, 12   unbelievable

das   Unglück, 14   misfortune; accident

uniformiert, 16   uniformed

die   Universität, -en, 4   university

unkonventionell, 13   unconventional

unmöglich, 18   impossible

unrecht (haben), 13   (to be) wrong

unser, unsere, unser, 10   our

unsozial, 18   unsocial

unter, 1/8   under; among

unterbrechen (unterbricht), unterbrach, unterbrochen, 18   to interrupt

die   Unterbrechung, -en, 18   interruption

unter·bringen, brachte unter, untergebracht, 14   to install

unterdrücken, 9   to suppress

die   Unterdrückung, 9   suppression

die   Untergrundbahn, -en, 14   subway

sich   unterhalten (unterhält), unterhielt, unterhalten, 10   to talk; to entertain

unterhaltend, 13   entertaining

die   Unterhaltung, -en, 14   entertainment

das   Unternehmen, -, 9   enterprise

unterschreiben, unterschrieb, unterschrieben, 4   to sign

unterstützen, 9   to support

unwohl, 13   unwell

der   Urlaub, 7   vacation; leave

das   Urlaubsgeld, 7   vacation money

V

der   Vampir, -e, 12   vampire

der   Vater, ̈:, 8   father

die   Verabredung, -en, 6   date; appointment

sich   verabschieden, 16   to say good-bye

verändern, 1   to change

verantwortlich, 12   responsible

verbessern, 7   to improve

verbieten, verbot, verboten, 17   to forbid

verbinden, verband, verbunden, 9   to connect

der   Verbrecher, 18   criminal

der   Verdacht, 18   suspicion

verdauen, 7   to digest

verdienen, 6   to earn

der   Verein, -e, 17   club

die   Vereinten Nationen, 14   United Nations

die   Verfolgung, -en, 18   pursuit; persecution

vergangen, 14   past

die   Vergangenheit, 10   past

vergeblich, 3   in vain

vergessen (vergißt), vergaß, vergessen, 3   to forget

der   Vergleich, -e, 10   comparison; im Vergleich mit, 10   in comparison to

das   Vergnügen, 9   pleasure; Viel Vergnügen!, 9   Have fun!

vergnügt, 18   delighted, happy

vergrößern, 17   to enlarge

verheiratet, 7   married

der   Verkauf, ̈-e, 12   sale

verkaufen, 18   to sell

der   Verkaufsstand, 17   stall, booth

der   Verkehr, 11   traffic

verkehrt, 11   wrong; reversed, perverted

die   Verkürzung, -en, 7   shortening; decrease

verlassen (verläßt), verließ, verlassen, 3   to leave

verleihen, verlieh, verliehen, 15   to grant

verletzt, 13   hurt

verlieren, verlor, verloren, 5   to lose

vermieten, 7   to rent (to someone)

das   Vermittlungsbüro, -s, 4   room rental agency

verneinen, 18   to negate

verrostet, 11   corroded

verrückt, 18   crazy

verschieden, 12   different

verschmutzen, 6   to pollute

die   Verschmutzung, -en, 6   pollution

verschwinden, verschwand, ist verschwunden, 16   to disappear

versetzen (in gute Laune), 17   to put in a good mood

verspätet, 12   late

das   Versprechen, -, 15   promise

versprechen (+ dat.) (verspricht), versprach, versprochen, 14   to promise

sich   versprechen (verspricht), versprach, versprochen, 15   to make a slip of the tongue; to make an error in speaking

verständlich, 15   understandable, comprehensible

verstärken, 14   to reinforce

verstehen, verstand, verstanden, 5   to understand

verstehen von, verstand, verstanden, 16   to know something about

versuchen, 8   to try

verteilen, 1   to distribute

das   Verwaltungszentrum, -zentren, 14   administration center

verwenden, 9   to use

verwirklichen, 17   to realize

verwurzelt, 9   rooted

die   Verzeihung, 2   pardon

der   Vetter, -n, 8   male cousin

viel, 2/3   much; Vielen Dank!, 3   Thank you very much!

viele, 5   many

vielleicht, 2   perhaps

die **vielversprechend, 15** very promising

die **Violine, -n, 2** violin

vier, IC four

Viertel vor drei, IC a quarter to three

vierzehn, IC fourteen

vierzig, IC forty

das **Visum, Visa, 16** visa

das **Volk, ⁻er, 9** people

die **Volkskammer, 16** East German Parliament

das **Volkslied, -er, 17** folk song

der **Volkspolizist, -en, 16** East German policeman

der **Volkstanz, ⁻e, 17** folk dance

voll, 6 full; **voll Gold, 6** full of gold

der **Volleyball, 2** volleyball

von, 1/3 from; of

Von wegen!, 7 No! Certainly not!

vor, IC before

voraus·sagen, 18 to predict, forecast

vorbei, 8 past; gone

vorbei·kommen, kam vorbei, ist vorbeigekommen, 8 to pass by

vorbei·fahren (fährt vorbei), fuhr vorbei, ist vorbeigefahren, 18 to pass

vor·bereiten, 15 to prepare

sich **vorbereiten, 15** to prepare oneself

vorerst, 16 for the time being

vorgestern, 10 day before yesterday

sich **vor·kommen (+ dat.), kam sich vor, ist sich vorgekommen, 11** to feel like

die **Vorlesung, -en, 1** lecture

die **Vorliebe, -n, 12** preference

vor·machen, 9 to pretend to

der **Vormittag, -e, 13** morning

vormittags, 13 in the morning

vorne, 8 in front

vorsichtig, 9 careful

vor·stellen, 14 to introduce

sich **vor·stellen, 14** to imagine

die **Vorstellung, -en, 9** performance; imagination; idea

vorwärts, 15 forward

vor·ziehen, zog vor, vorgezogen, 12 to prefer

W

die **Wachablösung, 16** change of the guard

der **Wächter, -, 10** guard

die **Waffe, -n, 18** weapon

der **Wagen, -, 6** car

wahr, 7 true

während, 7 while

die **Wahrheit, 8** truth

wahrscheinlich, 5 probable

die **Währung, -en, 16** currency

das **Wahrzeichen, -, 16** landmark

der **Wald, ⁻er, 8** forest

der **Walzer, -, 14** waltz

wandern, 14 to hike

wann, 2 when

warm, IC warm

warnen, 18 to warn, caution

die **Warnung, -en, 2** warning

warten, 8 to wait; **Wart mal!, 10** Wait a minute!

warum, 2 why

was, IC what

was für ein, 9 what a

das **Waschbecken, -, 4** washbasin

sich **waschen (wäscht), wusch, gewaschen, 10** to wash oneself

das **Wasser, 6/7** water

das **Wasserwerk, -e, 6** waterworks

der **Wechsel, 15** change

wechseln, 10 to exchange

wecken, 17 to wake up

der **Wecker, -, 17** alarm clock

der **Weg, -e, 11** way

wegen, 7 because of

das **Weihnachten, 15** Christmas

weil, 9 because

der **Wein, -e, 5** wine

der **Weinberg, -e, 10** vineyard

weinen, 17 to cry

die **Weise, -n, 18** way, kind, manner

weiß, 4 white

der **Weißwein, -e, 11** white wine

weit, 4 wide; far

weiter (+ verb), 3 further; to go on with

weiterer, 15 further, farther (adj.)

weiter·fahren (fährt weiter), fuhr weiter, ist weitergefahren, 3 to go on

weiter·gehen, ging weiter, ist weitergegangen, 3 to go on

weiter·kommen, kam weiter, ist weitergekommen, 3 to proceed

weiter·laufen (läuft weiter), lief weiter, ist weitergelaufen, 3 to run on

weiter·lesen (liest weiter), las weiter, weitergelesen, 3 to read on

weiter·machen, 3 to continue

weiter·reden, 8 to talk on and on

weiter·sprechen (spricht weiter), sprach weiter, weitergesprochen, 3 to speak on

welcher, welche, welches, 2/10 which

die **Welt, -en, 7** world

die **Weltanschauung, -en, 12** concept of the world

weltbekannt, 17 world-famous

der **Weltkrieg, -e, 10** world war

die **Weltzeituhr, -en, 13** global clock

wem, 4 to whom

wen, 2 whom

wenig, 8 little

wenige, 10 few

wenigstens, 6 at least

wenn, 2 if

wer, 1 who

die **Werbung, 18** advertising

werden (wird), wurde, ist geworden, 7 to become

werfen (wirft), warf, geworfen, 11 to throw

das **Werk, -e,** 14 work
werktätig, 11 working
wessen, 11 whose
die **Weste, -n,** 11 vest
der **Westen,** 8 west
westlich, 16 western
das **Wetter, IC** weather
wichtig, 7 important
wie, IC/9 how; like, as;
Wie bitte?, 5 Pardon me?;
wie lange, 1 how long
wieder, 3 again
wieder·finden, fand wieder,
wiedergefunden, 12 to
recover
wiederholen, 9 to repeat
die **Wiederholungsübung, -en,** 9
review exercise
wieder·kommen, kam
wieder, ist
wiedergekommen, 9 to
come back
wieder·sehen (sieht wieder),
sah wieder,
wiedergesehen, 9 to see
again
das **Wiedersehen, IC** reunion,
meeting again; **Auf**
Wiedersehen!, IC Good-
bye!
der **Wiener, -,** 14 Viennese
die **Wiese, -n,** 17 meadow
wieso, 17 why
wieviel, IC/4 how much
wieviele, 4 how many
willkommen, 16 welcome
sich **winden (durch), wand,**
gewunden, 10 to wind
(through)
windig, 7 windy
der **Winter, -, IC** winter
das **Wintersemester, -,** 15
winter term
wir, 1 we
wirklich, 1 real(ly)
die **Wirtschaft,** 10 economy
das **Wirtschaftsproblem, -e,** 10
economic problem
das **Wirtschaftswunder, -,** 10
economic miracle
wirkungsvoll, 18 effective
wissen (weiß), wußte,
gewußt, 6 to know
die **Wissenschaft, -en,** 18 science

der **Witz, -e,** 16 joke, wit
wo, 1 where
die **Woche, -n,** 4 week
das **Wochenende, -n,** 12
weekend
wöchentlich, 4 weekly
der **Wodka, -s,** 5 vodka
wofür, 7 what for
woher, 3 where from
wohin, 3 where(to)
das **Wohl,** 17 health; **Zum**
Wohl!, 17 Cheers!
wohl, 9/13 perhaps; well
wohlhabend, 15 well-to-do
wohnen, 4 to live
das **Wohnhaus, ¨er,** 16 home
die **Wohnung, -en,** 14
apartment
das **Wohnzimmer, -,** 5 living
room
die **Wolke, -n,** 7 cloud
wollen (will), wollte, gewollt,
6 to want
womit, 10 with which
wonach, 16 after which
woran, 16 at which
worauf, 16 on which
woraus, 14 out of which
worin, 16 in which
das **Wort, ¨er,** 4 word
die **Wortfamilie, -n,** 9 word
family
worüber, 8 about which
worunter, 16 under (among)
which
wovon, 7 from which
wozu, 16 to which
wünschen, 12 to desire,
wish
wütend, 18 mad, angry

Z

die **Zahl, -en,** 13 number
der **Zahn, ¨e,** 12 tooth
die **Zauberflöte,** 14 magic flute
der **Zeh, -en,** 12 toe
zehn, IC ten
zeigen, 4 to show
die **Zeit, -en,** 2 time
die **Zeitschrift, -en,** 7 periodical
die **Zeitung, -en,** 3 newspaper
der **Zenith,** 14 zenith
der **Zentimeter, -,** 17 centimeter

zerreißen, zerriß, zerrissen,
14 to tear apart
zerstören, 14 to destroy
sich **ziehen (durch), zog, gezogen,**
10 to extend (over)
ziemlich, 15 rather
die **Zigarette, -n,** 2 cigarette
die **Zigarre, -n,** 2 cigar
das **Zimmer, -,** 1 room
der **Zimmerschlüssel, -,** 4 room
key
die **Zimmervermittlung, -en,** 4
[room] rental agency
das **Zitat, -e,** 15 quotation
die **Zivilisation,** 12 civilization
der **Zivilschutzbunker, -,** 11 civil
defense shelter
zu, 3 to
zu (langsam), 3 too (slow, etc.)
der **Zucker,** 2 sugar
die **Zueignung, -en,** 14
dedication
zueinander, 13 to each other
zuerst, 4 at first
zufällig, 12 by chance
zufrieden, 15 content,
satisfied
der **Zug, ¨e,** 4 train
zu·hören (+ *dat.*), 10 to
listen
der **Zuhörer, -,** 10 listener; pl.:
audience
die **Zukunft,** 7 future
zukünftig, 18 future (*adj.*)
der **Zukunftsplan, ¨e,** 16 plan for
the future
zu·lassen (läßt zu), ließ zu,
zugelassen, 15 to admit;
to allow
die **Zulassung, -en,** 15
admission
zuletzt, 14 at last
zu·machen, 3 to close
zu·nehmen, (nimmt zu), nahm
zu, zugenommen, 12 to
gain
zurück, 9 back
zurück·fahren (fährt zurück),
fuhr zurück, ist
zurückgefahren, 6 to return
zurück·führen, 14 to lead
back
zurück·geben (gibt zurück)
gab zurück,

zurückgegeben, 14 to return, give back

zurück·gehen, ging zurück, ist zurückgegangen, 3 to go back

zurück·kehren, ist zurückgekehrt, 13 to return

zurück·kommen, kam zurück, ist zurückgekommen, 5 to come back

zurück·laufen (läuft zurück), lief zurück, ist zurückgelaufen, 3 to run back

zusammen, 7 together

zusammen·fließen, floß zusammen, ist zusammengeflossen, 10 to flow together

zusammen·kommen, kam zusammen, ist zusammengekommen, 6 to come together, to gather

zusammen·schrumpfen, ist zusammengeschrumpft, 16 to shrink

der Zustand, ¨e, 18 condition, situation

zuversichtlich, 13 confident, assured

zuviel, 2 too much

zwanzig, IC twenty

zwei, IC two

die Zweierbeziehung, -en, 13 relationship of two

zweihundert, IC two hundred

zweihundertfünfzig, 4 two hundred and fifty

zweimal, 3 twice

zweitens, 11 secondly

zweiter, 10 second

zwingen, zwang, gezwungen, 18 to force

zwischen, 8 between

zwitschern, 12 to chirp

zwölf, IC twelve

der Zyniker, -, 18 cynic

zynisch, 7 cynical

INDEX

Photograph Credits